International Law and Violence Against Women

This book offers an in-depth and critical analysis of the Istanbul Convention, along with discussions on its impact and implications.

The work highlights the place of the Convention in the landscape of international law and policies on violence against women and equality. The authors argue that the Convention with its emphasis on integrated and comprehensive policies has an important role in promoting equality, but they also note the debates on "genderism" that the Convention has triggered in some member states. The book analyses central concepts of the Convention, including violence, gender and due diligence. It takes up major commitments of the parties to the Convention, including support and services to victims, criminal law provisions and protection of migrant women against violence. The book thus makes a major contribution to the development of national laws, policies and practice.

It provides a valuable guide for policy-makers, students and academics in international human rights law, criminal and social law, social policy, social work and gender studies.

Johanna Niemi, Professor of Procedural Law, University of Turku, Finland.

Lourdes Peroni, Human Rights Lecturer, Sheffield Hallam University, UK.

Vladislava Stoyanova, Associate Professor, Lund University, Sweden.

Routledge Research in Human Rights Law

Civil and Political Rights in Japan
A Tribute to Sir Nigel Rodley
Edited by Saul J. Takahashi

Human Rights, Digital Society and the Law
A Research Companion
Edited by Mart Susi

Criminal Theory and International Human Rights Law
Women's Health and the Limits of Law
Steven Malby

Domestic and International Perspectives
Women and International Human Rights Law
Edited by Irehobhude O. Iyioha

Universal Periodic Review in Practice
Gayatri H. Patel

International Law and Violence Against Women
Europe and the Istanbul Convention
Edited by Johanna Niemi, Lourdes Peroni and Vladislava Stoyanova

The Human Rights Council
The Impact of the Universal Periodic Review in Africa
Damian Etone

Domestic Judicial Treatment of European Court of Human Rights Case Law
Beyond Compliance
Edited by David Kosař, Jan Petrov, Katarína Šipulová, Hubert Smekal, Ladislav Vyhnánek and Jozef Janovský

For more information about this series, please visit: www.routledge.com/Routledge-Research-in-Human-Rights-Law/book-series/HUMRIGHTSLAW

International Law and Violence Against Women

Europe and the Istanbul Convention

Edited by Johanna Niemi, Lourdes Peroni and Vladislava Stoyanova

Routledge
Taylor & Francis Group
LONDON AND NEW YORK

First published 2020 by Routledge

2 Park Square, Milton Park, Abingdon, Oxon OX14 4RN
605 Third Avenue, New York, NY 10017

Routledge is an imprint of the Taylor & Francis Group, an informa business

First issued in paperback 2021

British Library Cataloguing-in-Publication Data
A catalogue record for this book is available from the British Library

Library of Congress Cataloging-in-Publication Data
A catalog record has been requested for this book

ISBN: 978-0-367-25766-8 (hbk)
ISBN: 978-1-03-217353-5 (pbk)
DOI: 10.4324/9780429289736

Typeset in Galliard
by Wearset Ltd, Boldon, Tyne and Wear

Contents

Editors

Johanna Niemi is Professor of Procedural Law at the Faculty of Law, University of Turku, Finland. Formerly, she has served as Vice Dean of the Faculty of Law, University of Helsinki, as professor at Umeå University and as visiting professor at Lund University. She is Doctor Honoris Causa at Uppsala University and former Fulbright scholar at the University of Wisconsin, Madison. Niemi was a member of the Scientific Committee of the European Union Agency for Fundamental Rights and of the Academy of Finland Research Council for Culture and Society. She leads the research project ASLA: Actors, Structures and Law (2015–2019). She is co-editor of several books, including Nousiainen et al. (eds), *Responsible Selves. Women in the Nordic Legal Culture* (Ashgate, 2001); Svensson et al. (eds), *Nordic Equality at a Crossroads. Feminist Legal Studies Coping with Difference* (Routledge, 2004) and *Gendered Violence* (in Finnish, Vastapaino, 2017). She has published on topics in criminal procedure, violence against women and insolvency law.

Lourdes Peroni is Lecturer in Human Rights at the Helena Kennedy Centre for International Justice at Sheffield Hallam University, United Kingdom. Before joining Sheffield Hallam, Lourdes held positions at the Human Rights Centre of Ghent University (Postdoctoral Research Fellow), at Yale Law School (Fellow) and at the Inter-American Commission on Human Rights (Fellow). She holds an LLM from Harvard Law School and a PhD in Law from Ghent University. Her areas of teaching and research include equality and non-discrimination; gender and migration; gender-based violence against women; and legal feminism in the contexts of the United Nations, Council of Europe, and Organisation of American States. She has published among others in *Feminist Legal Studies*, *International Journal of Constitutional Law – I•CON* and *Human Rights Law Review*. Her most recent publications include "The Protection of Women Asylum Seekers under the European Convention on Human Rights: Unearthing the Gendered Roots of Harm" (*Human Rights Law Review*) and "The Borders that Disadvantage Migrant Women in Enjoying Human Rights" (*Netherlands Quarterly of Human Rights*). Lourdes held visiting research positions at

Emory Law School (The Vulnerability and the Human Condition Initiative) and at Melbourne Law School (The Institute of International Law and the Humanities).

Vladislava Stoyanova is Associate Professor in Public International Law at the Faculty of Law, Lund University, Sweden. She holds an LLM from Leiden Law School and a PhD from Lund University. Her research interests are within the areas of international migration law, international refugee law, international human rights law and EU law. Her publications include the monograph *Human Trafficking and Slavery Reconsidered: Conceptual Limits and States' Positive Obligations in European Law* (Cambridge University Press, 2017), two co-edited volumes *Seeking Asylum in the European Union: Selected Protection Issues Raised by the Second Phase of the Common European Asylum System* (Brill, 2015) and *The New Asylum and Transit Countries in Europe: During and in the Aftermath of the 2015–2016 Crisis* (Brill, 2018), various book chapters and articles published in international peer-reviewed law journals, such as the *International Journal of Refugee Law*, *Human Rights Law Review*, *Michigan Journal of International Law*, *Cambridge Journal of International and Comparative Law*, *Netherlands Quarterly of Human Rights*, and *European Human Rights Law Review*. She is the director of the Migration law courses at her faculty. Vladislava Stoynova is the holder of the Wallenberg Academy Fellowship (2019–2021) awarded by the Knut and Alice Wallenberg Foundation and the Royal Swedish Academy of Sciences.

Contributors

Daniela Alaattinoğlu is a Research Associate at the University of Turku, Finland, currently working on a project on sexual violence commissioned by the Finnish Ministry of Justice. She holds a PhD and an LLM in Law from the European University Institute and an LLM and LLB in Law from the University of Helsinki. She has been a Kathleen Fitzpatrick Visiting Fellow at Melbourne Law School in 2018 and a visiting fellow at the Max Planck Institute for Social Anthropology in 2019. Her publications include the co-edited volume *Contesting Femicide: Feminism and the Power of Law Revisited* (Routledge 2019, with Adrian Howe) and the Article "Redress for Involuntarily Sterilised Trans People in Sweden against Evolving Human Rights Standards: A Critical Appraisal" (*Human Rights Law Review* 2019, with Ruth Rubio-Marín). Alaattinoğlu has previously worked as a legal researcher for the Turkish human rights NGO TOHAV and as a criminal law lecturer at the Police College of Finland.

Ulrika Andersson is Professor of Criminal Law at the Faculty of Law, Lund University, Sweden. Her main research focuses broadly on questions concerning law and power. She is particularly interested in issues of sexuality and gender, in addition to power related to class, age and ethnicity. She has done research on sexual offences, highlighting the gendered structure of legal definitions, as well as the proof process. She has also done research on human trafficking regulations and juvenile crime and delinquency issues in connection with gang activity. Together with Professor Titti Mattsson, she has initiated the interdisciplinary research group Law and Vulnerabilities at Lund University, in collaboration with among others Professor Martha Fineman of Emory Law School, Atlanta. They have published M Fineman, T Mattsson and U Andersson (eds) *Privatization, Vulnerability and Social Responsibility: A Comparative Perspective* (Oxon, Routledge 2016). Andersson collaborates with Tata Institute of Social Sciences (TISS) in Mumbai, India, where she stayed as a visiting researcher and teacher in January 2016. She has recently published U Andersson, M Edgren, L Karlsson L and G Nilsson (eds) *Rape Narratives in Motion* (Palgrave Macmillan 2019), together with colleagues from the department of history, ethnology and English literature at Lund University.

Sara Bengtson holds an LLM and an LLM in International Human Rights Law from Lund University, as well as an LLM from Columbia University, where she studied as a Fulbright scholar. She is currently working as a lawyer at a law firm in Stockholm, where she advises clients on anti-corruption, anti-money laundering, and corporate sustainability.

Wojciech Burek is Assistant Professor (*Adiunkt*) at the Institute of European Studies, Jagiellonian University in Cracow, Poland. He holds a PhD in Legal Sciences with a specialisation in public international law (2008). He also obtained diplomas from the American Law Program organised by the Catholic University of America Columbus School of Law and Jagiellonian University (2004) and from the Helsinki Foundation for Human Rights School of Human Rights (2004). He was recipient of the Stanislaw Kutrzeba Human Rights in Europe Prize (2008) and The Ryoichi Sasakawa Young Leaders Fellowship (founded by Tokio Foundation – 2007). His current academic and professional interests include international migration and refugee law, diplomatic and consular law, human rights law, EU anti-discrimination law and gender.

Sara De Vido is Associate Professor of International Law and Vice-Director of the Centre for Human Rights (Cestudir) at Ca' Foscari University in Venice, Italy, where she teaches international law, human rights law and European Union law. She is also a professor at the Venice International University. She is an affiliate to the Manchester International Law Centre, where she co-founded the Women in International Law Network (Wilnet). Sara has spent several research periods abroad, including at the University of Manchester, and at the Hitotsubashi and Waseda universities in Tokyo. She teaches in Italian, English and French both in Italy and abroad. Her main research interests include the fight against transnational criminality and women's rights under international law. Among her publications is a monograph on the Council of Europe Istanbul Convention on *Donne, violenza e diritto internazionale* (Mimesis, 2016).

Minni Leskinen holds an LLM from the University of Helsinki (2015). She is a doctoral student at the University of Turku, Faculty of Law, Finland and member of the research project ASLA: Actors, Structures and Law (2015–2019). Before joining the project, she completed her court training at the District Court of Pirkanma and worked as a Senior Officer at the Ombudsman for Equality. She has previously published on Finnish law on sexual offences. Her research interests include equality law, legal theory and feminist philosophy.

Ruth M. Mestre i Mestre teaches Jurisprudence and Legal Theory at the University of Valencia, Spain, where she is a member of the Human Rights Institute. She holds a PhD from the University of Valencia (2005), a Master in Legal Theory (Brussels 1995) and a Master in Sociology of Law (Oñati 1997) and has been Marie Curie Fellow at CRER-Warwick University

(2003–2004). Her lines of research include feminist legal theory, equality and non-discrimination, gendered citizenship, multiculturalism and women's rights, sex work, trafficking in human beings, female genital mutilation/cutting, and sexual violence against women. With S. Johnsdotter, she coordinated the report *FGM in Europe: An Analysis of Court Cases*, European Commission-Directorate General-Justice (2015). Her publications include the monograph *La Caixa de Pandora. Introducció a la teoría feminista del dret* (PUV, 2006); the edited book *Mujeres, derechos y ciudadanías* (Tirant lo Blanch, Valencia 2009); the co-edited book *Democracia y participación política de las Mujeres. Visiones desde Europa y America Latina* (Tirant lo Blanch, 2013); various book chapters and articles published in peer-reviewed international law journals such as *Cuadernos electrónicos de filosofía del derecho, REMHU, International Journal of Law, Crime and Justice* and *Studies in Law, Politics and Society.*

Dolores Morondo Taramundi is Head of Research at the Human Rights Institute of the University of Deusto in Bilbao, Spain. She holds a PhD in Law from the European University Institute (EUI) with a thesis on feminist legal theory. Her main research areas include anti-discrimination law, critical legal theory, especially feminist legal theory, human rights and legal methodology. She has worked as an independent expert in EU projects on human rights and as a consultant for the Spanish Agency for International Cooperation. In that capacity she has prepared various reports on asylum and the antidiscrimination principle, among which *La situación de las personas LGBTI del Norte de Centroamérica con necesidades de protección internacional en Guatemala y México* (AECID 2018) and with Mustaniemi-Laakso et al., *The protection of vulnerable individuals in the context of EU policies on border checks, asylum and immigration*, 2016 (www.fp7-frame.eu).

Katarzyna Sękowska-Kozłowska is Assistant Professor and Head of the Poznań Human Rights Centre at the Institute of Law Studies of the Polish Academy of Sciences as well as member of the Scientific Board of the Interdisciplinary Centre for Cultural Gender and Identity Studies at Adam Mickiewicz University. Her field of research is international human rights law with a focus on gender issues, including reproductive rights, violence against women, temporary special measures, and gender stereotyping. She has authored academic publications, reports and analyses, and cooperates with numerous non-governmental organisations.

Lorena Sosa is Assistant Professor at the Netherlands Institute of Human Rights (SIM) at Utrecht University, the Netherlands. She holds an LLM (*cum laude*) and a PhD (*cum laude*) from Tilburg University. She has previously worked as a researcher and lecturer at the International Victimology Institute Tilburg (INTERVICT). Her research looks at the limits of law in relation to gender-based violence from a socio-legal perspective. She received a Marie Skłodowska Curie grant from the European Commission and a

VENI grant from the Dutch Scientific Organisation for her research on gender-based violence against trans and intersex persons. Her publications include the monograph *Intersectionality in the Human Rights Legal Framework on Violence Against Women: At the Centre or the Margins?* (Cambridge University Press, 2017), book chapters and articles published in peer-reviewed international law journals such as the *Netherlands Quarterly of Human Rights*, *Human Rights Quarterly*, *The International Review of Victimology* and *Victims & Offenders.*

Fulvia Staiano is Adjunct Professor of International Law and European Union Law at Giustino Fortunato University, Italy, and Associate at the Institute for Research of Innovation and Services for Development of the National Research Council of Italy. She holds a PhD in Law and an LLM in Comparative, European and International Laws from the European University Institute in Florence. She has published in international migration law, human rights law, environmental law as well as gender and the law. She is a member of the Coordinating Committee of the Feminism and International Law Interest Group of the European Society of International Law. Prior to her current role, she was a postdoctoral researcher at the Institute for Research on Innovation and Services for Development of the Italian National Research Council and an Irish Research Council postdoctoral fellow at University College Cork. In 2016, she published a monograph, *The Human Rights of Migrant Women in International and European Law* (Giappichelli Editore – Eleven International Publishing).

Amalia Verdu Sanmartin holds an LLM in Law and an LLM in Interdisciplinary Gender Studies from the University Autonoma of Madrid. She is a member of the Madrid Bar since 2010. She is a member of the research project ASLA: Actors, Structures and Law (2015–2019) at the University of Turku, Finland, and is currently finalising her PhD on the concept of gender in law and feminism.

Ingrid Westendorp is Senior Lecturer and researcher in International Law and Women and Law at Maastricht University, the Netherlands. She defended her PhD thesis on the right to housing from women's perspective in 2007. Since then, she has published on women's right to land, the link between domestic violence and adequate housing, the influence of culture on gender equality, and the right to adequate shelter for asylum seekers. Furthermore, she is the editor of the book *The Women's Convention Turned 30: Achievements, Setbacks, and Prospects* (Intersentia, 2013). She teaches on bachelor courses in International Law and a Master course on Human Rights of Women. She has been a guest lecturer at the universities of Lund, Denpasar, Yogyakarta, Bandung and Coimbra. Between 2008 and 2018 she was involved in capacity building projects on international law in Indonesia under the auspices of the Dutch Ministry of Foreign Affairs and Development Cooperation. She is Vice-Chair of the Association of Human Rights Institutes (AHRI) and a board member of the Maastricht Centre for Human Rights.

Acknowledgements

When this book started to take shape, we were fortunate to get funding from the Foundation of the Swedish Central Bank (*Riksbankens Jubileumsfond*) to organise a seminar to discuss the book and the draft chapters. The seminar was held in May 2018 at the University of Lund in Sweden. We thank all participants for the encouraging and engaged discussions during the two beautiful days. In particular, Rosa Logar, a participant in the negotiations of the Istanbul Convention and then a member of the monitoring body GREVIO, and Renée Römkens, an expert in the negotiations of the Convention, gave valuable insights into the preparation of the Convention and its first years in force. We would like to thank our home universities, Lund, Sheffield Hallam and Turku, and the Academy of Finland for the possibility to engage in the editing of this book and Turku law student, Emilia Taimi, for compiling the reference lists.

Abbreviations

CAHVIO	Ad Hoc Committee for Preventing and Combating Violence against Women and Domestic Violence
CAT	Committee against Torture
CEDAW	Convention on the Elimination of All Forms of Discrimination Against Women
CEDAW Committee	Committee on the Elimination of Discrimination against Women
CERD	Committee on the Elimination of Racial Discrimination
CESCR	Committee on Economic, Social and Cultural Rights
CoE	Council of Europe
CRC	Committee on the Rights of the Child
DEVAW	United Nations Declaration on the Elimination of Violence against Women
ECHR	European Convention for the Protection of Human Rights and Fundamental Freedoms (European Convention on Human Rights)
ECSR	European Committee of Social Rights
ECtHR	European Court of Human Rights
EIGE	European Institute for Gender Equality
EPAC VAW	European Policy Action Centre on Violence against Women
EU	European Union
EWL	European Women's Lobby
FGC	Female genital cutting
FGM	Female genital mutilation
FGM/C	Female genital mutilation/cutting
FRA	European Union Agency for Fundamental Rights
GREVIO	Group of Experts on Action Against Violence against Women and Domestic Violence
GU	Gazzetta Ufficiale
IACHR	Inter-American Court of Human Rights
IACmHR	Inter-American Commission of Human Rights
IC	Istanbul Convention

ICCPR	International Covenant on Civil and Political Rights
ICESCR	International Covenant on Economic, Social and Cultural Rights
ICJ	International Court of Justice
ILA	International Law Association
ILC	International Law Commission
ILGA	International Lesbian, Gay, Bisexual, Trans and Intersex Association
KKO	Korkein oikeus (Finnish Supreme Court)
LBT	Lesbian, bisexual and trans
LGBTI	Lesbian, gay, bisexual, trans and intersex persons
LGBTIQ	Lesbian, gay, bisexual, trans, intersex persons and queer
NGO	Non-governmental organisation
PiS	Prawo i Sprawiedliwość (Law and Justice, a party in Poland)
PO	Platforma Obywatelska (Civic Platform, a party in Poland)
ROKS	Riksorganisationen för Kvinnjourer i Sverige (National Organisation for Women's and Young Women's Shelters in Sweden)
ShGB	Strafgesetzbuch (Penal Code of Austria)
Skr	Sveriges Kvinnojourers Riksförbund (the Swedish Association of Women's Shelters and Young Women's Empowerment Centres)
SOU	Statens offentliga utredningar (The State's Public Investigations, Sweden)
TAR	Tribunale Amministrativo Regionale
TFEU	Treaty on the Functioning of the European Union
UN	United Nations
UNHCR	Office of the United Nations High Commissioner for Refugees
UNODC	United Nations Office on Drugs and Crime
VAW	Violence against women
VCLT	Vienna Convention on the Law of the Treaties

Table of cases

International Court of Justice

European Court of Human Rights

CEDAW Committee

UN Human Rights Committee

European Committee of Social Rights

Court of Justice of the European Union

The Inter-American Court of Human Rights

Nuremberg Military Tribunal

National Case Law

Finland

Italy

Poland

Spain

Sweden

United Kingdom

Table of legislation

International Treaties

United Nations

Council of Europe

European Social Charter CETS no 163, 1961 – revised 3 May 1996, 50, 60, 188, 193, 194
Convention for the Protection of Human Rights and Dignity of the Human Being with regard to the Application of Biology and Medicine: Convention on Human Rights and Biomedicine (Oviedo Convention) CETS no 164, 4 April 1997, 60
Protocol No 13 to the European Convention on Human Rights and Fundamental Freedoms, Concerning the Abolition of the Death Penalty in All Circumstances CETS no 187, 3 May 2002, 278
Council of Europe Convention on Action against Trafficking in Human Beings CETS no 197, 16 May 2005, 7, 228, 290

International Labour Organization

Convention Concerning the Elimination of Violence and Harassment in the World of Work C190, International Labour Organization (ILO), 21 June 2019, 5

Organization of American States

Inter-American Convention on the Prevention, Punishment and Eradication of Violence against Women (*Belém do Pará* Convention), the Organization of American States (OAS), 1994, 5, 43, 45, 48, 50, 51, 61, 62, 63

European Union Law

Council Directive 2000/78/EC of 27 November 2000 establishing a general framework for equal treatment in employment and occupation [2000] OJ L303/16, 68
Directive 2002/73/EC of the European Parliament and of the Council of 23 September 2002 amending Council Directive 76/207/EEC on the implementation of the principle of equal treatment for men and women as regards access to employment, vocational training and promotion, and working conditions [2002] OJ L269/15, 37
Directive 2004/38/EC of the European Parliament and of the Council of 29 April 2004 on the right of citizens of the Union and their family members to move and reside freely within the territory of the Member States amending Regulation (EEC) No 1612/68 and repealing Directives 64/221/EEC, 68/360/EEC, 72/194/EEC, 73/148/EEC, 75/34/EEC, 75/35/EEC, 90/364/EEC, 90/365/EEC and 93/96/EEC (Text with EEA relevance) [2004] OJ L158/77, 69, 70
Council Directive 2004/83/EC of 29 April 2004 on minimum standards for the qualification and status of third country nationals or stateless persons as refugees or as persons who otherwise need international protection and the content of the protection granted [2004] OJ L304/12 (replaced by Directive 2011/95/EU of 13 December 2011), 72

National Legislation

Austria

Denmark

Finland

Germany

Italy

Poland

Spain

Sweden

Introduction

The Istanbul Convention as a response to violence against women in Europe

Johanna Niemi, Lourdes Peroni and Vladislava Stoyanova

1 Background

The signing of the Council of Europe Convention on Preventing and Combating Violence against Women and Domestic Violence in Istanbul in May 2011 was a significant development in the protection of women against violence and in the development of international law. The Istanbul Convention confirms that States have an obligation to protect women and others against violence.

Violence against women is a persistent problem worldwide. A European Union survey showed that this problem is prevalent also in all EU Member States.[1] Violence against women takes many forms. Domestic violence, which disproportionally affects women, is well documented in many parts of the world. Women are killed in domestic violence more often than in other types of crime.[2] Violence in domestic and other close relationships can include physical violence, coercion and deprivation of liberty, psychological violence such as threats, defamation and degrading treatment, and also economic control. With the #MeToo movement, the media have focused on sexual harassment, which has turned out to be more common, more serious and more silenced than most people could have expected. In fact, the continuum of sexual violence from harassment to serious sexual crimes such as rape and child sexual abuse is known but not publicly discussed.[3] Stalking, trafficking in women and girls, honour-based violence, female genital mutilation (FGM), forced marriage, selective and forced

1 European Union Agency for Fundamental Rights (FRA), 'Violence against Women: An EU-Wide Survey' (2014) http://fra.europa.eu/sites/default/files/fra-2014-vaw-survey-main-results-apr14_en.pdf accessed 15 October 2019. See also World Health Organization (WHO), 'Global and Regional Estimates on Violence against Women: Prevalence and Health Effects of Intimate Partner Violence and Non-Partner Sexual Violence' (2013).

2 United Nations Office on Drugs and Crime (UNODC), Global Study on Homicide 2019. Executive Summary, 24 and Gender-related Killing of Women and Girls, 7.

3 Liz Kelly, 'The Continuum of Sexual Violence' in Jalna Hanmer and Mary Maynard (eds), *Women, Violence and Social Control* (MacMillan 1987).

abortion, denial of and maltreatment when seeking reproductive health services are all serious forms violence against women. In recent years, psychological violence has increasingly taken place in social media.[4]

Violence affects women's human rights in many ways. In addition to causing serious physical and psychological harm, violence prevents women from enjoying a whole range of human rights, including economic and social rights such as the right to work and the right to housing. Thus, violence against women is today seen as a discriminatory practice in itself.[5] However, responses to violence against women by national and local criminal justice organs and victim services have been lacking or inefficient and often not on par with responses to typical forms of violence that men encounter, multiplying the discriminatory effect of violence against women.[6] International human rights instruments have increasingly addressed gender-stereotypical assumptions of violence and the gendered passiveness of the criminal justice system.[7]

Feminist movements have assisted women victims of violence and, especially since the seventies, feminists have put pressure on States and the international community to recognise violence against women as a social and criminal problem. Also, a considerable amount of research has made the problem visible,[8] afforded theories to understand its root causes[9] and,

4 FRA, 'Challenges to Women's Human Rights in the EU' (2017) https://fra.europa.eu/sites/default/files/fra_uploads/fra-2017-challenges-to-women-human-rights_en.pdf accessed 15 October 2019.

5 Committee on the Elimination of Discrimination against Women (CEDAW Committee), General Recommendations No 19 on Violence against Women (1992) and No 35 on Gender-based Violence against Women, Updating General Recommendation No 19 (2017); United Nations General Assembly Declaration on Violence against Women (1993); Fourth United Nations Women's World Conference, Beijing Platform of Action (1995).

6 E.g. UN Division for the Advancement of Women, *Handbook for Legislation on Violence against Women* (United Nations 2010), 35; Beijing Platform of Action, 117; Stacey L Mallicoat, *Women, Gender, and Crime: Core Concepts* (Sage 2019).

7 CEDAW Committee, General Recommendation No 33 on Women's Access to Justice (2015), 26–28.

8 See FRA, WHO and UNODC (n 1 and n 2).

9 Carol Hagemann-White, Liz Kelly and Renee Romkens, 'Feasibility Study to Assess the Possibilities, Opportunities and Needs to Standardise National Legislation on Violence against Women, Violence against Children and Sexual Orientation Violence' (European Union 2010) 158–172 www.europarl.europa.eu/eplive/expert/multimedia/20110405MLT17038/media_20110405MLT17038.pdf accessed 15 October 2019. This meta-study is based on 140 research publications on the causal factors contributing to violence against women and children, including sexual violence. The authors distinguish four levels of explanations. The macro level relates to cultural, historical and economic structures, such as devaluing women and children, hierarchical power and impunity for violence. At the meso level, social institutions may contribute to violence by condoning violence in honour codes, hate groups or discriminatory practices, instead of setting limits or sanctions. The micro level refers to face-to-face groups, families, peer groups and so on that may approve or disapprove of violent behaviour. The ontogenic level includes personal life histories, personal traits and abuse of alcohol, drugs and pornography.

together with professionals and civil society organisations, developed best practices.[10]

The national and international human rights communities have not remained passive in the face of these problems. Since the nineties, violence against women has been introduced in the international human rights agenda and recognised as an issue in international law. However, only a few international documents or decisions have so far been legally binding. The Istanbul Convention is the first European instrument that sets clear and binding obligations on the States that ratify the Convention, thus contributing to the development of international law in this area.

2 Violence against women in international law

Violence against women was introduced in the agenda of international human rights institutions at the beginning of the nineties. Since then, it has gained increasing attention in international organisations and human rights bodies. The Committee on the Elimination of Discrimination against Women (CEDAW Committee) first paid attention to violence against women in 1989, signalling that the Convention on the Elimination of All Forms of Discrimination against Women (CEDAW), which does not specifically mention violence, must be interpreted in a way that requires States to take steps to protect women from and eradicate violence.[11] In 1992 the CEDAW Committee[12] and in 1993 the United Nations General Assembly[13] put violence against women in the context of discrimination and structural inequality. The UN Women's Conference in Beijing and its Platform of Action in 1995 characterised violence against women as an issue of inequality and women's subordinate position in society.[14] These documents have had a lasting impact on legal developments in national and international law.

10 E.g. United Nations, *Handbook for Legislation on Violence against Women* (2010). Liz Kelly and others, *Realising Rights: Case Studies on State Responses to Violence against Women and Children in Europe* (London Metropolitan University 2011) www.academia.edu/19483029/Realising_rights_Case_studies_on_state_responses_to_violence_against_women_and_children_in_Europe accessed 15 October 2019.

11 Convention on the Elimination of All Forms of Discrimination against Women (CEDAW) 1979; CEDAW Committee, General Recommendation No 12 Violence against Women (1989).

12 CEDAW Committee, General Recommendation No 19 on Violence against Women (1992).

13 Declaration on the Elimination of Violence against Women A/RES/48/104, 20 December 1993.

14 Fourth World Conference on Women, Beijing, China – September 1995: Action for Equality, Development and Peace. Platform of Action.

In Europe, both the Council of Europe[15] and the European Union[16] have paid attention to violence against women and promoted studies, programmes and recommendations to prevent such violence. The European Court of Human Rights (ECtHR) has developed a substantial body of case law on violence against women. Already in 1985, the Court noted that States must have sufficient criminal laws in place to protect individuals against sexual crimes.[17] State Parties to the European Convention on Human Rights (ECHR) can be found in violation of the ECHR due to gaps and insufficiencies in their national substantive criminal laws. The prime example is *M.C. v Bulgaria*,[18] where the crime of rape was interpreted narrowly by the national authorities to the effect that circumstances where victims who did not exercise physical resistance might be excluded from the definition of the crime. In light of the ECtHR's case law, States are also under the procedural obligation to effectively investigate claims of violence.[19] The Strasbourg Court has developed the standards against which the quality of the investigation can be assessed.[20] Importantly, States' positive obligations under the ECHR in the context of violence against women are not limited to the realm of criminal law. States have a positive obligation under the ECHR to protect persons against known and imminent threats of violence. This has been framed as a positive obligation to take protective operational

15 Especially Council of Europe Recommendation (2002) 5 on the protection of women against violence in Council of Europe member states. See also review of law and policies: Carol Hagemann-White, *Combating Violence against Women – Stocktaking Study on the Measures and Actions Taken in Council of Europe member States* (Council of Europe 2006). See e.g. Carol Hagemann-White, *Protecting Women against Violence* (Council of Europe 2010); Liz Kelly and others, *Realising Rights: Case Studies on State Responses to Violence against Women and Children in Europe* (London Metropolitan University 2011).

16 E.g. European Parliament, Resolution of 26 November 2009 on the elimination of violence against women 2010/C 285 E/07. The European Union has funded several studies from the Daphne programme, held numerous conferences and included topics on violence in its equality strategies over the years. The most recent Strategic Engagement for Gender Equality 2016–2019 document underlines data collection, prevention of female genital mutilation and enforcement of the Anti-trafficking Directive and Victims' Rights Directive. See https://ec.europa.eu/info/policies/justice-and-fundamental-rights/gender-equality/gender-equality-strategy_en accessed 15 October 2019. About the studies funded by the EU, see e.g. Carol Hagemann-White, Liz Kelly and Renee Romkens, *Feasibility Study to Assess the Possibilities, Opportunities and Needs to Standardise National Legislation on Violence against Women, Violence against Children and Sexual Orientation Violence* (European Union 2010).

17 *X and Y v the Netherlands* App no 8978/80 (ECHR, 26 March 1985).

18 *M.C. v Bulgaria* App no 39272/98 (ECHR, 4 December 2003).

19 *Durmaz v Turkey* App no 3621/07 (ECHR, 13 November 2014); *E.M. v Romania* App no 43994/05 (ECHR, 30 October 2012); *Valiuliene v Lithuania* App no 33234/07 (ECHR, 26 March 2013); *P.M. v Bulgaria* App no 49669/07 (ECHR, 24 January 2012); *I.G. v the Republic of Moldova* App no 53519/07 (ECHR, 15 May 2012).

20 See generally Vladislava Stoyanova, *Human Trafficking and Slavery Reconsidered. Conceptual Limits and States' Positive Obligations in European Law* (Cambridge University Press 2017) 360.

measures.[21] Another positive obligation that has been consistently used by the ECtHR to assess States' compliance with the ECHR is the positive obligation to adopt and apply in practice effective regulatory frameworks so that violence can be prevented or addressed.[22]

The Istanbul Convention builds on developments in regional and international human rights law. The ECHR is invoked in the first paragraph of its Preamble and, as the Explanatory Report clearly states, the ECtHR's case law "provided guidance to the drafters for the elaboration of numerous positive obligations and measures needed to prevent" violence.[23] CEDAW is also mentioned in the Preamble and, together with the work of the CEDAW Committee, has influenced different parts of the Istanbul Convention, including the definition of violence against women[24] and the provision on equality and non-discrimination.[25] The influence of international human rights law and the absorption of standards,[26] however, does not diminish the significance of the Istanbul Convention. Notwithstanding the growing body of international documents on the subject, only one previous international convention – the Inter-American Convention on the Prevention, Punishment, and Eradication of Violence against Women (*Belém do Pará* Convention) of 1994 – has directly addressed violence against women.

At the same time, the Istanbul Convention substantially contributes to the development of international norms on protection against violence, most recently to the ILO Violence and Harassment Convention (2019).[27] It sets clear

21 *Osman v UK* App no 87/1997/871/1083 (ECHR, 28 October 1998). For further elaboration see V Stoyanova in this volume. See also *Kontrova v Slovakia* App no 7510/04 (ECHR, 31 May 2007); *Branko Tomasic and Others v Croatia* App no 46598/06 (ECHR, 15 January 2009); *Civek v Turkey* App no 55354/11 (ECHR, 23 February 2016); *Talpis v Italy* App no 41237/14 (ECHR, 2 March 2017); *E.S. and Others v Slovakia* App no 8227/04 (ECHR, 15 September 2009).

22 For a review of the case law, see Stoyanova in this volume. See also Vladislava Stoyanova, 'Causation between State Omission and Harm within the Framework of Positive Obligations under the ECHR' (2018) 18 *Human Rights Law Review* 309–346. For relevant case law see *O'Keeffe v Ireland* App no 35810/09 (ECHR Grand Chamber, 28 January 2014); *Bevacqua and S v Bulgaria* App no 71127/01 (ECHR, 12 June 2008); *Hajduova v Slovakia* App no 2660/03 (ECHR, 30 November 2010); *Kalucza v Hungary* App no 57693/10 (ECHR, 24 April 2012).

23 Explanatory Report, para 29.

24 Explanatory Report, para 40.

25 Article 4. Explanatory Report, para 55. See Peroni in this volume.

26 For a detailed examination see Stoyanova in this volume.

27 Convention concerning the Elimination of Violence and Harassment in the World of Work C190, International Labour Organization (ILO), 21 June 2019. For example, the Istanbul Convention has been used by the ECtHR as an important point of reference. See *Talpis v Italy* App no 41237/14 (ECHR, 2 March 2017), para 129; *Bălşan v Romania* App no 49645/09 (ECHR, 23 May 2017); *Ž.B. v Croatia*, App no 47666/13 (ECHR, 11 July 2017) para 56.

aims and policies for the prevention of violence and the protection of victims. With these policy obligations, it offers a forward-looking perspective.

3 Drafting of the Istanbul Convention

The Istanbul Convention was drafted and negotiated during an intensive period between the spring of 2009 and December 2010. The Council of Europe set up the Ad Hoc Committee for Preventing and Combating Violence against Women and Domestic Violence (CAHVIO) in December 2008. CAHVIO was composed of governmental representatives of 47 Council of Europe Member States. Also, a good number of representatives of international organisations, including the European Union and the United Nations, non-governmental organisations and other observers attended the meetings of CAHVIO. Assisted by scientific experts, Professors Renée Römkens and Christine Chinkin, the Council of Europe Secretariat prepared the Convention text and the Explanatory Report. The country delegations actively participated in the preparation of the Convention making amendments discussed during the nine meetings of CAHVIO.[28] The drafters of the Convention drew on the work that had been done within the Council of Europe on violence against women and equality, especially on Recommendation 2002(5).[29]

The Convention was adopted by the Committee of Ministers and opened for signature in Istanbul on 11 May 2011. Following its 10th ratification by Andorra on 22 April 2014, it entered into force on 1 August 2014. By January 2020, 34 States had ratified the Convention and 12 had signed it but not yet ratified it. The Convention is open for accession by States that are not members

28 See in particular the Protocol of the 5th meeting of CAHVIO (2010)11, 15 July 2010, point 4. www.coe.int/en/web/istanbul-convention/cahvio accessed 15 October 2019.

29 Committee of Ministers, Recommendation 2002(5) on the protection of women against violence; see also Committee of Ministers, Recommendation No R (85) 4 on violence in the family and Recommendation No R (90) 2 on social measures concerning violence in the family; Parliamentary Assembly, Recommendations and Resolutions 1450 (2000) on Violence against women in Europe; 1247 (2001) on female genital mutilation; 1582 (2002) on domestic violence; 1327 (2003) on so-called "honour crimes"; 1723 (2005) on forced marriages and child marriages; 1847 (2008) on combating violence against women: towards a Council of Europe convention; 1777 (2007) on sexual assaults linked to "date-rape drugs"; 1654 (2009) on feminicides; 1691 (2009) on rape of women, including marital rape; 1868 (2009) on action to combat gender-based human rights violations, including abduction of women and girls; 1873 (2009) on sexual violence against women in armed conflict; 1881 (2009) on the urgent need to combat so-called "honour crimes"; 1891 (2009) on migrant women at particular risk from domestic violence; 1905 (2010) on children who witness domestic violence. Also, several reviews of the law and practice of Member States preceded the drafting process. See Carol Hagemann-White, *Combating Violence against Women* (Council of Europe 2006); Liz Kelly and Lorna Dubois, *Combating Violence against Women: Minimum Standards for Support Services* (Council of Europe 2008); Carol Hagemann-White, *Protecting Women against Violence* (Council of Europe 2010); Kelly and others (n 10).

of the Council of Europe but so far only Member States have joined. On 13 June 2017, the European Union signed the Convention but, as of January 2020, had not ratified it.[30]

While there seems to have been consensus in CAHVIO that a convention on violence against women was needed and timely, delegations expressed different opinions on the scope of the Convention during the preparatory meetings. While a majority of the delegations were in favour of a convention that covers all forms of violence against women, a minority of delegates wanted the Convention to focus on domestic violence irrespective of the victim's gender. The final wording of the Convention is a compromise between these two approaches: the Convention covers all forms of violence against women (Article 2.1) and encourages Parties to apply the Convention to "all victims of domestic violence" (Article 2.2). Part of the compromise was that the criminal law articles, with the exception of FGM, are gender neutral and do not refer to sex or gender.[31]

These disagreements have been reflected in the ratification processes. The Convention has a specific system that does not allow reservations to its key commitments. Reservations are only allowed to a limited number of articles listed in the Convention. Even so, two thirds of the States (22) that have ratified the Convention have made reservations. The most common reservations refer to international jurisdiction. Some States have made more general interpretative declarations that may reflect the tensions present in the preparation of the Convention.[32]

4 Scope and goals of the Convention

According to the Convention, violence against women means "all acts of gender-based violence that result in, or are likely to result in, physical, sexual, psychological or economic harm or suffering to women" (Article 3(a)). Specific forms of violence mentioned in the Convention are physical and psychological violence, including threats, coercion and arbitrary deprivation of liberty,[33] sexual violence and harassment, stalking, forced marriage, forced abortion and sterilisation, crimes committed in the name of so-called "honour" and female genital mutilation (Articles 33–42). The Convention and the Explanatory Report are, however, silent on the trafficking in women and girls and on the abuse of women in prostitution and pornography. The exclusion of human trafficking from the scope of the Istanbul Convention is understandable given the existence of a separate Council of Europe treaty on this subject.[34]

30 See De Vido in this volume.

31 CAHVIO 2nd meeting 2009 para 6; CAHVIO, Interim Report, para 39.

32 For more details, see Burek in this volume.

33 Preamble.

34 Council of Europe Convention on Action against Trafficking in Human Beings CETS No 197.

The goals of the Convention are ambitious and broad. The main goals are the elimination of violence against women and the protection of women against all forms of violence (Article 1(a)). Since violence against women is seen as a manifestation of unequal power relations between women and men and as discrimination against women, the Convention also aims at eliminating discrimination against women and at empowering women (Article 1(b)). The Convention puts violence against women in the context of inequality between the sexes and urges States to address inequality, cultural patterns and stereotypes on women and men that facilitate violence against women and hamper policies aimed at preventing violence and protecting women (Article 12(1)).

Under these overarching goals, the Convention has operational goals, which have been summarised as integrated and comprehensive policies against violence. The underlying understanding is that violence against women cannot be eliminated by isolated measures, let alone by criminal law only, but requires systematic and coordinated policies and programmes in many areas of social policy. Article 1(c) gives the Convention as a goal the design of "a comprehensive framework, policies and measures for the protection of and assistance to all victims of violence against women and domestic violence". The rest of the Convention explains, defines and prescribes what these comprehensive frameworks and policies should mean in practice but, at the concrete level, State Parties give content to the policies. However, it is important to underline that States have committed themselves to drawing up these policies, an obligation that is in line with the criteria set by the ECtHR in its case law on violence against women.[35]

5 Three Ps policy

The comprehensive and integrated approach of the Convention is further specified in the three Ps approach: prevention, protection and prosecution. This playful use of the letter P has evolved in human rights documents over the years and some documents add other Ps, such as policies[36] and punishment.[37] The P for policies may be the most important, since setting up consistent policies at the national level should be indispensable for fulfilling the Convention goals. It is also pertinent that these policies involve all relevant actors, such as "government agencies, the national, regional and local parliaments and authorities, national human rights institutions and civil society organisations" (Article 7(3)). The Convention pushes for cooperation among these actors (Article 9). In all policies, the victim should be placed at the centre (Article 7(2)).

35 Stoyanova (n 22).

36 CAHVIO (2009) 4 FIN, 4 May 2009, Interim Report II A "An additional main element ('P') will be included to represent the importance of integrated, holistic and coordinated policies in this field, without which measures to eliminate violence against women will be unsuccessful".

37 CEDAW Committee, General Recommendation No 35 on Gender-based Violence against Women, Updating General Recommendation No 19 (2017).

While the operative parts of the Convention give content to the policies, States must also allocate the necessary human resources and funding to counteract violence, including support to civil society organisations (Article 9). The State should also nominate a coordinating body for the policies, carry out fundamental data collection and support research on violence against women. The operational parts of the Convention are divided into Prevention; Protection and Support; Substantive Law; Procedures; and Migration and Asylum.

5.1 Prevention, protection and support

Prevention of violence covers general information and educational programmes as well as targeted training programmes for professionals. These programmes should improve knowledge on violence against women and equality. Like CEDAW,[38] the Istanbul Convention includes the obligation to eradicate prejudices, stereotypes, customs, traditions and practices based on the idea of the inferiority of women (Article 12(1)). Culture, custom, religion, tradition or so-called "honour" shall not be invoked as justifications for violence (Article 42).

Education is seen as key to eliminating violence. The curricula at all levels of education should cover themes such as "equality between women and men, non-stereotyped gender roles, mutual respect, non-violent conflict resolution in interpersonal relationships, gender-based violence against women and the right to personal integrity" (Article 14). Certainly, the teaching methods and exact content vary from primary to higher education. However, this commitment should lead to comprehensive assessments of curricula in educational institutions all over Europe.

Protection and support cover services to victims, which are divided into general and specialised services. The obligation to offer general services means that the authorities and agencies that may come into contact with victims in the course of their normal business must have the necessary knowledge and capability to respond to the needs of victims and to refer them to specialised services. States also commit themselves to provide specialised services to victims (Articles 22–25).

The formulations are mostly general, leaving the concrete design and content of programmes and services to the discretion of Member States. Also, the design of these programmes and services underlines the role of the Group of Experts on Action against Violence against Women and Domestic Violence (GREVIO), the body entrusted to monitor the implementation of the Convention. The general formulation of services also means that States should develop services covering the whole range of forms of violence against women. This should not be forgotten, even if the few concrete examples of services concern domestic violence, rape and sexual abuse, such as 24/7 helpline for victims, shelters, sexual violence referral centres and programmes for perpetrators, one of the few articles that mentions perpetrators (Article 16).

38 CEDAW Article 5(a); Istanbul Convention Article 12(1).

5.2 Civil and criminal law

In contrast to the generally formulated provisions on victim services, the substantive law part of the Convention contains concrete legislative requirements, a checklist for legislators, including both civil law and criminal law provisions.

Two obligations of the Convention go into the civil rights of the parties. First, a forced marriage must be possible to annul so that its consequences or the process do not burden the victim (Article 32). Second, violence must be taken into account in determining the custody of and visitation to children (Article 31). The Convention also notes that the withdrawal of parental rights can be possible if the safety of the victim cannot be guaranteed otherwise (Article 45(2)). Moreover, a victim must have recourse to civil remedies and compensation against both the perpetrator of violence and the State if the latter has failed to protect her against an immediate and known risk (Article 29).

The criminal law provisions of the Convention include the obligation to have adequate criminal laws against physical violence, psychological violence, stalking, sexual violence, sexual harassment, forced marriage, female genital mutilation, forced abortion and forced sterilisation (Articles 33–40). However, sexual harassment may be sanctioned by other than criminal law measures, as long as these measures are effective. The same applies to psychological violence and stalking but only as a reservation that has limited duration (Article 78(2) and 78(3)). There is no obligation to enact a specific crime with an honour-related motive but honour cannot be legitimate justification for any crime (Article 42). Aiding and abetting as well as attempting should also be a crime (Article 41). For sexual crimes, forced marriage, FGM and forced abortion and sterilisation the statute of limitation may not hinder the victim from initiating a process after she has come of age (Article 58).

Criminal sanctions must be effective, proportionate and dissuasive, taking into account the seriousness of the offences (Article 45(1)). The article on aggravating circumstances has turned out to be of particular importance. The law should allow judges to consider as aggravated circumstances that the crime was committed by a family member, or a person in a position of authority or in the presence of a child. Repeated crimes and crimes against a vulnerable victim can also make a crime aggravated. Likewise, crimes committed by two or more persons together, by the use or threat of a weapon or causing severe harm may be aggravated (Article 46).

The investigation of crimes should take place without delay and efficiently, including the collection of evidence. Victims must be protected throughout the proceedings and adequate risk assessments carried out (Article 50). There should be both emergency barring orders – to bar the suspect from the shared home in situations of immediate danger – and longer-term protection orders (Articles 52–53). In criminal proceedings, the victim's rights must be respected. Victims must be informed of their rights and of the release of the suspect/perpetrator. Victims have the right to be assisted by lawyers, support persons and organisations and the right to interpretation (Articles 56–57). If possible, they should be able to avoid contact with the suspect at the court house and be heard by electronic means. Their privacy and image should be protected (Article 56).

6 International dimensions

As an international instrument, the Convention goals include the promotion of international co-operation. The Convention promotes and provides a legal basis for mutual legal cooperation in the protection of victims, in the investigation and prosecution of crimes covered by the Convention and in the enforcement of judgements (Article 62). It includes regulation of jurisdiction to enable prosecution for most serious crimes in the Member State in which the perpetrator resides even if the crime was committed in another State (Article 44).

The Convention recognises the vulnerable situation of victims whose residence permit is dependent on that of their (violent) spouse. States are obliged to recognise that the victim is entitled to have her residence permit assessed independently from that of her spouse. In particular, the victim must have a right to a renewable residence permit if she is in a situation of particular vulnerability or if her stay is necessary to cooperate in the criminal investigation or procedure (Article 59).[39] Furthermore, the Convention enhances the recognition of gender-based persecution as a basis for asylum or humanitarian protection (Articles 60–61).[40] State Parties commit themselves to recognising the goals of the Convention in their development aid with third parties (Article 62(4)).

7 Impact

The Istanbul Convention has already had a remarkable impact in European countries.[41] This impact is supported by the implementation and monitoring system of the Convention. The monitoring bodies are GREVIO, an expert body of 15 members, and the Committee of the Parties, consisting of representatives of State Parties.

The monitoring process does not include an individual complaint mechanism but a state reporting mechanism. The process has two forms. First, Parties prepare a report on the implementation measures taken when they joined the Convention. This report, which is based on a detailed questionnaire, is submitted to GREVIO, which then discusses the report with the country representatives. Later, GREVIO designs monitoring rounds, focused on selected articles of the Convention (Article 68). GREVIO also gathers information and submissions from other sources, including civil society organisations, human rights bodies and country visits. Finally, GREVIO presents a report on the

39 See Staiano in this volume.

40 See Morondo Taramundi in this volume.

41 See Leskinen, Staiano, Sekowska-Kozolowska and Burek in this volume.

implementation of the Convention in the country. If needed, the Committee of the Parties may adopt recommendations.

The first report by State Parties has served as a benchmarking tool for States in evaluating their laws and policies. The Convention has contributed, among other things, to discussions on the elements of rape[42] – whether the essential element of force should be changed to lack of consent – on aggravating factors in criminal law and on *ex officio* prosecution of violence against women[43] and enhanced protection of victims.

In some Central and Eastern European countries, the Convention has received political attention and resistance because it has been understood as requiring States to change their concept of family.[44] While these worries seem to be unwarranted, this attention has greatly promoted the visibility of the Istanbul Convention in this part of Europe.

The impact of the Convention has been felt not only at the national level, but also at the regional EU level. The EU has signed the treaty, although it has not ratified it yet.[45] Despite the restrictions that follow from the limited competence of the EU as an international organisation,[46] the Istanbul Convention can have a wider impact by shaping the interpretation of EU secondary law. Two examples to this effect are offered in De Vido's chapter in this volume. The first concerns the interpretation of the term "sexual violence" in EU Directive 2014/41 regarding the European investigation order in criminal matters.[47]

42 See Leskinen in this volume.

43 See Niemi and Verdu Sanmartin in this volume.

44 See Sekowska-Kozolowska in this volume.

45 For a useful general overview of EU measures in the area of domestic violence and the legal basis invoked for the signature of the Istanbul Convention, see Ruth Lamont, 'Beating Domestic Violence? Assessing the EU's Contribution to Tackling Violence against Women' (2013) 50 *Common Market Law Review* 1787; See also Violence against Women and the EU Accession to the Istanbul Convention (European Parliament, 2017) available at www.europarl.europa.eu/RegData/etudes/STUD/2017/596815/IPOL_STU(2017)596815_EN.pdf accessed 15 October 2019; Sara De Vido, 'The Ratification of the Council of Europe Istanbul Convention by the EU: A Step Forward in the Protection of Women from Violence in the European Legal System' (2017) 9(2) *European Journal of Legal Studies* 69.

46 The EU can bind itself only to the extent of its competence. In light of this restriction, the EU signed the Convention in 2017 by adopting two decisions: one in relation to its competence in the area of asylum and *non-refoulement* (Council Decision 2017/866 of 11 May 2017 on the signing on behalf of the EU of the CoE Convention on preventing and combating violence against women and domestic violence with regard to asylum and *non-refoulement* OJ L 131/13) and one in relation to its competence in the area of judicial cooperation in criminal matters (Council Decision (EU) 2017/865 of 11 May 2017 on the signing, on behalf of the European Union, of the Council of Europe Convention on preventing and combating violence against women and domestic violence with regard to matters related to judicial cooperation in criminal matters OJ L 131/11). For an in-depth analysis see Vladislava Stoyanova, 'On the Bride's Side. Victims of Domestic Violence and their Residence Rights under EU and Council of Europe Law' (forthcoming).

47 Directive (EU) 2014/41 of the European Parliament and of the Council regarding the European investigation order in criminal matters [2014] OJ L130/1.

The second example concerns the circumstances in which migrant victims can be provided with autonomous residence permits, as envisioned in Directive 2004/38 on the rights of the citizens of the EU and their families,[48] and in Directive 2003/86/EC, which determines the conditions for the exercise of the right to family reunification by third country nationals residing lawfully in Member States.[49]

8 Aims and organisation of the book

This book brings much needed scholarly attention to the Istanbul Convention. Despite the importance of this major regional human rights development, surprisingly little has so far been said about it in the literature.[50] The book aims to explore the significance of the Istanbul Convention in the context of theoretical, international, and regional human rights law developments on violence against women. It further seeks to place the Convention within the context of gender equality and feminist movements, as violence against women has advanced on the international agenda largely thanks to these movements. In addressing these aims, the various chapters in this volume answer a number of questions, including:

- How has the Convention benefited from and contributed to prior international and regional human rights law developments?
- How does the Convention relate to feminist theoretical understandings of violence against women and in which ways does the Convention fall short of this project?
- While the Convention puts violence in the context of equality, does it really push for restructuring the gender and other power imbalances, and if so, in which ways?
- What impact has the Convention had so far in Member States and in EU and ECHR law?
- What is the Convention's potential to effectively combat violence against women and what are possible limitations to this potential?

The book presents the Convention but it also has a critical approach. The contributors are mainly young scholars with a background in international law and feminist legal studies. How does this generation view the Convention? While the authors' overall assessment of the Convention is positive – it is needed and

48 Article 13(2)(c), Directive (EC) 2004/38 of the European Parliament and of the Council on the right of citizens of the Union and their family members to move and reside freely within the territory of the Member States [2004] OJ L158/77.

49 Article 15(3), [2003] OJ L 251/12.

50 One of the few books on the Istanbul Convention is Ronagh McQuigg, *The Istanbul Convention, Domestic Violence and Human Rights* (Routledge, 2017).

it improves the protection of victims of violence – two cross-cutting critiques underlie the book contributions. First, the Convention is not seen as sufficient in itself to protect victims of violence. The Convention is a political compromise that could be stronger. At the level of implementation, the impact of the Convention depends on the role that GREVIO will take. Second, several contributors pay attention to the lack of intersectionality in the Convention, which draws its strength from the comprehensive and integrated policies on violence against women. Except for migrant women and women asylum seekers, the Convention does not pay particular attention to the problems of specific groups of women in vulnerable situations, nor to other genders but rather to women and men.

The volume is organised in six parts. In the first two parts, some authors contextualise the Convention within broader human rights developments on violence against women, including CEDAW and ECHR developments, and within feminist theoretical debates and movements. Other authors critically scrutinise central concepts linked to violence against women, most notably violence, equality, gender and due diligence. These concepts lie at the core of the Convention and are central to defining the obligations imposed on States. The interpretation of these concepts necessarily has an impact on the interpretation of the Convention as a whole and on the content and scope of state responses to violence against women, including obligations of prevention, protection, criminalisation and prosecution.

In the next four parts of the book, the authors focus on the Convention's more specific responses to violence against women – including support and criminal law responses – and on national responses to the Convention in various countries of the Council of Europe, including Poland and Sweden. Some authors discuss protection and support services, including the provision of shelters and housing to victims of violence. Others focus on the Convention's responses to specific forms of violence such as FGM, forced sterilisation and sexual offences and on its responses to violence against specific groups of women, namely migrant women and women asylum seekers. Another group of authors reflect on the challenges the Convention faces in some Council of Europe States because of political environments resistant to the cultural changes in gender roles pushed for by the Convention.

Part I "Context and role" opens with a chapter by Lorena Sosa who shows that feminist movements had great influence in the initial recognition of gender-based violence as a human rights issue. The author further shows that these movements continue to be relevant after the adoption of international norms by pointing to regulation gaps and to deficiencies in the implementation of these norms. In consequence, she argues, human rights instruments often show an imprint of the concerns flagged by social movements and civil society. Lorena Sosa additionally argues that, given that human rights treaties are "living instruments" that adapt to new social realities, attention to contemporary feminist claims could ensure that these treaties remain effective and compelling. Her chapter explores to what extent the Istanbul Convention is in line with feminist claims made at the time of its adoption and thereafter. It offers a reflection of the potential of the Istanbul Convention to adapt to changing times and, thus, to ensure the responsiveness of the gender-based violence paradigm.

In the second chapter, Lourdes Peroni argues that the Istanbul Convention holds great potential to combat the prejudices and stereotypes that have historically construed women as subordinate to men in society. However, in her view, it is less clear whether the Convention holds equally strong potential to advance women's actual power in the political and socio-economic spheres, including women's equal participation in politics and in the labour market. Her chapter argues that if the Convention is to fully realise its substantive equality aspiration and to effectively combat violence against women, it needs to be interpreted so as to promote women's de facto equality politically and socio-economically. The arguments in the chapter draw mainly on an international human rights instrument from which the Istanbul Convention drafters took inspiration: CEDAW, which brings together civil, political, social and economic rights in advancing women's equality.

In the last chapter of Part I, Sara De Vido explores the impact of the Istanbul Convention as an interpretative tool at the European level. The chapter suggests that this legal instrument can be used by European and national judges alike to set higher standards of protection of women's human rights while interpreting European and national law. In order to assess the potential of the Istanbul Convention, the chapter therefore proposes a threefold analysis of the Council of Europe, the European Union and the domestic levels with a focus on two Italian cases. It also critically investigates the complex legal issues related to the ratification of the Istanbul Convention by the EU and how an interpretation of EU law in light of the Istanbul Convention could overcome the political difficulties in the adoption of secondary legislation on combating violence against women. The chapter eventually encourages dialogue between European and national courts.

In Part II "Concepts" Johanna Niemi and Amalia Verdu Sanmartin show in their chapter that gender and violence against women are central concepts in the Istanbul Convention. They sustain that the Convention's conceptualisation of violence is important, as it guides the interpretation of measures and provisions of the Convention. This chapter offers a discourse analytic reading of the Convention text and its Explanatory Report to understand their approach to the concepts of violence against women and gender-based violence. It contends that gender is an integrated part of the definition of violence against women. The analysis presented in this chapter shows that the concept of gender in the Convention refers to a binary of sexes, namely to men and women and to their social roles as a reflection of biological differences. The authors argue that the concept of gender used in the Convention shapes the depiction of the subjects as victims or perpetrators. They additionally sustain that the Convention underlines women as victims of violence and the harm done to them, while perpetrators of violence remain mostly invisible and ungendered. Niemi and Verdu Sanmartin argue that the Convention does not address intersecting differences among women either, which the Convention refers to as vulnerabilities. According to the authors, the only reference to other gender identities, sexualities and differences among women is in the anti-discrimination clause, which forbids discrimination among victims. While the Explanatory Report defines a long list of vulnerabilities, neither the Explanatory Report nor the Convention text specifies special services to vulnerable groups of women. The only group specifically addressed in the Convention are women with a migrant background, as several articles mention crimes typically associated with this group. However, as the authors conclude, the services prescribed in the Convention should be available to all women, without discrimination.

Vladislava Stoyanova's chapter focuses on the standard of due diligence enshrined in Article 5 of the Istanbul Convention to frame States' obligations. This standard, the author argues, has been uncritically endorsed in the existing literature on violence against women because it has played a crucial role in the recognition of this violence as a human rights violation. The chapter offers an in-depth inquiry into the meaning of the due diligence standard, its limits and reasons to be cautious about it. It explores how due diligence has been framed in the Istanbul Convention. The chapter clarifies that, in general, the European Court of Human Rights does not use the concept of due diligence; rather, violence against women can trigger States' positive human rights obligations. The chapter underlines that all positive obligations are not obligations of due diligence and calls for better sensitivity between these two standards. The main argument is that it is important to be sensitive to the nuances and differences between the two frameworks. The author contends that a general reference to the due diligence standard, as can be found in Article 5 of the Istanbul Convention, poses the danger of ignoring these nuances.

In Part III "Criminal law responses", Minni Leskinen provides an overview and a critical assessment of the relevant provisions of the Istanbul Convention on sexual offences. Her chapter discusses these provisions in relation to the Explanatory Report of the Convention, to relevant case law of European Court of Human Rights and to the country monitoring carried out by GREVIO. In addition to the GREVIO reports that have been completed so far, she uses examples from Finland and Sweden to articulate various topical issues. With regard to the Istanbul Convention, the chapter investigates themes such as the lack and validity of consent to sexual intercourse, the sexual nature of sexual acts, vulnerability, marital rape, sentencing and sexual harassment. Eventually, the chapter asks to what extent the Istanbul Convention holds potential for challenging the ways we understand sexuality in the framework of criminal law.

Ruth M. Mestre i Mestre examines in her chapter the use of intersectionality in relation to violence against women in the Convention with a focus on female genital mutilation/cutting (FGM/C). Intersectionality, she reminds us, is a tool for exploring the different ways in which discriminatory systems interact. The consequences of intersectionality are manifested in institutions and legislation. According to the Istanbul Convention, gender-based violence against women is related to harm caused to a woman as a result of power relations that shape women's subordinate status in society. As Mestre i Mestre argues, violence against women needs to be addressed in the context of inequality and discrimination, existing stereotypes and gender roles in a particular society. She further reminds us that intersectional approaches claim that race, migration status, gender and class are not distinct and isolated realms of experience but come into existence in relation to one another and are mutually constructing. Her chapter asks what articulations of distinct systems of power the Istanbul Convention recognises and analyses the consequences of such articulations on racialised women. To approach these questions, the chapter analyses the ways in which race, migration and other power structures intersect with gender in shaping structural, political, and representational aspects of female genital mutilation/cutting in the Istanbul Convention.

In her chapter, Daniela Alaattinoğlu recalls that laws and practices allowing for sterilisation against the patient's will have existed in Europe for around a century, targeting different groups at different times. Groups particularly targeted by the practices today are Roma women, people with disabilities and trans people. Article 39(b) of the Istanbul Convention outlaws "performing surgery which has the purpose or effect of terminating a woman's capacity to naturally reproduce without her prior and informed consent or understanding of the procedure". But which practices are included in the scope of this provision? Who does it recognise as a victim? And how effective is the Istanbul Convention to combat contemporary practices of forced sterilisation in its ratifying States? The chapter renders visible how forced sterilisation has, modelled on the Nazi atrocities, developed from a violation of international criminal law to also a violation of human rights law, including in the ECHR. The chapter welcomes the explicit inclusion of forced sterilisation as a form of gender-based violence in the Istanbul Convention. Nevertheless, it points to three specific shortcomings that may undermine the Convention's effectiveness in this area. The first is the Convention's limited remedial scope and individual focus. The second is its failure to recognise the structural discrimination and stereotypes inherent in practices of forced sterilisation – which are not merely gender-based, but rather, intersectional. The last shortcoming concerns the Convention's inherent cis-exclusiveness, which hampers its potential to combat some of the currently most common coercive sterilisations in Europe.

Part IV "Victim services" starts with a chapter authored by Ingrid Westendorp who shows that, when the main human rights instruments recognising the right to adequate housing were drafted, there was no specific attention to women's perspective, let alone to the perspective of women in abusive relationships. Her chapter raises the question whether the Istanbul Convention is capable of changing this situation by offering women victims of domestic violence better protection and support services. In order to answer this question, first the content of the right to adequate housing is examined. Next, the different solutions offered to women victims of domestic violence are debated, i.e. sending battered women to shelters and evicting the perpetrator from the family residence as well as the housing situation of domestic violence survivors.

Subsequently, current international attention to the link between domestic violence and the right to housing is explored. Finally, the potential of the Istanbul Convention is examined, including the role that GREVIO can play in protecting and safeguarding the right to adequate housing of battered women.

The discussion in the fourth part continues with a discussion on the relationship between services provided by the State and those provided by civil society organisations. The Istanbul Convention puts great emphasis on civil society. It recognises their role and guides States to support and allocate resources to civil society organisations (Articles 7–9; 13; 68(5)). The division of roles between the State and civil society is not always a simple matter, as Ulrika Andersson and Sara Bengtson exemplify through an examination of the Swedish shelter support to battered women. Article 23 of the Istanbul Convention obliges State Parties to provide for easily accessible shelters but it does not take a stand on how shelters should be organised. The authors argue that violence against women in Sweden was considered to be a private matter until the eighties. The feminist movement pressed for more active policies and set up a number of feminist-oriented shelters. Once the non-interventionist attitude towards violence against women was abandoned, other tensions followed. Their chapter explores some of these tensions as they have played out in the context of the shelter movement and the professionalisation of support to battered women. The main tensions have concerned the conceptualisation of violence against women and the ways of organising society's response to such violence. The Istanbul Convention places violence against women in the context of gender inequality and requires that a contracting State acknowledges responsibility for combating this violence. The Swedish discussion, the authors argue, illustrates that increased public responsibility may entail dilemmas for feminist goals and perspectives.

In Part V "Migration and asylum", Fulvia Staiano argues that migrant women in Europe are particularly at risk of experiencing various forms of violence. She contends that, though the issue has been widely recognised in the European context and beyond, the main problem in this area is not merely the absence of protective norms. Rather, she further argues, the law in this field plays a complex role because of a narrow focus on criminal law responses, which has overshadowed the need for a more comprehensive approach that takes into account how immigration law contributes to migrant women's vulnerability to violence. The chapter claims that, in this context, family reunification and labour migration law are crucial areas in need of attention. A broader question concerns the capability of the human rights systems in Europe to shift their focus from moments of crisis (such as those already exacerbated phenomena of violence against women) to effectively addressing the socio-economic disenfranchisement experienced by migrant women as aggravated by norms in immigration law. The chapter explores the potential of the Istanbul Convention to do this by fostering a holistic approach to violence against women beyond a criminal law perspective.

Dolores Morondo Taramundi discusses the Istanbul Convention's responses to violence against another group of women: asylum seekers. She reminds us that international conventions and national asylum policies have tended to overlook the specific position of female asylum seekers and the gendered nature of refugee situations, thus failing to offer women adequate international protection. Morondo Taramundi shows that one of the obstacles for obtaining protection concerns the recognition of gender-based violence against women as grounds for claiming asylum. Her chapter reviews the main challenges to the recognition of gender-based violence as grounds for determining the status of refugees according to the definition in the Refugee Convention of 1951 and examines the contribution of the Istanbul Convention. The chapter looks at how Articles 60 and 61 of the Istanbul Convention address those challenges, reinforcing the claims of women victims of gender-based violence. It also identifies lingering issues and missed opportunities.

In Part VI "National responses to the Convention", the contribution of Katarzyna Sękowska-Kozłowska examines the resistance to and the changes promoted by the Istanbul Convention in Poland. Poland ratified the Istanbul Convention in 2015, after a heated public and political debate that focused on provisions of the Convention stipulating State Parties' obligations regarding the change of cultural patterns and gender stereotyping. Thereby, she argues, the Istanbul Convention became one of the key elements of the so-called "war on gender" between conservative and liberal movements. Her chapter further shows that other legal implications of the Polish accession remained overshadowed. It argues that, four years later, in the middle of the backlash against gender equality, human rights and democracy in Poland, the situation remains unchanged if not worse. According to the author, endangered by the risk of withdrawal, the Convention is still a subject of ideological rather than of substantive discussion. The chapter examines to what extent, despite these unfavourable circumstances, the Convention has been a tool of real changes in Polish law and practice, particularly with regard to sexual and domestic violence.

The book closes with a chapter authored by Wojciech Burek on reservations and declarations under the Istanbul Convention, which according to the author play an important role: so far, almost half of the 45 States (and the European Union) that have signed the Convention have formulated a reservation and/or an interpretative declaration. Burek shows that some States have objected to these reservations and declarations. Against this background, his chapter summarises the evolution of international law governing reservations to human rights treaties, and presents the partially unique system of reservations established by the Istanbul Convention. The chapter also critically appraises States' practice under the Convention. It gives special attention to the practice of some States (Croatia, Latvia, Lithuania and Poland) to formulate vaguely-worded interpretative declarations with reference to domestic law. The author concludes that the Convention's silence on the interpretative declarations is most unfortunate.

In sum, this book makes a significant contribution to the literature on international human rights law and violence against women by analysing the Istanbul

Convention's potential, limitations and challenges and by suggesting ways forward. Key areas of potential impact include advancing substantive equality between women and men,[51] and enhancing support for women victims of domestic violence.[52] However, and as many contributors emphasise, developing this potential will greatly depend on GREVIO's work.[53] Moreover, as some authors remark, civil society organisations[54] as well as judges and lawyers at the EU, Council of Europe and national levels[55] also play a crucial role in realising the Convention's potential.

The book also significantly exposes various limitations flowing from the Convention. One of these limitations arises from the Convention's very subject of protection. Including sexual orientation and gender identity as grounds of discrimination, according to Lorena Sosa, "seems insufficient to provide protection to lesbian and trans women". In turn, Johanna Niemi and Amalia Verdu Sanmartin note that the Convention "does not recognise violence against homosexuals, transmen or men who do not conform to the masculine standard as gender-based violence". As highlighted earlier, the Convention could have been stronger in addressing intersectional inequalities and violence. Another limitation, to which Vladislava Stoyanova draws our attention, concerns the due diligence standard embedded in Article 5 of the Convention, which may undermine rather than strengthen the positive obligations to prevent, investigate, punish and provide reparation developed by the ECtHR.[56] Also, if the Convention is to truly push for substantive equality, its understanding of economic violence and dependency may need to go beyond abusive partner relationships to problematise "the economic impact that gender inequality has on women".[57]

The Convention's criminal law responses to forms of violence such as FGM/C, forced sterilisation and sexual violence are generally welcomed by the authors, as these responses signal the need to take seriously forms of violence typically inflicted on women.[58] At the same time, however, the authors highlight some risks and challenges underlying these responses, including the risk of racialisation and stigmatisation in the case of FGM/C[59] and the challenge of respecting state discretion in defining the criminal law details while demanding effective criminalisation.[60] The provisions focusing specifically on migrant women and women asylum seekers are among the key additions in the Istanbul Convention. Yet challenges remain with respect to the Convention's potential

51 See Peroni in this volume, though note the limitations in the political and economic spheres.
52 See, for example, Westendorp in this volume.
53 See, for example, Peroni as well as Niemi and Verdu Sanmartin in this volume.
54 See Sosa in this volume.
55 See De Vido in this volume.
56 See Stoyanova in this volume.
57 See Sosa in this volume. See also Peroni.
58 See, for example, Alaattinoğlu in this volume.
59 See Mestre i Mestre in this volume.
60 See Leskinen in this volume.

to protect these groups of women.[61] One of these challenges is ensuring that the Convention's comprehensive approach, which includes prevention obligations, also benefits migrant women.[62] Another set of challenges highlighted in this volume relates to the strategies to avoid, undermine or limit the Convention's impact domestically. These strategies range from threatening to withdraw from the Convention to vaguely wording reservations and declarations.[63]

This book reinforces the link between advancing equality and combating violence against women that the Istanbul Convention emphasises. Thus, to eliminate violence against women, it is paramount to interpret substantive equality so as to promote women's de facto equality politically (e.g. women's participation in politics) and socio-economically (e.g. in the labour market).[64] As Niemi and Verdu Sanmartin remark "it is important that the general principles of the Convention, such as empowerment, non-discrimination and protection of vulnerable groups, are recognised in the interpretation of all articles of the Convention". If the Convention is to remain responsive to future feminist claims, its monitoring body as well as lawyers and academics will need to pay attention to social movements beyond NGOs.[65] Fulfilling the Convention's potential, addressing the risks and challenges and moving forward are a collective endeavour that will involve a wide range of social and legal actors besides GREVIO.

61 See Morondo Taramundi and Staiano in this volume.
62 See Staiano in this volume.
63 See Sękowska-Kozłowska and Burek in this volume.
64 See Peroni in this volume.
65 See Sosa in this volume.

Part I

Context and role

1 The Istanbul Convention in the context of feminist claims

Lorena Sosa

1 Introduction

The normative impact of social movements is particularly visible in the field of violence against women (VAW), including in the human rights instruments addressing this violence. Norms address violence according to the perceptions, considerations and reactions that seem prevalent in certain sectors of society at a given time.[1] Moreover, human rights treaties must take account of developing social conditions and perception of rights.[2] The adaptation of human rights norms to social claims regarding VAW can contribute to these norms' effectiveness and permanency.

Women's activism has a prominent part in the process of elaboration, implementation and monitoring of norms. It has contributed to defining the scope and meaning of VAW and to triggering and promoting the development of international norms, standards and monitoring mechanisms.[3] It contributes to monitoring the implementation of and compliance with norms by pointing out the gaps and flaws in policies.[4] That said, compliance with norms is most often assessed in relation to the presence of institutional factors, such as abolishing conflicting laws and passing legislation, allocating budget, creating dedicated agencies and including women in decision-making positions. Strategies for the implementation of norms may nevertheless fail to contribute to social transformation "if they lose their relation to women's movements and claims".[5]

1 Mary R Jackman, 'Violence in Social Life' (2002) 28 *Annual Review of Sociology* 387.
2 A Boyle and Christine Chinkin, *The Making of International Law* (Oxford University Press 2007) 154.
3 United Nations Secretary General (2006) p. 13.
4 Thomas Risse, Stephen C Ropp and Kathryn Sikkink (eds), *The Power of Human Rights: International Norms and Domestic Change* (Cambridge University Press 1999); Alison Brysk, 'The Persistent Power of Human Rights' in Thomas Risse, Stephen C Ropp and Kathryn Sikkink (eds) (Cambridge University Press 2013); Beth A Simmons, *Mobilizing for Human Rights: International Law in Domestic Politics* (2009).
5 Dolores Morondo Taramundi, 'Gender Machineries vs Feminist Movements? Collective Political Subjectivity in the Time of Passive Revolution' (2016) *Gender and Education* 1, 16.

The connection between social movements and the effectiveness of norms prompts the question to what extent contemporary feminist claims are addressed by the Council of Europe Convention on Preventing and Combating Violence against Women and Domestic Violence (the Istanbul Convention) and considered by its monitoring mechanism. By "feminist claims" I refer to challenges to systematic gender discrimination and the pursuit of gender equality, expressed through collective actions. These actions can range from spontaneous to organised forms of participation, including general subversiveness in the arts or academia.

Women have mobilised, raised their claims and organised their actions, before and after the adoption of the Convention. In spite of important achievements, recent times have witnessed a "redoing" of feminism and its "resurgence", with the participation of younger generations,[6] confirmed by the many organised campaigns against them.[7] The "revival" of feminism is in part due to the use of social media and the Internet for networking, coordinating actions and disseminating strategies.[8] A "spontaneous feminism" is emerging, incorporating women who "simply position themselves as the subject of rights and with rights equal to men".[9] This feminism is characterised by having "incidental" representatives, who emerge from women's participation in such different acts of resistance.[10] These "new" forms of feminist participation result in a diverse array of collective actions often originating from submerged, latent, and temporary networks, rather than centralised organisational forms.[11]

That said, there is great diversity within and among "feminisms" and only the most visible public protests, often by elite groups of women, are noticed, thus missing the activism of marginalised groups.[12] Nonetheless, there is a continuity between generations according to which "new" or emerging feminist elaborations are based on previously elaborated notions. In addition, despite the contemporary transnational character of feminist movements,[13] their content, structure and demands are heavily inflected by their specific contexts.

6 Hester Baer, 'Redoing Feminism: Digital Activism, Body Politics, and Neoliberalism' (2016) 16 *Feminist Media Studies* 17, 17; 34; Jonathan Dean and Kristin Aune, 'Feminism Resurgent? Mapping Contemporary Feminist Activisms in Europe' (2015) 14 *Social Movement Studies* 375.

7 Mieke Verloo and David Paternotte, 'The Feminist Project under Threat in Europe' (2018) 6 *Politics and Governance* 1.

8 Rachel F Seidman, 'Who Needs Feminism? Lessons from a Digital World' (2013) 39 *Feminist Studies* 549.

9 María Luisa Femenías, 'Feminismos Latinoamericanos: Una Mirada Panorámica' (2011) 6 *La manzana de la discordia* 53, 53; 59.

10 Graciela Di Marco, 'Los Movimientos de Mujeres En La Argentina y La Emergencia Del Pueblo Feminista' (2010) XIV *Segunda época* 51, 51; 67.

11 SM Buechler, 'New Social Movement Theories' (1995) 36 *The Sociological Quarterly* 441.

12 Nancy A Hewitt, 'Feminist Frequencies: Regenerating the Wave Metaphor' (2012) 38 *Feminist Studies* 658.

13 Laura Briggs, 'Trasnational' in Lisa Disch and Mary Hawkesworth (eds), *The Oxford Handbook of Feminist Theory* (Oxford University Press 2016).

Without attempting an exhaustive historical discussion, this chapter explores the main feminist claims in the European context during the drafting process and after the adoption of the Istanbul Convention, followed by a review of their incorporation into the final text. The chapter concludes with some reflections about the lessons learned.

2 Feminisms in Europe and the adoption of the Istanbul Convention

Feminisms in Europe seem characterised by three aspects. First, their heterogeneity. Europe has a long tradition of women's activism, addressing issues such as women's political participation, sexual violence, the gendered division of labour, pay equity and sex discrimination. However, the varied histories of feminism in different European countries confirm the diversity of goals among the movements. Feminisms in Europe have ranged from liberalism to materialism, including varying types of "difference" feminisms, some of them becoming more prevalent in some countries. The idea of a traditional flow of first-, second- and third-wave feminism that applies to Europe is also challenged by the historical development of each State.[14] For instance, while British women gained the right to vote in 1918, marking the end of the first wave, Swiss women did so only in 1971. Particularly, post-fascist and post-communist countries' expressions of feminism do not fit the wave framework.[15]

Second, the early reception of several feminist claims by the Council of Europe (CoE) is another characteristic. For instance, it recognised the political rights and legal position of women in the seventies,[16] and since the eighties, equality between women and men has been a leading principle of the organisation.[17] Moreover, in many European countries, feminist movements have undergone a process of "institutionalisation", partly as the consequence of the Council of Europe's broad agenda for promoting women's participation in all fields of decision-making.[18] For instance, in 2003, the Council of Europe adopted Recommendation Rec(2003)3 on balanced participation of women and men in political and public decision-making. Although the numbers of women elected and holding strategic positions within the Council

14 On feminism in Europe until the emergence of the Third Wave, see Gisela Kaplan, *Contemporary Western European Feminism* (New York University Press 1992).

15 Jonathan Dean and Kristin Aune, 'Feminism Resurgent? Mapping Contemporary Feminist Activisms in Europe' (2015) 14(3) *Social Movement Studies* 375–395.

16 Resolutions R (72) 22 and R (75) 606.

17 See Second Mid-Term Plan (1981–86).

18 Encouraging what Lovecey calls "the politics of presence". Jill Lovecy, 'Gender Mainstreaming and the Framing of Women's Rights in Europe – the Contribution of the Council of Europe' (2002) 10 *Feminist Legal Studies* 271.

has increased, "parity is still a distant goal for all aspects of political and public decision-making".[19]

Third, activism is channelled in women's organisations and NGOs, encouraged by the CoE's strategy for civil society participation. NGOs have become the pillar of civil society in dialogues with the Committee of Ministers, the Parliamentary Assembly and the Congress of Local and Regional Authorities. The European Union has also greatly encouraged the participation of civil society through NGO funding. Such NGO-isation of activism, however, has been criticised by some authors as leading to a "depoliticisation" and "delocalisation" of feminist claims.[20] That said, given the strategy to involve NGOs in the discussions of regulation, it is reasonable to expect NGOs participation as observers in the negotiations of the Istanbul Convention, and to convey some of the main feminist claims.

Considering the long history of women's movements in Europe, the adoption of a legally binding convention on violence against women a decade into the new millennium, may appear as a tardy one. However, several initiatives dating back to the eighties and nineties preceded the adoption of the Istanbul Convention, such as Recommendation No R (85) 4 on violence in the family adopted in 1985 by the Committee of Ministers,[21] and Recommendation No R (90) 2 on social measures concerning violence in the family in 1990.[22] In 1993, the third European Ministerial Conference on Equality between Women and Men focused on "Strategies for the elimination of violence against women in society: the media and other means", which resulted in the development of an Action Plan to Combat Violence against Women. Finally, recommendation (2002) 5 on the protection of women against violence was adopted.[23] National implementation of this recommendation has been monitored, showing many

19 Factsheets on Gender Equality, 'Achieving balanced participation of women and men in political and public decision-making: a gender equality and democratic requirement', available at: Achieving balanced participation of women and men in political and public decision-making. See also: Mercedes Mateo Diaz and Susan Millns, 'Parity, Power and Representative Politics: The Elusive Pursuit of Gender Equality in Europe' (2004) 12 *Feminist Legal Studies* 279; Daniel James Keith and Tania Verge, 'Nonmainstream Left Parties and Women's Representation in Western Europe' (2018) 24 *Party Politics* 397.

20 Islah Jad, 'The "NGOization" of the Arab Women's Movements' (2003) 20 *Al-Raida*; Islah Jad, 'NGOs – between Buzzwords and Social Movements' (2007) 17 *Development in Practice* 622; William F Fisher, 'Doing Good? The Politics and Antipolitics of NGO Practices' (1997) 26 *Annual Review of Anthropology* 439; Jael Silliman, 'Expanding Civil Society, Shrinking Political Spaces – The Case of Women's NGOs' (1999) 96 *Social Politics* 23.

21 Parliamentary Assembly of the Council of Europe, Recommendation No R (85) 4 of the Committee of Ministers to Member States on Violence in the Family (26 March 1985).

22 Parliamentary Assembly of the Council of Europe, Recommendation No R (90) 2 of the Committee of Ministers to Member States on Social Measures Concerning Violence within the Family (15 January 1990).

23 Council of Europe, Recommendation (2002) 5 of the Committee of Ministers to Member States on the Protection of Women against Violence Adopted on 30 April 2002 and Explanatory Memorandum (30 April 2002).

gaps in the provision of services for victims.[24] In December 2008, the Council of Europe set up the Ad Hoc Committee for Preventing and Combating Violence against Women and Domestic Violence (CAHVIO), which held nine meetings during the drafting process of the Istanbul Convention.

Following the European approach to civil society participation, several NGOs participated as observers during the meetings of CAHVIO. After the adoption of the Convention, NGOs continue to actively participate in the monitoring process by submitting shadow reports to the Group of Experts on Action against Violence against Women and Domestic Violence (GREVIO), the independent expert body responsible for monitoring the implementation of the Convention. Such interaction can contribute to keep the Convention receptive to social developments.

3 Contemporary feminist claims and their reception in the Convention

This section explores the theoretical construction of the subject of protection, the conceptualisations of violence and the economic aspects of feminist claims, and their incorporation in the text of the Istanbul Convention.

3.1 The feminist subject and the subject of protection in the Convention

At the time of adoption of the Istanbul Convention, feminist theories had dwelt for decades upon who was the subject of their claims. Naffine argued that law's construction of its subjects follows a set of characteristics – rational, in control of its cognitive capacities, inhabiting the public sphere – suggesting that the legal subject is implicitly a man, excluding and silencing women. Feminism thus points out such bias in the law and brings attention to "women". Yet the view of "men" and "women" as stable categories ("enduring bodies") with a fixed and "natural" content was also challenged by feminist theory.[25] Moreover, the idea of women as a constant and homogenous category, promoted by mainstream European feminism, was soon criticised for promoting issues that affected "white heterosexual middle class women" almost exclusively. Dissenting perspectives derived from critical race theory, postcolonial, chicana, and queer studies, emerged in the early eighties and approached a mature shape by the new millennium. Postcolonial feminism – critiquing colonial images of non-Western women as oppressed by their cultures – has been prevalent in

24 The analytical report of the fourth monitoring round is available at: https://rm.coe.int/CoERMPublicCommonSearchServices/DisplayDCTMContent?documentId=0900001680465f71.

25 Joan W Scott, 'Reflections on Women and Gender in Twentieth-Century Mexico Introduction' (2008) 20 *Gender & History* 149.

Europe, due to its colonialist past.[26] In addition, "intersectionality", highlighting the qualitatively different experience of discrimination that results from the intersection of gender with other socially constructed categories of distinction,[27] was quite widespread in European academic circles by the time the Convention was adopted,[28] while the European Union was engaged in tackling multiple discrimination. Intersectionality seemed particularly appealing to "young feminists".[29]

Similarly, the heterosexual assumptions that the notion of "woman" normally entails was also challenged.[30] The category of women was then reconfigured in Queer theory,[31] emphasising that sex is a cultural construct, regulated by a heteronormative discourse.[32] Discrimination against lesbian, gay, bisexual, trans and intersex persons (LGBTI) gained much attention in the so-called "Europeanization of social movements".[33] For instance, the International Lesbian, Gay, Bisexual, Trans and Intersex Association (ILGA), founded in 1978, gained access to the European Union (EU) in the nineties, and managed to get sexual orientation and gender identity issues on the EU agenda.[34] These claims gained momentum in 2006, following the adoption of the Yogyakarta Principles on the Application of International Human Rights Law in Relation to Sexual Orientation and Gender Identity, and contributing to the "normalisation" of homosexuality in Europe.[35] In September 2009, ILGA Europe, submitted a petition to CAHVIO recommending that the non-discrimination clause made explicit reference to sexual orientation, gender identity and gender expression, and the

26 Lourdes Peroni, 'Violence Against Migrant Women: The Istanbul Convention Through a Postcolonial Feminist Lens' (2016) 24 *Feminist Legal Studies* 49.

27 Kimberlé Williams Crenshaw, 'Demarginalizing the Intersection of Race and Sex: A Black Feminist Critique of Antidiscrimination Doctrine, Feminist Theory and Antiracist Policies' (1989) *The University of Chicago Legal Forum* 139.

28 See the special issue on Intersectionality of the *European Journal of Women's Studies* 13(3) (2006) and the *International Feminist Journal of Politics* 11(4) (2009).

29 See, for instance, Flavia Dzodan's blogpost 'My feminism will be intersectional or it will be bullshit' http://tigerbeatdown.com/2011/10/10/my-feminism-will-be-intersectional-or-it-will-be-bullshit/; *The Guardian* 'Are you too white, rich, able-bodied and straight to be a feminist?' www.theguardian.com/commentisfree/2013/apr/18/are-you-too-white-rich-straight-to-be-feminist; 'In defence of intersectionality': www.theguardian.com/commentisfree/2013/dec/23/in-defence-of-intersectionality.

30 Monique Wittig, *The Lesbian Body* (William Morrow, 1975).

31 Michel Foucault, *The History of Sexuality: An Introduction: Volume I* (1990); Michel Foucault, *The History of Sexuality, Vol. 2: The Use of Pleasure* (1985); Judith Butler, *Gender Trouble: Feminism and the Subversion of Identity* (Routledge 1990); Eve Kosofsky Sedgwick, *Epistemology of the Closet* (University of California Press 1990).

32 Judith Butler, *Bodies That Matter* (Routledge 1993).

33 Donatella Della Porta and Manuela Caiani, *Social Movements and Europeanization* (Oxford University Press 2009) 225.

34 Joke Swiebel, 'Lesbian, Gay, Bisexual and Transgender Human Rights: The Search for an International Strategy' (2009) 15 *Contemporary Politics* 19.

35 Kelly Kollman and Matthew Waites, 'The Global Politics of Lesbian, Gay, Bisexual and Transgender Human Rights: An Introduction' (2009) 15 *Contemporary Politics* 1.

obligation of States to prevent and combat violence against LBT women, including trans women who have not undergone gender reassignment.[36] "Without specific references in the Convention", ILGA Europe argued, "it remains all too possible that its measures will not be used to combat violence against LBT women".[37] The UN High Commissioner for Refugees also recommended to include sexual orientation as a ground for asylum, understood as a prevention and protection measure against violence.[38] In addition, ILGA asked CAHVIO to include LBT women as a "vulnerable group".[39]

The feminist claims and developments described above show that, at the time of drafting the Convention, the conceptualisation of women as a fixed category with certain characteristics was being challenged, recognising women's diversity, including their sexual orientation and gender identity, and parting from biological understandings of sex and heteronormative discourses. CAHVIO reports confirm the discussions about these issues during the process of negotiation of the Convention.[40]

The adopted text explicitly recognises the diversity of women through the equal treatment principle promoted in non-discrimination clauses, and to some extent, in the recommendation of certain policies. Article 4.3. states that the Convention provisions

> shall be secured without discrimination on any ground such as sex, gender, race, colour, language, religion, political or other opinion, national or social origin, association with a national minority, property, birth, sexual orientation, gender identity, age, state of health, disability, marital status, migrant or refugee status, or other status.

Although postcolonial views are somehow considered throughout the Convention,[41] this is the only reference suggesting that women can be discriminated against on multiple grounds, potentially resembling intersectionality.

The depiction of women, however, is not completely in line with the feminist claims previously outlined. Specifically, the challenges to cisnormative and heteronormative assumptions are captured superficially. For instance, although Article 4.3. reflects ILGA's recommendation to include sexual orientation and

36 https://rm.coe.int/CoERMPublicCommonSearchServices/DisplayDCTMContent?documentId=0900001680594272.

37 ILGA EUROPE Report to the Council of Europe Ad Hoc Committee on Preventing and Combating Violence Against Women and Domestic Violence (ILGA Report), available at: https://rm.coe.int/CoERMPublicCommonSearchServices/DisplayDCTMContent?documentId=0900001680594272.

38 UNHCR comments to the first Meeting of the Ad Hoc Committee on Preventing and Combating Violence against Women and Domestic Violence (6–8 April 2009), paras 3 and 4.

39 ILGA Report, p. 21.

40 Reports available at: www.coe.int/en/web/istanbul-convention/cahvio.

41 Peroni (n 26).

gender identity in the non-discrimination clause, there is no consideration of the ways in which lesbian and trans women are affected by violence. Lesbian and trans women are not considered as vulnerable groups, which has consequences for the provision of services, especially shelter, and in relation to granting refuge status. The special vulnerability of lesbian and trans women has also been pointed out in shadow reports to GREVIO:

> Sexual orientation and gender identity are not recognized in Turkey and there exist discriminatory practices against LGBTIQs in the admission to shelters, just as in all spheres of social services. There is no legal arrangement to prevent this discrimination, on the contrary, discriminatory discourse of service providers further cultivates it. Lesbian women are forced to hide their sexual orientation in shelters. LGTIs are subjected to discrimination on the ground of their outlook, attire, attitudes and behaviours etc. even when they do not make their sexual identities and orientations public. As such, they are easily subjected to mistreatment from both shelter staff and other women staying in the institution.[42]

The shadow report also provides a detailed account of the vulnerable position of LGBTIQ refugees, who are arbitrarily kept in deportation centres, charged with prostitution and later deported.[43] In its evaluation report, GREVIO recommended to "review existing laws and regulations to remove restrictions preventing access to shelters for certain groups of victims", yet lesbian and trans women were not explicitly mentioned among them.[44] It appears that the lack of explicit reference to lesbian and trans women in the provisions about shelters impacts on the interpretation of the norms.

Second, the Convention text and the Explanatory Report make no references to sexual orientation and gender identity as aggravating circumstances, disregarding the prevalence of domestic violence or sexual harassment against lesbian and trans women. Hate speech, which also affects them disproportionally, is not considered as a form of violence against women.[45] The cisnormative perspective toward violence also seems reinforced in the manner that bodily interventions are included in the Convention. Female genital mutilation implies having female

42 Contribution from the İstanbul Convention Monitoring Platform to the First Baseline Evaluation of Turkey, September 2017, p. 37. Available at: https://rm.coe.int/turkey-shadow-report-2/16807441a1.

43 Ibid., pp. 60–65.

44 1st Evaluation Report by Grevio on Turkey, October 2018, p. 64, para 180. b. Available at: https://rm.coe.int/eng-grevio-report-turquie/16808e5283.

45 See Recommendation No R (97) 20 of the Committee of Ministers on "hatespeech"; Recommendation CM/Rec(2010)5 of the Committee of Ministers on measures to combat discrimination on grounds of sexual orientation or gender identity. See also *Vejdeland and Others v Sweden* App no1813/07 (ECHR, 9 February 2012).

genitalia and forced sterilisation does not explicitly refer to trans women, although many forcibly undergo sterilisation before sex reassignment surgery.[46]

3.2 Violence against women: feminist and Convention's conceptualisations

This subsection discusses feminist claims on gender-based violence that particularly resonated in European women's movements during the negotiations and after the adoption of the Convention.

3.2.1 Domestic violence

Domestic violence is one of the types of violence with the longest presence in the feminist agenda, with most of its aspects explored and addressed by women's organised responses within many European States. The battered women's movement, which gained particular strength in the United Kingdom in the seventies, effectively mobilised resources to aid battered women by launching feminist actions at all levels, from grassroots to federal governments, and by adopting strategies that ranged from institutional to confrontational.[47] At the time of negotiation of the Convention, the European Women's Lobby (EWL) and the European Policy Action Centre on Violence against Women (EPAC VAW) submitted a petition (EPAC-EWL Statement) supporting that

> the convention should be a human rights instrument with an independent monitoring mechanism focusing on violence against women, including domestic violence, and that the core of the convention would thus cover a wide range of forms of violence typically experienced by women.[48]

The notion that "the home is the most dangerous place for women",[49] however, may not resonate with many women, particularly when we consider their class, race, sexual orientation and gender identity. Women's diversity impacts directly on their realities and experiences of violence, yet the Convention seems to focus on domestic violence at the expense of other forms of violence experienced by

46 See, for instance, *Y.Y. v Turkey* App no 14793/08 (ECHR, 10 March 2015).

47 Myra Marx Ferree and B Hess, *Controversy and Coalition: The New Feminist Movement across Four Decades of Change* (Routledge 2002) 126; Kathleen J Tierney, 'The Battered Women Movement and the Creation of the Wife Beating Problem' (1982) 29 *Social Problems* 207.

48 'Women's NGOs call on the Council of Europe to Move towards a Strong Instrument on Violence against Women', available at: https://rm.coe.int/CoERMPublicCommonSearchServices/DisplayDCTMContent?documentId=0900001680594273.

49 Ibid.

many women whose main exposure is outside the home/family, such as migrant women,[50] lesbians and trans women.[51]

Nevertheless, the definition and scope of domestic violence has broadened through the years. The "women battering" language, used in the seventies, was replaced in the eighties by the less political language of "domestic violence". Nonetheless, feminists continued to emphasise men's responsibility for these assaults and the structural nature of violence affecting women.[52] In addition, the profile of the victims of domestic violence has also changed, becoming more inclusive. ILGA's submission to CAHVIO described that regarding domestic violence, LBT women usually face violence committed by family members after disclosing their sexual orientation or gender identity. Their submission also pointed out that LBT women may face same-sex intimate partner violence.

These claims, however, are not fully captured by the Convention. While the preamble addresses violence as the result of the historical unequal position of men and women, recognising its gender-based and structural nature, this view varies depending on the type of violence being addressed. The gender dimension of domestic violence was one of the main points of contention during the negotiations. Since the first meeting in 2009, some of CAHVIO members agreed that most victims of domestic violence are women and that the gender dimension of domestic violence needed to be reflected in the instrument, while other members argued that domestic violence should be applicable to all victims irrespective of their gender or age.[53] Clarifying this aspect was not a minor one, considering that at the time of drafting, the European Court of Human Rights (ECtHR) was yet to interpret domestic violence as a form of gender discrimination for the first time. Hence, the Convention had the potential to guide the Court in its interpretation on the issue.

In a compromised position, reached by consensus, CAHVIO finally agreed that the Convention should deal with domestic violence "which affects women disproportionally",[54] as proposed by the Belgian delegation. Article 2.2 further calls State Parties to pay "particular attention to women victims of gender-based violence". This compromised position is also reflected in the preamble, which points out that "women and girls are exposed to a higher risk of gender-based violence than men", although it adds that "men may also be victims of domestic violence". Lesbian and transgender women facing domestic violence against women due to their sexual orientation or gender identity, despite the clear depiction of the problem made by ILGA during the

50 See Violence against women migrant workers – Report of the Secretary-General (A/72/215) [EN/AR].

51 See European Union Agency for Fundamental Rights, EU LGBT survey – European Union lesbian, gay, bisexual and transgender survey – Results at a glance.

52 Marx Ferree and Hess (n 47).

53 Report of the 2nd meeting, para 6.

54 Ibid.

negotiations, were not included in the final definitions nor recalled in the Explanatory Report. Ironically, the Convention includes men in the context of domestic violence, contrary to the claims and theoretical elaborations of the feminist movement.

While these negotiations were taking place, the European Court finally considered domestic violence as gender-based discrimination in *Opuz v Turkey*, understanding that the general and discriminatory judicial passivity in Turkey was conducive to domestic violence and thus affected mainly women.[55] That said, the judgment also stated that "men may also be the victims of domestic violence and, indeed, that children, too, are often casualties of the phenomenon, whether directly or indirectly".[56] The Court shows the same ambivalence toward the gender-dimension of domestic violence that we find in the Convention. Since *Opuz*, the Court has not consistently addressed violence against women as gender-based discrimination, and when it does, it is based on the authorities' passivity towards a woman's experience of domestic violence.[57]

Regarding the provision of services, since the seventies, the shelter movement in Europe was concerned with providing women with a safehouse for temporary protection and support. In relation to the protection measures needed in cases of violence, the Convention falls in line with feminist claims. It establishes the obligation of States to provide shelter to victims,[58] which in some States remained scarce as indicated in monitoring reports, despite decades of feminist claims and organisation on this matter and previous documents recommending it. As mentioned above, although the need to provide suitable shelter to LBT women was voiced by ILGA, no reference is made in the Istanbul Convention provisions to their vulnerability.[59]

More recently, women's movements have called for issuing protection orders and for keeping the woman at home and excluding the batterer. The Convention contemplates this possibility.[60] The Explanatory Report clarifies the reasoning behind the provision, echoing feminist claims:

55 *Opuz v Turkey* App no 33401/02 (ECHR 9 June 2009).
56 *Opuz v Turkey* para 132.
57 Cases recognising the gender-dimension of the violence: *Eremia and Others v The Republic of Moldova* App no 3564/11(ECHR, 28 May 2013); *Valiulienė v Lithuania* App no 33234/07 (ECHR, 26 March 2013); *B. v the Republic of Moldova* App no 61382/09 (ECHR, 16 July 2013) and *Mudric v the Republic of Moldova*, App no (ECHR, 16 July 2013); *N.A. v the Republic of Moldova* App no 13424/06 (ECHR, 24 September 2013): *T.M. and C.M. v the Republic of Moldova*, App no 26608/11 (ECHR, 28 January 2014); *Durmaz v Turkey* App no 3621/07 (ECHR, 13 November 2014); *M.G. v Turkey* App no 646/10 (ECHR, 22 March 2016); *Halime Kılıç v Turkey* App no 63034/11 (ECHR, 28 June 2016); *Bălşan v Romania* App no (ECHR, 23 May 2017).
58 Article 23, the Istanbul Convention.
59 ILGA statement, 25.
60 Article 52, the Istanbul Convention.

> Rather than placing the burden of hurriedly seeking safety in a shelter or elsewhere on the victim, who is often accompanied by dependent children, often with very few personal affairs and for an indefinite period of time, the drafters considered it important to ensure the removal of the perpetrator to allow the victim to remain in the home.[61]

The exclusion of the batterer is complemented by the issuing of protection and restraining orders,[62] aiming to prevent further acts of violence. The clarity of these measures has the potential to ensure that Europe moves toward a consistent system of protection across State Parties.

Feminist organisations have also highlighted the woman's right to self-defence when society fails to protect her.[63] This absence of state intervention is often the result of the lack of appropriate prosecution policies,[64] and other times the result of a biased perception of women's response to violence, regarding women's response as constitutive of "bidirectional" violence.[65] These complaints about the difficult access to justice and the deficient state response have undoubtedly contributed to the adoption of detailed provisions in the Convention. Although the Convention does not explicitly contemplate the right to self-defence, it calls for the prompt and efficient response of agents, systematically assessing the seriousness of the situation and the risk of repeated violence.[66]

Finally, feminist movements claim that an appropriate and effective prosecution of violence against women challenges the sense of impunity rooted in society and upsets the patriarchal order. The United Nations Special Rapporteur on Violence against Women also suggests this:

> [P]rosecutors working on cases of domestic violence have the potential and the obligation to change the prevailing balance of power [between men and women] by taking a strong stance to disempower patriarchal notions. Interventions at this level may have both consequential effects in that condemnations of patriarchy can lead to changes in socio-cultural norms, as well as intrinsic effects, in that prosecutors … can be considered to be the 'mouthpieces' of society, and strong statements condemning violence against women

61 Explanatory Report, Article 52, para 264.
62 Ibid., Article 53.
63 Myra Marx Ferree and B Hess, 'Two Steps Forward, One Step Back: Defending Gains, 1983–92', *Controversy and Coalition : the New Feminist Movement across Four Decades of Change* (Routledge 2000) 170.
64 Michelle Madden Dempsey, 'Toward a Feminist State: What Does "Effective" Prosecution of Domestic Violence Mean?' (2007) 70 *The Modern Law Review* 908.
65 Renée Römkens, 'Ambiguous Responsibilities: Law and Conflicting Expert Testimony on the Abused Woman Who Shot Her Sleeping Husband' (2000) 25 *Law and Social Inquiry* 355.
66 Articles 50 and 5, the Istanbul Convention.

made on behalf of society through the ... prosecutorial services will make that society less patriarchal.[67]

In this respect, the Convention has taken a significant step toward meeting feminist claims for a more proactive State. Yet it does not require public prosecution of violence against women. Instead, it establishes that investigations and prosecution of physical violence, sexual violence, forced marriage and female genital mutilation should not be "wholly dependent" on the complaint of the victim and that the proceedings may continue even if the victim withdraws the complaint.[68] This approach is meant to address procedural differences in legal systems, yet making clear that ensuring the investigation or prosecution of offences is the responsibility of the State and its authorities,[69] who need "to ease the burden of lengthy criminal investigations and proceedings".[70]

3.2.2 Sexual harassment

Sexual harassment has been conceptualised by feminist theories as part of the general pattern of gender discrimination and as a way of obstructing women from work.[71] It is thus no surprise that the European Union's attention to employment issues highlighted early on sexual harassment in the workplace, addressing it at first with soft-law measures such as the Council Declaration of 19 December 1991 on the protection of the dignity of women and men at work. By the time of drafting the Istanbul Convention, sexual harassment was addressed by binding EU law.[72]

Since 2006, women all over the world have organised and shared their experiences of sexual harassment using the hashtag #MeToo, showing that

67 Yakin Ertürk, 'Integration of the Human Rights of Women and the Gender Perspective: Violence Against Women – The Due Diligence Standards as a Tool for the Elimination of Violence Against Women' Report of the Special Rapporteur on Violence against Women, its Causes and Consequences, to the United Nations Commission on Human Rights, E/CN.4/2006/61, 20 January 2006, 20. On this, Madden-Dempsy, 'Toward a Feminist State, What Does Effective Prosecution Mean?' (2007) 70(6) *The Modern Law Review* 908–935.
68 Article 55, the Istanbul Convention.
69 Explanatory Report, para 280.
70 Explanatory Report, para 279.
71 Anita M Superson, 'A Feminist Definition of Sexual Harassment' (1993) 24 *Journal of Social Philosophy* 46; Jane Gallop, 'Sex and Sexism: Feminism and Harassment Policy' (1994) 80 *Academe* 16.
72 Directive 2002/73/EC of the European Parliament and of the Council of 23 September 2002 amending Council Directive 76/207/EEC on the implementation of the principle of equal treatment for men and women as regards access to employment, vocational training and promotion, and working conditions, OJ 2002 L 296; OJ 2006 L 204; Directive 2006/54/EC of the European Parliament and of the Council of 5 July 2006 on the implementation of the principle of equal opportunities and equal treatment of men and women in matters of employment and occupation (recast).

sexual harassment is a pervasive form of violence affecting women.[73] The EPAC-EWL Statement, submitted to CAHVIO after its first meeting, pointed out worrying statistics on sexual harassment. The submission by ILGA-Europe also pointed out that LBT women suffer sexual harassment because of their sexual orientation and gender identity both in the community and the private sphere.[74] After the adoption of the Convention, statistics have continued to show a very significant number of cases of sexual harassment, including on the grounds of sexual orientation and gender identity.[75] Recently, the #MeToo movement has gained yet more visibility and strength, with cases reported even within European Union and Council of Europe institutions.[76]

The CAHVIO meetings reports indicate that some members had expressed concern about the criminalisation of sexual harassment, while others called for criminal law sanctions for this behaviour. The co-chairs seemed inclined to limit the criminal scope of the issue, and called for a definition of sexual harassment that covers all types of situations where women are in a position of weakness – beyond the area of employment and education.[77] The Convention defines sexual harassment as any verbal, non-verbal and physical conducts of a sexual nature, carried out in a context of abuse of power, promise of reward or threat of reprisal, not limited to the field of employment. In this regard, it calls for the adoption of legal measures that allow for a criminal "or other" legal sanction against this type of violence.[78] Considering the specific nature of this conduct, the Explanatory Report points out that:

> While generally considering it preferable to place the conduct dealt with by this article under criminal law, the drafters acknowledged that many national legal systems consider sexual harassment under civil or labour law. Consequently, parties may choose to deal with sexual harassment either by their criminal law or by administrative or other legal sanctions, while ensuring that the law deals with sexual harassment.[79]

In addition, the Explanatory Report argues that Article 17.1, referring to policies, guidelines, and self-regulatory standards to prevent violence against

73 https://metoomvmt.org/about/.

74 ILGA Report, n 37.

75 EU Fundamental Rights Agency, 'Violence against Women: An EU-wide Survey. Main Results Report' (2014) 95; EU Fundamental Rights Agency 'EU Lesbian, Gay, Bisexual and Transgender Survey. Main Results' (2014); Inter-Parliamentary Union (IPU) study on Sexism, Harassment and Violence against Women in Parliaments in Europe (2018), available at: http://website-pace.net/documents/19879/5288428/20181016-Women-ParliamentIssues-EN.pdf/7d59e7c5-4a88-4d23-a6cd-7404449fd45f.

76 Sexual harassment plagues the EU body meant to fight it. Multiple complaints show difficulty of putting "zero tolerance" into practice. www.politico.eu/article/sexual-harassment-eu-gender-equality-agency/.

77 3rd Meeting Report, para 7.

78 Article 40, the Istanbul Convention. See also Explanatory Report, para 155.

79 Explanatory Report, para 207.

women, includes the adoption of protocols or guidelines on how to deal with cases of sexual harassment in the workplace.[80]

Sexual harassment in the public sphere has also gained attention, leading the Parliamentary Assembly to adopt a resolution calling CoE states to "put an end to impunity by prosecuting perpetrators of sexual violence and harassment in public space".[81] Moreover, "online sexual harassment" and misogynistic behaviour in the digital sphere, such as social media, blogs and other digital platforms, is increasing attention.[82] These forms of harassment, in addition to being violent, may result in discrimination against women in relation to their use of information and communication technologies, breaching their freedom of expression and in many cases their privacy. The debate on sexual harassment is ongoing, and it is also becoming clear that what used to be a form of violence connected to employment and education, it is also pervasive in a much broader sphere. Beyond the response provided by the Convention – criminal, civil, administrative or through soft measures like protocols – current feminist claims will broaden the scope of this form of violence to include the public space, social media and digital communications.

3.3 Economic dimensions of feminist claims: from labour inclusion to austerity policies

The construction of gender inequality by the economic system has been the target of feminist critique for decades.[83] Traditional claims included equal access to all sectors of the labour market and shared care-giving responsibilities,[84]

80 Explanatory Report, Article 107.

81 Parliamentary Assembly, Resolution 2177 (2017) Putting an end to sexual violence and harassment of women in public space, available at: http://assembly.coe.int/nw/xml/XRef/Xref-XML2HTML-en.asp?fileid=23977&lang=en.

82 See, for instance, www.amnesty.org/en/latest/news/2017/11/amnesty-reveals-alarming-impact-of-online-abuse-against-women/; www.forbes.com/sites/michelleking/2017/11/14/how-powerful-women-experience-extreme-online-sexual-harassment-and-what-you-can-do-to-stop-it/#118881e37b73; www.abc.net.au/news/2018-04-18/why-men-abuse-women-online/9666900.

83 C Delphy, 'The Main Enemy' (1980) 1 *Feminist Issues* 23; H Hartmann, 'The Unhappy Marriage of Marxism and Feminism: Toward a More Perfect Union' in L Sargent (ed.), *Women and Revolution: A Discussion of the Unhappy Marriage of Marxism and Feminism* (South End Press 1981); Nancy Fraser, *Fortunes of Feminism: From State-Managed Capitalism to Neoliberal Crisis* (Verso 2013).

84 J Gardiner, 'Women's Domestic Labor' (1975) 69 *New Left Review* 47–58; M Ferber, *Women and Work, Paid and Unpaid* (Garland Press 1987); M Hardt, 'Affective Labor' (1999) 26(2) *Boundary* 89–100; Caroline Straub 'A Comparative Analysis of the Use of Work–Life Balance Practices in Europe: Do Practices Enhance Females' Career Advancement?' (2007) 22(4) *Women in Management Review* 289–304; Torben Iversen and Frances Rosenbluth, 'The Political Economy of Gender: Explaining Cross-National Variation in the Gender Division of Labor and the Gender Voting Gap' (2006) 50(1) *American Journal of Political Science* 1–19.

underemployment[85] and precarious contracts.[86] Past generations achieved maternity leave, improved rights for part-time workers, anti-discrimination laws and legal protections against sexual discrimination. Despite such improvements, it has become clear that women's economic independence is not purely dependent on "getting a job". The economic structure still sustains gender inequality, particularly in some CoE Member States.[87] For instance, organisations like the "Gender Wage Watchers Network"[88] highlight persisting issues such as the average gender pay gap,[89] in spite of the economic improvement in the region, the increasing level of female employment and the adoption of "gender-sensitive" policies.

The urgency of attending to the economic aspects of women's status in Europe increased in the context of the post-2008 economic crisis, when the disproportionate impact of the austerity policies on women started to show.[90] The economic hardship that women faced became suddenly more visible, and anti-austerity movements in some CoE Member States were greatly supported by women's' movements.[91] In fact, organised action of European women's movements in relation to austerity policies and (structural) economic crisis are gaining ground internationally and in Europe, breathing new life to celebrations for International Women's Day on 8 March. Calls to join an "international women strike" on that date seem particularly strong among Spanish women.[92]

Feminist theory has long argued that the structural nature of the economic inequalities affecting women constitutes gender-based violence.[93] This notion echoes recent feminist claims. Capturing this claim in an instrument dedicated to violence against women is no doubt a challenge. The most evident way to do

85 Hans-Peter Blossfeld and Catherine Hakim, *Between Equalisation and Marginalization* (Oxford University Press 1997); M Marchand and A Runyan, *Gender and Global Restructuring: Sightings, Signs, Resistances* (Routledge 2000).

86 Judy Fudge and Rosemary Owens (eds), *Precarious Work, Women, and the New Economy* (Hart Publishing 2006).

87 Elzbieta Matynia, 'Polish Feminism between the Local and the Global: A Task of Translation' in *Women's Movements in the Global Era: the Power of Local Feminisms* (Westview Press 2010) 216.

88 http://genderpaygap.eu.

89 Paygap in Europe: https://ec.europa.eu/eurostat/tgm/table.do?tab=table&init=1&language=en&pcode=tesem180&plugin=1.

90 Maria Karamessini and Jill Rubery, *Women and Austerity: The Economic Crisis and the Future for Gender Equality* (Routledge 2013); JA MacLeavey, ' "New Politics" of Austerity, Workfare and Gender? The UK Coalition Government's Welfare Reform Proposals' (2011) 4 *Cambridge Journal of Regions, Economy and Society* 355.

91 María José Gámez Fuentes, 'Feminisms and the 15M Movement in Spain: Between Frames of Recognition and Contexts of Action' (2015) 14 *Social Movement Studies* 359.

92 See: www.bbc.com/news/world-europe-43324406; www.theguardian.com/world/2018/mar/08/international-womens-day-marked-by-protests-and-celebrations.

93 Rosemary Hennessy, 'Materialist Feminism and Foucault: The Politics of Appropriation' (1990) 3 *Rethinking Marxism* 251; Nancy Fraser, 'Feminism, Capitalism and the Cunning of History' (2012) 56 *New Left Review* 97.

so is including economic inequality in the definition of economic violence. However, the definitions of violence in the Convention do not replicate this broader scenario. "Economic violence" is only considered in the context of domestic violence and, although "economic independence (of the abuser)" appears as a preventive measure, the structural factors that prevent women from becoming "economically independent" are not considered. The notion of "economic harm" is also addressed as the result of domestic violence rather than gender inequality.

There is yet another possibility to address economic claims. The Convention aspires to establish "the link between achieving gender equality and the eradication of violence against women",[94] and thus attempts to promote the "substantive equality" of women.[95] Article 1 b. has the potential to address the underlying aspects of the unequal positioning of women, which leads to gender discrimination and violence. In addition, Article 4.2 calls for the adoption of measures to eliminate discrimination against women, although it requires formal measures to do so, such as enshrining in law the principle of equality between women and men. The Explanatory Report, however, holds that Article 4.2 also entails "the obligation to ensure the practical realisation of equality between women and men addresses the fact that enshrining it in law is often insufficient and that practical measures are required to implement this principle in a meaningful way".[96] The combination of Articles 4.2 and 6 on gender sensitive policies, suggests that the scope of "empowering policies" should go beyond domestic violence victims, aiming at substantive women's equality.[97]

4 Conclusions

From the perspective of past and current feminist claims, the Convention shows some shortcomings. Above all, the category of "women", as subject of protection under the Convention, calls for reconsideration. Although the diversity of women may appear as covered by the non-discrimination clause, the monitoring rounds have exposed the difficulties of resting the whole system on a non-discrimination clause. The inclusion of sexual orientation and gender identity as grounds for discrimination seems insufficient to provide protection to lesbian and trans women. Instead, it seems that incorporating them as vulnerable groups and specifically considering the types of violence that affect them disproportionally is needed.

Regarding domestic violence, although the Convention has provided a good basis to address the issue not only from a criminal approach but also ensuring the protection and provision of services to victims, it fails to consider the vulnerability of certain groups of women in the context of domestic violence. The

94 Explanatory Report, para 25.
95 Article 1(b), the Istanbul Convention.
96 Explanatory Report, para 52.
97 Explanatory Report, para 62.

vulnerability of some women in relation to sexual harassment is also limitedly recognised, while the expansion of the "public sphere" to include our online and digital existence reaffirms the urgent need of the Convention to adapt and to keep up with social developments.

Another challenging aspect relates to the understanding of economic violence and economic independence. In times of economic upheaval, the need to problematise economic dependency beyond an abusive partner relationship, recognising the economic impact that gender inequality has on women, seems needed if "substantive equality" is to be gained. In this respect, the assessment of gender-sensitive polices needs to enquire into labour policies, salary gap, irregular and part-time employment, the openness of the labour market to women and care activities.

It may be too soon to judge whether the Istanbul Convention has the potential to adapt to new claims. Despite the detailed provisions regarding criminalisation, protection and support of victims, the Convention needs to become highly adaptable to keep up with the rapid formation and fast dissemination of social claims. The adequacy of the Convention to address current feminist challenges will depend on the interpretation of its monitoring body. The interaction of civil society and GREVIO is thus crucial for the sustainability of the Convention. In this regard, one of the most positive aspects of the Istanbul Convention relates to the possibility of interaction of social movements with GREVIO, although it may be limited to NGOs. If all Convention interpreters, including lawyers and academics, remain conscious of the need to pay attention to social movements beyond NGOs and their potentially narrow agenda, we can contribute to pushing the boundaries of the instrument and to broadening its scope and responsiveness.

2 Unleashing the gender equality potential of the Istanbul Convention

Lourdes Peroni[1]

1 Introduction

The Council of Europe Convention on Preventing and Combating Violence against Women and Domestic Violence (the Istanbul Convention or the Convention) is one of the last instruments on violence against women to arrive in the human rights scene.[2] As a newcomer, the Convention has had the privilege to benefit from prior human rights developments on violence against women.[3] Following its international[4] and regional[5] predecessors, the Istanbul Convention understands violence against women as a problem of gender inequality, namely "a manifestation of historically unequal power relations between women and men, which have led to domination over, and discrimination against, women by men".[6]

1 I am thankful to Catrin Andersson, Jamie Grace, Dolores Morondo Taramundi, Johanna Niemi and Vladislava Stoyanova for their valuable comments on earlier versions of this chapter.

2 The Istanbul Convention was signed on 11 May 2011 and entered into force on 1 August 2014.

3 United Nations Committee on the Elimination of Discrimination against Women (CEDAW Committee); General Recommendation No 19 "Violence against Women" 1992 (CEDAW General Recommendation No 19); United Nations Declaration on the Elimination of Violence against Women, 20 December 1993 (DEVAW) and Inter-American Convention on the Prevention, Punishment and Eradication of Violence against Women, 9 June 1994 (*Belém do Pará* Convention). For the purposes of this chapter, I include among these developments only those of general character and application like conventions, declarations and general recommendations, as they render themselves to a more adequate comparison with the Istanbul Convention (an instrument of a general nature itself) than judgments, decisions and views adopted in individual cases.

4 CEDAW Committee General Recommendation No 19 (n 3) and DEVAW (n 3). Another important international human rights development on violence against women is CEDAW Committee, General Recommendation No 35 on Gender-based Violence against Women, Updating General Recommendation No 19, 26 July 2017. This General Recommendation, however, was adopted after the Istanbul Convention had entered into force.

5 E.g. *Belém do Pará* Convention (n 3).

6 Preamble of Istanbul Convention. For a similar wording, see Preambles of DEVAW and *Belém do Pará* Convention (n 3).

Two of the Convention's goals flow from this understanding of violence against women: eliminating discrimination against women and promoting substantive equality between women and men.[7] The drafters understood that "only substantive equality will prevent such violence in the future".[8] The Convention text, in turn, reaffirms its substantive approach to equality[9] by seeking to promote "de facto equality between women and men"[10] and by asking State Parties to realise this equality in practice.[11] The Convention's commitment to improving women's de facto equality is vital, as equality may be recognised in the law for decades but still remain unfulfilled in practice.

Yet, as I show in this chapter, the Istanbul Convention may fall short of its substantive equality promise unless its monitoring body – the Group of Experts on Action against Violence against Women and Domestic Violence (GREVIO) – pushes for advancing women's equality in enjoying *all* human rights, including political, social and economic rights. The Convention holds great potential to combat the prejudices and stereotypes that have historically construed women as subordinate to men in society. However, it is less clear whether the Convention holds equally strong potential to advance women's actual power in the political and socio-economic spheres, including women's equal participation in politics and the labour market.

I thus argue that, if the Convention is to fully realise its substantive equality aspiration and to effectively combat violence against women, it needs to be interpreted so as to promote women's de facto equality politically and socio-economically. My arguments draw mainly on an international human rights instrument from which the Istanbul Convention drafters drew significant inspiration: the United Nations Convention on the Elimination of Discrimination against Women (CEDAW), which brings together civil, political, social and economic rights in advancing women's equality.

2 Strong potential to combat subordinating gender stereotypes and prejudices

Embedded in the Convention's understanding of violence against women is a concern with the hierarchy of power and status between women and men in

7 Article 1(b).

8 Explanatory Report to the Council of Europe Convention on Preventing and Combating Violence against Women and Domestic Violence, Council of Europe Treaty Series No 210, 11 May 2011 (Explanatory Report) para 49.

9 The Convention understands equality substantively because it promotes women's *de facto* equality and because it tackles *gender hierarchy* (women's subordinate societal status in comparison to men's dominant status). On hierarchy as the substance of substantive equality, see Catharine A MacKinnon, 'Substantive Equality Revisited: A Reply to Sandra Fredman' (2016) 14(3) *International Journal of Constitutional Law I•CON* 739.

10 Preamble of Istanbul Convention.

11 Article 4(2).

society. The drafters define violence against women as "both the cause and the result of ***unequal power relations*** based on perceived differences between women and men that lead to ***women's subordinate status*** in both the private and public spheres".[12] It is thus hardly a surprise that eradicating violence against women and achieving gender equality are firmly tied together in the Convention's Preamble[13] and various of its provisions.[14]

In this part, I show that the Istanbul Convention holds great potential to redress what feminist scholar Nancy Fraser calls "misrecognition": value patterns that "constitute women as inferior, excluded, wholly other, or simply invisible, hence as less than full partner in social interaction".[15] This potential lies in the Convention's effort to challenge dominant societal attitudes, beliefs and behaviours that regard women as inferior to men and keep women in subordinate positions and roles in society. Indeed, following previous human rights developments on violence and discrimination against women[16] – most notably Article 5 CEDAW[17] – the Istanbul Convention seeks to eradicate the prejudices, customs, traditions and stereotypes that regard women as inferior to men and that perpetuate violence against women.[18] In the words of the drafters: "certain roles or stereotypes reproduce unwanted and harmful practices and contribute to make violence against women acceptable".[19]

In the next paragraphs, I show that the "Prevention" Chapter of the Istanbul Convention and to a lesser degree the "Substantive Law" and the "Investigation, Prosecution, Procedural Law and Protective Measures" Chapters – outline measures that may help subvert women's lesser status in society. I discuss two groups of measures through which the Convention challenges women's misrecognition: *societal* measures and *institutional* measures. The first set of measures seeks to transform the negative views on women prevailing in society at large, including in schools and the media. The second group aims to change these views in society's state institutions, such as laws and justice systems.

12 Explanatory Report, para 44. Emphasis mine.
13 Explanatory Report, para 25.
14 The Convention frames various measures "within the wider context of combating discrimination against women and achieving gender equality in law". Explanatory Report, para 25.
15 Nancy Fraser, *Fortunes of Feminism: From State Managed Capitalism to Neoliberal Crisis* (Verso 2013) 168.
16 CEDAW General Recommendation No 19, DEVAW and *Belém do Pará* Convention (n 3).
17 Article 5 of CEDAW states: "States Parties shall take all appropriate measures: (a) To modify the social and cultural patterns of conduct of men and women, with a view to achieving the elimination of prejudices and customary and all other practices which are based on the idea of the inferiority or the superiority of either of the sexes or on stereotyped roles for men and women".
18 Article 12.
19 Explanatory Report, para 43.

2.1 Tackling women's subordinate status in society at large

In an attempt to promote "changes in mentality and attitudes"[20] in society, Chapter III "Prevention" sets in motion a range of far-reaching measures to *prevent* violence against women from occurring in the first place. Through awareness-raising, education, professional training and perpetrator programmes, among other measures, the Convention targets different segments of society, including the public at large, children, relevant professionals, the private sector, the media, and perpetrators.[21] For example, the Convention pushes for disseminating "non-stereotyped gender roles" in school teaching materials[22] and public awareness-raising campaigns.[23] It also obliges States to encourage the media to "refrain from harmful gender stereotyping and spreading degrading images of women".[24] The Convention further demands States to train those working in law practice, law enforcement, health care, and social services so as to contribute to "changing the outlooks and the conduct of these professionals with regard to the victims".[25] The Istanbul Convention also seeks to promote attitudinal and behavioural changes in perpetrators to prevent further violence.[26]

The aforementioned measures tackle what the Convention considers a fundamental root cause of violence against women: "prevailing inequality between women and men, existing stereotypes, gender roles and discrimination against women".[27] Given the various societal levels they operate at, these prevention measures have the potential to advance systemic societal change:[28] changes in widely held views that legitimate women's unequal status and violent behaviour against them in society.

20 Explanatory Report, para 85.
21 Articles 13 to 17.
22 Article 14.
23 Article 13. Though the text of Article 13 is silent in this respect, the drafters explain that awareness-raising campaigns should include information on non-stereotyped gender roles. See Explanatory Report, para 91.
24 Article 17. The obligation to refrain from stereotyping and from using degrading images flows from the drafters' explanation rather than expressly from the text of Article 17. See Explanatory Report, para 107.
25 Article 15. The obligation to promote these attitudinal and behavioural changes flows from the Explanatory Report, para 98 rather than from the text of Article 15. See also Explanatory Report, para 100.
26 Article 16. The obligation to promote these changes flows from the Explanatory Report rather than from the text of Article 16. See Explanatory Report, para 102.
27 Explanatory Report, para 43.
28 Council of Europe, *Preventing Violence against Women: Article 12 of the Istanbul Convention, A Collection of Papers on the Council of Europe Convention on Preventing and Combating Violence against Women and Domestic Violence* (prepared by Marianne Hester and Sarah-Jane Lilley) 2014, 14.

2.2 Tackling women's subordinate status in society's state institutions

The Istanbul Convention also addresses women's inferior status in state institutional contexts conducive to and tolerant of violence against women.[29] Measures scattered mostly across Chapters V and VI essentially require that in their laws and justice systems States treat forms of violence commonly inflicted on women with the seriousness they deserve. These measures seek to ensure that state responses are not influenced by views and attitudes that regard women as lesser members of society and that therefore normalise, trivialise or justify forms of violence frequently experienced by women. There are two major ways in which the Istanbul Convention may be useful to redress women's unequal status reinforced by state institutions: (1) recognising as wrongs forms of violence typically inflicted on women and making these wrongs unlawful; and (2) tackling the attitudinal barriers that in practice prevent state actors from recognising and responding to these harms.

In Chapter V "Substantive Law", the Convention characterises as unacceptable and punishable – oftentimes criminally – various violent acts that injure women physically, sexually, psychologically and reproductively.[30] It requires that States make these acts "punishable by effective, proportionate and dissuasive sanctions"[31] so as to "match their action with the *seriousness* of the offences".[32] To avoid that state actors treat violence against women as unimportant or unworthy of immediate action, Chapter VI "Investigation, Prosecution, Procedural Law and Protective Measures", obliges States to carry out investigations and judicial proceedings promptly and effectively.[33] The drafters wanted this general obligation "to prevent that incidents of violence against women and domestic violence are assigned *low priority* in investigations and judicial proceedings".[34]

Chapter VI additionally eases the attitudinal barriers women victims of violence are up against when seeking justice by outlining anti-stereotyping measures in instances of sexual violence.[35] Thus, the Convention compels States to ensure that evidence related to victims' sexual conduct or history is prohibited unless

29 As human rights jurisprudence has recognised, impunity of violence against women suggests that this violence is acceptable, thereby contributing to its perpetuation. See Gonzalez et al. ("Cotton Field") v Mexico Series C 205 (16 November 2009) paras 163 and 167–168.

30 Articles 33–40. Examples include stalking, sexual violence, forced marriage, sexual harassment, forced abortion and forced sterilisation.

31 Article 45(1).

32 Explanatory Report, para 232. Emphasis mine.

33 Article 49.

34 Explanatory Report, para 255. Emphasis mine.

35 On the links between unequal access to justice of women victims of gender-based violence and judicial stereotyping, see Simone Cusack, 'Eliminating Judicial Stereotyping: Equal Access to Justice for Women in Gender-based Violence Cases' (2014) https://rm.coe.int/1680597b20 accessed 15 October 2019.

"relevant and necessary".[36] The motivation behind this prohibition is to avoid that a victim's past sexual behaviour is used to excuse violence.[37] This type of evidence, the drafters clarify, "may reinforce the perpetuation of damaging stereotypes of victims as being promiscuous and by extension immoral and *not worthy of the protection provided by civil and criminal law*".[38] The drafters make it clear that States should ensure that "the interpretations of rape legislation and the prosecution of rape cases are not influenced by gender stereotypes and myths about male and female sexuality".[39] These are the kinds of attitudes and beliefs that may prevent prosecutors and judges from treating rape allegations with the seriousness they deserve.

In tackling women's unequal status as manifested in views, attitudes and beliefs prevailing in state and other societal institutions, the Convention is not necessarily breaking new ground. It is standing firmly on a road long paved by previous human rights instruments combating discrimination and violence against women. Dismantling socially entrenched views that regard women as subordinate to men has been a key concern of international human rights law on violence against women. Already in the nineties, United Nations and Inter-American human rights instruments on violence against women demanded States to eliminate the stereotypes of and prejudices against women as a way of combating violence against women.[40] In other words, the Istanbul Convention's focus on eliminating gender stereotypes and prejudices does not come as a surprise given the way in which international human rights law has largely framed violence against women: as perpetuated, exacerbated and legitimised by attitudes and conducts that devalue and subordinate women.[41]

In sum, the breadth and depth of the measures discussed above hold great potential to rectify the lower status socially attributed to women through the workings of stereotypes and prejudices. The Convention challenges these stereotypes and prejudices in the public at large, in the law and in the justice system. More concretely, it demands States to promote attitudinal changes in schools, the media and relevant professions as well as in law/judicial responses to violence against women. However, as I explain in the next section, the Convention's attention to gender equality may remain limited to redressing "misrecognition" unless GREVIO also pushes for redressing socio-economic and political gender differentials.

36 Article 54.
37 Explanatory Report, para 278.
38 Explanatory Report, para 277. Emphasis mine.
39 Explanatory Report, para 192.
40 CEDAW General Recommendation No 19 para 24(f); *Belém do Pará* Convention Articles 5 and 8 and DEVAW Article 4(j) (n 3).
41 Ibid.

3 Increasing the potential to enhance women's political and socio-economic power

In this section, I propose that the Convention is interpreted so as to deepen the gender equality focus outlined in the previous section. In particular, I argue for GREVIO to pay strong attention to the political and socio-economic differentials between women and men in society. In making this argument, I rely on Nancy Fraser's notion of "parity of participation"[42] and on international human rights law, particularly CEDAW. Both Fraser's and CEDAW's frameworks allow for empowering women across several spheres, including the political and socio-economic ambits. I show that the Convention does offer some basis for furthering women's equality in these ambits and argue that, taking this basis as a point of departure, GREVIO may draw further inspiration from CEDAW and demand State Parties to promote women's equality politically and socio-economically.

3.1 Addressing political and socio-economic differentials: basis in the Istanbul Convention

Both the Istanbul Convention text and drafters hint at the need to advance women's equality politically and socio-economically. The hints come from the *empowerment* language and the *human rights* language. In its text – and consistent with its general goal of empowering women[43] – the Convention asks States to promote women's empowerment as part of the obligations to prevent violence against women[44] and to protect/support women victims of violence.[45] The drafters explain that the prevention obligation includes empowering women "in all aspects of life, including political and economic".[46] In turn, the Convention text makes it clear that protection and support obligations comprise advancing women's economic independence.[47]

As for the human rights language, the Convention text embraces it in various ways. It demands States to place the human rights of victims at the centre of both prevention[48] and protection/support[49] obligations. Its Preamble recalls *civil and political* human rights instruments as well as *social and economic*

42 Fraser (n 15) 164–167.

43 In the Istanbul Convention, empowering women is part of the equality purpose. See Article 1(b).

44 Article 12(1)6.

45 Article 18(3).

46 Explanatory Report, para 90. See also, Council of Europe (n 28) 8.

47 Article 18(3). According to the Explanatory Report, protection and support measures aimed at empowering and advancing victims' economic independence "need to instil in victims a sense of control of their lives, which in many cases includes working towards financial security, in particular *economic independence* from the perpetrator". Explanatory Report, para 118. Emphasis mine.

48 Article 12(3).

49 Article 18(3).

human rights instruments within the Council of Europe[50] and the United Nations,[51] including an instrument that combines both sets of rights: CEDAW. The Convention drafters, for their part, affirm that women will not be free from violence unless they equally "exercise and enjoy all civil, political, economic, social, and cultural rights", as recognised in instruments such as the European Social Charter and CEDAW.[52]

These indications, though important, are not as strong and clear as the equality signals discussed in the previous section. GREVIO, however, may take these indications as a point of departure and push for promoting women's equality politically and socio-economically, drawing inspiration from CEDAW and feminist scholarship, to which I now turn.

3.2 Addressing political and socio-economic differentials: CEDAW and feminist insights

A glance at the Convention's human rights predecessors confirms the importance given to advancing women's equal enjoyment of political, social and economic rights in order to effectively combat violence against women. These human rights precursors include General Recommendation No 19 of the United Nations Committee on the Elimination of Discrimination against Women (CEDAW General Recommendation 19), the United Nations Declaration on the Elimination of Violence against Women (DEVAW) and the Inter-American Convention on the Prevention, Punishment and Eradication of Violence against Women (*Belém do Pará* Convention). DEVAW, for example, recognises the negative impact of violence on women's social, political and economic equality[53] and the *Belém do Pará* Convention on women's exercise of civil, political, economic, social, and cultural rights.[54] CEDAW General Recommendation 19 notes even more specifically that violence against women contributes to lowering women's levels of political participation, education, and employment.[55] One key message flowing from these three human rights precursors is that elimin-

50 For example, Convention for the Protection of Human Rights and Fundamental Freedoms (ETS No 5, 1950) and its Protocols as well as the European Social Charter (ETS No 35, 1961, revised in 1996, ETS No 163).

51 For example, International Covenant on Civil and Political Rights (1966) and International Covenant on Economic, Social and Cultural Rights (1966).

52 Explanatory Report, para 50.

53 Preamble of DEVAW.

54 Article 5 of the *Belém do Pará* Convention states: "Every woman is entitled to the free and full exercise of her civil, political, economic, social and cultural rights, and may rely on the full protection of those rights as embodied in regional and international instruments on human rights. The States Parties recognize that violence against women prevents and nullifies the exercise of these rights".

55 CEDAW Committee, General Recommendation No 19 para 11. See also ibid. paras 17 (on the role of sexual harassment in impairing women's equality at work) and 23 (on the links between economic dependence and violence).

ating violence against women is essential to achieving women's equal participation "in all walks of life" – to use the words of the *Belém do Pará* Convention.[56]

These international human rights law concerns with women's equal participation in society resonate with the notion of "parity of participation" developed by Nancy Fraser.[57] To Fraser, participatory parity is the qualitative condition "of being a *peer*, of being on a *par* with others, of interacting with them on an equal footing".[58] For parity of participation to be possible, Fraser proposes three conditions: (1) material resources necessary to interact on a par with others ("redistribution"); (2) "institutionalised patterns" that culturally value all as full partners in society ("recognition"); and (3) membership criteria and decision rules necessary for voicing and resolving contests over redistribution and recognition ("representation").[59] While redistribution is about economically defined differentials in society, recognition is about "culturally defined hierarchies of status".[60] Representation, in turn, refers to "who" can make redistribution and recognition claims and "how" these claims are to be resolved.[61] The harm of "misrepresentation" involves denying the very possibility of participating as a peer in the political and other arenas.[62]

To understand how recognition, redistribution and representation are interlinked, let us examine an example used by Fraser and other feminists. Think of women's unequal access to economic resources because of a gendered division of labour, which does not remunerate or which offers low remuneration to work still predominantly performed by women (e.g. care work, domestic work).[63] In this example, realising women's right to equal pay (redistribution) requires revaluing work in those areas and eliminating the gendered assumptions that have historically justified its devaluation (recognition).[64] The redistribution and recognition dimensions are further linked to the representation dimension: the disparate division of housework and caregiving labour sustained socially[65] and

56 Preamble of *Belém do Pará* Convention.
57 Fraser (n 15) 193–200.
58 Nancy Fraser, 'Feminist Politics in the Age of Recognition: A Two-Dimensional Approach to Gender Justice,' (2007) *Studies in Social Justice* 1(1) 28. Emphasis hers.
59 Fraser (n 15) 193–200.
60 Fraser (n 58) 27–28.
61 Fraser (n 15) 195.
62 Ibid. 196.
63 See Fraser (n 58) 29; Jacqui True, 'The Political Economy of Violence against Women: A Feminist International Relations Perspective' (2010) (32) *The Australian Feminist Law Journal* 39, 44–45; and Dianne Otto, 'Gender Comment": Why Does the UN Committee on Economic, Social and Cultural Rights Need a General Comment on Women?' (2002) (14) *Canadian Journal of Women and the Law* 1. See also CEDAW Committee, General Recommendation No 23 (1997) Article 7 Political and Public Life, para 8 (noting that gender segregation in the workforce is a manifestation of the gendered public/private divide).
64 Otto (n 63).
65 By devaluing or under-valuing work coded as feminine.

economically[66] acts as a formidable obstacle to women's participation as peers in the political and other spheres of public life.[67] Women's inequivalent political power may, in turn, undermine their capacity to challenge this unequal *status quo*. Jacqui True nicely exemplifies the links between political and socio-economic gender differentials and gender-based violence:

> In a mutually constitutive way, the strict division of roles in the domestic sphere constrains women's public participation and their access to economic opportunities in the market, in turn creating inequalities in household bargaining power between men and women and entrapping women into potentially violent environments at home and at work.[68]

Fraser's "parity of participation" framework is helpful to think about gender equality across a range of spheres, including the political and socio-economic spheres. So is CEDAW, a human rights instrument that combines women's equal enjoyment of civil and political rights with that of social, economic and cultural rights. CEDAW prohibits discrimination against women and promotes women's equality across various fields, including political and public life,[69] education,[70] employment,[71] and "other areas of economic and social life".[72] Several of the CEDAW Committee's General Recommendations promote women's equality socio-economically (e.g. on unremunerated domestic activities[73] on women's right to education[74]) and politically (e.g. on women in political and public life).[75] What is more, in its recent update on gender-based violence, the CEDAW Committee includes "the neglect or denial of women's civil, political, economic, social and cultural rights" together with "patriarchal attitudes and stereotypes" among the underlying causes of this violence and asks States to address these causes.[76]

66 By denying pay or under-paying work coded as feminine.
67 Fraser (n 58) 29. See also CEDAW Committee (n 63).
68 True (n 63).
69 CEDAW Article 7.
70 CEDAW Article 10.
71 CEDAW Article 11.
72 CEDAW Article 13.
73 CEDAW Committee, General Recommendation No 17 (1991) Measurement and Quantification of the Unremunerated Domestic Activities of Women and their Recognition in the GNP.
74 CEDAW Committee, General Recommendation No 36 (2017) on the Right of Girls and Women to Education.
75 CEDAW Committee (n 63).
76 CEDAW Committee (n 4) para 34.

3.3 Deepening the Convention's commitment to tackle political and socio-economic differentials

GREVIO could take on board CEDAW's insights to strengthen the Istanbul Convention's concern with gender equality politically and socio-economically. While overseeing CEDAW is obviously not within GREVIO's mandate, the former can act as an interpretative reference in what concerns women's equality and non-discrimination. The Istanbul Convention has actually drawn inspiration from CEDAW: the equality and non-discrimination provision[77] echoes CEDAW Article 2.[78] Moreover, in asking State Parties to secure that women and men equally enjoy the civil, political, economic, social and cultural rights set out in human rights instruments, the Convention drafters emphasise "particularly CEDAW, to which they are parties".[79] All Council of Europe Parties to the Istanbul Convention are State Parties to CEDAW.[80]

77 See Article 4(2), which reads:

> Parties condemn all forms of discrimination against women and take, without delay, the necessary legislative and other measures to prevent it, in particular by: – embodying in their national constitutions or other appropriate legislation the principle of equality between women and men and ensuring the practical realisation of this principle; – prohibiting discrimination against women, including through the use of sanctions, where appropriate; – abolishing laws and practices which discriminate against women.

78 CEDAW Article 2:

> States Parties condemn discrimination against women in all its forms, agree to pursue by all appropriate means and without delay a policy of eliminating discrimination against women and, to this end, undertake: (a) To embody the principle of the equality of men and women in their national constitutions or other appropriate legislation if not yet incorporated therein and to ensure, through law and other appropriate means, the practical realization of this principle; (b) To adopt appropriate legislative and other measures, including sanctions where appropriate, prohibiting all discrimination against women; (c) To establish legal protection of the rights of women on an equal basis with men and to ensure through competent national tribunals and other public institutions the effective protection of women against any act of discrimination; (d) To refrain from engaging in any act or practice of discrimination against women and to ensure that public authorities and institutions shall act in conformity with this obligation; (e) To take all appropriate measures to eliminate discrimination against women by any person, organization or enterprise; (f) To take all appropriate measures, including legislation, to modify or abolish existing laws, regulations, customs and practices which constitute discrimination against women; (g) To repeal all national penal provisions which constitute discrimination against women.

79 Explanatory Report, para 50.

80 As of 3 March 2019, the time of writing, 33 Council of Europe States had ratified the Istanbul Convention. All of them have ratified CEDAW as well.

GREVIO's questionnaire for State Parties does incorporate in the "General Principles" part the Convention's substantive equality concerns.[81] In this part, GREVIO asks State Parties "to bear in mind" the equality and non-discrimination principles set out in Chapter I of the Convention and reminds States that these principles "apply to all substantive articles".[82] Recalling that equality between women and men should be "effectively realised in practice", GREVIO adds that States should implement policies promoting equality between women and men.[83] These equality efforts are no doubt valuable. Yet GREVIO could go further and zoom in on the specific areas on which States should report on the equality measures they are taking, including in the political and economic spheres. It could spell out these areas in the "General Principles" part and/or mainstream the different areas across state obligations in the questionnaire. GREVIO may also adopt a general recommendation[84] detailing the content and scope of measures to ensure gender equality's practical realisation[85] in areas like political participation, employment and education.

In offering more concrete guidance to State Parties, GREVIO could draw on CEDAW and the CEDAW Committee's work. For instance, the CEDAW Committee's General Recommendation on women's participation in political and public life identifies the barriers that need to be addressed to enable women to equally enjoy political rights. These impediments range from financial constraints to less information, stereotypes, and freedom of movement restrictions.[86] Some may argue that, unlike CEDAW, the Istanbul Convention is not as such an equality and non-discrimination instrument. While this is indeed true, it is equally true that the Convention has set itself to promote women's equality. In the words of the Convention drafters:

> Discrimination against women provides a breeding ground for tolerance towards violence against women. Any measures taken to prevent and combat violence against women need to promote equality between women and men as only substantive equality will prevent such violence in the future.[87]

81 GREVIO, Questionnaire on Legislative and Other Measures Giving Effect to the Provisions of the Council of Europe Convention on Preventing and Combating Violence against Women and Domestic Violence (Istanbul Convention), adopted on 11 March 2016 GREVIO/Inf(2016)1.
82 Ibid. "A. General Principles of the Convention" p 4.
83 Ibid.
84 Article 69. This provision draws inspiration from Article 21(1) of CEDAW. See Explanatory Report, para 359.
85 Article 4(2).
86 CEDAW Committee (n 63) para 20.
87 Explanatory Report, para 49.

In closing this section, the Istanbul Convention does offer a basis to advance substantive gender equality politically and socio-economically. Whether that basis will be developed far enough to render such a contribution significant will depend on GREVIO's work. To fully realise the Convention's purpose of promoting substantive equality GREVIO will need to pay attention to the political and socio-economic barriers women face in equally exercising their human rights. In so doing, GREVIO may look at the approach taken by the Istanbul Convention's human rights precursors, particularly by CEDAW given the inspirational role CEDAW played in the Convention's drafting process.

4 Conclusion

In promoting equality between women and men, the Istanbul Convention has greatly benefited from its human rights predecessors, particularly CEDAW. Like them, the Convention strongly combats the gender stereotypes and prejudices that disadvantage women and, in this way, pushes for dismantling the gender hierarchies at the root of gender-based violence in society. An impressive range of measures tackle the societal and institutional contexts conducive to and tolerant of violence against women. These measures flow from the Convention's understanding of violence against women as a gender inequality problem and from the Convention's substantive equality goal. The aim of these measures is to challenge gender-biased views prevalent in schools, the media and relevant professions as well as in the law and justice responses to violence against women.

Though these measures are crucial to advance women's equality, a fuller approach requires the Convention to additionally encourage state measures capable of transforming the arrangements that disadvantage women in exercising their human rights in various spheres of life. The stereotypes of and prejudices against women challenged by the Convention negatively affect women's enjoyment of human rights in employment, education, and politics, among other arenas. In turn, and in a mutually reinforcing way, women's unequal enjoyment of human rights across these spheres contributes to perpetuating women's subordinate status and stereotyped roles in society.

Much more can be learned from CEDAW in this regard, a human rights instrument that combats discrimination against women across civil, political, economic, social and cultural rights. In monitoring State Parties' compliance with the Convention, GREVIO may need to develop an approach that considers women's inequality in exercising all these human rights. This approach may take various forms. I have suggested roughly two approaches, which may be adopted together or separately. The first one is specifying the areas in which State Parties are expected to advance women's equality in GREVIO's questionnaire. The second suggested approach is mainstreaming women's equal enjoyment of all human rights across the questionnaire's different sections.

By adopting the Istanbul Convention, the Council of Europe has created a powerful women's equality instrument. The Convention does hold potential to transform what it views as one of the root causes of violence against women, namely gender hierarchies. Unleashing this transformative potential will involve rectifying gendered structures of power more widely and deeply so as to subvert women's subordinate status in "all walks of life".

3 The Istanbul Convention as an interpretative tool at the European and national levels

Sara De Vido

1 Introduction

This chapter will explore the impact of the Council of Europe Convention on Preventing and Combating Violence against Women and Domestic Violence (Istanbul Convention) as an interpretative tool at the European level. It suggests that this legal instrument can be used by European and national judges alike to set higher standards of protection of women's human rights while interpreting European and national law. The analysis is structured into three levels. First, I will argue that the provisions of the Istanbul Convention can constitute "relevant rules of international law" under Article 31(3)(c) of the Vienna Convention on the Law of Treaties (VCLT) in the interpretation of applicable articles of the European Convention on Human Rights (ECHR). In that respect, I will critically analyse the judgment rendered on 2 March 2017 by the European Court of Human Rights (ECtHR) in the *Talpis v Italy* case.[1] I will comment on the evolution of the well-known "Osman test", envisaging state positive obligations in situations of imminent risk to the right to life of an individual caused by a non-state actor with regard to peculiar situations, such as domestic violence. Second, I will move to the European Union (EU) level to appreciate the impact of the Istanbul Convention in terms of interpretation of EU secondary law. After briefly discussing the state of art of the process of EU adhesion to the Convention, the chapter will offer examples of what the entry into force of the Istanbul Convention for the European Union will entail. Third, I will explore the national level, critically commenting on two cases decided by Italian courts. The chapter eventually encourages dialogue between European and national courts.

1 *Talpis v Italy* App no 41237/14 (ECHR, 2 March 2017).

2 The provisions of the Istanbul Convention as "relevant rules of international law"

The provisions of the Istanbul Convention can constitute "relevant rules of international law" under Article 31(3)(c) VCLT that the ECtHR should use in order to interpret the provisions of the European Convention on Human Rights, in particular Articles 2, 3, 8 and 14 (namely the right to life; the prohibition of torture, or inhuman or degrading treatment; the right to respect for private and family life; and non-discrimination). To support the above argument, I will first explain the meaning of "relevant rules of international law" before delving into the potential and the risks of systemic interpretation from an international law perspective. Finally, I will focus on the recent *Talpis v Italy* judgment, decided by the ECtHR, as an example of systemic integration. The analysis will allow me to highlight the importance of a gender-sensitive interpretation of international human rights legal instruments.

2.1 "Relevant rules of international law" in the VCLT and systemic integration

Interpretation is a practice that "gives meaning to norms and that generates legal normativity".[2] The metaphor of a game describes the activity of interpretation in international law: there are players who are supposed to interpret the law, there are rules and there is an object, which ultimately consists in "persuad[ing] one's audience that [a given] interpretation of the law is the correct one".[3] Article 31(3)(c) VCLT, which expresses the general principle of treaty interpretation known as "systemic integration within the international legal system",[4] is one of the cards that lawyers and courts use in their game. Even though it is not the purpose of this chapter to dwell upon the considerable

2 Ingo Venzke, *How Interpretation 'Makes' International Law: on Semantic Change and Normative Twists* (OUP 2012) 18.

3 Andrea Bianchi, 'The Game of Interpretation in International Law' in Andrea Bianchi, Daniel Peat and Matthew Windsor (eds), *Interpretation in International Law* (OUP 2013) 36.

4 This is the starting point of the reflection by Campbell McLachlan, 'The Principle of Systemic Integration and Article 31(3)(c) of the Vienna Convention' (2005) 54 ICLQ 280.

literature on the matter,[5] it is worth highlighting that systemic integration of other rules of international law in the interpretation of international treaties in force presupposes a dynamic look at international law. This look is meant to "provide a contemporary interpretation of the ordinary meaning of a term".[6] In the Advisory Opinion on the case of Namibia, when interpreting Article 22 of the constitutive treaty of the League of Nations, the International Court of Justice argued that the interpretation of the provision "cannot remain unaffected by the subsequent development of the law", and that "an international legal instrument must be interpreted in the framework of the entire legal system prevailing at the time of the interpretation".[7] This argument reminds us of the position of the European Court of Human Rights that the European Convention is a *living instrument*. In the *Goodwin* case, the ECtHR pointed out that it must consider "the changing conditions within the respondent State and within contracting States generally and respond, for example, to any evolving convergence as to the standards to be achieved" and that the Convention must be "interpreted and applied in a manner which renders its rights practical and effective, not theoretical and illusory".[8]

2.2 *Potential of systemic integration*

The potential of systemic integration can be appreciated in analysing the jurisprudence of regional human rights courts. This approach is not new to courts

5 See, *inter alia*, Hersch Lauterpacht, 'Restrictive Interpretation and the Principle of Effectiveness in the Interpretation of Treaties' (1949) 26 BYIL 48; Mustafa Kamil Yasseen, 'L'intérpretation des traités d'après la convention de Vienne sur le droit des traités' (1976) 151 RCADI 1; Richard Gardiner, *Treaty Interpretation* (OUP 2011); Eirik Bjorge, *The Evolutionary Interpretation of Treaties* (OUP 2014); Rudolf Bernhardt, 'Evolutive Treaty Interpretation. Especially of the European Convention on Human Rights' (1999) 42 *German Y.B. Int'l L.* 11; Vaughan Lowe, 'The Politics of Law-Making: Are the Method and Character of Norm Creation Changing?' in Michael Byers (ed.), *The Role of Law in International Politics* (OUP 2000) 207; Christine Chinkin, 'Human Rights and the Politics of Representation: Is There a Role for International Law?' in Byers (ed.), *The Role of Law in International Politics*, 131; Ulf Linderfalk, 'Is Treaty Interpretation an Art of Science? International Law and Rational Decision-Making' (2015) 26 *EJIL* 1; Alexander Orakhelashvili, 'Restrictive Interpretation of Human Rights Treaties in the Recent Jurisprudence of the European Court of Human Rights' (2003) 14 *EJIL* 3; Ulf Linderfalk, *On the Interpretation of Treaties* (Springer 2008); Malgosia Fitzmaurice, 'Dynamic Interpretation of Treaties' (2010) 21 *Hague Yearbook of International Law* 101; Mark E. Villiger, *Commenting on the 1969 Vienna Convention on the Law of the Treaties* (Martinus Nijhoff 2009); Jean-Marc Sorel and Valérie Boré Eveno, 'Article 31' in Olivier Corten and Pierre Klein (eds), *The Vienna Convention on the law of the Treaties* (OUP 2011) 804; Antonio Cançado Trindade, *International Law for Humankind: Towards a New Jus Gentium* (Martinus Nijhoff 2010).

6 Mark Villiger, 'The Rules of Interpretation: Misgiving, Misunderstanding, Miscarriage? The "Crucible" Intended by the International Law Commission' in Enzo Cannizzaro (ed.), *The Law of Treaties beyond the Vienna Convention* (OUP 2011), 111.

7 ICJ Reports (1971) 31.

8 *Christine Goodwin v UK* App no 28957/95 (ECHR, 11 July 2002) para 6.

and can be used in the interpretation of relevant provisions of the ECHR in light of the Istanbul Convention. Some examples can be provided in that respect. The ECtHR specifically referred to Article 31(3)(c) VCLT to determine and expand the scope of application of Article 6 of the European Convention. In *Golder v United Kingdom*,[9] for example, the Court referred to the provision of the VCLT and mentioned Article 38 of the Statute of the International Court of Justice, while acknowledging that the relevant rules of law included general principles of law. Since the right to have access to civil courts can be considered as a general principle of law, it was deemed useful in the interpretation of Article 6 ECHR.[10]

In another case, the Court used a provision of the Convention for the Protection of Human Rights and Dignity of the Human Being with regard to the Application of Biology and Medicine (Oviedo Convention)[11] as relevant international law in order to clarify the content of the right to informed consent.[12] Similarly, the ECtHR relied on the (Revised) European Social Charter in a case concerning the application of the freedom of assembly and association (Article 11 ECHR) to municipal civil servants; in the judgment, the Charter was used as a means of interpretation, even though the respondent State was not a State party.[13] In *RMT v United Kingdom*, the Court referred to the International Labour Organization Convention No 87 and to the European Social Charter to conclude that secondary strike action – meaning a strike organised by trade union members in one company to support a strike in another company – formed part of trade union freedom and therefore could be brought within the terms of Article 11 ECHR.[14]

Other international courts and tribunals have considered "relevant rules of international law", both customary and treaty law, as means of interpretation.[15] In the jurisprudence of the Inter-American Court of Human Rights (IACHR), for example, the systemic integration approach emerged in a case addressing

9 *Golder v UK* App no 4451/70 (ECHR, 21 February 1975).

10 McLachlan (n 4) 294.

11 4 April 1997, CETS No 164.

12 *Evans v United Kingdom* App no 6339/05 (ECHR, 10 April 2007). Francesco Seatzu and Simona Fanni, 'The Experience of the European Court of Human Rights with the European Convention on Human Rights and Biomedicine' (2015) 31 *Utrecht Journal of International and European Law* 5.

13 *Demir and Baykara v Turkey* App no 34503/97 (ECHR, 12 November 2008) para 85. See Cesare Pitea, 'Interpreting the ECHR in Light of "Other" International Instruments: Systemic Integration or Fragmentation of Rules of Treaty Interpretation?' in Nerina Boschiero, Tullio Scovazzi, Cesare Pitea, Chiara Ragni (eds), *International Courts and the Development of International Law* (Springer 2013) 545. Cfr. A/CN.4/L.682, para 472.

14 *National Union of Rail, Maritime and Transport Workers v The United Kingdom* App no 31045/10 (ECHR, 8 April 2014) para 78.

15 Some examples mentioned by McLachlan (n 4) 279. In particular, the Iran–US Claims Tribunal and Permanent Court of Arbitration, *Ireland v United Kingdom*, final 2 June 2003 (2003) 42 ILM 1118.

violence against women. In *Fernández Ortega v Mexico*,[16] the Court specifically referred to the *Belém do Parà* Convention on the Prevention, Punishment and Eradication of Violence against Women of 1994 to point out that violence against women not only constitutes a violation of human rights, but also "an offence against human dignity", and "a manifestation of the historically unequal power relations between women and men".[17] The rape of Inés, a young member of the indigenous group Tlapanec, committed by military officers in the State of Guerrero, amounted to torture, inhuman, degrading treatment or punishment. Importantly, the Court stressed how the general obligations stemming from the American Convention on Human Rights were "complemented and enhanced" by the *Belém do Parà* Convention.[18]

The potential of systemic integration can also be appreciated with regard to treaties that protect the international *utilitas publica*; these are, according to Kolb, the treaties that will tend to be more often than others interpreted in an effective, evolutive and teleological manner.[19] As evolutive as it can be, however, an interpretation constitutes a "clarification" of existing norms, not law-making.[20] Human rights conventions might be considered an expression of international *utilitas publica*, meaning that they constitute an expression of the interest of the whole international community, a fact that explains, in Kolb's view, the attempt to broaden their scope of application by means of interpretation.[21]

2.3 Risks related to systemic integration

In international law, interpretation is about finding "what parties to a treaty had intended the text to mean, or what international law or what the international community requires the law to be – its true sense, or the force behind it".[22] In classical liberalist theory, the meaning of a given text must correspond to the

16 *Fernández Ortega et al. v Mexico* (IACHR, 30 August 2000).
17 *Ortega* (n 16) para 118.
18 *Ortega* (n 16) para 193.
19 Robert Kolb, *Interprétation et création du droit international. Esquisse d'une herméneutique juridique moderne pour le droit international public* (Bruylant 2006) 202–203.
20 Kolb (n 19) 920–926. See also Gerald Fitzmaurice, *Law and Procedure of the International Court* (Cambridge University Press 1986) 345:

> [T]reaties are to be interpreted with reference to their declared or apparent objects and purposes; and particular provisions are to be interpreted so as to give them their fullest weight and effect consistent with the normal sense of the words and with other parts of the text, and in such a way that a reason and a meaning can be attributed to every part of the text.

21 Robert Kolb, 'The Jurisprudence of the Permanent Court of International Justice between *Utilitas Publica* and *Utilitas Singulorum*' (2015) 14 *The Law and Practice of International Courts and Tribunals* 17.
22 Venzke (n 2) 52.

will of the parties.[23] Nonetheless, Venzke suggested that the interpreter should look at the practice that "shapes and shifts the meaning of norms, that generates legal normativity";[24] this does not mean that interpretation must be arbitrary or indeterminate, but that it must be developed in a space that accommodates major developments in international law, including an increasing consideration of humanitarian values.[25] Systemic integration, as already seen, pursues this objective. Yet systemic integration is not devoid of risks. As Dupuy pointed out, "there is a solid tradition of viewing dynamic interpretation with some suspicion on the basis that it risks giving the judge too much licence not to scrupulously respect the will of the parties as expressed in the treaty instrument".[26] In that respect, courts have adopted different approaches and it does not come as a surprise that the ECtHR has been the one more willing to commit to evolutive interpretation.

Another author warned against the uncritical use of systemic integration, which may result in "the indirect application and supervision of other treaties [meaning treaties belonging to other legal systems] under the guise of interpretation".[27] Rachovitsa especially questioned the application of the principle of systemic integration in the context of international human rights law by providing concrete examples of the reasoning of both the ECtHR and the IACHR. With regard to the former, one judgment that the author criticised – *Opuz v Turkey*, rendered by the ECtHR in 2009[28] – is relevant for my discussion. The applicant's mother was murdered by the husband of the latter in one of the numerous and recurrent episodes of domestic violence. She had reported the violence to the police prior to the murder, but had then been forced to withdraw the complaint due to the death threats received from her husband. In analysing the case, the Court mentioned several international, regional and national legal materials, including the CEDAW Convention of 1979 and related quasi-jurisprudence of the Committee established by the Convention, the *Belém do Parà* Convention – which at the time of the decision was the only convention on violence against women in force – and national laws. When deciding the merits of the case, the Court found that Turkey violated Articles 2, 3 and 14 ECHR. The Court considered that the local authorities had not displayed due

23 Alexander Orakhelashvili, *The Interpretation of Acts and Rules in Public International Law* (OUP 2008).

24 Venzke (n 2) 197.

25 Venzke refers to Lowe, 'The Politics of Law-Making', and to Ruti G Teitel, 'Humanity's Law: Rule of Law for the New Global Politics' (2002) 35 *Cornell International Law Journal* 355.

26 Pierre-Marie Dupuy, 'Evolutionary Interpretation of Treaties: Between Memory and Prophecy' in Enzo Cannizzaro (ed.), *The Law of Treaties Beyond the Vienna Convention* (OUP 2011) 123, 127.

27 Adamantia Rachovitsa, 'The Principle of Systemic Integration in Human Rights Law' (2017) 66 *ICLQ* 561.

28 *Opuz v Turkey* App no 33401/02 (ECHR, 9 June 2009).

diligence to prevent violence against the applicant and her mother. Contrary to what was argued,[29] however, the Court did not use the systemic integration approach here because it did not rely on legal documents "outside" the European legal system to interpret the ECHR – a procedure that could be reasonably objected. The Court rather implemented a form of "transjudicial communication" or "cross-fertilisation" among legal systems.[30] In other words, the ECtHR did not use in the merits CEDAW or the *Belém do Parà* Convention *to interpret* the ECHR, but *took into account* the experience developed at the international and regional levels to make its own and authentic interpretation of the European Convention on Human Rights.

2.4 The systemic integration approach in the Talpis v Italy case

Against this backdrop, I am arguing that the provisions of the Istanbul Convention can constitute "relevant rules of international law" in the interpretation of the ECHR. These provisions will be, for example, fundamental in the determination of the content of due diligence obligations in preventing and combating violence against women. Even though the ECtHR did not expressly mention Article 31(3)(c) VCLT, it seemed to use the principle of systemic integration in *Elisaveta Talpis v Italy*, a case of domestic violence which culminated in the murder of the applicant's son by his own father (who was the applicant's husband).[31] The ECtHR found, by a majority of six votes to one, that Italy had violated Article 2 ECHR, as a consequence of the death of the applicant's son and the attempted murder of the applicant. The Court unanimously found that the State had breached Article 3 ECHR due to the failure of the authorities to protect the applicant from violence. The Court declined to analyse the case under Articles 8 and 13 ECHR, but found a violation of the principle of non-discrimination (Article 14 ECHR) taken in conjunction with Articles 2 and 3 ECHR by a majority of five votes to two.

An interesting aspect of the judgment concerns the application of the so-called "Osman test" in the assessment of the violation of Article 2 ECHR.[32] In order to avoid an excessive burden on the authorities, the test elaborated by the ECtHR provides that the positive obligation to protect the right to life requires that the authorities "knew or ought to have known at the time of the existence

29 Rachovitsa (n 27) 567.

30 See the interesting analysis by Anne-Marie Slaughter, 'A Typology of Transjudicial Communication' (1994) *University of Richmond Law Review* 101. With regard to domestic courts, see Antonios Tzanakopoulos, 'Judicial Dialogue as Means of Interpretation' in Helmut Philipp Aust and Georg Nolte (eds), *The Interpretation of International Law by Domestic Courts: Uniformity, Diversity, Convergence* (OUP 2016) 72.

31 Sara De Vido, 'States' Positive Obligations to Eradicate Domestic Violence: The Politics of Relevance in the Interpretation of the European Convention on Human Rights' (2017) 6 ESIL Reflection http://esil-sedi.eu/?p=1815 accessed on 15 October 2019.

32 *Osman v United Kingdom* App no 23452/94 (ECHR, 28 October 1998).

of a real and immediate risk to the life of an identified individual or individuals from the criminal acts of a third party", and that "they failed to take measures within the scope of their powers which, judged reasonably, might have been expected to avoid that risk".[33] According to the majority of judges, the immediacy requirement was met in the *Talpis* case, despite the fact that a year had passed between the initial police intervention and the murder.[34] Given the circumstances of the case – especially the fact that the woman had called the authorities the night of the murder and that the husband had been stopped by the police a second time that night in the streets before going back home and killing his son – the Court considered that the husband constituted a real threat to the applicant and that the State had an obligation to adopt concrete measures in order to protect her. In the *Talpis* case, the Court did not refer to different techniques of interpretation but was well aware of the impact of the Istanbul Convention when it noted that States – in particular ratifying States such as Italy, which is party to the Convention as of 2013 – have "particular" (*particulière*) due diligence obligations and that the peculiarity of acts of domestic violence, as acknowledged in the preamble of the Istanbul Convention, "must be taken into account" during domestic proceedings.[35]

Article 49 of the Istanbul Convention provides that "Parties shall take the necessary legislative or other measures to ensure that investigations and judicial proceedings in relation to all forms of violence [...] are carried out without undue delay", and Article 50 aims to ensure that the "responsible law enforcement agencies respond to all forms of violence covered by the scope of this Convention promptly and appropriately by offering adequate and immediate protection to victims". These are "relevant rules of international law" that need to be considered in the interpretation of the European Convention in cases of domestic violence.

More specifically, in the *Talpis* case, the above quoted provisions from the Istanbul Convention are pertinent in the assessment as to whether the threshold of "immediate risk" was met. The "Osman test" as applied in the context of Article 2 ECHR and the implied due diligence requirement must be read in light of the Istanbul Convention in the sense that national authorities must consider the specific conditions of vulnerability of women victims of domestic violence and must adopt preventive measures even in the absence of strict immediacy of the harm. In other words, in a situation similar to the one brought before the Court, the immediacy requirement should be satisfied even when the risk of violence is only "present" but not yet imminent. In particular, the fact that the woman had previously found refuge in a shelter for women and that

33 Osman (n 32) para 116.

34 See the two divergent partly dissenting opinions by Judge Eicke and Judge Spano. The latter in particular stressed that the requirement of the immediacy of the risk was not met (para 11 of the opinion).

35 Talpis (n 1) para 129.

she had called the police the night of the murder should have been enough for meeting the requirement of "present risk", which, in turn, would have triggered the obligation upon the State to take protective measures. Accordingly, the ECtHR challenged – although not explicitly – the "Osman test" (and more specifically the immediacy of the harm requirement) through the provisions of the Istanbul Convention, which play the role of "relevant rules of international law". In this way, it followed the pioneering position of Judge De Albuquerque in the *Valiuliene* case, where he emphasised that in the "particular context of violence" and "repeated violence" to which women are subjected, the immediacy requirement as normally applied in the Osman test could be very problematic.[36]

2.5 Gender-sensitive interpretation of human rights legal instruments

The Istanbul Convention also holds the potential to encourage a gender-sensitive approach in the jurisprudence of the ECtHR. As it has been observed by Sjöholm, the Court has not so far adopted an overt gender-sensitive method in its case-law, although "it has successfully integrated several forms of violence [of which women are victims], as human rights violations".[37] A gender-sensitive approach means considering the gendered causes and effects of violence and recognising that harm exclusively or mainly affects women. It also implies acknowledging the gendered effects of a violation, such as the social stigma that women might face as a consequence of violence. It might also mean identifying the element of sex discrimination inherent in State omissions with regard to the investigation of domestic violence.[38] By referring to the Istanbul Convention, the ECtHR can "gender" its legal reasoning and recognise that violence against women is a form of discrimination against women and a violation of human rights.

The Istanbul Convention would be useful to "gender" reparations as well, which means relying on the "transformative potential of reparations", which is capable of disrupting the domino effect that condemns victims/survivors to continue suffering.[39] As Margaret Urban Walker argued, the project of gendering reparations does not aim at disregarding men's suffering but rather at

36 *Valiuliene v Lithuania* App no 33234/07 (ECHR 26 March 2013) 31. See the reasoning I developed in Sara De Vido (n 31).

37 Maria Sjöholm, *Gender-Sensitive Norm Interpretation by Regional Human Rights Law Systems* (Brill 2018) 116.

38 Sjöholm (n 37) 111.

39 Colleen Duggan and Ruth Jacobson, 'Reparation of Sexual and Reproductive violence. Moving from Codification to Implementation', in Ruth Rubio-Marin (ed.), *The Gender of Reparations* (Cambridge University Press 2009) 121, 148.

considering that, with regard to women, "the original violation is extended, ramified and augmented in multiple ways".[40]

The *Talpis* case, which I analysed in the previous paragraph, goes in this direction only partly. The Court emphasised the "particular context of domestic violence" and referred to "vulnerable individuals" such as the applicant, but failed to use the definition of violence against women provided in the Istanbul Convention, according to which this violence is a form of violence which affects women *because* they are women or affects them *disproportionately*. The Istanbul Convention was useful in the identification of the imminent and real risk under Article 2 ECHR and, in this way, it was relevant for the re-conceptualisation of the so-called "Osman test", as I contended above. This is an achievement that should not be underestimated. However, even though an attempt to use a gender-based approach can be traced in the Court affirmation of the existence of particular due diligence obligations, the Court did not take a further step in terms of elaboration of targeted States' obligations. The latter may include, for example, "educational and social obligations beyond the traditional ones of legislation, investigation and operational measures", and "particular expediency and sensitivity in investigations".[41]

3 The Istanbul Convention as a tool for interpreting EU law

I will now turn to the EU legal system to explore the possible "dialogue" and interaction between this system and the Istanbul Convention. Article 75 of the Istanbul Convention provides the legal basis for the accession of the European Union to the Convention. The process started in 2015, when the European Commission issued a roadmap on the possible ratification of the Istanbul Convention by the EU.[42] In 2016, the Commission presented two proposals for Council Decisions, one related to the signature of the Convention and the other one to its conclusion.[43] The European Parliament has strongly encouraged EU

40 Margaret Urban Walker, 'Gender and Violence in Focus: A Background for Gender Justice in Reparations', in Rubio-Marin, *The Gender of Reparations* (n 39) 18, 50 and 53.

41 Sjöholm (n 37) 117. The Court does not even take into account the impact of violence on the woman's health. See, in that respect, Sara De Vido, *Violence against Women's Health in International Law* (forthcoming Manchester University Press).

42 '(A possible) EU Accession to the Council of Europe Convention on preventing and combating violence against women and domestic violence (Istanbul Convention)', JUST – JUST.D.1 (LEGAL ASPECTS) AND JUST D.2 (POLICY ASPECTS) 2015/JUST/010 (2015).

43 Proposal for a Council Decision on the signing, on behalf of the European Union, of the Council of Europe Convention on preventing and combating violence against women and domestic violence, COM/2016/0111 final – 2016/063 (NLE). Proposal for a Council Decision on the conclusion, by the European Union, of the Council of Europe Convention on preventing and combating violence against women and domestic violence, COM/ 2016/0109 final – 2016/062 (NLE), 4 March 2016.

accession since the beginning.[44] The Council of the European Union adopted in 2017 two Decisions on the signature: one regarding matters related to judicial cooperation in criminal matters and the other one on asylum and *non-refoulement*.[45] The legal bases are, respectively, Articles 82(2) and 83(1) of the Treaty on the functioning of the EU (TFEU) and Article 78(2) TFEU.[46] The European Union signed the Convention on 13 June 2017, but has not ratified it yet. Once it enters into force for the European Union, the Convention will become EU law (Article 216 TFEU). The ratification is, however, hampered by the reluctance showed by some Member States regarding the notions of gender and gender-based violence.[47] At the same time, the European Parliament has asked the European Court of Justice for an opinion on the validity of the legal bases for ratification, raising doubts on the decision of the Council to adopt two different legal instruments for the signature of the Istanbul Convention.[48] In the next paragraphs, I will investigate the impact of the Convention in terms of interpretation of EU secondary law.

3.1 Impact of the Istanbul Convention in terms of interpretation of EU secondary law

My analysis will now consider the Istanbul Convention as a means of interpreting EU secondary law. I am convinced that in this field the role of the Convention can be appreciated at its best.[49] The mechanism of using international treaties for interpreting EU law is not new. For example, the definition of

44 See, for example, European Parliament resolution of 24 November 2016 on the EU accession to the Istanbul Convention on preventing and combating violence against women (2016/2966(RSP)), P8_TA(2016)0451.

45 Council Decision (EU) 2017/865 on the signing, on behalf of the European Union, of the Council of Europe Convention on preventing and combating violence against women and domestic violence with regard to matters related to judicial cooperation in criminal matters [2017] OJ L131/11. Council Decision (EU) 2017/866 on the signing, on behalf of the European Union, of the Council of Europe Convention on preventing and combating violence against women and domestic violence with regard to asylum and *non-refoulement* [2017] OJ L131/13.

46 See the complete analysis in terms of legal bases and possible developments in the legislation of the EU in Sara De Vido, 'La violenza di genere contro le donne nel contesto della famiglia: sviluppi nell'Unione Europea alla luce della Convenzione di Istanbul' (2017) 3 *Federalismi* 1, 9.

47 That is what the European Commission acknowledged in its 2019 Report on Equality between Women and Men in the EU, 47. The European Commission was confident of the possibility to conclude the ratification process before 2019 European Parliament election.

48 European Parliament, 'Resolution seeking an opinion from the Court of Justice on the compatibility with the Treaties of the proposals for the accession by the European Union to the Council of Europe Convention on preventing and combating violence against women and domestic violence and on the procedure for that accession' (2019/2678(RSP).

49 See also the application of the Convention in the European Court of Human Rights judgment *Talpis v Italy*, and the comment in De Vido (n 31).

disability included in Directive 2000/78 on equal treatment in employment and occupation[50] has been interpreted in light of the UN Convention on the Rights of Persons with Disabilities (although the UN Convention had not been ratified by all EU Member States).[51]

I will now propose two examples of how the Istanbul Convention can be useful for interpreting EU law. First, the legal instrument might be useful in the interpretation of the expression "sexual violence" included in Directive 2014/41 regarding the European investigation order in criminal matters.[52] The Directive contains the expression "sexual violence" without defining it. Paragraph 36 of the preamble reads that "categories of offences listed in Annex D" [including sexual violence] "should be interpreted consistently with their interpretation under existing legal instruments on mutual recognition". Since "sexual violence" is defined neither in Directive 2014/41 nor in Directive 2011/99 on the European protection order[53] – concerning mutual recognition of decisions on protection measures for victims of crime in EU countries – Article 36 of the Istanbul Convention could be used as a means to interpret the expression *for the purposes* of the European investigation order.

Another example of how the Istanbul Convention could be useful when interpreting EU law concerns the residence status of victims of violence. Article 59(1) of the Istanbul Convention, in relation to which several State Parties appended reservations, provides that:

> Parties shall take the necessary legislative or other measures to ensure that victims whose residence status depends on that of the spouse or partner as recognised by internal law, in the event of the dissolution of the marriage or the relationship, are granted in the event of particularly difficult circumstances, upon application, an autonomous residence permit irrespective of the duration of the marriage or the relationship. The conditions relating to the granting and duration of the autonomous residence permit are established by internal law.

According to Article 59(3), States shall issue a renewable residence permit to victims in one of the two envisaged cases or in both, in particular "where the competent authority considers that their stay is necessary owing to their personal situation". As correctly argued, the provision is not devoid of criticism and

50 Council Directive (EC) 2000/78 establishing a general framework for equal treatment in employment and occupation [2000] OJ L303/16.

51 Case C-335/11 and C-337/11 *HK Danmark v Dansk almennyttigt Boligselskab*, and *HK Danmark v Dansk Arbejdsgiverforening* [2013] paras 35–38.

52 Directive (EU) 2014/41 of the European Parliament and of the Council regarding the European investigation order in criminal matters [2014] OJ L130/1.

53 Directive (EU) 2011/99 of the European Parliament and of the Council on the European protection order [2011] OJ L338/2.

surely does not expressly cover all cases[54] but this does not jeopardise its relevance for the interpretation of EU law. Reference to this provision does not imply the creation of new laws or the attempt to overcome EU Member States' reservations; rather, it aims to exploit the potential of a provision that, despite its not straightforward text, had a clear purpose in the minds of the drafters of the Convention: to protect women from violence when their migration status depends on the migration status of their spouse or partner. Furthermore, the wording of Article 59(1) of the Istanbul Convention is identical to a key provision of Directive 2004/38 on the rights of the citizens of the EU and their families.[55]

If Article 59 of the Istanbul Convention is used to interpret secondary EU legislation, this could overcome the limits of judgments such as *Secretary of State for the Home Department v NA* decided by the European Court of Justice in 2016 upon request for preliminary ruling sent by the Court of Appeal (England & Wales) (Civil Division).[56] In *NA*, the applicant was a Pakistani woman who lived in the United Kingdom with her husband, self-employed, of German nationality. Their children were European citizens. She survived several abuses by her husband, who decided to leave the country before starting the proceedings to get a divorce. The man was a European citizen; hence he did not lose his rights of residence but, rather, exercised his right to freedom of movement. These details are fundamental. Article 13(2)(c) of Directive 2004/38 provides that "divorce, annulment of marriage or termination of the registered partnership […] shall not entail loss of the right of residence of a Union citizen's family members who are not nationals of a Member State", where "this is warranted by particularly difficult circumstances, such as having been a victim of domestic violence while the marriage or registered partnership was subsisting". The European Court of Justice contended that the victim lost the right of residence when the perpetrator left the country before the beginning of the divorce proceedings and that to interpret otherwise would contradict the spirit of the Directive. The woman in the end could retain her status of residence, but *not* because she was a victim of domestic violence but because she was the sole caregiver of her children who were EU citizens. The judgment did not follow the opinion of Judge Wathelet who argued that the "particularly difficult circumstances" mentioned

54 Vladislava Stoyanova, 'A Stark Choice: Domestic Violence or Deportation?' (2018) 20 *European Journal of Migration and Law* 53.

55 Directive (EC) 2004/38 of the European Parliament and of the Council on the right of citizens of the Union and their family members to move and reside freely within the territory of the Member States [2004] OJ L158/77.

56 Case C-115/15 *Secretary of State for the Home Department v NA* [2016] ECLI:EU:C:2016:487. See the comment by Steve Peers, who defined the judgment as one of 'the most shameful judgments' of the European Court of Justice http://eulawanalysis.blogspot.it/2016/07/domestic-violence-and-free-movement-of.html accessed on 15 October 2019.

in Article 13(2) of Directive 2004/38 must be appreciated in the context of the entire Directive. In particular, he found that

> the loss of the derived right of residence, by a spouse who is a third country national, in the event of the Union citizen's departure could be used as a means of exerting pressure to stop the divorce at a time when the circumstances are in themselves enough to wear the victim down psychologically and, in any event, to engender fear of the perpetrator of the violence.[57]

He added that it is not the act of divorce to grant the residence status *but* the specific situation detailed in subparagraph c) of the Directive, namely domestic violence. He pointed out indeed that:

> An interpretation requiring a Union citizen spouse to be present in the territory of the host Member State until the commencement of divorce proceedings would not only be restrictive but would also deprive the provision of its effectiveness, which lies in converting the *derived* right of residence of a family member of a Union citizen into a personal right of residence in particular circumstances warranting protection.[58]

Having in mind the judgment and the position of Judge Wathelet, the Istanbul Convention can be used for the interpretation of Article 13(2)(c) of Directive 2004/38. The first sentence of this sub-paragraph should be read in the sense that "divorce, annulment of marriage or termination of the registered partnership" do not constitute an exhaustive list but examples of dissolution of relationships, as envisaged by Article 59(1) of the Istanbul Convention. Thus, the departure of the husband and his separation from the family should be considered as a case of dissolution of the relationship. Article 59(1) of the Istanbul Convention does seem to exclude cases in which the woman has lost her residence status[59] but, as correctly argued by Wathelet, the particular situation triggering the possibility to retain the residence status is not the act of divorce as such but *domestic violence*.[60] In other words, the woman who was a victim of domestic violence should be entitled to an autonomous residence permit notwithstanding other circumstances that might deprive her of this status. To argue otherwise would lead to a discriminatory outcome: on the one hand, women victims of violence who can retain their status because, for example, they are the sole caregiver of their (European citizens) children; on the other hand, women who lose their residence status without any possibility to invoke domestic violence as a reason for retaining that status. As far as the length of the residence permit is concerned, it is up to the domestic legislator to decide.

57 Opinion of 14 April 2016, para 70.
58 Opinion (n 57) para 75.
59 Stoyanova (n 54) 72.
60 Opinion (n 57) para 59.

In the case of the applicant, it could have been easily argued that Article 59(3)(a) of the Istanbul Convention could have supported her request for residence status, since her stay was "necessary owing to [her] personal situation". But this option was not the most gender-sensitive if the purpose is to disrupt the stereotypes linked to the classic role of the woman as a caregiver and to consider her as an agent for change capable of applying for an autonomous residence permit that allows her to take her life back. In the specific case at issue, the Court concluded that the woman qualified for a right to residence, but this conclusion is unsatisfactory in questioning the traditional gender imbalances between women and men.

4 The Istanbul Convention as a tool for interpreting national law

As a third level of analysis envisaged in this chapter, I am arguing that the Istanbul Convention can influence the interpretation of domestic law by national judges. Italy can be used as a case study in that respect. The country ratified the Convention in 2013 and soon thereafter adopted a law on violence against women, which preceded the entry into force of the Convention itself.[61] Even though some of the provisions of the Convention have not been implemented yet – and concerns have been raised by NGOs on the scarcity of resources made available by the government[62] – the Council of Europe legal instrument has had a huge impact in terms of interpretation of provisions of national law.

In the context of a case of stalking, for example, the *Cassazione* – the Italian Supreme Court – argued that this offence falls under the category of "delitti commessi con violenza alla persona" (offences committed using violence against an individual).[63] In order to decide whether stalking should be considered in this category of crimes, the Court referred to the Istanbul Convention and to EU Directive 2012/29 on the rights, support and protection of victims of crime.[64] The Convention contains the definitions of domestic violence, violence against women and gender-based violence (Article 3); whereas the Directive ensures a specific protection for victims of gender-based violence, violence in a close relationship and sexual violence (Article 22). The *Cassazione* acknowledged that these definitions are not included in domestic law; however, "by virtue of international law, they have entered the national legal system", and

61 *Decreto-Legge* of 14 August 2013 No 93 that became Law 15 October 2013 No 119.

62 See also the shadow report prepared by Italian NGOs for GREVIO (2018): www.direcontrolaviolenza.it/wp-content/uploads/2018/11/GREVIO.Report-inglese-finale.pdf.

63 *Cassazione penale*, sez un (Italian Cassazione, criminal division, unified sessions), No 10959 [29 January 2016].

64 Directive (EU) 2012/29 of the European Parliament and of the Council establishing minimum standards on the rights, support and protection of victims of crime, and replacing Council Framework Decision 2001/220/JHA [2012] OJ L315/57.

have an impact on the application of national law.[65] By invoking the requirement that the Italian legislative power must be exercised in compliance with international and EU obligations as enshrined in Article 117 of the Italian Constitution, the Court argued in favour of the principle of consistent interpretation. This means that where the domestic norm might allow more than one interpretation, there is an obligation for the judge to choose the interpretation that better corresponds to the international and EU obligations Italy must abide by. The national court concluded that the expression "violence against a person" defined in international legal instruments such as the Istanbul Convention is a broad concept that includes both physical and psychological violence and that stalking is a "grave" case of gender-based violence.[66] Accordingly, stalking falls under the category of "delitti commessi con violenza alla persona".

In another case, decided on 5 December 2016, the *Cassazione* considered the appeal of a woman of Moroccan nationality whose request for international protection had been denied by the competent authorities. Her request for reconsideration of the case had been dismissed by the court of first instance and later by the court of appeal in Rome. The woman asked for international protection because she feared she would be subjected to domestic violence perpetrated by her former husband once back home. The authorities rejected the application, arguing that she could receive protection in her country of origin. She did not only obtain divorce in Morocco, but her former husband also was criminally prosecuted and convicted for the perpetrated violence in the home State. The applicant complained that the protection offered by the Moroccan authorities was not adequate and that the Moroccan system did not grant forms of protection such as restraining or protection orders. The Court referred to Article 60 of the Istanbul Convention on gender-based asylum claims, pointing out that violence against women is a form of persecution under the 1951 Convention on refugee status and that the domestic violence suffered by the woman clearly falls under the notion of violence against women. Accordingly, the Court interpreted the notion of "inhuman and degrading treatment" under the Italian legislative Decree No 251/2007,[67] concerning international protection, as encompassing domestic violence. Such interpretation – the Court stressed – is not contrary to the text of the provision of domestic law, on the one hand, and is *compulsory* according to Article 60(1) of the Istanbul Convention, on the other hand. The

65 *Cassazione penale* (Italian Cassazione, criminal division), No 10959, para 6.2.

66 *Cassazione penale* (n 65) para 6.2.

67 *Decreto legislativo* 19 novembre 2007 No 251, Attuazione della direttiva 2004/83/CE recante norme minime sull'attribuzione, a cittadini di Paesi terzi o apolidi, della qualifica del rifugiato o di persona altrimenti bisognosa di protezione internazionale, nonché norme minime sul contenuto della protezione riconosciuta. (Legislative Decree n 251 of 19 November 2007, implementation of Council Directive 2004/83/EC of 29 April 2004 on minimum standards for the qualification and status of third country nationals or stateless persons as refugees or as persons who otherwise need international protection and the content of the protection.)

Cassazione quashed the Court of Appeal's judgment and referred the case back to the lower court to decide on the merits.

These two examples show how the Istanbul Convention can not only induce the legislator to enact new laws or amend existing laws, but also prompt national judges to broaden the scope of application of relevant national law without adopting an interpretation that leads to *contra legem* outcomes.[68] Regrettably, not all national courts have proved to be capable of advancing such a progressive interpretative approach.[69]

5 Concluding remarks

The purpose of my analysis was to find ways through which the Istanbul Convention might play a pivotal role in the enhancement of the protection of women from violence at the European level. The three levels along which the main argument was constructed, namely the Council of Europe legal system, European Union law and the domestic level – have confirmed the expectations. In all cases, the Istanbul Convention can be used as an instrument of interpretation of, respectively, the European Convention on Human Rights, EU law and national law, to strengthen the mechanisms of protection of women from gender-based violence. It is undisputable that the Istanbul Convention is binding only on its State Parties, as all international treaties are. Nonetheless, its impact can be appreciated both in terms of interpretation of the legal instruments in force and in terms of "transjudicial communication"[70] between courts. It means that the Istanbul Convention can be invoked, although not directly applied, by other regional human rights courts, national courts and UN treaty bodies as well to support an interpretation of the legal instruments in force in a more gender-sensitive way. It would also mean to acknowledge the evolution of women's rights at the international level and the role played by international legal instruments such as the Istanbul Convention, which is both a human rights and a criminal law convention, in dismantling rooted stereotypes stemming from the unequal power relations between women and men. Furthermore, I do believe, even though there is no space to develop this argument further, that the application of the Istanbul Convention by European and national courts alike

68 In a report, HL 106, HC 594 – Violence Against Women and Girls, prepared by the Joint Committee on Human Rights, it is written that the Report could be cited by UK Courts as "persuasive authority with regard to legal decision-making". Furthermore, when there is some ambiguity as to what the law requires, the Courts shall assume that the law should be interpreted in a way that complies with UK's international obligations (p. 6).

69 See some recent examples in Italian jurisprudence (decisions not yet published): the Tribunal in Rome acknowledged a form of "cultural defence" as mitigating circumstance in a brutal case of rape in the streets. News reported by the press. https://roma.corriere.it/notizie/cronaca/18_aprile_20/roma-resta-incinta-la-violenza-termini-la-mia-vita-distrutta-3dfa33b4-4402-11e8-8c6c-5ab8ac5380d3.shtml accessed on 15 October 2019.

70 Anne-Marie Slaughter (n 30).

constitutes relevant State practice and *opinio juris* capable of consolidating an incipient custom in international law prohibiting gender-based violence against women, especially inter-personal violence.[71]

Interpretation can truly make international law more effective in the protection of women from violence and courts can play a pivotal role in that respect. To that purpose, judges and lawyers alike must be aware of the potential of the Convention and trained to fully comprehend the provisions of the Istanbul Convention, which, in one of its landmark provisions, stresses the importance of "training [...] the relevant professionals [...] dealing with victims and perpetrators of all acts of violence". The implementation of the Convention is a process which aims to instil gender-sensitiveness at different levels, requiring the development of law and practices capable of eradicating gender stereotypes.

71 See General Recommendation No 35 on gender-based violence against women adopted in July 2017 by the CEDAW Committee which refers to the Istanbul Convention as "practice of State". General recommendation No 35 on gender-based violence against women, updating general recommendation No 19, 14 July 2017, CEDAW/C/GC/35. The Committee stressed that "the *opinio juris* and State practice suggest that the prohibition of gender-based violence against women has evolved into a principle of customary international law".

Part II

Concepts

4 The concepts of gender and violence in the Istanbul Convention

Johanna Niemi and Amalia Verdu Sanmartin[1]

1 Introduction

The Council of Europe Convention on Violence against Women and Domestic Violence (2011; Istanbul Convention) is the last word, at least in Europe, in a chain of international documents on violence against women (VAW) that started with the United Nations Declaration on VAW in 1993[2] and the Peking Platform of Action in 1995.[3] These documents use the concept violence against women, according to which VAW is seen as a manifestation of power imbalances between men and women.[4] This view of VAW is based on extensive research,[5] which has led to the understanding that there is no simple solution to this persistent problem. Thus, the Istanbul Convention promotes a comprehensive and integrated policy to counteract VAW[6] and contains the most extensive list of measures that the contracting countries agree to undertake.

1 This article has been written within the research project ASLA: "Actors, Structures and Law", funded by the Academy of Finland, decisions 281788 and 312497. We thank the members of the project and the editors of this book for valuable comments.
2 United Nations Declaration on Violence against Women 1993, GA 48/104.
3 Beijing Platform of Action. Fourth World Conference on Women 1995.
4 Declaration 1993, Preamble; Beijing Platform of Action 1995 para 118.
5 See European Union Agency for Fundamental Rights (FRA), 'Violence against Women: An EU-Wide Survey' (European Union Agency for Fundamental Rights 2014) http://fra.europa.eu/sites/default/files/fra-2014-vaw-survey-main-results-apr14_en.pdf; FRA, 'Challenges to Women's Human Rights in the EU (2017)'. Research points out different types of VAW and domestic violence in particular. However, control is an important aspect in assessing domestic violence and especially dominant in serious and repetitive violence. See Sylvia Walby and Jude Towers, 'Untangling the Concept of Coercive Control: Theorizing Domestic Violent Crime' (2018) 18 *Criminology and Criminal Justice* 7; Ryan G Carlson and K Dayle Jones, 'Continuum of Conflict and Control: A Conceptualization of Intimate Partner Violence Typologies' (2010) 18 *The Family Journal* 248. Michael P Johnson, 'Conflict and Control: Gender Symmetry and Asymmetry in Domestic Violence' (2006) 12 *Violence Against Women* 1003; Andy Myhill, 'Measuring Coercive Control: What Can We Learn From National Population Surveys?' (2015) 21 *Violence Against Women*, 55; Evan Stark, *Coercive Control: How Men Entrap Women in Personal Life* (OUP 2007).
6 Istanbul Convention (2011) Article 1.1(e) and Chapter 2.

The aims of the Convention, as presented in Article 1, are complex. They include the elimination of violence against women, the prevention of, the protection against and the prosecution of violence, referred to as "three P approach".[7] In addition, the aim of the Convention is to eliminate discrimination against women, to promote substantive equality and to empower women. The Convention also presents a broad set of policies and measures.

In this chapter, we ask what kind of violence is in the focus of the Convention. The Convention defines violence in several ways. Besides the explicit definitions of violence, we are interested in the representation and implicit understandings of violence embedded in the Convention, in its comprehensive and integrated approach to violence and in the aims, policies and measures that the Convention prescribes.

We think that such analysis is needed because the conceptualisation of violence guides the interpretation of measures included in the Convention when it is implemented in State Parties and monitored by GREVIO. We also argue that the conceptualisation of violence has had an impact on the measures that the Convention is proposing and advocating.

This chapter is structured so that in Section 2 we explain the theoretical basis of our research, the method and how we approach the Convention as data. In Section 3 we analyse the definition(s) of violence against women, gender-based violence and domestic violence in the Convention. The subsequent sections analyse the three P policies of the Convention: Section 4 examines the preventive policies in Chapters II and III of the Istanbul Convention; the content and the target groups of prevention. Section 5 looks at the protection of the victim. In particular, in this section we analyse how the victim is conceptualised, because the depiction of the victim is closely connected with the understanding of violence throughout the chapter. Sections 6–7 look at prosecution, first the criminal law part and then the procedural part of the Convention.

2 Theory, method and data

Violence hurts, diminishes, excludes and may even kill. It is real but, yet, it is important how we talk about it. We adhere to the social constructionist approach to social problems, according to which the underlying understanding of the problem has an influence on what kind of measures a legal instrument envisions. Thus, the understanding of a problem, such as violence against women, has important consequences. According to Carol Bacchi the way social

7 Explanatory Report to the Council of Europe Convention on Preventing and Combating Violence against Women and Domestic Violence. Istanbul, 11.V.2011 (Explanatory Report), para 116. See also CEDAW General Recommendation No 35 on gender-based violence against women, updating general recommendation No 19, para 28, adding punishment to the list of Ps.

problems are presented, framed and constructed in professional discourses and social practices has a pertinent effect on what solutions are offered. Vice versa, the solutions to a problem also contribute to the framing of the problem. That is, the problem is framed to fit the proposed solution.[8] Based on a Foucauldian understanding of knowledge being produced in social interaction and social processes,[9] Bacchi states that the representation of a social problem has effects on how it is talked about (discursive effects), on how the subjects who are related to the problem are represented and defined (subjectification effects) and on how material resources are allocated (lived effects).[10]

Legal issues are also social issues but a legal analysis all too seldom focuses on how the legal issue in question has been framed.[11] A reference to the social construction of legal issues is found in Kaarlo Tuori's "the hidden social theory of a legal institution"; the idea is that each legal institution is based on or reflects a view (theory) about how social relations are constituted,[12] in this case, what the construction of violence is. The construction of violence is closely connected to how its subjects are represented. As Butler notes, the linguistic representation of the subject is a result of juridical notions of power.[13] Thus, the construction of violence, victims and perpetrators are intertwined in our analysis.

With these theoretical starting points, this chapter presents a discourse analytical reading of the Istanbul Convention. The focus of the analysis is on the Convention text but we have of course looked also at the Explanatory Report, which reflects the intentions of the drafters and plays a crucial role in the interpretation of the Convention. It fulfils the gaps in the Convention text and it is much more detailed than the Convention.

We have coded the expressions that define and describe violence, victims, perpetrators, actors and measures in the Convention. We utilise Bacchi's approach in looking at what kinds of solutions the Conventions offers and at the representations of violence reflected in these measures. Further, we look at what type of identity is constructed for the victim and what kind of presence the Convention gives to the perpetrator. Besides gender studies, our reading is influenced by critical race studies given their interest in how race or ethnicity is

8 Carol Lee Bacchi, *Analysing Policy: What's the Problem Represented to Be?* (Pearson 2009); Carol Lee Bacchi, *Women, Policy and Politics: The Construction of Policy Problems* (SAGE 1999).

9 This theme permeates Foucault's work and is explicated for example in Michel Foucault, 'Truth and Juridical Forms' in James Faubion (ed.), *Power. Essential Works of Michel Foucault 1954–1984* (Penguin Books, 1994), 14.

10 Carol Lee Bacchi, *Women, Policy and Politics*, 40.

11 Johanna Niemi, 'Law and Crisis: Reflections on How Legal Problems Are Constructed and How They Can Be Studied' (2018) *Retfaerd* 75.

12 Kaarlo Tuori, *Critical Legal Positivism* (Ashgate, 2002).

13 See Judith Butler, *Gender Trouble: Feminism and the Subversion of Identity* (Routledge 2006) 3.

constructed. Our analysis is intersectional in that it looks at how intersecting grounds of discrimination, such as age, disability and ethnicity, are represented in the text.

3 Defining VAW and gender in the Istanbul Convention

3.1 All forms of violence

In research on violence against women, several studies have analysed the construction of the concept of VAW. For example, VAW is often constructed as another kind of violence as compared to ordinary violence. Especially domestic violence is seen as more interactional, less serious and more private than "normal" or standard violence between men.[14] A further distinction is the juxtaposition between ordinary violence, especially in the domestic sphere, and cultural or honour violence within ethnic and migrant minorities. In Suvi Keskinen's analysis, violence against ethnic migrant women is constructed as a problem of violence, migration and national security.[15] Analysing European politics on violence, Montoya and Agustin find that violence against ethnic minority women is either dismissed in mainstreaming policies or presented as a specific minority problem of honour, migration and culture.[16]

The Istanbul Convention defines VAW in several articles. These definitional articles underline gendered power relations, women and men as the basic sex/gender categories and women as victims. VAW is seen as "a manifestation of the historically unequal power relations between women and men",[17] as "a violation of human rights and a form of discrimination against women …"[18] and as an obstacle to achieving equality:[19]

> … these forms of violence need to be addressed in the context of the prevailing inequality between women and men, existing stereotypes, gender roles and discrimination against women in order to adequately respond to the complexity of the phenomenon.[20]

14 Johanna Niemi-Kiesiläinen, 'Sukupuoli ja Rikosoikeuspolitiikka' (Gender and Criminal Law Policy) (2005) *Oikeus* 230; Minna Ruuskanen, '"The Good Battered Woman": A Silenced Defendant' in Kevät Nousiainen and others (eds), *The Responsible Selves. Women in the Nordic Legal Culture* (Ashgate 2001) 311–330.

15 Suvi Keskinen, 'Securitized Intimacies, Welfare State and the "Other" Family' (2017) 24 *Social Politics: International Studies in Gender, State & Society* 154.

16 Celeste Montoya and Lise Rolandsen Agustín, 'The Othering of Domestic Violence: The EU and Cultural Framings of Violence against Women' (2013) 20 *Social Politics* 534.

17 UN Declaration on Violence against Women 1993, Preamble. CEDAW Recommendation 1993; Beijing Platform for Action; Council of Europe Recommendation 2002.

18 Istanbul Convention Article 3(a).

19 Istanbul Convention Preamble.

20 Explanatory Memorandum, para 43. See Peroni in this volume.

Notwithstanding the emphasis on gender inequality, the Convention remains gender neutral when it comes to domestic violence. According to Article 3(b) domestic violence is defined as all acts of physical, sexual, psychological or economic violence that occur within the family or domestic unit or between former or current spouses or partners. The preamble notes that domestic violence affects women disproportionately, and that men and children may also be victims of domestic violence.[21] However, the Convention does not put domestic violence explicitly in the context of control that is typical to situations of serious and repeated domestic violence. Serious cases of domestic violence, particularly those that have ended with the killing of or serious physical damage to the woman, are often a consequence of a long relationship of violence and control of the victim by the perpetrator. The authorities often have difficulties in recognising such spirals of violence.[22] Certainly, the focus on inequality, all forms of violence, proportional sanctions[23] and domestic violence affecting disproportionally women gives the possibility to State Parties and GREVIO to interpret the Convention so that the context of domestic violence is taken into account. However, neither the Convention nor the Explanatory Report contextualise domestic violence as a form of control and a sequence of controlling acts and processes. Thus, the focus of the Convention is not on the most serious form of domestic violence but on all forms of violence. In Sections 4–7 of this chapter we look at how this approach affects the proposed measures.

3.2 The gender of the Convention

A key concept in the Convention is gender, as the expression gender-based violence is used interchangeably with VAW. According to Article 3 "'gender-based violence against women' shall mean violence that is directed against a woman because she is a woman or that affects women disproportionately" and gender is "socially constructed roles, behaviours, activities and attributes that a given society considers appropriate for women and men" (Article 3.c).[24]

Thus, the Convention recognises two genders, women and men, and adheres to theories on gender that understand gender as the social organisation of

21 Explanatory Report, paras 41, 45.

22 This is evident in the case law of the European Court of Human Rights (e.g. *Opuz v Turkey* App no 33401/02 (ECHR, 9 June 2009) and CEDAW Committee (e.g. *Goecke v Austria* 5/2005; *Yildirim v Austria* 6/2005). See Heidi Stöckl and others, 'The Global Prevalence of Intimate Partner Homicide: A Systematic Review' (2013) 382 *Lancet* 836; Jill Radford and Diana Russel, *Femicide: The Politics of Woman Killing* (1992); Adrian Howe and Daniela Alaattinoğlu (eds), *Contesting Femicide: Feminism and the Power of Law Revisited* (Routledge 2018). See also references in footnote 5.

23 See subchapter 6.

24 See also CEDAW General Recommendation No 35 on gender-based violence against women, updating general recommendation No 19, paras 9–10.

relations and power structures between men and women.[25] The only references to persons with a different sex or gender identity are found in the non-discrimination clause in Article 4. Otherwise the text is firmly embedded in the heteronormative binary of women and men as the genders.[26] Thus, gender is used as a substitute of sex, sex being women and men.

The Convention does not structurally recognise LGBTI rights, which are still insufficiently recognised in international and national law[27] and the Istanbul Convention does not change that. The political movements against "genderism" in Eastern European countries[28] seem to be misplaced in the light of the Convention text. The Convention does not recognise as gender-based violence such violence that is directed at men because of their sexual orientation or gender-identity. Literally, the Convention does not recognise as gender-based violence such violence that is directed at a man because of whom he loves. This is illustrated by the case of Abbas in Sweden in which the family – it is still unclear who actual killed him – killed an unwanted boyfriend of their daughter.

> Abbas Rezai was a 19-year old asylum seeker from Afghanistan. He met his beloved, a girl of the same age and from the same country, over the internet. The girl was strictly controlled by her family but, having found a soulmate, decided to meet Abbas in the north of Sweden where he was staying. After a while the girl missed her family who convinced them to come over. After the girl had been given a substance to faint, Abbas was cruelly killed. The 17-year-old brother of the girl confessed the murder and was sentenced to four years in an institution for young offenders and to life-long expulsion. In 2011 his conviction was cancelled and the parents were tried and convicted of murder.[29]

25 About the power gendered structure, see e.g. Gayle Rubin, 'The Traffic in Women: Notes on the "Political Economy" of Sex' in Linda Nicholson (ed.), *The Second Wave: a Reader in Feminist Theory* (Routledge 1997).

26 On gender referring to the binary see e.g. Joan Scott, 'Gender: A Useful Category of Historical Analysis' (1986) 91 *The American Historical Review* 1053.

27 However, see the Yogyakarta Principles that seek to clarify that human rights law covers all persons: Yogyakarta Principles and State Obligations on the Application of International Human Rights Law in Relation to Sexual Orientation, Gender Identity, Gender Expression and Sex Characteristics to Complement the Yogyakarta Principles. https://yogyakartaprinciples.org/

> Ali Miller, 'Fighting over the Figure of Gender' (2011) 31 *Pace Law Review* 837; Ali Miller, 'Sexuality, Violence against Women, and Human Rights: Women Make Demands and Ladies Get Protection Author' (2004) *Health and Human Rights;* Dianne Otto, 'Queering Gender [Identity] in International Law' (2015) 33 *Nordic Journal of Human Rights* 299.

28 Sekowska-Kozolowska in this volume. The roots of the conservative attack on gender were seen already at the United Nations Women's Conference in Peking 1995. See Sally Baden and Anne Marie Goetz, 'Who Needs [Sex] When You Can Have [Gender]?' (1997) *Summer Feminist Review* 3.

29 The Local, www.thelocal.se/20110808/35416.

As to the roles of women, the Convention views them as victims because they are women.[30] Violence is defined in the Convention with reference to the harm and suffering it causes to women, which may be physical, sexual, psychological or economic in nature.[31] Women are seen as victims of human rights violations and discrimination, as sufferers of harm and even as the cause of violence.

Among the policies against violence, the Convention calls for the eradication of social and cultural patterns of behaviours, customs and traditions that are based on stereotypes and inferiority of women.[32] The Explanatory Report specifies "… certain roles or stereotypes reproduce unwanted and harmful practices and contribute to make violence against women acceptable".[33] We agree with the drafters of the Convention that it is important to reveal and counteract the stereotypes that are embedded in the legal norm systems and their implementation.[34] However, underlining the role of stereotypes in the processes of violence may obscure the fact that it is actually people who use violence.

The perpetrators of violence and their sex are not visible in the Convention. Thus, men are mentioned as possible victims of domestic violence but not as perpetrators of violence. The invisibility of the sex of the perpetrators also avoids the question about the gender-based or gendered nature of men's violence against other men. Men's violence against other men is prevalent, probably as prevalent as men's violence against women, it just takes place in different contexts and it is equally embedded in the cultural roles of men.[35]

Thus, when the Convention focuses on VAW in a heteronormative context, it excludes many forms of violence, many kinds of victims and mostly the role of perpetrators. As important as dismantling stereotypes is, there is a real risk that the view on stereotypes that the Convention offers is a narrow one, focused on stereotypes of women, and one that does not really challenge the most fundamental problem, that is, men's role in violence.

30 Article 3(d) "'gender-based violence against women' shall mean violence that is directed against a woman because she is a woman …".

31 In comparison to earlier international documents on VAW, economic harm is added to the definition.

32 Article 12(1). The article echoes Article 5 of the United Nations Convention on the Elimination of All Forms of Discrimination against Women 1979. CEDAW Article 5, however, mentions both "the inferiority or the superiority of either of the sexes" while the Istanbul Convention only refers to the inferiority of women. CEDAW General Recommendation No 35 refers more explicitly to the norms of masculinity, male control and power and men's entitlement and privilege over women, para 19.

33 Explanatory Report, para 43.

34 Rebecca J Cook and Simone Cusack, *Gender Stereotyping: Transnational Legal Perspectives* (University of Pennsylvania Press 2010); Eva Brems and Alexandra Timmer (eds), *Stereotypes and Human Rights* (Intersentia 2016).

35 Jeff Hearn, *Violences of Men* (Sage 1998). Jeff Hearn, *Men of the World: Genders, Globalizations, Transnational Times* (1st ed, Sage Publications 2015). Michael S Kimmel, *Guyland: The Perilous World Where Boys Become Men* (Harper 2008).

4 Prevention: trust on education

Prevention of violence is one of the central aims of the Istanbul Convention. Chapter II of the Istanbul Convention describes a broad set of policies and a holistic approach to prevention. Both public and private actors are mentioned and special emphasis is placed on civil society organisations and on co-operation among different actors (Articles 7–9).[36] State Parties must set up a national authority for the co-ordination, monitoring and evaluation of policies (Article 10), collect data on VAW and finance research.

The core issue in prevention is education. Education should be directed at the general public (Article 13; 17), at students at all levels, at people participating in sports, leisure and cultural activities (Article 14), at professionals (Article 15), at men and boys in general (Article 12.4) and at perpetrators in particular (Article 16). Parties should also encourage the private sector, especially the information and communication sectors and the media (Article 17),[37] to develop self-regulation to prevent violence.

According to the Convention, the educational project should include gender equality (Articles 14.1 and 15), the empowerment of women (Article 12.6) and counteracting stereotypes and cultural and religious justifications of violence (Articles 12.1, 12.5 and 14.1). The school curricula and teaching materials should include mutual respect, non-violent conflict resolution in interpersonal relationships, gender-based violence against women and the right to personal integrity (Article 14).

The training of professionals should include prevention and detection of violence, the needs and rights of victims, referral to specialised services and multi-agency cooperation. Also, professionals are to be informed about equality between women and men (Article 15). Relevant professionals to be educated are the judiciary, including judges, prosecutors, lawyers, law enforcement agencies, health care staff, social workers and educators.[38] However, in contrast to school curricula, the Convention does not require that the degree curricula for the relevant professions include VAW or equality training. Though professional training may be enough, even this requirement is mitigated by reference to the independence of judges and voluntary participation. [39]

Article 16 on perpetrator programmes is directed towards persons who have already committed violent crimes. Thus, its purpose is to prevent re-offending.

36 For more see Andersson and Bengtson in this volume.
37 A non-exhaustive list is provided in Explanatory Report, para 91.
38 Explanatory Report, para 100.
39 Ibid.

State Parties should set up or support programmes to teach perpetrators of domestic violence and of sex offences to adopt non-violent behaviour.[40]

To conclude, the Convention includes a comprehensive and ambitious programme to prevent violence through educational measures. However, the obligations of State Parties are at the level of encouragement and recommendations. The concrete educational standards are not specified, not even for key actors in the services and the criminal justice system. Thus, GREVIO shall have the responsibility for setting standards.

5 Protection and support

5.1 Victim at the centre

As promised in Article 7.2, the victim is put at the centre in Chapter IV of the Convention, dedicated to victim services. This chapter has two main goals: to protect[41] and to support the empowerment of victims (Article 18.1–3).

The Chapter makes a distinction between general and specialised services. General services encounter victims as part of their general mandate, such as health care, housing, education, employment or social services, and they should be able to assist and refer victims to special services (Article 20). Among the specialist services, the most important concrete commitments are the setting up of a sufficient number of accessible shelters,[42] a 24/7 helpline for victims and rape crisis and/or sexual violence referral centres (Article 21–25.[43]

5.2 Anti-discrimination, vulnerabilities and special needs

The comprehensive policies are aimed at covering all victims of VAW. The emphasis is either on all victims of VAW or women as victims. Intersectionality is not underlined but difference among women are mentioned as grounds of discrimination and as vulnerabilities.

40 The scientific evidence on the effects of such programmes, especially aggression control programmes, is ambiguous. Marianne Hester and Sarah-Jane Lilley, *Domestic and Sexual Violence Perpetrator Programmes: Article 16 of the Istanbul Convention* (Council of Europe 2014). Jeff Hearn and Susan Edwards, *Working Against Men's "Domestic Violence": Priority Policies and Practices for Men in Intervention, Prevention and Societal Change* (Council of Europe, Strasbourg, 2005). The Explanatory Report (paras 102–105) discusses the criteria for a successful programme.

41 Istanbul Convention, Articles 1(1)(a) and 5.

42 The Explanatory Report (p. 135) refers to the Council Europe Task Force recommendation of one family place per 10,000 inhabitants. While it is difficult to give an exact figure, this figure has been used as a benchmark.

43 A helpline should be around the clock, toll-free and the caller should remain anonymous if she so wishes (Explanatory Report, paras 136–137). *Rape crisis centres* provide counselling, therapy, support and legal aid. *Sexual violence referral centres* offer immediate medical care and secure forensic evidence. Explanatory Report, paras 138–142.

As the leading principle of the Convention, gender equality is complemented by the prohibition against discrimination in the access to services and protection secured by the Convention.[44] The anti-discrimination clause is the only article that mentions differences: race, colour, language, religion, political or other opinion, national or social origin, national minority, property, birth, sexual orientation, gender identity, age, health, disability, marital status, migrant or refugee status, or other status (Article 4.3). The clause is complemented by a clause on positive measures that are necessary to protect women and cannot be considered discriminatory (Article 4.4).[45]

Specific groups of victims are addressed under the concept of vulnerability in Articles 12(3), 18(3) and 46(c). What vulnerability means is not explained in the Convention,[46] but the Explanatory Report includes an extensive list of vulnerabilities:

> pregnant women and women with young children, disabilities, including those with mental or cognitive impairments, persons living in rural or remote areas, substance abusers, prostitutes, persons of national or ethnic minority background, migrants – including undocumented migrants and refugees, gay men, lesbian women, bi-sexual and transgender persons as well as HIV-positive persons, homeless persons, children and the elderly.[47]

However, the Convention does not explicate what measures should be taken to protect vulnerable groups. There is one exception: migrant women are explicitly mentioned in Part VII of the Convention (Migration and Asylum) and in some of the criminal law articles.[48]

The Convention pays attention to children. However, they are seen as an appendix to their mothers, either as witnesses to (Article 26) or as secondary sufferers of violence against their mothers.[49] Thus, the paramount issue whether a child, who witnesses his or her mother being beaten, should be considered a victim is avoided altogether.[50] Girls are included in the protection of the Istanbul Convention but the specific problems of girls who are sexually and violently abused are not addressed, with the exception of female genital mutilation (Article 38).

44 Explicitly so in Explanatory Report, para 53.

45 According to the Explanatory Report, this clause refers to specific protections of women as opposed to men, "measure which would benefit women only", not to intersecting grounds of discrimination. Explanatory Report, para 55.

46 Vulnerability is a contested concept that is increasingly used in international human rights law. However, Martha Fineman understands vulnerability as a part of the human condition, not as a feature of groups. Martha A Fineman, *The Autonomy Myth: A Theory of Dependency* (The New Press 2004).

47 Explanatory Report, paras 87, 120.

48 See section 6 of this chapter.

49 Articles 13, 18, 22, 23, 31, 45.

50 Yet we know that children usually know about the violence and that it is very harmful to them even if they are not themselves beaten.

6 Criminal law

6.1 Serious and less serious violence

The Convention obliges States to make a national benchmarking exercise when the Convention is ratified.[51] Interesting discussions have ensued in many countries with their accession to the Convention.[52] Even in the Nordic countries, known for their high level of gender equality, the requirement of having lack of consent as the central element of rape as required by the Convention (Article 36), has provoked discussions between the criminal law establishment and women's movements. For example, Sweden has recently changed the law so that the essential element of rape is lack of consent.[53] Similarly, definitions of domestic violence and seeing the domestic context as an aggravating circumstance of violence (Article 46a) have been reformed in several European countries.[54]

As discussed earlier, the Convention does not place domestic violence in the context of repeated cycle of violence and control.[55] Such contextualisation is found in the Explanatory Report concerning psychological violence, which is seen as a course of conduct rather than a single event. The aim has been to capture the criminal nature of an abusive pattern of behaviour occurring over time, whether within or outside the family.[56] The Convention itself defines psychological violence as intentional coercion and threat seriously impairing a person's psychological integrity (Article 33).[57] There is an obvious discrepancy between the text of Article 33 and the Report, and together they narrow the crime. While the Convention narrows the crime to conduct that seriously impairs a person's integrity, the Report narrows it into a continuing pattern of violence. Thus, the scope of psychological violence is a narrow one and does not necessarily cover threats to use violence if they are not very serious or part of a pattern. This problem is a real one, first, because the seriousness of threats can be difficult to assess and, second, because evidence of threats is often available even when there is no evidence of the repeated pattern.

51 Article 68(1–2).

52 See Burek, Möschl and Sekowska-Kozolowska in this volume.

53 Helena Jokila and Johanna Niemi, 'Rape Law and Coercive Circumstances' in Marie B Heinskou, May-Len Skilbrei and Kari Stefansen (eds), *Rape in the Nordic countries* (Routledge 2019).

54 Liz Kelly, Carol Hagemann-White, Thomas Meysen and Renée Römkens, *Realising Rights: Case Studies on State Responses to Violence against Women and Children in Europe* (London Metropolitan University 2011).

55 See above at 3.1.

56 Explanatory Report, para 181.

57 Similarly, stalking is defined as threatening conduct causing fear for safety (Article 34). The contextualisation and description of the activity is done in Explanatory Report, paras 182–186.

The decision not to contextualise psychological violence is even more problematic since the Convention and the Explanatory Report do not discuss mutual violence. In domestic violence, allegations that the wife/female partner uses psychological violence (nagging, defamation, planning to leave etc.) are typical.[58] While they are not acceptable in the spirit of the Convention, they may still today affect the criminal procedures and, therefore, should be mentioned in this context.

Even if the Convention underlines the obligation to prevent all forms of violence, some forms of violence are downplayed as crimes. Psychological violence (Article 33), stalking (Article 34), sexual harassment (Article 40) and breach of protection orders (Article 53.3) need not be criminal offences at all but can be dealt with other than criminal sanctions (Articles 40 and 78.3). Given the narrow scope and high threshold of psychological violence, the repeated nature of stalking, the abuse of power in sexual harassment[59] and that violence or threat has preceded protection orders, the efficiency of other sanctions than criminal is in doubt.

Generally, the level of sanctions is addressed in Article 45.1 requiring that sanctions for crime must be effective, proportionate and dissuasive, including deprivation of liberty, which can give rise to extradition.[60] The Convention does not include minimum sentences for serious crime.[61] However, Article 46 on aggravating circumstances goes along with the general European trend to recognise a close relationship between the victim and the perpetrator as an aggravating factor.[62] Also the vulnerability of the victim due to particular circumstances or in the presence of a child make a crime aggravated.

In conclusion, the most important contribution of the Convention to generic criminal laws is the introduction of victim-related factors as aggravating factors. Notwithstanding the gender equality approach of the Convention, domestic violence is not seen in the context of control and use of power that is typical to seriously violent relationships. Moreover, behaviours that are typically directed

58 E.g. Kris Henning and Robert Holdford, 'Minimization, Denial, and Victim Blaming by Batterers' (2006) 33 *Criminal Justice and Behavior* 110.

59 The obligation to have measures against sexual harassment is not limited to working life and education as in Gender Equality Directive (Dir 2006/54/EU) but the effect is formulated in a similar vein as creating an intimidating, hostile, degrading, humiliating or offensive environment. The abuse of power in sexual harassment is explicitly mentioned in Explanatory Report, para 209.

60 The formulation is the same as in the Council of Europe Convention on Child Sexual Abuse, Article 27.1.

61 Such requirements rarely exist in international conventions. However, the EU Directive on preventing and combatting trafficking in human beings and protecting its victims, 2011/36/EU, includes minimum sentences for traffickers in Article 4.

62 Carol Hagemann-White, Liz Kelly and Renée Römkens, Feasibility Study to Assess the Possibilities, Opportunities and Needs to Standardise Legislation on Violence against Women, Violence against Children and Sexual Orientation Violence (European Union 2010) 62.

to any woman and include gendered use of power, such as stalking, sexual harassment and psychological violence, do not need to be crimes at all.

6.2 Specific crimes

The Convention contains three articles on specific crimes: forced marriages (Article 37),[63] female genital mutilation (FGM; Article 38), forced abortion and sterilisation (Article 39). These four gender-specific crimes focus on "others", that is, on migrant populations and national minorities in European countries.[64] They are also related to the reproductive capacity of these women.

While the prohibition of forced marriage and FGM seeks to protect women within "their" group or culture,[65] the prohibitions of forced abortion and sterilisation refer to state intervention into the privacy and fertility of minority women, which has sad historical roots in many European countries.[66] It is interesting to note that forcing a woman to carry a child she has not wanted to conceive is not recognised as violence by the Convention.[67]

The tendency to "othering" is present also in provisions of the Convention on international criminal jurisdiction. According to the generic principles of international law on jurisdiction in criminal matters, prosecution in another country than where the crime was committed requires double criminality, that is, that the act is stipulated as a crime in both countries. This requirement is excluded for some crimes, such as rape, forced marriage, FGM and forced abortion and sterilisation (Article 46.3) in the Istanbul Convention, but not for domestic violence, however serious the violence might be. Nor does the

63 In addition, a forced marriage should be voidable, Article 32.

64 See Lourdes Peroni, 'Violence against Migrant Women: The Istanbul Convention through a Postcolonial Feminist Lens' (2016) *Feminist Legal Studies* 49.

65 See Mestre in this volume. Also, Anja Bredal, 'Ordinary v Other Violence? Conceptualising Honour-Based Violence in Scandinavian Public Policies' in Aisha K Gill, Carolyn Strange and Karl Roberts (eds), *'Honour' Killing and Violence* (Palgrave MacMillan 2014).

66 The history of forced sterilisations shows that it has been performed on minority women, such as Roma, other ethnic minorities, disabled women and HIV-positive women. See e.g. Re-mapping women's testimonies into networked subjectivities: The Quipu Project.

67 In contrast, CEDAW General Recommendation No 35 considers forced pregnancy, forced continuation of pregnancy and criminalisation of abortion as forms of gender-based violence, at paras 18 and 31(a). While international law has not whole heartily embraced the right to abortion as part of the right to privacy, it is today considered as part of the right to reproductive health. See Committee on Economic, Social and Cultural Rights, General comment No 22 (2016) on the right to sexual and reproductive health (Article 12 of the International Covenant on Economic, Social and Cultural Rights). The European Court of Human Rights, which is of the opinion that abortion is a matter to be regulated by national law (*A, B and C v Ireland* App no 25579/05, 16 December 2010, para 214), has held that the procedures may put a woman seeking abortion in a position that amounts to violation of her human rights. See e.g. *R.R. v Poland* App no 27617/04 28 (ECHR, 28 November 2011); *Tyciąc v Poland* App no 5410/03 (ECHR, 24 March 2007). Rachel Rebouché, 'Abortion Rights as Human Rights' (2016) 25 *Social & Legal Studies* 765.

exclusion of the requirement for double criminality concern the crime of serious stalking. Again, the Convention does not put VAW into the context of continuous control and repetitive violence, which is often the reality of these crimes. Furthermore, the omission is deplorable because stalking and harassment are increasingly done over the internet and do not require presence in the same country.

6.3 Defences

The Convention states that the so-called "honour" may not be invoked as a justification for violence and underlines that such justification is related to culture, religion, tradition and customs (Articles 12(5) and 40). This "cultural defence" is the only criminal law defence that is mentioned in the Convention. Nothing is said about the justifications that are commonly invoked by many perpetrators, such as substance abuse, provocation, mutual violence, self-defence[68] and jealousy. Typically, perpetrators claim that the violence was justifiable or that any sanctions should be mitigated because the victim had provoked them. This kind of victim blaming has many forms, such as "she did not cook, consent to sex, she nagged, danced with another man".[69] These kinds of defences are mostly legally irrelevant, but common. Likewise, mutual violence and self-defence are used to belittle violence. In a document that has a strong educational ethos such as the Istanbul Convention, one would expect these defences to be mentioned.

6.4 Concluding on criminal law

The list of criminal offences in the Istanbul Convention is a useful benchmarking tool for States especially when they prepare to accede to the Convention and to submit their first reports to GREVIO. The list has contributed to discussions in all countries, including those that flag gender equality, on issues of rape, aggravating factors and stalking. The Convention addresses the most serious forms of violence in aggravating factors but does not specifically mention measures to prevent the most serious forms of violence, such as femicides. It does not even mention femicides. The Istanbul Convention puts the threshold of psychological violence and stalking high and does not connect those to the continuous use of control and power. As a consequence, the Convention does not add much to existing tools to fight domestic violence and stalking, forms of

68 Self-defence is fleetingly mentioned in Explanatory Report, para 156.

69 Solveig Lelaurain, David Fonte and Pierluigi Graziani, 'French Validation of the Domestic Violence Myth Acceptance Scale (DVMAS)' (2018) *Affilia* 237–258; Deborah A Levesque, Patricia H Castle, Wayne F Velicer and R Neil Greene, 'Resistance among Domestic Violence Offenders: Measurement Development and Initial Validation' (2008) 14 *Violence against Women* 158; LynnMarie Sardinha and Héctor E. Nájera Catalán, 'Attitudes towards Domestic Violence in 49 Low- and Middle-Income Countries: A Gendered Analysis of Prevalence and Country-Level Correlates' (2018) 13 *PLOS ONE*.

violence that are common in all parts of the population. In contrast, the Convention highlights the crimes associated with migrant families and underlines how they are embedded in the cultures, traditions and customs that perpetuate the oppressed position of women in these cultures.

7 Ambiguous rules on the criminal procedure

7.1 Victim's complaint or ex officio *prosecution*

The procedural Articles of the Convention are ambiguous on the role of the victim's complaint versus the *ex officio* duty of the justice system actors to respond to violence. Chapter VI starts with a firm position that the authorities have a duty to promptly and appropriately respond, investigate and process all forms of VAW, while taking into account the rights and protection of the victims (Articles 49–51). When it comes to prosecution, one of the three Ps[70] of the Convention, the picture becomes more ambiguous. The prosecution and investigation of sexual crimes, forced marriages, FGM, forced abortions and sterilisations should "not be *wholly dependent* upon a report or complaint filed by a victim" (Article 55(1)). The expression "wholly dependent" is open to interpretation, but the Explanatory Report clarifies that the purpose is to make these offences *ex officio* prosecuted[71] and investigated.[72] Supposedly, the expression has to mean something and, as its meaning is not "wholly" explained, the regulation remains ambiguous.

However, there is specific possibility of reservations to the main rule of requiring public prosecution regarding minor physical violence (Article 78 with reference to Article 55). Thus, a State may require a complaint by the victim for the purposes of the investigation and prosecution of minor violent offences. The Explanatory Report defines the meaning of minor violence as not "serious offences of physical violence resulting in severe bodily harm or deprivation of life".[73] This definition puts the threshold of *ex officio* very high indeed. It would allow to make a reservation to *ex officio* prosecution regarding physical violence that causes bodily harm, as long as such harm is not considered severe. We would argue that the interpretation offered in the Explanatory Report goes too far. Since the Convention only allows reservation to minor offences of physical violence, the main rule of *ex officio* prosecution holds for violence that causes bodily harm, even if that bodily harm is not severe.

70 See introduction to this chapter.

71 *Ex officio* prosecution means that the prosecutor brings the charges irrespective of the request of the victim. Usually, it also means that the police have the obligation to investigate the crime *ex officio*.

72 Explanatory Report, paras 279–280.

73 Explanatory Report, para 281.

7.2 Protection in criminal procedure

The dominant discourse in Part VI of the Convention is protection. However, the means of protection are not sufficiently spelled out. The most concrete means of protection are protection orders (Articles 52–53). Notably, the Istanbul Convention is the first international instrument specifically committed to protection orders,[74] including both emergency barring orders, making it possible to remove the perpetrator from the shared home, and longer-term protection orders. The latter bars the perpetrator from approaching the victim in any way, including through electronic means.[75] As other measures of protection, the Convention mentions the conduction of risk assessments, in which access to firearms is taken into account, giving information to the victim about the release of the suspect/perpetrator and affording procedural rights to the victim.[76]

The Convention is mysteriously silent on criminal sanctions and coercive measures, such as arrest and detention. This is mysterious because the Convention is about violent crime. It does not say anything about pre-trial arrest and detention to secure the investigation. It is also silent on the issues of prosecution and trial. This is peculiar because the only truly protective measure against serious violence is pre-trial detention, and many if not all national laws mention risk of repetition of crime as one of the reasons to arrest and detain a suspect. However, the implementation of coercive measures in cases of VAW is often not as rigorous as in cases of other violent crimes.[77] Therefore, several US states and Canada enforced mandatory arrest and pro-arrest laws in domestic violence cases during the nineties and the United Nations has recommended pro-arrest and pro-prosecution policies.[78] These policies have been researched and widely discussed,[79] but these discussions are seldom referred to in European policy making. Nevertheless, the silence on arrest and detention as a response to domestic violence seems to be a conscious European policy, even if not openly

74 EU law recognises the cross-border effects of protection orders in Directive 2011/99/EU on the European protection order and Regulation 606/2013 on mutual recognition of protection measures in civil matters.

75 Suzan van der Aa, Johanna Niemi, LPA Sosa, Ana Ferreira and Anna Baldry, *Mapping the Legislation Ond Assessing the Impact of Protection Orders in the European Member States* (Wolf Legal Publishers 2015).

76 Articles 51 and 56.

77 United Nations, *Handbook for Legislation on Violence against Women* (United Nations 2010) 37–38.

78 Ibid. 37.

79 Susan L Miller, LeeAnn Iovanni and Kathleen D Kelley, 'Violence against Women and the Criminal Justice Response' in Claire M Renzetti, Jeffrey L Edleson and Raquel Kennedy Bergen (eds), *Sourcebook on Violence against Women* (Sage 2017) 267. Stacy L Mallicoat, *Women, Gender, and Crime: Core Concepts* (SAGE Publications, Inc 2018) 73. Evan Stark, 'Mandatory Arrest of Batterers' (1993) 36 *American Behavioral Scientist* 651; David Eitle, 'The Influence of Mandatory Arrest Policies, Police Organizational Characteristics, and Situational Variables on the Probability of Arrest in Domestic Violence Cases' (2005) 51 *Crime & Delinquency* 573.

discussed. In this line, the Convention systematically refrains from saying anything about the most robust means of protection, such as detention, arrest and mandatory prosecution. The tendency to treat VAW and domestic violence as special forms of violence,[80] which require special procedures is still present in the procedural provisions of the Convention, leaving a great deal of discretion to State Parties.

8 Conclusion

The Istanbul Convention has great potential, which has already been partly realised. It provides a good benchmarking tool for States when they accede to the Convention. GREVIO is tasked to ensure that the Convention's ambitious aims and its integrated and comprehensive policies are followed. However, we should not shut our eyes to the fact that it is not a very progressive convention. It is firmly embedded in a world with fixed and binary genders, men and women, using the term gender merely as a substitute for sex. Thus, it does not recognise violence against homosexuals, transmen or men who do not conform to the masculine standard as gender-based violence.

It underlines all forms of violence against women, forbids discrimination against different groups of women and requires that particular circumstances that make women vulnerable are taken into account in services. Women who do not conform to the standard heteronormative model are categorised as vulnerable. Elderly, young, disabled, pregnant and rural women or women abused in prostitution are not mentioned in the Convention, only in the Explanatory Report. However, neither of these two documents includes concrete provisions detailing how violence against vulnerable groups should be addressed.

The measures the Convention obliges States to focus on are prevention and protection, services and empowerment. The comprehensive and integrated package underlines the services available to victims in welfare States. The focus on victims means that the Convention is all but silent on perpetrators. Even if it sees VAW as grounded in inequality between the genders, it does not address violence as predominantly male or masculine behaviour.

The criminal law provisions of the Convention do not challenge generic criminal law. It does not put domestic violence into the context of control and continuity of violence, nor does it address the most serious forms of violence. When it comes to "less serious" forms of violence, such as sexual harassment, stalking and psychological violence, the Convention does not even require that these forms are crimes at all. Furthermore, its articles on *ex officio* prosecution are ambiguous and open to interpretation. The Convention does not urge State Parties to use arrest and detention when VAW is under investigation. Mandatory arrest and no-drop prosecution are policies that have been extensively discussed in Anglo-Saxon countries and the United Nations but this discussion is

80 Johanna Niemi-Kiesiläinen (n 14).

completely absent in the Convention and its Explanatory Report. The Convention constructs the problem of violence as one in which the empowerment of the woman, support and services are key to stopping violence. The violence thus constructed is not an immediate threat to a woman's life and limb.

Thus, the Convention does not seriously address all forms of violence that perpetuate gender inequality and that are prevalent in the majority population. In contrast, the Convention highlights cultural practices harmful to women who belong to cultures other than our "own".

None of the above should be read as saying that we would be better off without the Istanbul Convention. It has already proved to be a useful tool for law reform. In the future, it is important that the general principles of the Convention, such as empowerment, non-discrimination and protection of vulnerable groups, are recognised in the interpretation of all articles of the Convention. A big responsibility for this falls on GREVIO. At best, the Convention will turn out to be a strong protective tool for victims of violence. At worst, it will offer States excuses not to address violence seriously.

5 Due diligence versus positive obligations

Critical reflections on the Council of Europe Convention on Violence against Women

Vladislava Stoyanova

1 Introduction

With its 65 substantive provisions, the Council of Europe Convention on Preventing and Combating Violence against Women and Domestic Violence (the Istanbul Convention or the Convention) is impressive not only in terms of its length, but also in terms of the amount of details. This stands in sharp contrast with general human rights treaties, like the European Convention on Human Rights (ECHR) that describes abstract rights that need to be subject to interpretation so that their corresponding obligations can be transformed into relatively more precise and certain rules.[1] In addition to its detailed and concrete provisions (e.g. Article 23 (shelters), Article 24 (telephone helplines), Article 16 (teaching perpetrators to adopt non-violent behaviour)), the Istanbul Convention also contains general provisions. Two of these are particularly notable. First, Article 3(a) defines "violence against women" as "a violation of human rights".[2] Second, Article 5 enshrines the principle of state responsibility that is important for conceptualising this violence as a human rights law issue. In particular, under the heading "State obligations and due diligence" Article 5 contains the following two paragraphs:

> 1. Parties shall refrain from engaging in any act of violence against women and ensure that State authorities, officials, agents, institutions and other actors acting on behalf of the State act in conformity with this obligation.

1 M Addo, *The Legal Nature of International Human Rights* (Martinus Nijhoff Publishers, 2010) 187.

2 This is also reflected in the preamble of the Istanbul Convention: "[...] women and girls are often exposed to serious forms of violence [...], which constitute a serious violation of the human rights of women and girls".

> 2. Parties shall take the necessary legislative and other measures to exercise due diligence to prevent, investigate, punish and provide reparation for acts of violence covered by the scope of this Convention that are perpetrated by non-State actors.[3]

Clearly the detailed provisions in Chapter II (Integrated policies and data collection), Chapter III (Prevention), Chapter IV (Protection and support), Chapter V (Protection and support), Chapter VI (Investigation, prosecution, procedural law and protective measures), Chapter VII (Migration and asylum) and Chapter VIII (International cooperation) of the Istanbul Convention inform what measures States are expected to undertake to comply with the standard of due diligence as required by Article 5(2).[4] However, this provision also imposes a more general obligation of due diligence that extends beyond the more concrete measures as outlined in the above-mentioned chapters of the Convention. This calls for an inquiry as to the meaning of the due diligence standard, its limits and any reasons to be cautious about it. Are there any peculiarities as to how it has been framed in the Istanbul Convention, which could be a reason for concern? How does the obligation of due diligence compare with positive human rights obligations, their scope and the standards for determining the circumstances when they are triggered as developed by the ECtHR?[5]

In the existing literature in the area of violence against women, the adoption of the standard of due diligence has been uncritically endorsed;[6] the reason is that it has played a crucial role in the recognition of this violence as a human

3 In my analysis, I will ignore the definitional divergence between Articles 5(1) and 5(2): the first one referring more narrowly to "violence against women", while the second one referring more broadly to "acts of violence covered by the scope of this Convention". Generally, this chapter does not address the definitions contained in Article 3 of the Istanbul Convention.

4 It needs to be also taken into account that many of the detailed provisions contain qualifiers, which also denotes some flexibility as to how States can comply with them. For example, Article 20(1) stipulates that "Parties shall take the *necessary legislative or other measures* to ensure that victims have access to services facilitating their recover from violence. These measures should include, *when necessary,* services such as legal and psychological counselling, financial assistance, housing, education, training and assistance in finding employment. [emphasis added]"

5 The EtCHR has developed a very complex framework of positive obligations. See Mowbray, *The Development of Positive Obligations under the European Convention on Human Rights by the European Court of Human Rights* (Hart, 2004). The ECHR is part of the Council of Europe human rights law standards like the Istanbul Convention, which further justifies the comparative parallels between the two treaties.

6 J Sarkin, 'A Methodology to Ensure that States Adequately Apply Due Diligence Standards and Processes to Significantly Impact Level of Violence against Women around the World' (2018) 40(1) *Human Rights Quarterly* 1, 4.

rights issue.[7] This endorsement,[8] accompanied by efforts to push the boundaries of this standard and to "re-imagine" it for advancing broad interpretations,[9] has happened without an in-depth engagement with the actual meaning of the due diligence standard, the circumstances when it is triggered and any negative ramifications for using it as the yardstick.[10]

Sufficient efforts have not been made to better understand the interrelationship between the standard of due diligence and positive obligations under human rights law. Chinkin's position is illustrative; she maintains that "States' obligation to respect, protect and fulfill women's rights to be free from violence have been conceptualised and *made more concrete* through the duty and

7 R McQuigg, 'What Potential does the Council of Europe Convention on Violence against Women Hold as Regards Domestic Violence?' (2012) 16(7) *International Journal of Human Rights* 947, 951; K Bourke-Martignoni, 'The History and Development of the Due Diligence Standard in International Law and Its Role in the Protection of Women against Violence' in C Benninger-Budel (ed.), *Due Diligence and Its Application to Protect Women from Violence* (Brill, 2008) 47, 52: the "use of the standard [of due diligence] by the women's movement has been crucial to the advancement of our understanding of state responsibility for violence perpetrated by non-state actors".

8 Committee on the Elimination of Discrimination against Women, General Recommendation No 19, UN Doc. A/47/38, para 9: "Under general international law and specific human rights covenants, States may also be responsible for private acts if they fail to act with due diligence to prevent violations of rights or to investigate and punish acts of violence, and for providing compensation". See also Article 4(c), Declaration on the Elimination of Violence against Women, UN General Assembly Resolution 48/104, 20 December 1993.

9 Special Rapporteur on Violence against Women, its Causes and Consequences, The Due Diligence Standard as a Tool for the Elimination of Violence against Women, UN Doc. E/CN.4/2006/61 (20 January 2006) (by Yakin Ertürk); Y Ertürk, 'The Due Diligence Standard: What does it entail for Women's Rights?' in C Benninger-Budel (ed.), *Due Diligence and its Application to Protect Women from Violence* (Brill, 2008) 27; Special Rapporteur on Violence against Women, its Causes and Consequences, Report on Violence against Women, its Causes and Consequences, UN Doc. A/HRC/23/49 (14 may 2013) (by Rashida Manjoo) (where all possible measures are subsumed under the due diligence obligation and it is argued that '[t]he State responsibility to act with due diligence must continue to evolve in a cumulative and inclusive approach.'); S de Vido, 'States' Due Diligence Obligations to Protect Women from Violence: A European Perspective in Light of the 2011 CoE Istanbul Convention' 14 *European Yearbook of Human Rights* 365, 368: "the trend at the international level is to push the boundaries of the standard of due diligence […]".

10 For rare exceptions see J Goldscheid and D Liebowitz, 'Due Diligence and Gender Violence: Parsing Its Power and its Perils' (2015) 48 *Cornell International Law Journal* 301 (the authors warn of "state overreach", including the risks of stronger criminal justice responses, and of the risk of "situating the State as the entity charged with program delivery when other entities would be more effective".); see also M Kamminga, 'Due Diligence Mania' in I Westendorp (ed.), *The Women's Convention Turned 30* (Intersentia, 2012) 407: "Due diligence in general international law therefore is rather weak standard with a high threshold".

standard of due diligence [emphasis added]".[11] It is doubtful whether the reference to due diligence adds any concreteness and, in any case, Chinkin fails to show how due diligence does this. I would contend that the reference to due diligence obscures, rather than injects concreteness. An additional danger is that the reference to due diligence in Article 5(2) of the Istanbul Convention lowers the standards expected of States as regards violence performed by non-state actors.

Bourke-Martignoni has specifically looked into the interaction between due diligence and positive obligation and has posited that "the positive obligation to protect, respect and fulfil human rights that are contained in human rights treaty law imply a duty to act with due diligence to protect individuals against human rights violations by private persons or entities".[12] It follows that she assumes some form of convergence and, in a move similar to the one made by Chinkin, superimposes the standard of due diligence on the positive obligations. Sarkin can be also added to this group of authors since he argues that

> [...] due diligence is not about undermining positive obligations but about reinforcing them. It is about ensuring compliance with positive obligation that a state already has. Thus, due diligence is really an oversight tool. It is about what states need to do, and how they comply with their obligations. It is simply a devise to ensure that states do what they need to in their quest to carry out their obligations. It does not subtract from their positive obligations.[13]

The Explanatory Report to the Istanbul Convention also assumes the indistinguishability of due diligence and positive obligations.[14]

This chapter attempts to challenge the assumption in the literature that the reference to the standard of due diligence makes a positive contribution to the framework of positive obligations. This assumption appears to reign due to insufficient exploration of how the standard of due diligence and the framework of positive human rights obligations relate to each other. As an attempt to address this insufficiency, the chapter first clarifies the difficulty in basing state responsibility on failure to perform an act (i.e. an omission) and in making

11 C Chinkin, 'Addressing Violence against Women in the Commonwealth within States' Obligations under International Law' (2017) 40(3) *Commonwealth Law Bulletin* 471, 479.

12 J Bourke-Martignoni, 'The History and Development of the Due Diligence Standard in International Law and its Role in the Protection of Women against Violence' in C Benninger-Budel (ed.), *Due Diligence and Its Application to Protect Women from Violence* (Brill, 2008) 47, 52.

13 J Sarkin, 'A Methodology to Ensure that States Adequately Apply Due Diligence Standards and Processes to Significantly Impact Level of Violence against Women around the World' (2018) 40(1) *Human Rights Quarterly* 1, 16.

14 The Explanatory Report, para 58.

the distinction between the existence of the obligation to act, on the one hand, and the *post facto* assessment whether this obligation has not been performed (Section 2), on the other. Then the two frameworks (due diligence versus positive obligations) are juxtaposed against each other in Section 3. This exercise necessarily requires a better understanding of each one of them which is also offered in Section 3.1 as to the standard of due diligence and in Section 3.2 as to the types of positive obligations and the different tests that they invoke.

2 Due diligence, omissions and positive obligations

Inadequate efforts have been invested in developing an in-depth analysis of the conceptual framework underpinning the due diligence standard. This standard has been injected in the discussion about violence against women for addressing the relationship between violence and the State given that perpetrators are likely to be non-state actors. Since harm inflicted by non-state actors is not attributable to the State,[15] "due diligence" provides the framework for linking the harm to the State by making the claim that the state ought to have adopted certain conduct to prevent the harm. The State can thus be held responsible for its omission to adopt a specific conduct. Within this frame, human rights lawyers understand "due diligence" as a standard of conduct required to discharge an obligation.[16] At this point, it is crucial to make the following analytical distinction: the existence of an obligation as such to act needs to be distinguished from the question as to the failure to fulfil this obligation. First, one needs to identify a separate legal obligation to act; only then, can one ask the question about the failure of the State to act. I will return to this distinction in the text below.

Since "due diligence" directs our attention to state omissions, it is important to also clarify that generally the law on state responsibility under international law for omissions is not well developed and that specific literature on the notion of "omission" in the law of state responsibility is rare.[17] Any more profound engagement with the issue has to start with Article 2 of the International Law Commission (ILC) Draft Articles on Responsibility of States for Internationally Wrongful Acts. This article stipulates that "[t]here is an internationally wrongful act of a State when conduct consisting of an action or omission: (a) is attributable to the State under international law; and (b) constitutes a breach of an

15 For the rules on attribution see ILC Draft Articles.

16 For a useful discussion, see J Bonnitch and R McCorquodale, 'The Concept of "Due Diligence" in the UN Guiding Principles on Business and Human Rights' (2017) 28(3) *European Journal of International Law* 899, 900.

17 J Klabbers, 'Reflections on Role Responsibility: The Responsibility of International Organizations for Failing to Act' (2017) 28(4) *European Journal of International Law* 1133, 1135.

international obligation". The Commentary to the ILC Draft Articles clarifies that "[...] no difference in principle exists between the two [an action and an omission]".[18] This, however, is an oversimplification. True, certain conduct can be simultaneously framed as both action and omission depending on the baseline that one chooses to adopt and on certain normative standpoints.[19] As Pogge has observed, the application of the distinction between acts and omissions to collective agents and social institutions i.e. the State, is baffling, if we do not have "baseline comparisons".[20] Still, normally an omission cannot cause harm in the same way as a positive action.[21] This fundamental difference has been well developed in the context of national administrative law and tort law. In contrast to public international law and international human rights law, domestic administrative law and tort law have developed complex analytical frameworks for measuring and assessing when state authorities can be held liable for omissions.[22] The issue of causation has played a major role here, i.e. the causal connection between the omission and the harm.[23] However, causation is far from being the single criteria; policy and other considerations (knowledge and foreseeability of the harm, the reasonableness of imposing a positive duty to act etc.) also intervene in the assessment required by the national legislation,[24] which clearly demonstrates that establishing responsibility for omissions is an exercise fraught with complications.

Basing state responsibility on omission is problematic because there are numerous omissions that a State might have committed. Many of these might

18 ILC Commentary, p. 35.

19 For example, often, the ECtHR refuses to explicitly say whether it will review the case from the perspective of States' negative or positive obligations. See L Lavrysen, *Human Rights in a Positive State. Rethinking the Relationship between Positive and Negative Obligations under the European Convention on Human Rights* (Intersentia, 2016) 241.

20 T Pogge, 'Recognized and Violated by International Law: The Human Rights of the Global Poor' (2005) 18(4) *Leiden Journal of International Law* 717, 728.

21 Generally on the complexities surrounding causation between harm and state omissions in the context of human rights law, see V Stoyanova, 'Causation between State Omission and Harm within the Framework of Positive Obligations under the European Convention on Human Rights' (2018) 18(2) *Human Rights Law Review* 309; V Stoyanova, 'Common Law Tort of Negligence as a Tool for Deconstructing Positive Obligations under the European Convention on Human Rights' *International Journal of Human Rights* (forthcoming).

22 J Plunkett, *The Duty of Care in Negligence* (Hart Publishing, 2018); see also the contributions in D Fairgrieve, M Andenas and J Bell (eds), *Tort Liability of Public Authorities in Comparative Perspectives* (The British Institute of International and Comparative Law, 2002).

23 S Steel, *Proof of Causation in Tort Law* (Cambridge University Press, 2015).

24 C Booth and D Squires, *The Negligence Liability of Public Authorities* (Oxford University Press, 2006) 165.

not even be cognisable.[25] It will be absurd to suggest that every single omission that can be somehow related to the harm suffered by an individual (or risk of harm), should be a basis for establishing state responsibility. In this connection, the assertion in the Istanbul Convention that all "violence against women" is "a violation of human rights" cannot be correct. The assertion assumes that in all instances of violence against women, the State has necessary failed to fulfil its obligations. While one can be certainly sympathetic to any efforts of preventing violence, showing disregard of some basic principles underlying state responsibility in international law is hardly helpful. There must be an obligation to act in the first place that has remained unperformed, against which state responsibility can be assessed. As Crawford has framed it:

> [...] omission is more than simple 'not-doing' or inaction: it is legally significant only when there is a legal duty to act which is not fulfilled, and its significance can only be assessed by reference to the content of that duty. So an omission is the failure to do that which should be done; the absence of any primary obligation 'to do' will mean that no omission may be complained of.[26]

This brings us back to the above-mentioned distinction between the existence of an obligation to act and the *ex post facto* assessment whether this obligation has been performed. The challenge is framing this primary obligation to act *ex ante*. At the same time, this primary obligation can be framed at different levels of abstraction and with different level of concreteness,[27] an issue to which I will also return below in the text. The level of abstraction and concreteness is important because it has an impact on the mere possibility of making an assessment whether the State has failed to fulfil it.[28]

25 To make the omissions cognisable, a reference to the national legislation might be useful since it sets detailed standards. See V Stoyanova, 'Causation between State Omission and Harm within the Framework of Positive Obligations under the European Convention on Human Rights' (2018) 18(2) *Human Rights Law Review* 309, 332. Since national authorities operate in accordance with detailed legal frameworks, their omissions are more easily cognisable. See Lehner, 'Judicial Review of Administrative Inaction' (1983) 83 *Columbia Law Review* 627.

26 J Crawford, *State Responsibility. The General Part* (Cambridge University Press, 2013) 2018.

27 On the framing of positive obligations, see generally V Stoyanova, 'The Disjunctive Structure of Positive Rights under the European Convention on Human Rights' (2018) 87(3) *Nordic Journal of International Law* 344.

28 For example, Article 5(2) of the Istanbul Convention that contains the obligation of due diligence to "prevent, investigate punish and provide reparation" is very abstract. The same level of abstraction can be found in Article 12(2) of the same Convention: "Parties shall take the necessary legislative and other measures to prevent all forms of violence covered by the scope of this Convention by any natural or legal person". In contrast, Article 16(1) (support programs for perpetrators) that also aims at prevention of violence is framed in more concrete terms.

Framing the primary obligation is a challenge because general human rights treaties are not framed in terms of obligations; rather rights have been used as the organising principles (the right to life; the right not to be subjected to torture, inhuman or degrading treatment; the right to private life etc.). There has been, however, an increased interest in the "supply side" of human rights,[29] i.e. in the corresponding obligations,[30] because of the awareness that framing the obligations is crucial for the realisation of rights. If we take rights seriously and see them as normative, we must take obligations seriously.[31] In other words, rights have to be matched by obligations.[32]

Due diligence as a standard of conduct that requires the discharge of an obligation helps in this respect. It has been "a fundamental feature of many disparate areas of international law";[33] however, international treaty law rarely uses the term "due diligence".[34] Similarly, human rights treaties do not generally explicitly contain the term "due diligence". Article 5(2) of the Istanbul Convention is thus exceptional in this sense. Within the UN human rights treaty system, the framework of the obligations to respect, protect and fulfil is rather used.[35] This has a basis in the text of the treaties. The International Covenant on Civil and Political Rights (ICCPR) stipulates that "Each Party to the present Covenant undertakes to respect and to ensure [...] the rights recognised in the

29 J Griffin, *On Human Rights* (OUP, 2008) 111.

30 J Nickel, 'How Human Rights Generate Duties to Protect and Provide' (1993) 15(1) *Human Rights Quarterly* 77; J Nickel, *Making Sense of Human Rights* (Blackwell 2007) 37–41; S Besson, 'The Bearers of Human Rights' Duties and Responsibilities for Human Rights: A Quiet (R)evolution' (2015) 32(1) *Social Philosophy and Policy* 244; A Kuper, Introduction: The Responsibilities Approach to Human Rights in A Kuper (ed.), *Global Responsibilities. Who Must Deliver on Human Rights?* (Routledge, 2005).

31 O O'Neill, 'The Dark Side of Human Rights' (2005) 81(2) *International Affairs* 427, 430; H Shue, 'The Interdependence of Duties' in P Alston and K Komasevski (eds), *The Right to Food* (Matinus Nijhoff, 1984) 83, 84:

> The bottom line of the intellectual enterprise, [], must be the specific designation of what should be done by whom at a level of detail that will permit assessments of compliance by responsible agents themselves and, where appropriate, by others charged with supervision over their compliance.

32 "Identifying the multiple duties that may be relevant to any one rights sharpens an understanding of what is distinctive to and necessary to realize that right". HR Steiner, P Alston and R Goodman, *International Human Rights in Context: Law, Politics, Morals* (Oxford University Press) 186.

33 D French and T Stephens (Rapporteurs), International Law Association Study Group on Due Diligence in International Law, First Report, 7 March 2014, 6; J Kulesza, *Due Diligence in International Law* (Brill, 2016).

34 D French and T Stephens (Rapporteurs), International Law Association Study Group on Due Diligence in International Law, First Report, 7 March 2014, 6.

35 There is no consistency among the different UN treaty bodies though. This corresponds to the taxonomy originally developed in H Shue, *Basic Rights* (Princeton University Press, 1996) 52.

present Covenant".[36] Article 1 of the ECHR also stipulates that "The High Contracting Parties shall secure to everyone within their jurisdiction the rights and freedoms defined in Section 1 of this Convention". The obligation to secure the right has been interpreted by the European Court of Human Rights (ECtHR) as imposing positive obligations upon States to take positive measures.[37] The ECtHR has thus adopted the terminology of positive and negative obligations. Brief clarification is necessary at this juncture as to the conceptual framework of the obligations to respect, protect and fulfil and its relationship to the positive versus negative obligations dichotomy.

The obligation to respect refers to circumstances when the State has to refrain from infringing human rights and, in this sense, the State is under a negative obligation. Responsibility does not pivot here on due diligence,[38] since the issue is one of state action, not a failure to act. At this junction, it is pertinent to observe that Article 5(1) of the Istanbul Convention has somehow sown confusion in this respect since it uses the term "ensure" (not "respect") with reference to state agents' activities that will *normally* give rise to negative obligations.[39] Pursuant to Article 5(1), State Parties have to ensure that state agents act in conformity with the obligation to refrain from engaging in any act of violence. The clearer formulation would rather be that state agents have to respect the obligation, i.e. they shall not commit any acts of violence.

The text of Article 5(1) of the Istanbul Convention also introduces a distinction between actions of State Parties, on the one hand, and actions of "State authorities, officials, agents, institutions and other actors acting on behalf of the State", on the other. This distinction is non-existent from the perspective of international law that assumes the unity of the State.

An importation qualification is immediately due here. Negative obligations in human rights law are usually relevant when state agents cause harm. However, positive obligations might be also relevant in these circumstances: States are under the obligation to "structure their relationship between their agents and individuals in such a way that harm is prevented and, if it occurs, is adequately addressed".[40] This has been particularly relevant in the context of the right to life, where human

36 Article 2(1) ICCPR.

37 *Opuz v Turkey* App no 33401/02 (ECHR, 9 June 200) para159. It needs to be acknowledged that in some judgments the ECtHR has used the term "due diligence". See, for example, *Talpis v Italy* App no 41237/14 (ECHR, 2 March 2017) para 124 and *Opuz v Turkey* paras 137–149), however, not as a general standard and without prejudice to the detailed elaboration of the concrete tests applicable under the positive obligations framework.

38 R Pisillo-Mazzeschi, 'Due Diligence Rule and the Nature of International Responsibility of States' (1992) 35 *German Yearbook of International Law* 9, 23.

39 This confusion can be perhaps resolved by reading Article 5(1) as a whole to the effect that States have to ensure that state authorities refrain from engaging in any act of violence against women.

40 V Stoyanova, 'Causation between State Omission and Harm within the Framework of Positive Obligations under the European Convention on Human Rights' (2018) 18 *Human Rights Law Review* 309.

rights law assumes that state agents can legitimately use lethal force under certain circumstances (see Article 2(2) ECHR) and that there is a need to regulate these circumstances.[41] However, in the context of violence that cannot be justified as, for example Article 2(2) ECHR justifies it, harm caused by state agents is a breach of negative obligations and no issues of due diligence arise. This means that, for instance, the standard of reasonableness that will be discussed in the next section, is not pertinent.

In contrast to the negative obligation to respect, the obligations to protect and fulfil can be generally framed as positive obligations. These raise some of the same challenges as those discussed above in relation to the concept of due diligence; namely, framing the obligations *ex ante* and then using them to assess state conduct *post factum*. However, generally the ECtHR does not use the concept of due diligence and, as I will show below, not all positive obligations are obligations of due diligence. Better sensitivity as to the divergences and their implications is called for.

3 Due diligence contrasted to positive human rights obligations

The attempt to disentangle and better understand the relationship between due diligence and positive obligations in human rights law has to start with the emphasis that the classification of positive obligations under the ECHR is much more complex and nuanced than the general standard of due diligence. The ECtHR has made important advances in framing the positive obligations at a more concrete level. These can be generally systematised as (1) the obligation to criminalise harmful conduct, (2) the procedural obligation to investigate allegations of criminal conduct, (3) the obligation to take protective operational measures, (4) the obligation to adopt effective regulatory frameworks for general prevention and (5) the obligation to offer remedies.[42] To some extent, these are

41 *McCann and Others v United Kingdom* [GC] App no 18984/91 (ECHR, 27 September 1995) para 194. A similar argument can be made under Article 5 ECHR (the right to liberty) that exhaustively indicates circumstances when the State can inflict harm upon individuals in the form of detention.

42 For this systematisation see V Stoyanova, *Human Trafficking and Slavery Reconsidered. Conceptual Limits and States Positive Obligations in European Law* (Cambridge University Press, 2017) 329. For other systematisations see C Dröge, *Positive Verpflicchtungen der Saaten in der Europäischen Menschenrechtskonvention* (Springer, 2003), who frames two dimensions of positive obligations: horizontal dimension and social dimension. The horizontal dimension covers obligations of protecting individuals against interferences by other private parties (the obligations to criminalise and to take protective operational measures fall here). According to Dröge, the social dimension is very versatile since it includes "obligations of the state to realize the effective enjoyment of human rights in social reality". See also L Lavrysen, *Human Rights in a Positive State. Rethinking the Relationship between Positive and Negative Obligations under the European Convention on Human Rights* (Intersentia, 2016) 45.

reflected in the text of Article 5(2) of the Istanbul Convention that refers to prevention, investigation, punishment and provision of reparation. Article 5(2) of the Istanbul Convention, however, subjects all of these to the standard of due diligence. This implies that the text of the treaty assumes convergence between due diligence and positive obligations. As I will show below, this should be a reason for concern. A meaningful effort to juxtapose the two frameworks (due diligence versus positive obligations) requires a better understanding of each one of them, which is attempted below.

3.1 Factors relevant to the due diligence assessment

When it comes to the standard of due diligence, perhaps the most in-depth study so far has been conducted by the International Law Association (ILA) that has issued two reports on due diligence.[43] In contrast to the first report that is thematic (i.e. how the standard of due diligence is applied in distinctive areas of international law, including human rights law),[44] the second report aims to address broader analytical questions as to what functions due diligence serves, why it is employed as a standard of conduct and what factors influence the variability of the standard.[45] As to the first two questions, the second ILA report highlights that since due diligence triggers obligations of conduct, rather than of result, it preserves for States "a significant measure of autonomy and flexibility in discharging their international obligations".[46] The ILA report contends that it is possible to identify certain factors when making an assessment whether the State has acted with due diligence: (1) reasonableness, (2) control, (3) degree of risk and (4) state knowledge about the harm or the risk of harm. As to the first one, it implies that the State is only required to take reasonable measures, which necessarily presuppose a context-specific assessment and hardly any *in abstracto ex ante* determination can be made as to what is reasonable to expect from the State.[47] This relates to the second factor mentioned above, namely control. This factor implies that the more control the State has over non-state actors, the more reasonable it is to impose higher expectations on the State in terms of measures taken.[48] The control factor can be linked to state capacities and resources. The less resources the State has, the less control it is likely to have, which might relax the actual conduct required. As to the risk, the measures expected from the State have to be appropriate and proportionate to

43 See the Due Diligence Study Group www.ila-hq.org/index.php/study-groups.

44 ILC Study Group on Due Diligence in International Law, First Report, Duncan French (Chair) and Tim Stephens (Rapporteur) 7 March 2014.

45 ILC Study Group on Due Diligence in International Law, Second Report, Tim Stephens (Rapporteur) and Duncan French (Chair) July 2016.

46 ILC Second Report, 2.

47 ILC Second Report, 9.

48 ILC Second Report, 11.

the degree of risk of harm.[49] The higher the risk, the more demanding obligations of diligence can be imposed on the State. The element of state knowledge is also crucial: the State can be expected to take measures only when it knew or should have known about the harm or the risk of harm.[50]

Given these factors, it is clear that it cannot be ascertained with certainty in advance whether the State's conduct meets the standard of due diligence. Once harm materialises, an *ex post facto* review can be made given the circumstances.[51] This inevitably creates a great deal of uncertainty since nobody can know in advance what is required for satisfying the due diligence obligation. This uncertainty, however, also denotes flexibility, which, as mentioned above, is a reason as to why the standard of due diligence in international law has been attractive.

It is also crucial to highlight that these four factors determine both the existence of an obligation and the question whether the obligation has been breached.[52] The factors also determine the *scope* of the obligation, understood as how demanding the obligation should be. For example, the higher the degree of risk, the higher the demands that can be imposed upon the State to prevent it. As to the *content* of the obligation, understood as the concrete measures that the State should have adopted but failed to do so, it is also dependent on these four factors. For example, given the circumstances, the expectation from the State to take the concrete measure of, say, a restraint order, might not be reasonable.[53] However, in the process of making the *ex post facto* assessment as to the existence of a breach, the decision maker needs to have some idea as to the concrete measures that could have been adopted. Otherwise, it will be difficult to measure the omission. The decision maker still needs to ask the question of

49 ILC Second Report, 12.

50 ILC Second Report, 12. See also M Hakimi, 'State Bystander Responsibility' (2010) 21(2) *European Journal of International Law* 341, who has developed a framework with factors that determine the identification and the requirements raised by the obligation to protect from abuses committed by third parties. The factors that she proposes are (1) control (it corresponds to the factor proposed in the ILA report); (2) severity of harm; and (3) reasonableness (it corresponds to the factor proposed in the ILA report). As to the second factor that is absent from the ILA report, Hakimi contends that "[s]tates must protect only against conduct that: (1) causes serious physical or psychological harm; or (2) affects people because they belong to vulnerable group." While it might be correct that the severity of the harm might influence the assessment what measures are reasonable and, thus, this factor needs to be taken into account, the starting assumption in human rights law is that fundamental and important interests are protected and framed in terms of rights.

51 *Application of the Convention on the Prevention and Punishment of the Crime of Genocide* (Bosnia v Serbia) (ICJ February 2007) para 430: "the notion of 'due diligence' [...] calls for an assessment *in concreto*".

52 See English law of state negligence where a similar overlap can be observed. C Booth and D Squires, *The Negligence Liability of Public Authorities* (Oxford University Press, 2006), where the questions asked for establishing the existence of a duty of care (i.e. the obligation to take positive action) and the questions asked for determining whether this duty has been breached are explained.

53 Restraint and protection order are regulated by Article 53, Istanbul Convention.

what measures should have been taken (if no measures whatsoever were actually undertaken) or what alternative protective measures could have been undertaken (if some protective measures were undertaken, but they arguably turned out to be ineffective). Despite the *ex post factum* inquiry as to any concrete alternatives, generally the State preserves its discretion and flexibility as to how it fulfils its due diligence obligations.

It has to be, however, acknowledged that there might be cases where the particular circumstances are such that no other but a specific measure is called for. In addition, there might be general agreement that in certain type of circumstances certain measures are required (e.g. support programs for teaching perpetrators to adopt non-violent behaviour;[54] locating victim support services on the same premises[55]). The concrete provisions of the Istanbul Convention provide a good example in this respect.[56] The Convention is an expression of the coalescence around certain more specific measures that States have to undertake, which clearly shapes the standard of reasonableness. In particular, it is harder to make an argument that it is not reasonable to undertake those specific measures. It is also harder to make an argument that since the State has less control and fewer resources, a relaxation of the obligation should follow.

Not only does the State preserve its flexibility as to what measures to adopt to fulfil its due diligence obligations, but these measures, as the State has chosen to take, are not required to achieve particular outcomes. As already mentioned above, the due diligence obligation is an obligation of conduct, not of end result.[57] This implies that even if the harm has actually materialised, this is far from enough for establishing state responsibility under human rights law with reference to the due diligence standard. It is simply not reasonable to expect from the State to prevent *any* domestic violence inflicted by private parties. The materialisation of the harm (i.e. suffering domestic violence) will likely trigger the *ex post factum* concrete assessment whether the state conduct (the range and the sequence of measures taken) has actually lived up to the due diligence standard in the concrete circumstances.

Another question that has to be raised is whether the materialisation of harm is a *necessary* requirement so that a State can be found to have failed to fulfil its due diligence obligation. The judgment of the International Court of Justice

54 Article 16(1), Istanbul Convention.

55 Article 18(3), Istanbul Convention.

56 It needs to be, however, also acknowledged that these concrete provisions also allow for considerable state discretion and flexibility. See, for example, the qualifiers "where appropriately" (used in Article 4(2), 13, 16(3), 18(3), 44(6), 45(1), 56(2), 62(4) of the Istanbul Convention) and 'under appropriate conditions' (used in Article 28 of the Istanbul Convention).

57 J Knox, 'Horizontal Human Rights' (2008) 102 *American Journal of International Law* 1, 21–24; Pisillo-Mazzeschi, 'The Due Diligence Rule and the Nature of the International Responsibility of States' (1992) 35 *German Yearbook of International Law* 9, 30.

(ICJ) in the *Bosnia Genocide* case offers some insights.[58] The ICJ found that a State can be held responsible for a failure to prevent genocide (an obligation that the ICJ framed as one of due diligence) only if genocide is actually committed.[59] To substantiate this, the ICJ referred to a general rule of the law of state responsibility as codified in Article 14(3) of the ILC Draft Articles on State Responsibility: "The breach of an international obligation requiring a State to prevent a given event occurs when the event occurs and extends over the entire period during which the event continues and remains not in conformity with that obligation".

It is crucial, however, to clarify that "a State's obligation to prevent, and the corresponding duty to act, arise at the instant that the State learns of, or should normally have learned of, the existence of a serious risk that genocide will be committed".[60] As Milanovic has remarked,

> There is a slight, if unavoidable, contradiction in defining the scope of the duty to prevent genocide as arising whenever there is awareness of a serious risk of genocide, yet requiring that genocide actually be committed in order that state responsibility for a breach of the obligation to prevent should ensue.[61]

It follows that the obligation of due diligence has a "dual nature": it arises whenever there is a serious risk of harm, but is capable of being breached only when the harm has already materialised.[62] Therefore, it is crucial to clarify the distinction between the arising and the existence of the due diligence obligation, on the one hand, and the assessment of whether the State is responsible for its failure to fulfil it, on the other. An assessment affirming failure and thus responsibility implies the materialisation of harm. The trigger of the obligation of due diligence requires only a risk of harm, which intimately relates to the whole rationale behind the due diligence standard, namely the prevention of harm.[63]

58 Case Concerning the Application of the Convention on the Prevention and Punishment of the Crime of Genocide (Bosnia and Herzegovina v Serbia and Montenegro) (ICJ, 27 February 2007) (hereinafter *Bosnia Genocide* Case).

59 *Bosnia Genocide*, para 431.

60 *Bosnia Genocide*, para 431.

61 M Milanovic, 'State Responsibility for Genocide: A Follow-Up' (2007) 18(4) *European Journal of International Law* (2007) 669, 687.

62 Ibid. 688.

63 Prevention has been the main reason as to why "due diligence" has been invoked in the context of violence against women. See Special Rapporteur on Violence against Women, its Causes and Consequences, *The Due Diligence Standard as a Tool for the Elimination of Violence against Women*, UN Doc. E/CN.4/2006/61 (20 January 2006) (by Yakin Ertürk) 6, para 15; Special Rapporteur on Violence against Women, its Causes and Consequences, *Report on Violence against Women, its Causes and Consequences*, UN Doc. A/HRC/23/49 (14 May 2013) (by Rashida Manjoo) 7, para 20.

To recapitulate, the standard of due diligence implies that States have to act without achieving any certain results; the standard allows a wide margin of flexibility as to the substance of conduct (i.e. the measures); the assessment as to the sufficiency of the conduct is influenced by the following factors: reasonableness, degree of control, degree of risk and knowledge about the risk of harm. No assessment in advance can be made on whether the state conduct complies with the standard of due diligence. True, the standard is triggered and applies whenever there is a risk of harm and in this way has preventive functions. However, the assessment that aims at determining whether a State carries international responsibility for its omissions to exercise due diligence requires the materialisation of harm.

3.2 Positive human rights obligations

I will review the five positive human rights obligations already identified above in the introductory paragraph to Section 3. Although this review will be extensively based on the case law of the ECtHR in the area of violence against women, judgments from other areas where similar analytical issues arise are also used. Article 2 (the right to life), Article 3 (the right not to be subjected to torture, inhuman or degrading treatment) and Article 8 (the right to private life) have been the main ECHR provisions under which the Court has engaged with violence against women. Therefore, the judgments cited below have been decided based on these articles.

The main objective here is to see whether indeed the above described factors and characteristics of the due diligence standard have any role to play in the context of *all* positive obligations without any variations. How do these factors and characteristics manifest themselves in the context of positive obligations?

The establishment of state responsibility for breaches of ECHR requires the materialisation of harm. Before engaging with the issue of obligations, the Court has to assess whether the specific ECHR provision has been engaged, i.e. whether the definitional threshold of Article 3 or Article 8 has been passed,[64]

64 This has been referred as the bifurcated structure of rights. See J Gerards and H Senden, 'The Structure of Fundamental Rights and the European Court of Human Rights' (2009) 7 *International Journal of Constitutional Law* 619; J Gerards and E Brems, 'Introduction' in E Brems and J Gerards (eds), *Shaping Rights in the ECHR. The Role of the European Court of Human Rights in Determining the Scope of Human Rights* (Cambridge University Press) 1.

in the first place.[65] This corresponds to one of the characteristics of the due diligence standards as clarified in Section 3.1 above; namely, the requirement that the harm has actually materialised so that the state responsibility can be established.

3.2.1 Obligation to criminalise

It has been firmly established in the ECtHR's case law that States have the positive obligation to criminalise abuses.[66] The leading judgments in this respect are *X. and Y. v the Netherlands*[67] and *M.C. v Bulgaria*,[68] both of them involving violence against women reaching the threshold of Article 3 and Article 8 ECHR. In the context of Article 2, the Court has held that this provision requires from States

> to take appropriate steps to safeguards the lives of those within its jurisdiction. This involves a primary duty on the State to secure the right to life by putting in place effective criminal law provisions to deter the commission of offences against the person backed up by law-enforcement machinery for the prevention, suppression and punishment of breaches of such provisions.[69]

It is important to observe here that the obligation to criminalise does not require an engagement with any of the factors the shape the due diligence standard. More specifically, no issue arises as to whether a criminal law measure should be available in light of any assessment as to its reasonableness or

65 This assessment done by the ECtHR has to be clearly distinguished from the substantive obligation that implies that at the time when the events were unfolding risk of harm was enough to trigger the national authorities' obligation to take preventing operational measures (see Section 3.2.2). For an example of this confusion, see L Grans, 'The Istanbul Convention and the Positive Obligation to Prevent Violence' (2018) 18 *Human Rights Law Review* 142. It needs to be also mentioned that judgments can be identified where the Court does not make a definitive determination that the definitional threshold of the invoked provision has been passed. An example of such a judgment is *Rantsev v Cyprus and Russia* App no 25965/04 (ECHR 7 January 2010). For elaboration see V Stoyanova, 'Dancing on the Borders of Article 4: Human Trafficking and the European Court of Human Rights in the Rantsev Case' (2012) 30(2) *Netherlands Quarterly of Human Rights* 163.

66 For general analysis as to the relationship between human rights law and criminal law see F Tulkens, 'The Paradoxical Relationship between Criminal Law and Human Rights' (2011) 9 *Journal of International Criminal Justice* 577; L Lazarus, 'Positive Obligations and Criminal Justice: Duties to Protect or Coerce' in L Zadner and J Roberts (eds), *Principles and Values in Criminal Law and Criminal Justice: Essays in Honour of Andrew Ashworth* (Oxford University Press, 2012) 136.

67 *X. and Y. v the Netherlands* App no 8978/80 (ECHR, 26 March 1985) para 27.

68 *M.C. v Bulgaria* App no 39272/98 (ECHR, 4 December 2003) para 153.

69 *Kontrova v Slovakia* App no 7510/04 (ECHR 31 May 2007) para 49; *Branko Tomašić and Others v Croatia* App no 46598/06 (ECHR, 15 January 2009) para 49.

knowledge about the risk of harm.[70] In *Valiuliene v Lithuania*, the ECtHR clarified that

> [...] the choice of means to secure compliance with Article 3 in the sphere of relations of individuals between themselves is in principle a matter that falls within the domestic authorities' margin of appreciation, *provided that criminal-law mechanisms are available to the victim* [emphasis added].[71]

The assumption is that criminalisation aims at specific and general deterrence. In *Valiuliene v Lithuania*, the Court framed this objective in the following way: "[...] one of the purposes of imposing criminal sanctions is to restrain and deter the offender from causing further harm".[72] The clarification in *A. v Croatia* that "[b]ringing to justice perpetrators of violent acts serves mainly to ensure that such acts do not remain ignored by the relevant authorities and to provide effective protection against them"[73] suggests that criminalisation also aims at general deterrence.[74]

The relevance of the due diligence standard emerges if an assessment has to be made as to the *actual application* of the criminal law at national level. In circumstances where no issues arise as to the scope of the criminalisation (i.e. there are relevant criminal law offences and they are interpreted in a sufficiently broad way), but an assessment needs to be made as to any deficiencies in the application of the criminal law. As it becomes clear from *A. v Croatia* and *M.C. v Bulgaria*, there might be deficiencies as to the way the criminal law was applied.[75] Although, "it is not the Court's task to verify whether the domestic courts correctly applied domestic criminal law",[76] the Court can review the implementation of

70 This has also given a basis for a critique see by L Lazarus, 'Positive Obligations and Criminal Justice: Duties to Protect or Coerce', in L Zadner and J Roberts (eds), *Principles and Values in Criminal Law and Criminal Justice: Essays in Honour of Andrew Ashworth* (Oxford University Press 2012) 136, who refers to the "coercive duties on the state to criminalise, prevent, police, and prosecute harmful acts". See also F Tulkens, 'The Paradoxical Relationship between Criminal Law and Human Rights' (2011) 9 *Journal of International Criminal Justice* 577.

71 *Valiuliene v Lithuania*, App no 33234/07 (ECHR, 26 March 2013) para 85; *X and Y v the Netherlands* App no 8978/80 (ECHR, 26 March 1985) para 27: "This is a case where fundamental values and essential aspects of private life are at stake. Effective deterrence is indispensable in this area and it can be achieved only by criminal-law provisions".

72 *Valiuliene v Lithuania*, para 85.

73 *A. v Croatia* App no 55164/08 (ECHR, 14 October 2010) para 67.

74 J Rogers, 'Applying the Doctrine of Positive Obligations in the European Convention on Human Rights to Domestic Substantive Criminal Law in Domestic Proceedings' (2003) *Criminal Law Review* 690, 695.

75 *A. v Croatia* App no 55164/08 (ECHR, 14 October 2010) para 67; *M.C. v Bulgaria* App no 39272/98 (ECHR 4 December 2003) para 150.

76 *A. v Croatia* para 66.

the national criminal law.[77] The ECtHR has also acknowledged that States retain some flexibility as to the application of the national criminal law.

In sum, the obligation to criminalise is not an obligation of due diligence. States are, however, allowed flexibility as to the actual application of the national criminal law.

3.2.2 Obligation to investigate

The positive obligation to investigate alleged crimes is intimately related to the implementation and effectiveness of the criminal law. A proper assessment of the obligation to investigate requires the introduction of the following conceptual distinction: the conditions under which the obligation is triggered and the criteria for making the assessment of whether the investigation (once triggered) was effective.[78]

I TRIGGERING OF THE OBLIGATION

As to the first issue, i.e. the triggering of the obligation, some nuances in the framing can be identified in the case law under Article 2 (the right to life), on the one hand, and under Article 3 and 8, on the other. In relation to the right to life in *Branko Tomašić and Others v Croatia*, the Court use the following framing:

> [...] the obligation to protect life under Article 2 of the Convention requires that there should be some form of effective official investigation when individuals have been killed as a result of the use of forced, either by State officials or private individuals. [...] Whatever mode is employed, *the authorities must act of their own motion once the matter has come to their attention* [emphasis added].[79]

The obligation to investigate is set into motion once the matter comes to the attention of the authorities, which is a low threshold, and no issues of due diligence arise as to the triggering of the obligation. The State is under a concrete obligation to initiate the investigation.

77 *Bălşan v Romania* App no 49645/09 (ECHR, 23 May 2017) para 64.

78 For an elaboration, see V Stoyanova, *Human Trafficking and Slavery Reconsidered. Conceptual Limits and States' Positive Obligations in European Law* (Cambridge University Press, 2017) 351. For the clear distinction between the positive obligation to investigate as such and the positive obligation to conduct effective investigation, see *M.C. v Bulgaria* App no 39272/98 (ECHR, 4 December 2003) paras 151 and 152.

79 *Branko Tomašić and Others v Croatia* App no 46598/06 (ECHR, 15 January 2009) para 62.

In relation to Article 3 and 8 ECHR, the Court has referred to the tests of "an arguable claim of ill-treatment"[80] and "reasonable suspicion"[81] of ill-treatment for assessing the circumstances as to when the obligation to investigate should have been set into motion. The reference to these tests implies that once allegations of ill-treatment are made that are "arguable" and "raise a reasonable suspicion", the obligation to investigate is triggered. The reference to the standard of reasonableness (i.e. "reasonable suspicion") seems to imply certain level of state discretion and flexibility that are suggestive of the due diligence standard. If the Court makes a *post factum* assessment that given the circumstances, the positive obligation to investigate should have been triggered but it was not, the State is directly in violation of the ECHR.

II OBLIGATION OF CONDUCT, NOT OF RESULT

In most circumstances, the State would have conducted some sort of an investigation into the allegations of ill-treatment. This triggers the assessment at the level of the ECHR whether the domestic investigation was effective. In making this assessment, the Court has referred to the standard of reasonableness:

> The authorities must take the *reasonable steps* available to them to secure the evidence concerning the incident. Any deficiency in the investigation which undermines its ability to establish the cause of death, or identify the person or persons responsible, will risk falling foul of this standard [emphasis added].[82]

The same standard has been framed in relation to Article 3:

> The authorities must have taken *the reasonable steps* available to them to secure the evidence concerning the incident, such as by taking witness statements and gathering forensic evidence, and a requirement of promptness and reasonable expedition is implicit in this context.[83]

80 *Dimitar Shopov v Bulgaria* App no 17253/07 (ECHR, 16 April 2013) para 47.

81 *M.C. v Bulgaria* App no 39272/98 (ECHR 4 December 2003) para 151; *Beganovic v Croatia* App no 46423/06 (ECHR, 25 June 2009) para 66; *C.A.S. and C.S. v Romania* App no 26692/05 (ECHR, 20 March 2012) para 69; *Milanovic v Serbia* App no 44614/07 (ECHR 14 December 2010) paras 85–86; *M. and Others v Italy and Bulgaria* App no 40020/03 (ECHR, 31 July 2012) paras 101 and 113. It has to be, however, acknowledged that there has not been firm consistency as to how the test that triggers the obligation to investigate is formulated in the judgments. For example, in some judgments, the Court simply says: "Article 3 requires that the authorities conduct an effective official investigation into the alleged ill-treatment even if such treatment has been inflicted by private individuals". See *Eremia v the Republic of Moldova* App no 3564/11 (ECHR, 28 May 2013) para 51; *Denis Vasilyev v Russia* App no 32704/04 (ECHR, 17 December 2009) paras 98–99.

82 *Branko Tomašić and Others v Croatia* App no 46598/06 (ECHR, 15 January 2009) para 62.

83 *M.A. v Slovenia* App no 3400/07 (ECHR, 15 January 2015) para 47; *N.D. v Slovenia* App no 16605/09 (ECHR, 15 January 2015) para 57.

The Court has also added that the investigation should be "capable of leading to the establishment of the facts of the case and to the identification and punishment of those responsible. This is not an obligation of result, but one of means".[84] *D.M.D. v Romania* shows that even though the essential purpose of the investigating might be achieved (i.e. conviction of the perpetrator), the State can still be found responsible because of the manner in which the investigation was conducted. This confirms that it is the conduct that is under scrutiny, not necessarily the final result as such.[85]

III RELEVANCE OF THE RESULT FROM THE INVESTIGATION

The qualification that the obligation to investigate as "not one of result, but one of means" has to be, however, subjected to some further analysis. The Court has never held that States are under the concrete positive obligation to prosecute a specific individual, who might have inflicted harm.[86] Nor has it framed a positive obligation to punish.[87] This certainly supports the assessment of the obligation as one of means and thus one of due diligence, given the analysis in Section 3.1 above, where it was clarified that the standard of due diligence allows States flexibility and imposes no demands of achieving particular outcomes (e.g. prosecution and conviction of a particular individual).

However, the Court has also added that it will maintain "a certain power of review and the power to intervene in cases of manifest disproportion between the gravity of the act and the results obtained at domestic level".[88] The Court has also added that

> [...] *in so far as the investigation leads to charges being brought before the national courts*, the procedural obligations under Article 3 of the Convention extend to the trial stage of the proceedings. In such cases the proceedings as a whole, including the trial stage, must satisfy the requirements of

84 *Eremia v the Republic of Moldova* App no 3564/11 (ECHR, 28 May 2013) para 51; *P.M. v Bulgaria* App no 49669/07 (ECHR, 24 January 2012) para 64; *W v Slovenia* App no 24125/06 (ECHR 23 January 2014) para 64; *Mikkeyev v Russia* App no 77617/01 (ECHR, 26 January 2006) paras 107–109: "[...] the failure of any given investigation to produce conclusions does not, by itself, mean that it was ineffective".

85 *D.M.D. v Romania* App no 23022/13 (ECHR, 3 October 2017).

86 For detailed analysis and reference to case law and relevant literature, see V Stoyanova, *Human Trafficking and Slavery Reconsidered. Conceptual Limits and States' Positive Obligations in European Law* (Cambridge University Press, 2017) 367.

87 The severity of the punishment meted is often part of the assessment as to the effectiveness of the criminal proceedings when these included the trial stage extending beyond the investigation stage. *W. v Slovenia* App no 24125/06 (ECHR 23 January 2014) para 68: "Moreover, it is worth noting that the defendants who were eventually convicted of the criminal acts against the applicant received prison sentences of between eight month and a year, which amounted to less than the minimum sentences prescribed by law, [...]".

88 *Valiuliene v Lithuania* App no 33234/07 (ECHR, 26 March 2013) para 76.

> the prohibition of ill-treatment [references omitted]. In this respect, the Court has already held that, regardless of the final outcome of the proceedings, the protection mechanisms available under domestic law should operate in practice in a manner allowing for the examination of the merits of a particular case within a reasonable time [emphasis added].[89]

The expression "the procedural obligations under Article 3 of the Convention extend to the trial stage of the proceedings" suggests that the result of the investigation (i.e. the initiation of the trial stage and any outcomes from this stage) might matter. Accordingly, and despite the rhetoric used in the text of the judgments themselves, the statement that the obligation to investigate is just one of means and not of result is too simplistic. More specifically, the above quotation does suggest that the Court's assessment might include a review as to whether there have been any results from the investigation in terms of bringing criminal charges and any actual criminal trials.

IV CRITERIA FOR ASSESSING THE QUALITY OF THE INVESTIGATION

The Court has framed the criteria for assessing the quality of the investigation (i.e. independence, promptness,[90] thoroughness, capabilities of leading to the establishment of the facts).[91] These certainly denote more concreteness that any general references to due diligence. At the same time, the Court has also cautioned against the general applicability of the above-mentioned criteria.[92]

Finally, it is crucial to underscore that despite the flexibility as to the manner in which the State conducts investigations and criminal trials, the Court has identified certain factors that *cannot* be used by the State as justification for any delays:

> [...] the failure of the State to ensure effective prosecution of rape cannot be justified by the backlog of cases in the relevant court [reference omitted]. Neither can it be justified by the frequent changes of the sitting judges who were dealing with the applicant's case. Namely, as the Court has already emphasised on many occasions, it is for the State to organise its judicial system in such a way as to enable its courts to comply with the requirements of the Convention.[93]

89 *W v Slovenia* App no 24125/06 (ECHR, 23 January 2014) para 65; *M.A. v Slovenia* App no 3400/07 (ECHR, 15 January 2015) para 48.

90 *D.M.D. v Romania* App no 23022/13 (ECHR, 3 October 2017) para 40; *M.C. and A.C. v Romania* App no 12060/12 (ECHR, 12 April 2016) para 111.

91 J Chevalier-Watts, 'Effective Investigation under Article 2 of the European Convention on Human Rights: Securing the Right to Life or an Onerous Burden on a State?' (2010) 21(3) *European Journal of International Law* 701.

92 *Velikova v Bulgaria* App no 41488/98 (ECHR, 18 May 2000) para 80.

93 *W. v Slovenia* App no 24125/06 (ECHR, 23 January 2014) para 69.

In *N.D. v Slovenia*, the Court took the view

> [...] that the failure of the State to ensure effective prosecution of rape cannot be justified by a backlog of cases in the relevant courts [reference omitted], cannot accept this argument [the government argument of systemic backlog], especially as, even in the face of difficulties, a prompt response by the authorities is vital in maintaining public confidence in their adherence to the rule of law and in preventing any appearance of collusion in, or tolerance of, unlawful acts.[94]

As the above quotations show, certain standards (e.g. prompt response, availability of judges and consistency in dealing with the case) for measuring the effectiveness of the criminal trials are quite concrete and not susceptible to due diligence assessment. It follows that while certain standards for measuring the effectiveness and the quality of the investigation might be subject to a due diligence assessment; others might not. It is important to be sensitive to these nuances and differences. A general reference to the due diligence standard poses the danger of ignoring these divergences.

3.2.3 Obligation to take protective/preventive operational measures

Under certain circumstances, the State is under the positive obligation to take protective operational measures to prevent harm against a *specific* individual who is *at risk* from the criminal act of another individual. The first judgment where this positive obligation was developed was *Osman v the United Kingdom*.[95] Since *Osman*, the obligation of taking protective operational measures has been applied by the Court in different contexts, including domestic violence and violence against women.[96] Similarly to my analysis in relation to the obligation to investigate, the following analytical distinction has to be made from the outset: the circumstances when the obligation is triggered and, once triggered, the criteria for assessing how effectively the State has fulfilled its obligation to protect the specific individual.

I TRIGGERING OF THE OBLIGATION

As to the first threshold, i.e. the triggering of the obligation, the Court has observed that

> [...] it must be established to its [the Court's] satisfaction that the authorities knew or ought to have known at the time of the existence of a real and immediate risk to the life of identified individual or individuals from the

94 *N.D. v Slovenia* App no 16605/09 (ECHR, 15 January 2016) para 60.
95 *Osman v the United Kingdom* [GC] App no 23452/94 (ECHR, 28 October 1998) para 116.
96 *Kontrova v Slovakia* App no 7510/04 (ECHR, 31 May 2007) paras 49–50.

> criminal acts of a third party and they failed to take measures within the scope of their powers which, judged reasonably, might have been expected to avoid the risk.[97]

The following standards can be extracted from the above quoted paragraph: (1) state knowledge and (2) "real and immediate risk" of harm. The requirement of "knew or ought to have known" is clearly reflected in the due diligence standard (see Section 3.1). It is enough if the State knew or ought to have known about the *risk* of harm. In this sense, the obligation is one of prevention: no requirement is raised that the harm should have already materialised at the time when the events were unfolding and when the relevant national authorities had to make an assessment whether to intervene. At the same time, it needs to be acknowledged that these three elements (knowledge, risk of harm and actual harm) can be intertwined. In particular, if some form of harm has already materialised at the time when the national authorities might and/or should have undertaken protective operational measures, it will be easier to support an argument that the State should have known. This reveals the importance of bringing violent incidents to the attention of the authorities.[98]

The triggering of the obligation requires that the risk be "real and immediate". The Court has not offered further clarification as to the meaning of these two terms. It can be proposed that "real" risk is risk that is objectively given.[99] This presupposes some objective factual circumstances that can substantiate the existence of the risk. As to the standard of "immediate", it refers to the temporal dimension of the risk: how near or far in the future is it (i.e. the future from the perspective of the point in time when the events were unfolding)? The term "immediate" presupposes more temporal proximity: the risk is present "now" (i.e. "now" from the perspective of the point in time when the state authorities arguably should have taken measures). For this reason, "immediate risk" has been interpreted as "present and continuing" risk.[100]

II IMMEDIACY OF THE RISK

The requirement for immediacy of the risk has been found problematic in the context of domestic violence. Judge Pinto De Albuqerque in his Separate Opinion in *Valiuliene v Lithuania* has explained the underlying reasons. He has observed that "at the stage of an 'immediate risk' to the victim it is often too

97 *Osman v the United Kingdom* [GC] App no 23452/94 (ECHR, 28 October 1998) para 116.

98 *Irene Wilson* App no 10601/09 (ECHR decision on inadmissibility, 23 October 2012) para 48; *Bălşan v Romania* App no 49645/09 (ECHR, 23 May 2017) para 62.

99 V Stoyanova, *Human Trafficking and Slavery Reconsidered. Conceptual Limits and States' Positive Obligations in European Law* (Cambridge University Press, 2017) 402.

100 Re W's Application [2004] NIQB 67; Re Officer L [2007] UKHL 36, Lord Carswell; *Smith v Chief Constable of Sussex* [2008] EWCA Civ 39.

late for the State to intervene". For this reason, he has proposed revision of the test to the effect that the positive obligation of taking protective operational measures should be triggered when the risk is only present. Arguably, "present" risk implies a lower standard than "immediate" risk. As a consequence, he has formulated the following positive obligation:

> If a State knows or ought to have known that a segment of its population, such as women, is subject to repeated violence and fails to prevent harm from befalling the members of that group of people when they face a present (but not yet imminent risk), the State can be found responsible by omission for the resulting human rights violation.

Two observations are pertinent in relation to this proposal for revision of the *Osman* test. First, in general, the Court has been quite flexible as to how it applies the "immediate" risk requirement.[101] Risks that could have materialised within months or even years have been accepted to be "immediate", which ultimately has stretched the notion of "immediacy" to a breaking point.[102] Therefore, it is doubtful whether the "immediate" risk requirement, as applied in the practice of the Court, is problematic.

We should rather ask ourselves the question about the theoretical underpinning behind this requirement. More specifically, if "the state were to take protective actions against any potential risk *regardless of its immediacy*, then we might be confronted with the problem of a too intrusive state [emphasis in the original]".[103] There might thus be reasons to resist a development that implies undertaking protective *operational* measures regardless of the immediacy of the risk.[104]

The second observation in relation to the above quotation from Judge Pinto De Albuqerque's Separate Opinion concerns his proposal for a modification of another segment of the "Osman test". In particular, according to his proposal, the obligation is triggered not in relation to "identified individual or individuals"

101 Ebert and Sijniensky, 'Preventing Violations of the Right to Life in the European and Inter-American Human Rights Systems: From the *Osman* Test to a Coherent Doctrine on Risk Prevention?' (2015)15 *Human Rights Law Review* 343.

102 V Stoyanova, 'Causation between State Omission and Harm within the Framework of Positive Obligations under the ECHR' (2018) 18(2) *Human Rights Law Review* 309.

103 V Stoyanova, 'Causation between State Omission and Harm' (2018) 18(2) *Human Rights Law Review* 309, 341; see Partly Dissenting Opinion of Judge Spano, para 13 in *Talpis v Italy* App no 41237/14 (ECHR, 2 March 2017).

104 *Talpis v Italy* App no 41237/14 (ECHR, 2 March 2017) paras 116–118, a case that exposed the problems ensuing from the application of the immediacy test in the context of domestic violence. In *Talpis*, however, the Court added a procedural twist; namely, as the Court's reasoning is framed, the failure by the authorities to 'conduct any assessment of the risks facing the applicant, including the risk of renewed assaults' played a crucial role.

but in relation to "a segment of its [the states'] population, such as women" who are subjected to repeated violence.

In relation to this part of Judge Pinto De Albuqerque's proposal, it is pertinent to clarify that the Court has attempted to make a distinction between the positive obligation of taking preventive operational measures and the positive obligation of adopting effective regulatory frameworks that can more generally ensure the prevention of harm.[105] The second one will be reviewed in more detail in the next subsection. Still, it is appropriate here to illustrate and explain the distinction.

The reasoning in *Rantsev v Cyprus and Russia* offers a good illustration of the distinction between the positive obligation of taking preventive operational measures and the positive obligation of adopting effective regulatory framework.[106] This case was about a young woman who was arguably trafficked from Russia to Cyprus. Under Article 4 of the ECHR (the right not to be subjected to slavery, servitude and forced labour), Cyprus was found in violation of its positive obligation to "to put in place an appropriate legislative and administrative framework" that could afford to Ms Rantseva "practical and effective protection against trafficking and exploitation".[107] In particular, the Court found weaknesses in the Cypriot immigration legislation that regulated the visa regime conditions under which Ms Rantseva entered and stayed in the country. Cyprus was also found in violation of its positive obligation to take protective operational measures. In particular, by applying the "Osman test", the Court concluded that "in circumstances which gave rise to a credible suspicion that Ms Rantseva might have been trafficking and exploited", the Cypriot authorities failed to take measures to protect Ms Rantseva.[108] In the reasoning of the Court, these circumstances referred to the individual circumstances of Ms Rantseva against the general background of the situation in Cyprus characterised by serious concerns about exploitation of migrant women coming to the country to work as dancers. It follows that some form of individualisation of the harm is necessary for triggering the positive obligation of taking protective operational measures.

It might be correct that when one individual is part of a group of individuals identified as vulnerable at a more general level, this might make the triggering

105 *Mastromatteo v Italy* [GC] App no 37703/97 (ECHR, 24 October 2002); *Maiorano and Others v Italy* App no 28634/06 (ECHR, 15 December 2009); *Eremia v the Republic of Moldova* App no 3564/11 (ECHR, 28 May 2013) para 56.

106 For an analysis of the case see V Stoyanova, 'Dancing on the Borders of Article 4: Human Trafficking and the European Court of Human Rights in the Rantsev case' (2012) 30(2) *Netherlands Quarterly of Human Rights* 163.

107 *Rantsev v Cyprus and Russia* App no 25965/04 (ECHR 7 January 2010) paras 290–293.

108 *Rantsev v Cyprus and Russia* para 498. It needs to be acknowledged, though that the framing of the *Osman* test in *Rantsev v Cyprus and Russia* does reveals some idiosyncrasies. See V Stoyanova, *Human Trafficking and Slavery Reconsidered* (CUP, 2017) 401.

of the obligation to take protective operational measures easier.[109] Still, annihilation of the distinction between the two types of positive obligations (the obligation of taking preventive operational measures and the obligation of adopting an effective regulatory framework), which might ensue from Judge Pinto De Albuqerque's proposal mentioned above, is hardly desirable. There might be circumstances where a person is just a representative victim of certain deficiencies in the national regulatory framework that operates at a general level. In these circumstances, he or she is not identifiable in advance and, in this sense, no requirement should be raised that the State knew or should have known that he or she has specifically been at immediate risk of harm. Conversely, these requirements are pertinent in relation to the positive obligation of taking protective operational measures.[110] When there is no immediacy of the risk, but rather the applicant is a representative victim of some general deficiencies at the national level, the positive obligation of adopting an effective regulatory framework is the relevant one. *Rantsev v Cyprus and Russia* and the specific visa regime reviewed therein exemplify this relevance. In particular, Ms Rantseva was a representative victim of the deficiencies in the national legislation regulating the visa regime; these deficiencies made migrant women very vulnerable to abuses by employers.[111]

If the two types of positive obligations (to take protective operational measures and to adopt effective regulatory frameworks) are merged, there is a danger of transposing certain requirements from the first one upon the second one, which might lead to unfavourable results.[112] In the context of violence against women, a woman might suffer harm as a result of some general deficiencies in the national legislation (for example, how protection orders are administered) without necessarily the state authority knowing that she in particular will suffer from these deficiencies. Therefore, the individualisation of the risk should not be raised as a requirement here. In contrast, in circumstances that call for protective operational measures, individualisation seems pertinent, which is reflective of the standards of "real and immediate risk" to an "identified individual" as entrenched in the ECtHR's case law.

109 L Peroni and A Timmer, 'Vulnerable Groups: The Promise of an Emerging Concept in European Human Rights Convention Law' (2013) 11 *International Journal of Constitutional Law* 1056.

110 See also V Stoyanova, 'L.E. v Greece: Human Trafficking and the Scope of States' Positive Obligations under the ECHR' (2016) 2 *European Human Rights Law Review* 290, where a concrete example is discussed as to the distinction between these two positive obligations and the negative consequence from using one of them rather than the other. V Stoyanova, 'Fault, Knowledge and Risk within the Framework of Positive Obligations under the European Convention on Human Rights' *Leiden Journal of Human Rights* (2020 forthcoming).

111 *Rantsev v Cyprus and Russia*, paras 292–293.

112 See the Partly Dissenting Opinion of Judge Bonello in *Mastromatteo v Italy* [GC] App no 37703/97 (ECHR, 24 October 2002).

III ASSESSMENT OF THE MEASURES

Once the positive obligation of taking protective operation measures is triggered, what is required from the State to do? The State has discretion as to what protective operational measures to undertake:

> In verifying whether the national authorities have complied with their positive obligations under Article 3 of the Convention, the Court must recall that it will not replace the national authorities in choosing a particular measures designated to protect a victim of domestic violence.[113]

The language in relation to Article 8 has been even softer and more lenient to the State:

> The Court reiterates that its task is not to take the place of the relevant national authorities in determining the most appropriate methods for protecting individuals from attacks on their personal integrity, but rather to review under the Convention the decisions that those authorities have taken in the exercise of their discretion.[114]

Despite these quotations, in its judgments, the Court engages with an evaluation as to what measures could have been undertaken. As mentioned in Section 2 above, without such an evaluation it is difficult to assess the omission. For example, in *Kontrova v Slovakia*, the ECtHR enumerated the specific measures the authorities could have undertaken to protect the life of the applicant's children.[115] In *Opuz v Turkey* and *Branko Tomasic and Others v Croatia*, a similar enumeration was made.[116] It has to be also highlighted that despite the discretion that the national authorities have, in the domestic violence cases the

113 *Eremia v the Republic of Moldova* App no 3564/11 (ECHR, 28 May 2013) para 58.

114 *Eremia v the Republic of Moldova* para 76; *Hajduova v Slovakia* App no 2660/03 (ECHR, 30 November 2010) para 47.

115 In the case of *Konrova v Slovakia*, para 53, after finding that the situation of the applicant's family was known to the police, the following measures were enumerated in the judgment as incumbent upon the authorities to undertake:

> [...] accepting and duly registering the applicant's criminal complaint; launching a criminal investigation and commencing criminal proceedings against the applicant's husband immediately; keeping a proper record of the emergency calls and advising the next shift of the situation; and taking action in respect of the allegation that the applicant's husband had a shotgun and had made violent threats with in.

116 In *Branko Tomasic and Others v Croatia* paras 54–59, the authorities failed to search M.M.'s premises although he claimed that he had a bomb. No adequate psychiatric treatment was provided to M.M., there was no assessment of his psychiatric condition prior to release from prison, nor was psychiatric treatment administered after his release.

Court has consistently emphasised the importance of the speedy and timely manner in which the authorities have to act.[117]

To assess the adequacy of the measures undertaken or the reasonableness of the failure to take any measures, the Court has invoked the following standards:

> Bearing in mind the difficulties in policing modern societies, the unpredictability of human conduct and the operational choices which must be made in terms of priorities and resources, the scope of the positive obligations must be interpreted in a way which *does not impose an impossible or disproportionate burden on the authorities.* [...] they [the authorities] failed to take measures within the scope of their powers which, *judged reasonably*, might have been expected to avoid the risk. Another relevant consideration is the need to ensure that the police exercise their powers to control and prevent crime in a manner which fully respects the due process and other guarantees which *legitimately place restraint on the scope of their action* to investigate crime and bring offenders to justice, [...].[118]

In sum, the measures required have to be "within the scope of their [the authorities'] powers", expected to avoid the risk,[119] and not disproportionately burdensome for the State. The requirement of "within the scope of their powers" requires some further elaboration. It cannot be interpreted to the effect that if the national legal framework has a gap and, as a consequence, does not require certain measures, the measures cannot be relevant in the assessment. In this sense, the scope of the powers conferred by the national regulatory framework might be too limited and this limitation cannot be used by the State to its advantage to argue that protection could not have been extended. "Within the scope of their powers" rather means that to protect individuals, the national authorities cannot be expected to violate human rights law. In this sense, conflicting interests might have to be taken into account.[120]

In sum, the obligation of taking protective operation measures raises a set of complex questions. These correspond to some of the factors identified in

117 *Kowal v Poland* App no 2912/11 (ECHR decision on inadmissibility, 18 September 2012) para 51.

118 *Opuz v Turkey* App no 33401/002 (ECHR, 9 June 2009) para 129.

119 The Court has referred to the standard of "real prospect": "A failure to take reasonably available measures which could have had a real prospect of altering the outcome or mitigating the harm is sufficient to engage the responsibility of the State". *E and Others v the United Kingdom* App no 33218/96 (ECHR, 26 November 2002) para 99.

120 "[...] the Court is aware that in respect of a measure of restraint ordered against an individual, the interest of protection of a person's physical integrity conflicts with the other person's right to liberty." *Kalucza v Hungary* App no 57693/10 (ECHR, 24 April 2012) para 63. In *Talpis v Italy* para 123, the Court stated that "in domestic violence cases perpetrators' rights cannot supersede victims' human rights to life and to physical and psychological integrity".

Section 3.1 (i.e. degree of risk and state knowledge about the harm or the risk of harm) that are of relevance in making the determination whether a State has exercised due diligence. However, in contrast to the due diligence standard, in the context of positive obligations important nuances have been introduced as to the individualisation and the immediacy of the risk. While the positive obligation of taking protective operational measures requires such an individualisation and immediacy, the positive obligation of adopting effective regulatory, to which I will turn in the next section, does not.

3.2.4 Obligation to adopt effective regulatory framework

States are not only under the obligation to protect specific individuals who are at "real and immediate" risk of harm. States also have the positive obligation to ensure general prevention by adopting effective regulatory frameworks that structure the relationships between private parties in such a manner that harm can be prevented.[121] The Court has reiterated that "States are to maintain and apply in practice an adequate legal framework affording protection against acts of violence by private individuals".[122]

I STRONG FOCUS ON CRIMINAL LAW

Generally, in the domestic violence and violence against women cases there has been a strong focus on the criminal law framework; however, the Court has made it explicit that protection by the legal framework extends beyond the realm of criminal law.[123]

Now, it is pertinent to reiterate the warning message that Judge Tulkens expressed in her Concurring Opinion in *M.C. v Bulgaria*:

> Admittedly, recourse to the criminal law may be understandable where offences of this kind [rape] are concerned. However, it is also important to emphasise *on a more general level*, as, indeed, the Court did in *X and Y v. the Netherlands* itself, that "[r]ecourse to the criminal law is not necessary the only answer". I consider that criminal proceedings remain, both in

121 See generally L Lavrysen, 'Protection by the Law: The Positive Obligation to Develop a Legal Framework to Adequately Protect the ECHR Rights' in E Brems and Y Haeck (eds), *Human Rights and Civil Rights in the 21st Century* (Springer, 2014) 69; V Stoyanova, *Human Trafficking and Slavery Reconsidered* (Cambridge University Press, 2017) 369.

122 *Eremia v the Republic of Moldova* para 52; *Bevacqua v Bulgaria*, App no 71127/01 (ECHR, 12 June 2008) para 65.

123 *Bălşan v Romania* App no 49645/09 (ECHR, 23 May 2017) para 63, where the Court referred to the Romanian Law No 217/2003 on preventing and combating domestic violence that ensured shelter, power of the national courts to order the aggressors to be held in psychiatric institutions or bans from entering the family home, and issuance of protection order.

> theory and in practice, a last resort or subsidiary remedy and that their use, even in the context of positive obligations, calls for a certain degree of "restraint". [124]

In practice, however, the nature of the cases involving violence against women are such that usually the application and the effectiveness of the national criminal law and criminal proceedings are at the heart of the issues raised. It is also interesting to observe how the Court has generally framed States' positive obligation in violence against women cases. In particular, the starting assumption seems to be that criminal law and criminal proceedings offer the structures within which responses are to be sought. For example, the Court has summarised the positive obligations in the context of domestic violence in the following way:

> the States' positive obligations under Article 3 include, on the one hand, setting up a legislative framework aimed at preventing *and punishing* ill-treatment by private individuals and, on the other hand, when aware of an imminent risk of ill-treatment of an identified individual or when ill-treatment has already occurred, to apply the relevant laws in practice, thus affording protection to the victims *and punishing* those responsible for ill-treatment [emphasis added].[125]

Another general formulation that can be extracted from the case law is that

> [...] it goes without saying that the obligation on the State under Article 1 of the Convention cannot be interpreted as requiring the State to guarantee through its legal system that inhuman or degrading treatment is never inflicted by one individual on another or that if it is, *criminal proceedings* should necessarily lead to a particular sanction. In order that a State may be held responsible it must, in view of the Court, be shown that the domestic legal system, *and in particular the criminal law application* in the circumstances of the case, failed to provide practical and effective protection of the rights guaranteed by Article 3 [emphasis added].[126]

Yet, if Judge Tulkens' position is seriously considered, then other regulatory frameworks should be not simply of equal, but of higher importance. In this way, the preventive functions of positive obligations can be strengthened. Although criminal law it intended to act as a deterrent and thus to have

124 Concurring Opinion of Judge Tulkens in *M.C. v Bulgaria* App no 39272/98 (ECHR, 4 December 2003) para 2.
125 *Eremia v The Republic of Moldova* App no 3564/11 (ECHR, 28 May 2013) para 56.
126 *Valiuliene v Lithuania* App no 33234/07 (ECHR, 26 March 2013) para 75; *Beganovic v Croatia* App no 46423/06 (ECHR, 25 June 2009) para 71.

preventive functions at a more abstract societal level, from the perspective of victims, it is a reactive tool that can deter further violence and/or offer a remedy.[127]

II RELEVANCE OF OTHER REGULATORY FRAMEWORKS

Besides criminal law, how are other regulatory frameworks relevant for compliance with positive obligations under the ECHR? The Grand Chamber judgment of *O'Keefee v Ireland* is a leading authority that can help us engage with this question.[128] The applicant complained under Article 3 ECHR that the system of primary education in Ireland failed to protect her from sexual abuse by a teacher in 1973. The ECtHR held that the question that needs to be answered to resolve the case is

> [...] whether the State's framework of laws, and notably its mechanisms of detection and reporting, provided effective protection for children attending a National School against the risk of sexual abuse, of which risk it could be said that the authorities had, or ought to have had, knowledge in 1973.[129]

The Court clarified that

> there was no evidence before the Court of an operational failure to protect the applicant [references omitted]. Until complaint about L.H. were brought to the attention of the State authorities in 1995, the State neither knew nor ought to have known that this particular teachers, L.H., posed a risk to this particular pupil, the applicant.[130]

In this way, the Court clearly distinguished the positive obligation of taking protective operational measures from the positive obligation of adopting an effective regulatory framework, a distinction whose value was already clarified in Section 3.2.2 above.

As to the standards for assessing any failure to fulfil the latter obligation, the Court held that:

> The positive obligation to protect is to be interpreted in such a way as not to impose an *excessive burden on the authorities*, bearing in mind, in particular, the unpredictability of human conduct and operational choices

127 The question of the actual deterrent effect of the criminal law has never been profoundly discussed by the ECtHR. In the ECtHR's judgments, it is simply assumed that the establishment of criminal offences can act as deterrence.

128 *O'Keefee v Ireland* [GC] App no 35810/09 (ECHR, 28 January 2014).

129 Ibid. para 152.

130 Ibid. para 148.

> which must be made in terms of priorities and recourses. Accordingly, not every risk of ill-treatment could entail the authorities a Convention requirement to take measures to prevent the risk from materializing. However, the required measures should, at least, provide protection in particular of children and other vulnerable persons and should include *reasonable steps* to prevent ill-treatment of which *the authorities had or ought to have had knowledge* [emphasis added].[131]

The Court also added that

> it is not necessary to show that "but for" the State omission the ill-treatment would not have happened. A failure to take *reasonably available measures* which could have had a *real prospect of altering the outcome or mitigating the harm* is sufficient to engage the responsibility of the State [emphasis added].[132]

When these principles were applied to the case at hand, the issue of state knowledge was an important initial threshold question. However, there is an important difference with the way that this threshold operates in comparison with the positive obligation of taking protective operational measures. In *O'Keefee v Ireland*, it was sufficient that the State had general criminal laws on the subject of sexual abuses against children for the Court to conclude that the knowledge test was passed. Having established state knowledge, the ECtHR determined that since there was no "effective protective connection between the State authorities and primary-school children and/or their parents",[133] the State failed and was in violation of Article 3. Crucially, no requirement was raised that the State knew or ought to have known that specifically the applicant was at risk of being sexually abused.

Various national regulatory frameworks can come under scrutiny depending on the factual circumstances of the particular case. Any aspect or branch of the national regulatory structures could be found deficient. In this sense, the Court has clarified that "it is for the national authorities to organise their legal systems so as to comply with their obligations under the Convention, including their obligation to ensure effective protection of victims of domestic violence".[134]

At the same time, States have discretion on how to organise their legal systems, which is certainly reflective of the flexibility implied by the due diligence standard, as mentioned in Section 3.1 above. The factors of reasonableness and knowledge that are of relevance in the assessment of any failure to comply with the positive obligation of adopting effective regulatory frameworks

131 Ibid. para 144.
132 Ibid. para 149.
133 Ibid. para 165.
134 *Kowal v Poland* App no 2912/11 (ECHR, decision on inadmissibility 18 September 2012) para 48.

are also suggestive of the due diligence standard. However, as already emphasised, these factors operate differently in the context of the different positive obligations (e.g. the obligation of taking protective operational measures versus the obligation of adopting effective regulatory frameworks). These are differences that any general references to due diligence risk ignoring.

III CAUSATION

A factor that was not mentioned in Section 3.1 where the due diligence standard was examined, but that might be of importance in the context of the positive obligation of adopting effective regulatory framework, is causation. This factor implies a causal link between any risk of harm and any deficiencies in the national regulatory framework. The standard of causation required can be a vexing issue since it raises the question to what extent the deficiencies should have contributed to the harm.[135] A separate question that might also intervene is to what extent it was possible for any alternative formulations of the national regulatory framework (that are arguably more protective for the individual) to prevent the harm.[136] In *O'Keefee v Ireland*, the Court referred to the "real prospect" test, but this test is far from being consistently applied in the case law.[137] The Court has thus not determined a specific standard as to the requirement for causation, it has rather been quite flexible.

Since establishing lines of causation might be an exercise fraught with difficulties, it is easier when there are certain standards that can be used as initial baselines. The detailed provisions in the Istanbul Convention relating to, for example, training of professionals (Article 15) or cooperation between all relevant state agencies (Article 18) can be helpful in this respect. This implies that when a case manifests a national regulatory framework that does not ensure or sufficiently well regulates the coordination between the relevant national authorities or the training of professionals, the Court might be more ready to find a violation without going into a complex investigation whether and how the absence of coordination and training caused or was contributory to harm.

3.2.5 Obligation to provide remedies

It will be far beyond the scope of this section to engage with all the relevant issues revolving around the right to remedy in human rights law. The following

135 See V Stoyanova, 'Causation between State Omission and Harm within the Framework of Positive Obligations under the European Convention on Human Rights' (2018) 18(2) *Human Rights Law Review* 309. See also L Lavrysen, *Human Rights in a Positive State* (Intersentia, 2016) 137.

136 V Stoyanova, 'Causation between State Omission and Harm within the Framework of Positive Obligations under the European Convention on Human Rights' (2018) 18(2) *Human Rights Law Review* 309.

137 *O'Keefee v Ireland* para 149.

observation is pertinent in light of the subject matter of this chapter. "Remedies" can be understood as "the process by which arguable claims of human rights violations are heard and decided".[138] "Remedies" can also refer to the outcome of the proceedings and the actual relief afforded when the claim is successful.[139] The relevant provisions from the ECHR are Article 13 (the right to effective remedy) and Article 6 (the right to fair trial).[140]

Article 5(2) of the Istanbul Convention uses the term "reparation" and stipulates that States have to exercise due diligence "to provide reparation for acts of violence covered by the scope of this Convention that are perpetrated by non-State actors". In the law of state responsibility, "reparation" is used in the context of inter-state claims[141] and its forms are restitution, compensation and satisfaction.[142] In contrast, Article 5(2) of the Istanbul Convention limits reparation to circumstances where violence is committed by private individuals. This is, however, rectified with Article 29(2):

> Parties shall take the necessary legislative or other measures to provide victim, in accordance with the general principles of international law, with adequate civil remedies against State authorities that have failed in their duty to take the necessary preventive or protective measures within the scope of their powers.

Contrary to what Article 5(2) of the Istanbul Convention suggests, the existence of procedures and institutions at the national level for affording remedies (against the State and against private individuals) is not subject to the due diligence standard. This is, in fact, also supported by the text of both Article 29(2) and Article 30(1) of the Istanbul Convention.[143] States are under a *concrete* obligation to have such procedures and institutions. The due diligence standard is of relevance, however, in relation to the way these procedures are organised and the way institutions function. These might require contextualisation in every concrete case.

As to the result of any remedial procedures, the obligation of the State is one of due diligence. Article 30(2) of the Istanbul Convention, however, might be

138 D Shelton, *Remedies in International Human Rights Law* (Oxford University Press, 2006) 7.
139 Ibid. 7.
140 See *D.M.D. v Romania* App no 23022/13 (ECHR, 3 October 2017) paras 61–69 where the ECtHR found that the omission of the domestic courts to examine whether compensation should have been awarded to the applicant (a child victim of domestic violence) amounted to denial of justice, which amount to violation of Article 6 ECHR.
141 D Shelton, *Remedies in International Human Rights Law* (Oxford University Press, 2006) 7; Article 31, ILC Draft Articles on State Responsibility.
142 Article 34, ILC Draft Articles on State Responsibility.
143 Article 30(1) of the Istanbul Convention stipulates: "Parties shall take the necessary legislative or other measures to ensure that victims have the right to claim compensation from perpetrators for any of the offences established in accordance with this Convention".

perceived as a departure from this proposition. It stipulates that "[a]dequate state compensation *shall be awarded* to those who have sustained serious bodily injury or impairment of health, to the extent that the damage is not covered by other sources [...] [emphasis added]". Two observations are pertinent here. First, the personal scope of the right to compensation as formulated by Article 30(2) is limited to victims with "serious bodily injury or impairment of heath", which implies that victims whose injuries do not meet the seriousness threshold are excluded from the scope of this provision. Second, Article 30(2) is open to reservation and many States have taken advantage of this possibility.[144] The mere fact that Article 30(2) has been left open for reservation is indicative of the reluctance of States to endorse an obligation to afford remedies (understood as the actual outcome from the remedial proceedings) that goes beyond the due diligence standard.

4 Conclusion

Article 5(2) of the Istanbul Convention causes confusion since it subjects all four types of obligations it refers to, namely the obligation "to prevent, investigate, punish and provide reparation" to the standard of due diligence. Given the practice of the ECtHR in the area of positive human rights obligations, the standards under which the obligations to prevent harm, to investigate, to punish and to provide remedies are triggered and the standards as to when the State is found to have failed to fulfil them, vary. Article 5(2) of the Istanbul Convention seems to be oblivious of these variations. Another source of concern emerging from Article 5(2) of the Istanbul Convention is that it textually limits these four obligations to prevent, investigate, punish and provide reparation to circumstances when violence is "perpetrated by non-State actors". In fact, the same obligations are of equal relevance when state actors inflict harm. I contend that the confusion arising from this conceptual slippage is problematic and I call for better analytical rigour. I hope that this chapter has contributed in this respect.

144 Article 78(2), Istanbul Convention. The following State Parties have submitted reservations in relation to this provision: Andorra, Armenia, Cyprus, Georgia Malta, Monaco, Poland, Romania, Serbia, Slovenia and Macedonia. See www.coe.int/en/web/conventions/full-list/-/conventions/treaty/210/declarations?p_auth=XfwEqXdj See also W Burek in this volume.

Part III

Criminal law responses

6 The Istanbul Convention on sexual offences

A duty to reform the wording of national law or the way we think?

Minni Leskinen[1]

1 Introduction

The Istanbul Convention is without doubt a remarkable document of international law in many ways. Even though violence against women has been internationally recognised as both a human rights violation and discrimination since the nineties,[2] the Convention is the first extensive list of measures in Europe that State Parties agree to undertake in order to prevent and combat the problem.[3] In the Convention, violence against women is understood both as a violation of human rights and as a form of discrimination against women, including all acts of gender-based violence that result in, or are likely to result in, physical, sexual, psychological or economic harm or suffering to women, both in public and in private life (Article 3). Thus, the understanding of violence is broad – broader than ever before – and the aim of the Convention is to prevent, prosecute and *eliminate* it altogether (Article 1).

The Convention is also a unique document of criminal law as it lists and defines a range of crimes belonging under the phenomenon of violence against women, including sexual violence. Whereas some of the definitions, such as that

1 This chapter has been written within the research project ASLA: Actors, Structures and Law, funded by the Academy of Finland, decision 312497, University of Turku.

2 See e.g. Committee on Elimination of All Forms of Discrimination against Women (CEDAW Committee), General Recommendation No 19: Violence against Women, HRI/GEN/1/Rev.7 (1992); United Nations Declaration on the Elimination of Violence against Women, A/RES/48/104 (1993); World Conference on Women, Beijing Declaration and Platform for Action, A/CONF.177/20 (1995) and A/CONF.177/20/Add.1 (1995). In the European context, the first document to state this was the Council of Europe Committee of Ministers (2002) Recommendation Rec (2002) 5 of the Committee of Ministers of the Council of Europe on the Protection of Women Against Violence. Under the European Convention of Human Rights, Violence against women has been construed either as torture and degrading treatment (Article 3 of ECHR) or as a violation of the right to respect for private life (Article 8). See e.g. P Londono, 'Defining Rape under the European Convention on Human Rights: Torture, Consent and Equality' in Clare McGlynn and Vanessa E. Munro (eds), *Rethinking Rape Law. International and Comparative Perspectives* (Routledge, 2010) 109–121.

3 See Niemi and Verdu Sanmartin in this volume.

of rape, have been debated in international law for some time already,[4] in other cases, there was no previous international ground to start from. The Convention provides the first international legal definitions of e.g. psychological violence, stalking, forced marriage and sexual harassment.[5] Traditionally, criminal law has been thought to belong to the very heart of national laws and state sovereignty.[6] Any attempts to harmonise the national criminal laws have been met with suspicion, and only gradually have serious forms of international crime such as terrorism, torture, trafficking with human beings, and the border-crossing sexual exploitation of children convinced the Member States of the need of more harmonised rules.[7] It should not be understated that the Istanbul Convention, with its obligations to criminalise certain crimes on a national level, places violence against women into a framework of serious criminality.

Despite its tone and ambitious aims, the Convention has been criticised for not living up to its potential. According to Niemi and Verdu Sanmartin, the Convention is not very progressive and the criminal law provisions do not succeed in challenging national criminal laws. Some forms of violence, such as sexual harassment, they state, are even "downplayed as crimes".[8] I do agree with Niemi and Verdu Sanmartin that, in all its ambitiousness, the Convention rather repeats some tensions than solves them. Whereas Lourdes Peroni praises the Convention's commitment to de facto equality,[9] in the field of criminal law there is still a lot of work to be done at the textual level that should not be dismissed. From this point of view, the crucial question seems to be to what extent the Istanbul Convention sets a standard for national laws while the formulation of the elements of crimes is still left to the domain of national sovereignty.

In this chapter, I will focus on the duty of State Parties to criminalise sexual violence (Article 36) and sexual harassment (Article 40) in Chapter V "Substantive Law" of the Convention. This decision does not reflect a stance that e.g. the support systems for rape victims, such as rape crisis centres (Article 25), telephone helplines (Article 24) or general support including legal counselling (Article 20), required by the Convention would not be of utmost importance, on the contrary. What I claim is that the formulation of a substantive criminal law is crucial for the legal recognition of victims and the effective prosecution of

4 On the formulations by international criminal courts, see e.g. A Cole, 'International Criminal Law and Sexual Violence: An Overview' in Clare McGlynn and Vanessa E Munro (eds), *Rethinking Rape Law. International and Comparative Perspectives* (Routledge, 2010) 47–60.

5 K Nousiainen and C Chinkin, Legal implications of EU Accession to the Istanbul-Convention. European Commission, Directorate-General for Justice and Consumers, Directorate D – Equality (2016) 44.

6 M Kimpimäki, *Kansainvälinen rikosoikeus* (Kauppakamari, 2015) 25.

7 The notion of international crime is used here in the meaning of crimes that are provided for in international treaties, whereas some sources use the notion more restrictively. See A Cassese, *International Criminal Law* (Oxford University Press, 2003) 23–25.

8 See Niemi and Verdu Sanmartin in this volume.

9 See Peroni in this volume.

sexual offences. The Group of Experts monitoring the implementation of the Istanbul Convention (GREVIO) has in its report on Finland emphasised the importance of identifying and addressing the reasons for high attrition rates of domestic violence and rape cases.[10] In the Finnish context, they are to a great extent due to how the law is written and interpreted in different phases of the criminal process.[11]

In interpreting sexual offences under the Istanbul Convention, three important relationships can be identified. The relationship of the Convention, first, with its Explanatory Report, second, with the case law of the European Court of Human Rights (ECtHR), and third, with its monitoring procedure as established in Chapter IX. The monitoring procedure can further be divided into two intertwining mechanisms. GREVIO is an independent expert body (Article 66) whereas the Committee of the Parties is a political body consisting of representatives of State Parties (Article 67).[12] GREVIO is in charge of carrying out country-specific evaluations in dialogue with State Parties, but it also has authority to adopt general recommendations on the implementation of the Convention (Article 69).[13] The Committee of the Parties offers a political dimension to the procedure. It may adopt country-specific recommendations based on the observations of GREVIO and demand information on their implementation by a due date.[14] The Convention also establishes the role of NGOs, civil society and national institutions for the protection of human rights, by explicitly stating that GREVIO may receive information from them on the implementation of the Convention (Article 68(5)).

At present, the first round of country-by-country monitoring is still ongoing. So far, it has been completed on Albania, Austria, Denmark, Monaco, Montenegro, Portugal, Sweden and Turkey.[15] Therefore, it is not possible to gain a full picture of the compatibility of the contracting States' sexual offences legislation with the Convention. Nevertheless, some preliminary remarks can be

10 GREVIO's (Baseline) Evaluation Report on legislative and other measures giving effect to the provisions of the Council of Europe Convention on Preventing and Combating Violence against Women and Domestic Violence (Istanbul Convention) Finland, 8.

11 Amnesty International, Finnish Section: Oikeuksien arpapeli: Naisiin kohdistuvat raiskausrikokset ja uhrin oikeuksien toteutuminen Suomessa. Published 6 March 2019, 19–24. Available at: https://s3-eu-west-1.amazonaws.com/frantic/amnesty-fi/2019/03/06061152/Oikeuksien-arpapeli_final.pdf (visited on 15 October 2019).

12 Explanatory Report, paras 337–338 and 345.

13 Explanatory Report, para 359.

14 Explanatory Report, para 357.

15 For more information on the completed, ongoing and upcoming processes, including all related documents, see: www.coe.int/en/web/istanbul-convention/country-monitoring-work (visited on 15 October 2019). In addition to already published country reports, the draft report on Finland will be used as an example. It will be published on the official web site after its adoption together with any comments received from the party. Currently it is available at: https://rm.coe.int/grevio-report-on-finland/168097129d (visited on 15 October 2019).

made. The completed reports of the first round of GREVIO country-by-country monitoring show that e.g. the debate on the question how the law on rape should be formulated, which started with the ECtHR ruling in *M.C. v Bulgaria* (2003), is still going on. In this regard, GREVIO seems to have taken the stance that it prefers the wording of the Convention and recommends legislation based on the lack of freely given consent. On the priority scale created by GREVIO, changes towards a consent-based legislation have been rated to be urgent or expected to be done in the near future.[16]

Regarding sexual harassment, the stance taken by GREVIO has not been as strict. For example, in its evaluation report on Finland, GREVIO has prioritised changes regarding sexual violence but possible changes in harassment legislation are not seen as urgent. Also, the discussion on compliance is quite superficial.[17] This is unfortunate since Article 40 leaves great room for national discretion and there seems to be a need for further discussion on the effectiveness of national laws in combatting sexual harassment. Sexual harassment has not come up in the ECtHR and there is no key case that would guide the interpretation of Article 40, similar to what e.g. *M.C. v Bulgaria* has been regarding sexual violence or *Opuz v Turkey* (2009)[18] regarding domestic violence. Following the interpretation of the Court in *M.C. v Bulgaria*, sexual harassment might fall under the protection of private life (Article 8 ECHR) and possibly under the prohibition of discrimination in enjoying this right (Article 14 ECHR), but so far this question has not been addressed. Therefore, the country-by-country monitoring and possibly a general recommendation by GREVIO would be the more probable context for discussing the phenomenon and developing the ways to tackle it.

In addition to providing an overview of the sexual offences under the Convention, my aim is to provide the reader with starting points for evaluation and critical discussion. The critical remarks are directed towards national legislators, the Convention itself and the interpretations made by GREVIO. In addition to the country reports adopted by GREVIO, I will use the Nordic framework, mainly Finland and Sweden, as an example when needed. The main questions

16 In its recommendations, GREVIO has adopted the use of four different verbs relating to the urgency of the State Party action. The verb "urges" means that immediate action is required to bring the Party's legislation into compliance with the Convention. "Strongly encourages" is used when remedies are required in the near future. "Encourages" is used in case of shortcomings that require attention, but the changes can be postponed to a later stage. Lastly, the verb "invites" is used when the gaps in implementation are small or GREVIO's intention is to provide guidance in the implementation process. See e.g. GREVIO's (Baseline) Evaluation Report on legislative and other measures giving effect to the provisions of the Council of Europe Convention on Preventing and Combating Violence against Women and Domestic Violence (Istanbul Convention) ALBANIA, GREVIO/Inf(2017)13, Published on 24 November 2017, 5.

17 GREVIO's (Baseline) Evaluation Report on legislative and other measures giving effect to the provisions of the Council of Europe Convention on Preventing and Combating Violence against Women and Domestic Violence (Istanbul Convention) Finland, paras 181–182.

18 *Opuz v Turkey* App no 33401/02 (ECHR, 9 June 2009).

addressed are: To what extent can the Istanbul Convention challenge national legislation? Is there room for further discussion on the content of the Convention itself? In which direction is GREVIO taking the interpretation of the Convention and where does it set its priorities? So far, the discussion on e.g. rape seems to focus on demanding consent-based legislation whereas other questions such as vulnerability have gained less attention. I will also refer to other Articles of the Convention and try to provide the reader with a holistic reading of the relevant articles and their context. In conclusion, the questions I will pose are: Are we looking at a duty to reform the wording of national law? Or, does the Convention have potential to challenge the ways we think about the role of criminal law in protecting one's sexual dignity and integrity?

2 Sexual violence

2.1 The duty to criminalise and effectively prosecute sexual violence

Article 36 of the Convention requires the criminalisation of (a) engaging in non-consensual vaginal, anal or oral penetration of a sexual nature of the body of another person with any bodily part or object; (b) engaging in other non-consensual acts of a sexual nature with a person; (c) causing another person to engage in non-consensual acts of a sexual nature with a third person. What qualifies as a non-consensual act is not further elaborated, but it is stated that consent must be given voluntarily, as the result of the person's free will assessed in the context of the surrounding circumstances. It is noteworthy that Article 36 covers a broad spectrum of non-consensual sexual acts, including rape. The Convention does not clearly state which of these acts should be defined as rape and which as sexual offences of a lesser degree, e.g. as coercion into a sexual act. In light of Article 36, it seems to suffice that all of these are criminalised, but as I will argue later, Article 45 on proportionate and effective sanctions should be taken into account when assessing the categorisation of different acts.

Any discussion on rape at the international level should be done cautiously, since there is no shared understanding of which acts exactly fall into this category. For example, in Finland, one element in the crime of rape is sexual intercourse. Traditionally, intercourse has meant only vaginal penetration. At the end of the nineties, the definition was broadened to cover all types of penetration performed with a sexual organ or directed at a sexual organ. Today, the definition of intercourse also covers anal penetration. In Finland, the definition is precise and exhaustive, whereas e.g. in Sweden rape covers both sexual intercourse and other sexual acts that in view of the seriousness of the violation are comparable to sexual intercourse.[19] It is interesting that the line between rape

19 Chapter 6 of the Swedish Penal Code (unofficial translation), Section 1. Available at: www.government.se/4a95e7/contentassets/602a1b5a8d65426496402d99e19325d5/chapter-6-of-the-swedish-penal-code-unoffical-translation-20181005 (visited on 15 October 2019).

and other sexual offences is left fully undefined in the Istanbul Convention, despite the symbolic value of recognising certain acts as rape. This should be kept in mind in the course of the discussion, even though the focus is shifted to other elements of the crime, first and foremost to the concept of non-consensuality.

As many national laws today, the Istanbul Convention takes as a starting point everyone's right to decide whether to engage in any type of sexual act (*sexual self-determination*). Basically, this means that every person is assumed to possess and be able to use their free will unless incapable or impaired to do so due to specified circumstances.[20] From the point of view of the legislator, there are two legal questions to be distinguished from each other relating to the use of free will: (1) a total lack of consent and (2) the validity of the given consent. According to paragraph 193 of the Explanatory Report, State Parties are required to provide legislation that specifies the lack of consent, but the exact wording of the legislation is left to national discretion. It is also left to the national legislators to decide the factors that make a given consent invalid. The only thing that the Convention specifies is that there needs to be *free will*, which is both philosophically and legally an empty shell, unless further specified.

As the country-by-country monitoring has already shown, there are many national variations, all claiming to fill the standard set by the Convention. In Austria and Germany, the signing of the Convention started a debate that lead to amending their respective legislation on sexual violence. For example, the new German rape law criminalises all sexual acts against the recognisable will of another person, whereas the old rape law only criminalised sexual acts coerced by force, by threat of imminent danger to life or limb, or by exploiting a situation in which the victim was unprotected and at the mercy of the offender. The new model is based on consent, whereas the old one is a coercion-based model. As Tatjana Höernle emphasises, the old law put a lot of pressure on the victim to give evidence of resistance or experiencing fear for their life. A verbal expression of "no" was not sufficient to establish a crime.[21] The new law is an achievement of German female Members of Parliament who brought to vote their own draft law instead of the rather conservative, still coercion-based one from the Ministry of Justice.[22]

In the Nordic countries, Finland and Denmark have not made any changes to their rape laws due to the Convention. Both countries represent the

20 On the problematics of this approach, see J Nedelsky, *Law's Relations: A Relational Theory of Self, Autonomy, and Law* (Oxford University Press, 2011); N Lacey, *Unspeakable Subjects. Feminist Essays in Legal and Social Theory* (Hart Publishing, 1998).

21 T Höernle, 'The New German Law on Sexual Offences' (2016). Available at: https://ssrn.com/abstract=2999677 (visited on 15 October 2019), 1–3.

22 T Höernle, 'The New German Law on Sexual Offences' (2016). Available at: https://ssrn.com/abstract=2999677 (visited on 15 October 2019), 4.

coercion-based model with little variation in wording.[23] In Finland, a person who forces another to have sexual intercourse by the use or threat of violence directed against the person, or has sexual intercourse with another person by taking advantage of the fact that this other person, due to unconsciousness, illness, disability, state of fear or other state of helplessness, is unable to defend himself or themselves or formulate or express his or their will, shall be sentenced for rape.[24] The question is: Does this type of legislation cover all cases where the other party has not consented? In Sweden, rape law was similar to the Finnish and Danish ones until 2018. Today, Swedish law covers all cases in which other party has not participated voluntarily, but the reason for the amendment was more likely the strong *#MeToo* movement in the country and the growing political will than any international pressure.[25] I will return to the question on formulating rape law in Section 2.2 addressing the issue of consent and in Section 2.4 addressing the issue of vulnerability.

The conducts listed in Article 36 are to be criminalised only when committed intentionally. The interpretation of intention is left to domestic law, but the requirement for intentional conduct relates to all the elements of the offence.[26] It is noteworthy that, depending on the specific national jurisdiction, there are differences in the doctrines of intention.[27] Intention is the mental or subjective part of the crime (*mens rea*), covering basically what the perpetrator desired, knew or should have known in relation to the act. Especially in relation to consent-based rape law, there has been a lot of discussion about how the intention of the perpetrator can cover for the lack of consent, which seems to be a subjective state of the victim. If the threshold for intent is that the perpetrator should have known, it very easily becomes a responsibility of the victim to express their will. For example, in Sweden the solution to this was to criminalise negligent rape.[28] Negligent rape covers cases in which the perpetrator acts in

23 See Report submitted by Denmark pursuant to Article 68, paragraph 1 of the Council of Europe Convention on preventing and combating violence against women and domestic violence (Baseline Report), GREVIO/Inf(2017)2 Published on 19 January 2017, 37–38.

24 The Criminal Code of Finland, Chapter 20, Section 1, translation in English available at: www.finlex.fi/fi/laki/kaannokset/1889/en18890039 (visited on 15 October 2019).

25 In the *travaux preparatoires* it is stated that the amendment will take away any grounds to doubt whether Sweden lives up to its international obligations, but it is only one among many arguments for the amendment. See SOU 2016:60 Ett starkare skydd för den sexuella integriteteten. Betänkande av 2014 års sexualbrottskommitté, 185.

26 Explanatory Report to the Council of Europe Convention on preventing and combating violence against women and domestic violence, Council of Europe Treaty Series – No 210, Istanbul, 11.V.2011, para 189.

27 On the Swedish discussion on intent and consent, see K Berglund, 'Uppsåt till bristande samtycke' in *Festskrift till Per Ole Träskman* (Norstedts Juridik, 2011) 66–75.

28 Chapter 6 of the Swedish Penal Code (unofficial translation), Section 1 a. Available at: www.government.se/4a95e7/contentassets/602a1b5a8d65426496402d99e19325d5/chapter-6-of-the-swedish-penal-code-unoffical-translation-20181005 (visited on 15 October 2019).

uncertainty, taking the risk that the other party is not voluntarily involved. I will come back to this question in the next Section. In addition to the perpetrator, also aiders and abettors have to be made liable for intentional conduct (Article 41). The attempt of the conducts listed in Article 36 shall be criminalised as well. Aiding, abetting and attempt are not defined further in the Convention or in the Explanatory Report, thus leaving room for national variations in their definitions.

Another important definition that is common to all forms of sexual violence relates to the *sexual nature* of the acts. Article 36 of the Convention applies to "penetration of sexual nature" (Article 36(1)(a)) and "acts of sexual nature" (Article 36(1)(b) and (c)). According to paragraph 190 of the Explanatory Report, the requirement of the act being of a sexual nature is a limitation seeking to avoid problems of interpretation, limiting Article 36 to acts with a "sexual connotation" or "undertone". It seems to be taken for granted that everyone knows when there is such an undertone; there is no explanation or examples given. However, this might lead to an unnecessary restriction of the applicability of Article 36. As I have stated in the Introduction, one of the main questions is how the Istanbul Convention could work in challenging national laws. Because the Convention leaves great room for national discretion on what counts as sexual and what does not, it does not contribute to this important discussion.

For example, in Finnish law, the definition is as tautological as the one given in the Explanatory Report. A sexual act is defined as "an act which, with consideration to the offender, the person at whom the act was directed and the circumstances of commission, is sexually significant".[29] The question of sexual significance has been taken up by the Finnish Supreme Court many times, often in relation to children. In a recent case, KKO:2016:52, a male teacher had hugged his 12-year-old girl pupil several times, held her in his lap at least once, called her so beautiful that he could eat her, and sent her e-mails during evenings and days off with similar content, giving her an impression to be his "number one pupil", "a treasure", and an "uncrowned queen of the class". The Supreme Court came to the conclusion that the acts, even when considered as a whole, did not meet the requirement of being sexually significant.[30] It is rather unfortunate that the Istanbul Convention does not take a specific position on this discussion facilitating the understanding of "sexual nature".

29 Criminal Code, Chapter 20, Section 10. Before 2014, a sexual act was defined in Finland as "an act whose purpose is sexual arousal or satisfaction, and which is sexually significant in view of the circumstances and the persons involved". The perspective was the perpetrator's and the definition led to the dismissal of the charges, especially in cases where a subjective seeking of sexual arousal or satisfaction could not be proved (see e.g. KKO:2005:93; KKO:2011:34).

30 Precedents of the Finnish Supreme Court are available at: https://korkeinoikeus.fi/fi/index/ennakkopaatokset.html (mainly in Finnish only, visited on 15 October 2019).

Even when rape has been a topical theme in the international arena, there has not been much legal discussion on sexuality or its value as such. This has to do with the fact that violence against women needed to be addressed through other concepts such as war crimes or violation of human rights. In the ECtHR's case law, rape has been conceptualised both as torture and as degrading treatment (Article 3 of the ECHR),[31] whereas other less severe acts, such as unnecessary strip-search, have been regarded as degrading treatment (also falling under Article 3)[32] or as a violation of the right to respect for private life (Article 8 of the ECHR),[33] depending on the circumstances such as the gender of the official conducting the search.[34] Article 8 of the ECHR offers protection to one's physical and moral integrity under respect for private life.[35] I see no obstacle to extending this to sexual integrity, even if the Court has not (yet) done so.

In the case *Wainwright v United Kingdom*, the two applicants, Ms Wainwright and her son, were strip-searched when they wanted to visit Ms Wainwright's other son in prison. The aspect of sexual integrity was not touched upon in the ruling even though the prison officers required, against normal procedure, the second applicant to strip completely naked and the first applicant to be practically naked at one instant. They did not bother to draw the blinds, so the first applicant was visible through a window during the search. The applicants were not informed of the applicable procedure, and the second applicant even believed that he was going to experience anal penetration.[36] After the incident, the first applicant cried and vomited, and the second applicant developed post-traumatic stress disorder.[37] However, the treatment did not, in the Court's view, reach the minimum level of severity prohibited by Article 3 of the ECHR, but it was found to be in breach of Article 8 of the ECHR. This case indicates that there might be more possibilities to discuss violations of sexual integrity and dignity under Article 8 than Article 3.

In the Explanatory Report of the Istanbul Convention, more is said on sexuality regarding procedural questions when assessing evidence in cases of sexual violence. According to the Report, assessment of the evidence should be

31 See *Aydin v Turkey* App no 23178/94 (ECHR, 25 September1997); *Maslova and Nalbandov v Russia* App no 839/02 (ECHR, 24 January 2008). In both cases, the applicants claimed that they had been raped by police officials while in custody. As Patricia Londono points out, the Court was originally reluctant to acknowledge rape by other than state officials as a violation of Article 3, and even in later cases, rape by non-state actors has been labelled as degrading treatment, not as torture. P Londono, 'Defining Rape under the European Convention on Human Rights: Torture, Consent and Equality' in Clare McGlynn and Vanessa E Munro (eds), *Rethinking Rape Law. International and Comparative Perspectives* (Routledge, 2010) 111–113.

32 *Valašinas v Lithuania*, App no 44558/98 (ECHR, 24 July 2001).

33 *Wainwright v the United Kingdom*, App no 12350/04 (ECHR, 26 September 2006).

34 *Wainwright v the United Kingdom*, paras 41–43.

35 *Wainwright v the United Kingdom*, para 43.

36 *Wainwright v the United Kingdom*, paras 19 and 45.

37 *Wainwright v the United Kingdom*, paras 16–20.

(a) context-sensitive, (b) done on a case-by-case basis, (c) not based on assumptions of typical behavioural responses to sexual violence and (d) not influenced by gender stereotypes or myths about male and female sexuality.[38] This also relates to Article 54 of the Convention, according to which evidence relating to the sexual history and conduct of the victim shall be permitted only when it is relevant and necessary. This is a welcomed provision since the sexual history and conduct of the victim has traditionally been a way to discredit the victim and to justify the act of the perpetrator, dividing victims into morally respectable and unrespectable, not worthy of protection.[39]

On the other hand, in jurisdictions based on free provision of evidence (unless fully unrelated to the case) and free evaluation of this evidence by judges, any process-related rules that would restrict or guide the process in the way imagined in the Explanatory Report are scarce. The admissibility of any evidence belongs to the discretion of judges and this applies also to Article 54. According to paragraph 278 of the Explanatory report, if a judge admits evidence regarding the previous sexual history of the victim, it should only be presented in a way that does not lead to secondary victimisation. The question is: How can judges evaluate in advance which evidence should not be permitted or how should they regulate its presentation, as they should know the content of the evidence only in the course of the proceedings? It seems to be left to the individual judges to be aware of and well educated on questions of harmful stereotypes and secondary victimisation, as well as to create their own ways to prevent them. The Convention does not offer either too many concrete solutions to the judiciary on how a more sensitive approach could enter the court room.

2.2 Lack of consent in light of the Convention

The question of whether to define rape as use of coercion or as lack of consent is an old one, but it was refuelled in Europe by the ECtHR judgment in *M.C. v Bulgaria*, delivered in 2003. In defining rape and sexual violence in Article 36, the drafters of the Istanbul Convention rely heavily upon this ruling. As stated in the Explanatory Report, State Parties should take into consideration this judgment when assessing the constituent elements of sexual offences. In the *M.C. v Bulgaria* judgment, the ECtHR stated that

38 Explanatory Report, para 192.

39 See e.g. C McGlynn, 'Rape Trials and Sexual History Evidence. Reforming the Law on Third-Party Evidence' (2017) 81(5) *Journal of Criminal Law* 367–392; in relation to the Finnish context, see e.g. H Jokila, *Tahdonvastainen suostumus ja liiallisen luottamuksen hinta. Raiskauksen ja muiden seksuaalirikosten oikeudellisen tiedon konstruktiot* (Suomalainen lakimiesyhdistys 2010).

> the member states' positive obligations under Articles 3 and 8 of the Convention [on Human Rights] must be seen as requiring the penalisation and effective prosecution of any non-consensual sexual act, including in the absence of physical resistance by the victim.[40]

Thus, the obligation to criminalise all non-consensual sexual acts as required by the Istanbul Convention must be interpreted in light of *M.C. v Bulgaria*.

NGOs and academics in many countries have used this case to promote consent-based rape legislation.[41] Despite the seemingly strict obligation, however, neither the case law of the ECtHR nor the Istanbul Convention requires the use of the word "consent" or "non-consensual" as a constituent element of the crime of rape at the national level. In *M.C. v Bulgaria*, the ECtHR compared national rape laws and came to the conclusion that "in a number of countries the prosecution of non-consensual sexual acts in all circumstances is sought in practice by means of interpretation of the relevant statutory terms", such as force.[42] Similarly, the Istanbul Convention leaves it to State Parties to decide whether they wish to define rape with reference to violence, coercion and threat, or with reference to the lack of consent of the victim. In the Nordic countries, there has, nevertheless, been a strong feminist movement in promoting (the) lack of consent as a constituent element of rape, enhanced by the *#MeToo* movement. For example, in Sweden, although initially no need was seen for amending rape law after *M.C. v Bulgaria* and after the ratification of the Convention, rape law was ultimately modified in 2018 to encompass all acts in which the other party has not participated voluntarily.

In *M.C. v Bulgaria*, a 14-year-old-girl (just above the age of consent in Bulgaria) filed a report of two rapes against two perpetrators. One of the rapes allegedly took place in a car after an evening at a local disco; the second one allegedly in a private apartment later that night. In both cases, the prosecutor decided to drop charges since there was no evidence of threats or violence having been used in the act.[43] The national prosecutor interpreted the elements of the crime to the effect that coercion would imply resistance from the side of the victim, and that the establishment of criminal responsibility required both the use of force and knowledge of lacking consent, communicated by this resistance.[44] There was expert evidence presented on the so-called frozen fright phenomenon and the victim's possible inability to act in the situation, but it did not affect the prosecutor's decision to eventually close the case.

40 Explanatory Report, para 191.

41 In Sweden, one of the main advocates was professor Madeleine Leijonhufvud. See, M Leijonhufvud, *Samtyckesutredningen. Lagskydd för den sexuella integriteten* (2008). For the opposite approach, see P Asp, 'M.C. v Bulgaria – a Swedish Perspective' (2009) (54) *Scandinavian Studies in Law* 191–211.

42 Explanatory Report, para 191.

43 *M.C. v Bulgaria* App no 39272/98 (ECHR, 4 December 2003) paras 55 and 60.

44 *M.C. v Bulgaria*, para 64.

What the ECtHR emphasised in its reasoning is "the meaning given to words such as 'force' or 'threats' or other terms used in legal definitions".[45] According to the Court, national courts in a number of countries have developed their interpretation so as to try to encompass any non-consensual sexual act, despite the concrete wording of the legislation. In this case, the Bulgarian Government failed to convince the Court (by e.g. providing relevant case law and legal commentaries) that every sexual act carried out without the victim's consent is punishable under Bulgarian law. It sufficed for the ECtHR that "the applicant's allegation of a restrictive practice is based on reasonable arguments and has not been disproved by the Government".[46]

In conclusion, I claim that the interpretative value of *M.C. v Bulgaria* for the Istanbul Convention does not derive from the use of the word *non-consensual*, but from the fact that State Parties need to prove that (a) their law on sexual offences does, despite the chosen wording, encompass all non-consensual acts covered by Article 36, and (b) that all these cases are effectively prosecuted. For example, in relation to the latest legislative amendment in Sweden, the government commissioned a case law study that revealed cases of non-consensual sexual intercourse that did not qualify as rape.[47] This was one of the reasons for the study to recommend a new rape law based on lack of voluntariness. In the framework of the Istanbul Convention, it is inadequate when State Parties claim that their legislation is sufficient; rather, they should provide proof, such as studies on case law and prosecutorial decisions, that all non-consensual sexual acts are encompassed by their criminal laws.

The obvious forum to discuss the challenges related to the elements of the crime of rape is the country-by-country monitoring by GREVIO. So far, it seems that GREVIO has chosen the strategy to recommend consent-based rape laws to be implemented in the near future.[48] In the case of Finland, GREVIO strongly encourages Finland to reform the entire Chapter 20 of the Finnish Criminal Code on sexual offences "to fully incorporate the notion of freely given consent" and "to ensure appropriate sanctions for all sexual acts without the consent of the victim, including where the circumstances of the case preclude valid consent".[49] A working group has already been set up by the Ministry of Justice to prepare this reform, so the recommendation will not be subject to objections even though there have previously been reluctant attitudes towards

45 *M.C. v Bulgaria*, para 171.
46 *M.C. v Bulgaria*, paras 173–174.
47 SOU 2016:60, 179.
48 GREVIO has recommended consent-based legislation in its reports on Albania, Denmark, Portugal and Turkey. Finland has received a similar recommendation in the draft evaluation report. GREVIO's (Baseline) Evaluation Report on legislative and other measures giving effect to the provisions of the Council of Europe Convention on Preventing and Combating Violence against Women and Domestic Violence (Istanbul Convention) FINLAND, para 169.
49 GREVIO's Evaluation Report on Finland, para 169.

consent-based legislation.[50] Another example is Denmark, where rape is defined not as lack of consent of the victim; rather, the definition refers to certain means used by the perpetrator such as violence, threats and duress. In its baseline report on Denmark, GREVIO strongly encouraged Denmark to move away from the current sexual violence legislation and to base it on the notion of freely given consent.[51] In its response, Denmark disagreed with GREVIO's recommendation. It also reminded GREVIO that the Explanatory Report does not require that domestic law include the word "consent".[52] In the light of Denmark's response, it will be difficult for GREVIO to efficiently encourage State Parties to implement consent-based legislation if there is no evidence such as a case study to back up its argument that a current piece of legislation is not all-encompassing.

The discussion on the meaning of consent seems more fruitful in cases in which the country in question already has adapted consent-based legislation. As stated in the baseline report on Austria, the country was one of the first parties to adapt its criminal law to the requirement of Article 36 of the Istanbul Convention.[53] It is not evident from the baseline report, but the amendment was a result of a campaign introduced by Austrian NGOs.[54] In addition to the criminal offence of rape, a provision entitled "violation of sexual integrity" was introduced, covering sexual intercourse or equivalent conduct against the will of a person.[55] Germany introduced a similar amendment in relation to the ratification of the Convention after intense debates on the matter in 2015 and 2016.[56] The new law on rape and sexual assault encompasses all sexual acts

50 Chapter 20 of the Finnish Criminal Code was last amended in 2014 and the reluctant attitudes were clearly expressed in the *travaux preparatoires*. See the Government Bill HE 216/2013 vp, 38.

51 GREVIO's (Baseline) Evaluation Report on legislative and other measures giving effect to the provisions of the Council of Europe Convention on Preventing and Combating Violence against Women and Domestic Violence (Istanbul Convention) DENMARK, GREVIO/Inf(2017)14, Published on 24 November 2017, para 177.

52 Comments submitted by Denmark on GREVIO's final report on the implementation of the Council of Europe Convention on preventing and combating violence against women and domestic violence (Baseline Report), GREVIO/Inf(2017)16, Published on 24 November 2017, 16.

53 GREVIO's (Baseline) Evaluation Report on legislative and other measures giving effect to the provisions of the Council of Europe Convention on Preventing and Combating Violence against Women and Domestic Violence (Istanbul Convention) AUSTRIA, GREVIO/Inf(2017)4, Published on 24 September 2017, para 140.

54 Austrian NGO Shadow Report to GREVIO. Coordination: Association of Austrian Autonomous Women's Shelters, AÖF & Domestic Abuse Intervention Centre Vienna, IST. Vienna, September 2016, 69–70.

55 GREVIO's Evaluation Report on Austria, para 140.

56 R Heike, Rabe and B Leisering, *Die Istanbul-Konvention. Neue Impulse für die Bekämpfung von geschlectsspezifischer Gewalt* (Deutsches Institut für Menschenrechte, 2018) 49.

against the recognisable will of another person.[57] In Germany, the requirement of an expression of will is clearly stated in the law through the expression "recognisable".

In the NGO Shadow Report on Austria, NGOs took up the fact that legislation did not protect persons who remained passive or did not have time to express their will.[58] GREVIO took up this in its report on Austria, stating that Article 36 of the Istanbul Convention applied also to victims who remained fully passive.[59] The stance of GREVIO is that the concept of non-consensuality used in the Istanbul Convention does not require that the victim should resist even verbally. Austria responded to GREVIO stating that the intent of the perpetrator has to comprise non-consensuality as well. Therefore, if a victim remains passive, the perpetrator must be aware of the fact that this behaviour is not implicit consent.[60] It seems to remain the victim's responsibility to ensure that his or her will is not unclear.

When Sweden amended its rape law in 2018, passivity and its meanings were discussed.[61] The Swedish solution was to criminalise also negligent rape that applies in cases of uncertainty. In a recent ruling of the Swedish Supreme Court, the relationship between passivity and *mens rea* was made decisive.[62] In the case, the victim remained fully passive during the penetration. The perpetrator, on the other hand, claimed that the victim had turned towards him and helped him to take off her underpants, which he interpreted as willingness. This was denied by the victim. The Supreme Court assessed the testimonies of the parties and came to the conclusion that there was no intent from the side of the perpetrator to rape the victim, but as he was acting in uncertainty about the will of the victim, it was a question of negligent rape.[63] The ruling seems to confirm the position of the Austrian government in their answer to GREVIO; namely, the perpetrator's intent must cover the question of will and in case of full

57 Strafgesetzbuch (StGB) § 177 Sexueller Übergriff; sexuelle Nötigung; Vergewaltigung. Available in German at: www.gesetze-im-internet.de/stgb/__177.html (visited on 15 October 2019).

58 Austrian NGO Shadow Report to GREVIO, 69–70.

59 GREVIO's Evaluation Report on Austria, para 141.

60 Comments submitted by Austria on GREVIO's final report on the implementation of the Council of Europe Convention on preventing and combating violence against women and domestic violence (Baseline Report). GREVIO/Inf(2017)11, Published on 27 September 2017, 23.

61 In the GREVIO evaluation report on Sweden, it is stated that this being a very recent development, GREVIO has not had the opportunity to assess its implementation by the judiciary. GREVIO's (Baseline) Evaluation Report on legislative and other measures giving effect to the provisions of the Council of Europe Convention on Preventing and Combating Violence against Women and Domestic Violence (Istanbul Convention) SWEDEN, GREVIO/Inf(2018)15, Published on 21 January 2019, para 183.

62 Högsta Domstolen, nr B 1200-19, 11.7.2019. Available at: www.hogstadomstolen.se/Avgoranden/Vagledande-domar-och-beslut-prejudikat/2019/ (visited on 15 October 2019).

63 Högsta Domstolen, nr B 1200-19, 11.7.2019, paras 38–45.

passivity the will of the victim remains uncertain. It will be interesting to see if GREVIO will continue to advocate the stance that Article 36 applies also to victims who have remained fully passive. This is crucial, since there seems to be no shared understanding among State Parties about what meaning should be given to passivity in the consent-based model.

2.3 Sexual violence and intimate partner relationships

According to Article 36(3) of the Istanbul Convention, State Parties have to ensure that the crimes of sexual violence also apply to acts committed against former or current spouses or partners. This might seem self-evident in the 21st century, however, the traditional view on marriage, that partners give an ongoing consent to sexual intercourse, is still visible in many jurisdictions. For instance, Finland criminalised rape in marriage as late as in 1994, and even at this point, the decision was not unanimous, thus giving the State's commitment to the protection of married women a sense of ambivalence.[64] In 2010, Denmark received strong criticism from Amnesty International for not equally protecting married women. Non-consensual sex with a victim in a helpless state was not punishable within marriage and if the perpetrator entered or continued a marriage with the victim after the rape, the punishment could be reduced or fully remitted.[65] The Danish Penal Code was amended in 2013.

Article 36 (3) of the Istanbul Convention needs to be evaluated against the background that, globally, in 58% of countries, marital rape is not explicitly criminalised.[66] In Europe, however, States Parties to the Convention seem to have amended their legislation, and the problem is more related to the actual application of the law. For example, GREVIO noted in its baseline report regarding Montenegro that many cases of marital rape were prosecuted not as rape but as sexual abuse of a family member, leading to extremely low sanctions and suggesting a lesser gravity of the offence. According to GREVIO, the actual situation in which sexual violence in intimate relationships is systematically routed to the misdemeanour courts and handled as a minor offence is not in

64 R Kotanen, *Näkymättömästä näkökulmaksi: Parisuhdeväkivallan uhrit ja oikeudellisen sääntelyn muutos Suomessa* (University of Helsinki, 2013) 80. See also R Kotanen, 'From the Protection of Marriage to the Defence of Equality – The Finnish Debate over the Sexual Autonomy of Wives' in M Bruvik Heinskou, May-Len Skilbrei and K Stefansen (eds), *Rape in the Nordic Countries. Continuity and Change* (Routledge, 2019).

65 Case Closed. Rape and Human Rights in the Nordic Countries. Summary Report, 9–10 (Amnesty International, 2010). Available at: www.amnesty.org/en/documents/ACT77/001/2010/en/ (visited on 15 October 2019).

66 UN Women (2019): Progress of the World's Women 2019–2020: Families in a Changing World, 26–27. Available at: www.unwomen.org/en/digital-library/progress-of-the-worlds-women (visited on 15 October 2019).

line with Article 36 (3).[67] Despite taking this stance, no proposal or suggestion was made by GREVIO as to how the situation should be improved.

Article 46 of the Convention, dealing with aggravating circumstances, should also be taken into account in the context of sexual violence occurring in a marital relationship. The first of the therein stipulated aggravating circumstances concerns cases in which the offence was committed against a former or current spouse or partner. The aggravating circumstances need not be part of the elements of the crime and their application by courts is not mandatory, but they should be available to judges when considering the sentence.[68] As Niemi and Verdu Sanmartin claim, the victim-related aggravating circumstances are the most important contribution of the Convention to generic criminal laws.[69] Surprisingly, the implementation of Article 46 into national laws has so far been discussed by GREVIO only in some of the reports, and in a controversial manner.

Some of the differences are understandable whereas others seem incoherent. For example, both in Finland and in Montenegro GREVIO noted a tendency to judge cases more mildly if the perpetrator was previously known to the victim.[70] Since in Montenegro no sentencing guidelines exist, GREVIO could only recommend legislative measures on a general level as well as an effective training of judges.[71] In the case of Finland, GREVIO could have urged the authorities to include all the aggravating circumstances in the Criminal Code that already entails both crime-specific and general rules on aggravating factors. Instead, GREVIO only strongly encouraged the Finnish authorities to take appropriate measures to ensure that all the circumstances listed in Article 46 are considered as aggravated circumstances by the judiciary. It is not clear why in the case of Finland the choice of measure is left to the Finnish authorities knowing that the judges might be reluctant to apply factors outside the explicit wording of the Criminal Code and that an addition to the law would clarify the situation. Quite the contrary, in the case of Portugal, GREVIO did not hesitate to urge the Portuguese authorities "to amend their criminal legislation to ensure that the circumstances described in Article 46 of the Istanbul Convention may be taken into consideration as aggravating circumstances for all forms of violence covered by the convention".[72]

67 GREVIO's (Baseline) Evaluation Report on legislative and other measures giving effect to the provisions of the Council of Europe Convention on Preventing and Combating Violence against Women and Domestic Violence (Istanbul Convention) MONTENEGRO, GREVIO/Inf(2018)5, Published on 25 October 2018, para 182.

68 Explanatory report, para 235.

69 See Niemi and Verdu Sanmartin in this volume.

70 GREVIO's Evaluation Report on Montenegro, para 204; GREVIO's Evaluation Report on Finland, para 187.

71 GREVIO's Evaluation Report on Montenegro, Appendix I, para 34.

72 GREVIO's (Baseline) Evaluation Report on legislative and other measures giving effect to the provisions of the Council of Europe Convention on Preventing and Combating Violence against Women and Domestic Violence (Istanbul Convention) Portugal. GREVIO/Inf(2018)16, Published on 21 January 2019, para 181.

Finally, for the effective prosecution of sexual violence in marital and intimate relationships, provisions on *ex officio* prosecution are crucial. According to Article 55(1) of the Istanbul Convention, State Parties shall ensure that investigations into or the prosecution of sexual violence that falls within the scope of Article 36 shall not be wholly dependent upon a report or complaint filed by the victim, and that the proceedings may continue even if the victim withdraws her or his statement or complaint. The withdrawal of charges or statements is a common feature between spouses, usually under pressure by the perpetrator. For example, in Finland, victims of rape and sexual violence have traditionally had the possibility to influence the prosecutor's decision whether or not to proceed with the case. Even though rape today is a crime to be prosecuted *ex officio*, the victim has the right not to testify in cases in which there is or has been a marital or similar intimate relationship between the parties.[73] To what extent the State should investigate whether there has been inadmissible pressure if the victim decides not to testify remains vague in the light of the wording of the Convention. So far, GREVIO has noted that, in three of the eight countries, gaps remained in the implementation of this article. The recommendations to bring all sexual violence under public prosecution, including in the case of Turkey even marital rape, have been given the highest priority.[74]

2.4 Vulnerability especially in the light of validity of consent and effective punishment

In the laws on sexual offences, it is recognised that certain types of victims, such as minors or the disabled, need more protection from sexual abuse than others. This Section focuses on the question of to what extent the Istanbul Convention recognises the need to protect vulnerable persons by means of criminal law. Vulnerability is mentioned in two articles of the Convention. According to Article 12(3), any preventive measures [taken under the Convention] shall take into account and address the specific needs of persons made vulnerable by particular circumstances. The limitation of Article 12 is that its paragraph 3 seems to refer only to Chapter III.

In relation to Chapter IV of the Convention that addresses substantial law, vulnerability is taken up in Article 46 on aggravating circumstances. According to Article 46, State Parties shall take the necessary legislative or other measures to ensure that vulnerability, insofar as it does not already form part of the constituent elements of the offences listed in Chapter IV, may be taken into consideration as aggravating circumstances in the determination of the sentence.

73 Code of Judicial Procedure, Chapter 17, Section 17. English translation available at: www.finlex.fi/fi/laki/kaannokset/1734/en17340004 (visited on 15 October 2019).

74 GREVIO's Evaluation Report on Albania, paras 197–198; GREVIO's Evaluation Report on Portugal, paras 222–223; GREVIO's Evaluation Report on Turkey, paras 312–313.

It is left to State Parties to decide how this is to be done. Thus, vulnerability can be part of the elements of the crime itself, a factor that qualifies the sexual crime as aggravated or a factor that can be taken into account when measuring the sentence, usually listed in the general part of the Criminal Code. Again, the Convention leaves State Parties with a broad set of options to choose from.

There is no universal definition of vulnerability. For the purposes of the Convention, the Explanatory Report provides a list of persons made vulnerable by particular circumstances.[75] They include pregnant women and women with young children, persons with disabilities, including those with mental or cognitive impairments, persons living in rural or remote areas, substance abusers, prostitutes, persons of national or ethnic minority background, migrants, including undocumented migrants and refugees, gay men, lesbian women, bisexual and transgender persons, as well as HIV-positive persons, homeless persons, children and the elderly. The Explanatory Report notes that perpetrators often choose to target persons in vulnerable situations because they know that they are less likely to be able to defend themselves or seek prosecution and other forms of reparation.[76]

A crucial question not taken up in the Convention concerns whether and to what extent vulnerability should be taken into account when assessing the validity of the victim's consent to participate in sexual intercourse or sexual acts. Article 36(2) only specifies that consent must be given voluntarily as a result of the person's free will, as assessed in the context of the surrounding circumstances. According to paragraph 193 of the Explanatory Report, it is left to State Parties to decide on the factors that can preclude freely given consent. There is no clear link between the list of circumstances given in relation to Article 46 (as listed above) and the duty to criminalise sexual violence. In its Evaluation Report on Finland, GREVIO notes that

> the capacity to consent to sexual acts varies on the basis of a number of factors, including for example age, dependency and victim-perpetrator-relationship. In many circumstances, they preclude valid consent, resulting in sexual intercourse without the woman's consent in the same way as the use of force and threats does.[77]

The discussion how vulnerability should be taken into account is a very important one, since there is a very fine line between demanding protection for vulnerable victims and denying the right to sexual self-determination. On the other hand,

75 Explanatory Report, para 87. According to paragraph 238 of the Explanatory Report, the list also applies to vulnerability in aggravating circumstances.

76 Explanatory Report, para 87.

77 GREVIO's Evaluation Report on Finland, para 166.

guaranteeing sexual self-determination to, for example, teenagers[78] or to the disabled should not leave them without proper protection by criminal law.

Another topical question is how the circumstances where a victim's vulnerability has been abused should affect the sentencing. According to Article 45, the offences established in accordance with the Convention shall be punishable by effective, proportionate and dissuasive sanctions, taking into account their seriousness. The drafters decided to leave it to State Parties to decide which offences merit a prison sentence.[79] Neither the Convention nor the Explanatory Report take a clear stance on how State Parties should judge the seriousness of different criminal conducts listed in Article 36.[80] For example, in Finland, the sexual abuse of a person in a vulnerable position is typically considered less serious than rape committed using violence. This seems to be in contradiction with both Article 45 on effective sanctions and Article 46 of the Convention on aggravating circumstances.[81] In its Evaluation Report on Finland, GREVIO took up this question warning "against the creation of a hierarchy of victims on the basis of their characteristics such as young age, helplessness, dependence, illness or other circumstances, and calls for appropriate legislative measures to send the message that rape is rape".[82]

In other country reports, GREVIO has taken up the question of sentencing, but not coherently. In its report on Denmark, GREVIO noted that "lenient sentences in domestic violence cases and other forms of violence against women do not serve the principle of ensuring justice for victims and ending impunity of perpetrators", and encouraged the Danish authorities "to ensure understanding among the Danish judiciary" on this fact.[83] In this example, it seems that the experts are in favour of stricter sentencing. Finland also received criticism on the fact that "the criminal penalties that may be imposed for any of the sexual offences in Finland are very low".[84] But in its country report on Austria, GREVIO dismissed the criticism by NGOs that the newly amended law had created a major difference between maximum sentences depending on whether non-consensual penetration was committed by force (maximum of ten years

78 The Istanbul Convention also applies to girls. However, the only criminal-law related provision where minors are specifically considered is Article 58, according to which initiating any legal proceedings with regard to the offences established in accordance with Articles 36, 37, 38 and 39 of this Convention shall continue for a period of time that is sufficient to allow for the efficient initiation of proceedings after the victim has reached the age of majority.

79 Explanatory Report, para 232.

80 However, it is clear that sexual harassment is seen as less of a crime, since according to Article 40 sanctions other than criminal ones suffice.

81 Amnesty International 2019, 9. See also M Leskinen, 'Raiskaus 2010-luvulla. Yhä vain väkisinmakaamista?' in J Niemi, H Kainulainen and P Honkatukia (eds), *Sukupuolistunut väkivalta. Oikeudellinen ja sosiaalinen ongelma* (Vastapaino 2017) 194, 204.

82 GREVIO's Evaluation Report on Finland, para 167.

83 GREVIO's Evaluation Report on Denmark, para 182.

84 GREVIO's Evaluation Report on Finland, para 166.

imprisonment) or otherwise against the will of the other party (maximum of two years).[85] It is interesting that Article 36 of the Istanbul Convention basically covers all types of non-consensual penetration but it seems to allow for sentencing that is based on the old discourse of violence being the most severe breach of sexual self-determination.

In its report on Denmark, GREVIO took up the question of vulnerable victims and sentencing. It noted that

> it seems inappropriate to issue a lesser sentence (maximum of four years imprisonment) for sexual intercourse following the exploitation of a "mental illness/disability" compared to sexual intercourse with an intoxicated woman incapable of consenting to the act, which currently carries a maximum prison term of eight years.[86]

GREVIO strongly encouraged the Danish authorities to bring these sanctions to the same level.[87] This recommendation was not commented on by the Danish Government, nor taken up by the Committee of the Parties. Hopefully, GREVIO will continue to take up similar questions, since it is important to discuss how different types of acts should be evaluated in relation to each other and why some vulnerable groups seem to be more easily neglected than others. As the ECtHR emphasised already in *X and Y v Netherlands*, there is a need for practical and effective protection of the mentally disabled from sexual violence by means of criminal law.[88] It seems that also the question of vulnerability is best approached by demanding effective protection.

3 Sexual harassment

The Istanbul Convention mentions sexual harassment twice. First, it is stated in the preamble that

> women and girls are often exposed to serious forms of violence such as [...] sexual harassment [...] which constitute a serious violation of the human rights of women and girls and a major obstacle to the achievement of equality between women and men.

Second, according to Article 40, State Parties shall take the necessary legislative or other measures to ensure that any form of unwanted verbal, non-verbal or physical conduct of a sexual nature with the purpose or effect of violating the dignity of a person, in particular when creating an intimidating, hostile, degrading, humiliating or offensive environment, is subject to criminal or other

85 Austrian NGO Shadow Report to GREVIO, 70.
86 GREVIO's Evaluation Report on Denmark, para 178.
87 GREVIO's Evaluation Report on Denmark, para 179.
88 *X. and Y. v the Netherlands* App no 8978/80 (ECHR, 26 March 1985) paras 27 and 30.

legal sanction. Even though harassment is violence according to the preamble, the choice to place it in an article of its own implies that it has a different status from other forms of sexual violence.

The Istanbul Convention, especially when read together with the Explanatory Report, leaves State Parties with a broad margin of appreciation regarding how to bring their legislation on par with the Convention. As stated in Article 40, measures other than legislative are sufficient for fulfilling the requirements of the Convention. In addition, the sanctions for sexual harassment do not need to be criminal. Paragraph 207 of the Explanatory Report recommends the criminalisation of sexual harassment; at the same time, other sanctions, such as administrative or civil law sanctions are possible as well, as long as the "the law deals with sexual harassment". This approach is not in harmony with the preamble of the Convention that emphasises the severity of sexual harassment. In addition, it makes it difficult for the monitoring body to ensure that State Parties have implemented Article 40 effectively. GREVIO has noted this in its report on Finland stating that "in the absence of data on the number of cases brought under the different regimes/laws, it is difficult to assess the effectiveness of the existing legal framework".[89]

Sexual harassment is further defined in the Explanatory Report. According to paragraph 208 of the Explanatory Report, any behaviour regarded as sexual harassment (1) must be of a sexual nature, (2) must be unwanted on the part of the victim and (3) must have the purpose or effect of violating the dignity of the victim. The dignity of the victim is violated if the conduct in question creates an intimidating, hostile, degrading, humiliating or offensive environment. As stated in the same paragraph, the concept of "environment" is intended to capture a pattern of behaviour whose individual elements may not reach the level of what is usually considered punishable. Typically, sexual harassment is a combination of acts, not a singular act. Verbal conduct refers to jokes, questions, and remarks, and may be expressed orally or in writing. Non-verbal conduct covers for example facial expressions, hand movements or symbols. Physical conduct refers to any sexual behaviour of the perpetrator and may include situations involving contact with the body of the victim.[90]

Sexual harassment is a very intriguing phenomenon since it mixes two discourses, namely sexual violence and discrimination, that are not always clearly distinguished. First, it can be understood as the least severe sexual offence with a distinct sexual purpose. This is the case, for example, in Austria and Denmark, where sexual harassment is criminalised with a general clause for all sexually offensive acts not falling into other categories.[91] Sexual harassment can also

89 GREVIO's Evaluation Report on Finland, para 181.

90 Explanatory Report, para 208.

91 Straffeloven §232, available at: https://danskelove.dk/straffeloven/232 (visited on 15 October 2019); § 218 Österreichisches Strafgesetzbuch, available at: www.jusline.at/gesetz/stgb/paragraf/218 (visited on 15 October 2019).

present abuse of power typically related to working life, with the purpose and/or effect of humiliation and degradation. This type of harassment is in the Nordic countries usually tackled in equality legislation and in the framework of safety at work. The main difference from the victim's point of view is that criminal law is typically more state-driven and there is a prosecutor in charge of bringing the case forward, whereas equality law is a hybrid of administrative, civil and labour law with less clear roles. Demanding civil law remedies based on equality law involves also risks which might take the form of high litigation costs. From the point of view of the State, the means used in improving equality in working life are often softer, such as awareness raising campaigns and multi-stakeholder initiatives, encouraging the private sector into zero tolerance rather than punishing for non-compliance. In relation to the Istanbul Convention, these measures fall into the scope of Article 17 on participation of the private sector.[92]

Both of these two discourses, the one emphasising the sexual crime and the other emphasising the imbalance of power, are present in the Explanatory Report, but they are not clearly distinguished from each other. One of the problems I see here is that the Convention requires the acts to be of a sexual nature, but it does not define what counts as sexual. The intent of the perpetrator can differ significantly depending on the context of the act, as stated above. The question remains whether the point of view should be that of the perpetrator or that of the victim, or whether we can perhaps find an objective, shared standard of what counts as sexual. Does it suffice that a person is victimised due to their sex/gender or must there be a sexual intention or undertone in the act, as is the case regarding Article 36? For example, in the Finnish Equality Act that concerns working life, there is a distinction between sexual and gender-based harassment, marking that not even all harassment directed against women bears a clear sexual marker. This is a controversy that the Convention does not recognise and tackle.

So far, it is not possible to distinguish a coherent stance regarding sexual harassment in the country-by-country monitoring by GREVIO. This might have to do with the fact that legislation in countries such as Albania, Austria,[93] Denmark and Sweden seem to be in line with Article 40 of the Convention.[94]

92 See e.g. GREVIO's Evaluation Report on Portugal, paras 111–113, in which the Portuguese Working Conditions Authority and Commission for Equality in Labour and Employment are praised for their initiatives in this field.

93 The Austrian NGOs, however, pointed out that the wording of the § 218 StGB (1)(2)(1a) does not include a definition of which areas are to be viewed as belonging to a person's sexual sphere (in German "eine der Geschlechtssphäre zuzuordnenden Körperstelle"). Only the explanatory report published with the amendment of the law lists specific parts of the body (in particular the buttocks and thighs) as meeting this definition. (Austria NGO Shadow Report to GREVIO, 71). See also the Austrian State Report, 47.

94 See e.g. GREVIO's (Baseline) Evaluation Report on legislative and other measures giving effect to the provisions of the Council of Europe Convention on Preventing and Combating Violence against Women and Domestic Violence (Istanbul Convention) ALBANIA, GREVIO/Inf(2017)13, Published on 24 November 2017, para 155.

The definition of sexual harassment has only been discussed in the baseline report regarding Portugal, in which GREVIO criticised the Portuguese Criminal Code for being too restrictive. As stated in the report, sexual harassment is defined in Article 170 of the Portuguese Criminal Code as the conduct of importuning the victim "by way of performing exhibitionist acts, formulating sexual proposals or compelling [the victim] to a contact of a sexual nature". GREVIO found that the wording was not aligned with Article 40 since this provision covers any verbal, non-verbal or physical conduct of a sexual nature unwanted by the victim, regardless of whether it qualifies as "exhibitionist" behaviour or a sexual "proposal".[95] Both GREVIO and the Committee of the Parties recommended Portugal to amend its criminal law.[96]

In Finland, there is strong consensus among feminist scholars that the implementation of the Istanbul Convention in regard to sexual harassment has been a failure.[97] In light of this position, it will be interesting to see to what extent GREVIO will challenge the Finnish legislation in this respect. Finland is the only Nordic country that has left out verbal and non-verbal acts from the criminalisation of sexual harassment. Rather, only "sexually significant acts by touching",[98] described by the Finnish government as the "most severe form of harassment",[99] are punishable by criminal law. I do agree that this is insufficient. Verbal and non-verbal harassment are sanctioned only by the Equality Act and Occupational Safety and Health Act addressing the employer.[100] In light of the Finnish situation, it would be possible to discuss to what extent civil law sanctions against the employer can be considered as sufficient implementation of Article 40 that does emphasise the responsibility of the harasser. Finally, the twofold legislative approach might also open up the discussion of whether sexual harassment is, in the end, about violating the sexual self-determination of

95 GREVIO's Evaluation Report on Portugal, para 174.

96 GREVIO's Evaluation Report on Portugal, para 175; Committee of the Parties: Recommendation on the implementation of the Council of Europe Convention on Preventing and Combating Violence against Women and Domestic Violence by Portugal. IC-CP/Inf(2019)3, Published on 28 January 2019, 4.

97 K Nousiainen and M Pentikäinen, 'Naisiin kohdistuva väkivalta ihmisoikeuskysymyksenä. Suomi alisuorittajana' in J Niemi, H Kainulainen and P Honkatukia (eds), ***Sukupuolistunut väkivalta. Oikeudellinen ja sosiaalinen ongelma*** (Vastapaino 2017) 51 and 63–64; F Pihlström, 'Kriminalisering av sexuella trakasserier – i gränsområdet mellan folkrättsliga plikter och kriminaliseringsprinciper' JFT 2/2018, 95–122, 107–108.

98 In the Criminal Code Chapter 20 on sexual offences, a new amendment, 5a§, was made in 2014. Before this, sexual harassment was not criminalised. In Finland, the harassing act needs to be sexually significant. T Ojala, ***Seksuaalirikokset*** (Edita 2014) 190; F Pihlström, 'Kriminalisering av sexuella trakasserier – i gränsområdet mellan folkrättsliga plikter och kriminaliseringsprinciper' JFT 2/2018, 95–122, 100 and 113.

99 Baseline report by the Government of Finland on measures giving effect to the provisions of the Council of Europe Convention on Preventing and Combating Violence against Women and Domestic Violence, April 2018, para 345.

100 See, Baseline report by the Government of Finland, paras 345–356.

the victim or about hindering women from taking an active part in the society, and in which ways these two intertwine.

4 Conclusion

The Istanbul Convention is remarkable and ambiguous, yet incomplete and controversial at the same time. It addresses many important questions; at the same time, however, it does not sufficiently offer concrete legal solutions. On the one hand, the Convention imposes many obligations on State Parties; on the other hand, it is intended to act only as an impulse for national legislators. It provides an exhaustive list of crimes but leaves significant room for national variations in the exact wordings of the elements of crimes. The question from the point of view of the Convention is more about *what*, and *not how*. This is a double-edged sword: it is perhaps more difficult to monitor the effectiveness of national implementation today, but at the same time the Convention itself may be interpreted in an evolutive way in the future.

Thus, leaving room for national variations is not necessarily a bad thing. It would not be realistic or even desirable to harmonise, for example, rape law in all State Parties. True, some commentators and GREVIO have recommended a consent-based rape law as the preferred solution; however, it should not be ignored that consent also has its weaknesses. For example, too little attention has been paid to questions such as the responsibility to communicate consent, the passivity of the victim, the validity of consent, vulnerability, and the use of free will in specific circumstances. Not to mention the problems of *mens rea* in this context. In addition, there are also other things, such as the procedural rules and principles of sentencing that need attention in the assessment of the protection that criminal law can provide. By having these variations and by comparing national laws, the problems can be identified, and best practices found.

The country-by-country monitoring conducted by GREVIO provides a great forum for discussion on what works best. This process is important for the further interpretation of the Istanbul Convention and for challenging the national solutions of implementation. This work is not made easy by the fact that, at least regarding sexual violence and sexual harassment, State Parties that do not want to amend their laws can always claim that the choice of the exact wording and sanctions is left to their discretion. There is a need for sophisticated analyses to bring together the two aims: on the one hand, ensuring that State Parties have discretion, and on the other, demanding effective solutions against sexual violence against women.

7 Exploring intersectionality

Female genital mutilation/cutting in the Istanbul Convention

Ruth M. Mestre i Mestre

1 Introduction

In recent decades, intersectionality has become a *buzzword* of feminist theory[1] with many and disparate uses of the term. It was coined by Kimberlé Crenshaw to denote the ways in which race and gender interact to shape the multiple dimensions of black women's employment experiences.[2] She criticised how anti-discrimination law failed to address black women's needs and reality, contributing to their further marginalisation. Many of the experiences black women face do not fit within the boundaries of race or gender discrimination as they are understood, and the intersection of racism and sexism required new framings. She later explored the ways in which race and gender intersect in shaping "structural, political and representational aspects" of violence against women of colour,[3] specifically rape and battering.[4]

Crenshaw's approach to intersectionality is adopted in this chapter. Intersectionality is not a policy goal, but an analytical tool that aims at understanding structural power relations. It considers that major social divisions (e.g. gender, class, race, migration status)[5] in a given time and society do not operate as

1 Linda Gordon, 'Intersectionality, Socialist Feminism and Contemporary Activism: Musings by a Second-Wave Socialist Feminist' (2016) 28(2) *Gender & History* 340.

2 Kimberlé Crenshaw, 'Demarginalizing the Intersection of Race and Sex: A Black Feminist Critique of Antidiscrimination Doctrine, Feminist Theory, and Antiracist Politics' in Katharine T Bartlett and Rosanne Kennedy (eds), *Feminist Legal Theory. Readings in Law and Gender* (Westview Press 1991). For a complete history of 'intersectionality' see Patricia Hill Collins and Sirma Bilge, *Intersectionality* (Polity Press 2016).

3 This chapter uses the terms "racialised women" and "women of colour" indistinctively; and uses "VAW of colour" to refer to "violence against women of colour". Racialisation is a process that attaches social meaning to certain group features and installs boundaries which are used to naturalise hierarchical power relations. See Floya Anthias and Nira Yuval-Davis, *Racialized Boundaries. Race, Nation, Gender, Colour and Class and the Anti-racist Struggle* (Routledge 1992).

4 Kimberlé Crenshaw, 'Mapping the Margins: Intersectionality, Identity Politics, and Violence Against Women of Color' (1991) 43 *Stan L Rev* 1241.

5 Given its actual relevance in EU countries, migration status is necessarily a social division to consider, intertwined with race, gender, and class.

exclusive entities, but work together, are intertwined, and mutually constructing. As Pragna Patel explains:

> the idea of intersectionality seeks to capture both the structural and dynamic consequences of the interaction between two or more forms of discrimination or systems of subordination. It specifically addresses the manner in which racism, patriarchy, economic disadvantage and other discriminatory systems contribute to create layers of inequality that structure the relative positions of women and men.[6]

In relation to violence against women, intersectionality is a tool for exploring the specific articulations of different discriminatory systems and their consequences, as expressed in institutions and legislation.[7] According to the Istanbul Convention (IC), gender-based violence against women refers to any harm caused to a woman as a result of the power relations that shape women's subordinate status in society.[8] As such, violence against women (VAW) needs to be addressed in the context of inequality and discrimination, existing stereotypes, and gender roles in a particular society. Because racism is always a gendered phenomenon,[9] gender roles and stereotypes are racialised and crucial in determining the distribution of resources and are therefore intertwined with class. Race, migration status, gender, and class are not distinct and isolated realms of experience but come into existence in relation to each other.[10]

Different women are located in different positions across the social web of power relations, and such positions affect the ways women experience violence. One could ask what is the articulation of the distinct systems of power that the IC expresses and what are the consequences of such articulation on racialised women. To approach these questions, this chapter analyses the ways in which race, migration, age, and other power structures intersect with gender in shaping structural, political, and representational aspects of female genital mutilation/cutting (FGM/C)[11] in the IC.

6 Quoted in United Nations, *15 Years of the UN Special Rapporteur on Violence Against Women (1994–2009) A Critical Review* (UN 2010).

7 Stefan Wallaschek indicates as a distinctive feature of postcolonial theory and intersectionality the fact that intersectionality addresses practices and experiences of people through laws and court decisions, whilst postcolonial theory works on a meta-level of representation. Stefan Wallascheck, 'In Dialogue: Postcolonial Theory and Intersectionality' (2015) 4(4) *Momentum Quarterly* 218. Precisely, the representational aspects of VAW that Crenshaw refers to constitute "research material" for postcolonial theory.

8 Explanatory Report para 44.

9 Avtar Brah, 'Reframing Europe: En-gendered Racism, Ethnicities and Nationalisms in Contemporary Western Europe' (1993) (45) *Feminist Review* 9, 12.

10 Avtar Brah and Ann Phoenix, 'Ain't I a Woman? Revisiting Intersectionality' (2004) 5(3) *Journal of International Women's Studies* 75, 76.

11 The acronym FGM (female genital mutilation) is widely used for the legal context but many researchers prefer circumcision and/or cutting (FGC). The terminological compromise FGM/C will be used in this chapter.

2 Exploring intersectionality in anti-racist feminist literature

This chapter uses Crenshaw's work as a starting point to understand intersectionality[12] within the context of a wider ongoing project[13] developed since the eighties and nineties by many anti-racist feminist groups and academics.[14] Anti-racist feminism addresses the ways in which racism and sexism operate simultaneously to oppress racialised women. Race and gender are key in the generation of class differences since they are two of the primary determinants for the distribution of social resources.[15] As gender relates to the way in which sexual difference is represented and organised, it is a product of social relations – including those of class and ethnicity that are time and space specific.[16] Anti-racist feminism rejects additive approaches to oppression:[17] "to be a Black woman is not another way of being working class, or even a particular type of working-class person" since everybody has a race/gender/class specific social location.[18] The replacement of additive models of oppression by interlocking models is crucial as it enables inclusive thinking about oppressions and the recognition of the varying amounts of privilege and penalty every group receives in a particular

12 Such as a "*body of normative theory and empirical research* in which more than one *category of difference* plays a role in the examination of complex political problems and processes." See Ange-Marie Hancock, 'Intersectionality as a Normative and Empirical Paradigm' (2007) 3(2) *Politics & Gender* 248, 251. Intersectionality is also a *frame* for "detecting whether gender is seen to intersect and if so, how, and with which inequalities in policies addressing VAW." See Emanuela Lombardo and Lise Roladsen Agustín, 'Framing Gender Intersections in the European Union: What Implications for the Quality of Intersectionality in Policies?' (2011) 19(4) *Social Politics* 482, 488. Intersectionality is also a *policy design* that draws attention to the needs of particular groups of women. See Celeste Montoya and Lise Roladsen Agustín, 'The Othering of Domestic Violence: The EU and Cultural Framings of Violence against Women' (2013) 20(4) *Social Politics* 534, 537. Intersectionality is also "[a] *concept* that captures the interaction between gender, race, and other categories of difference in individual lives, social practices, institutional arrangements, and cultural ideologies, and the outcomes of these interactions in terms of power". See Shazia Choudry, 'Towards a Transformative Conceptualisation of Violence Against Women – A Critical Frame Analysis of the Council of Europe Discourse on Violence Against Women' (2016) 79 (3) *Modern Law Review* 406, 437.

13 Patricia Hill Collins, 'Intersectionality's Definitional Dilemmas' (2015) 41 *Annual Review of Sociology* 1.

14 See Angela P Harris, *Critical Race Theory*, University of California, Davis 2012 (Available at https://works.bepress.com/angela_harris/17/).

15 According to Gordon (n 1, 342) in the eighties "only radical feminists saw sexism as the main injustice (…) the majority of feminists understood that racial, class, and international injustices had sources independent of male dominance, although usually intertwined with and strengthened by male dominance".

16 Anthias and Yuval-Davis (n 3)101.

17 Bell Hooks, *Ain't I a Woman? Black Women and Feminism* (Pluto Press 1981); Patricia Hill Collins, *Black Feminist Thought. Knowledge, Consciousness, and the Politics of Empowerment* (Routledge 1991).

18 Nira Yuval-Davis, 'Intersectionality and Feminist Politics' (2006) 13(3) *European Journal of Women's Studies* 193.

society.[19] In other words, depending on the context, or the social relation at stake, an individual can be an oppressor or oppressed.[20]

The distinctive systems of oppression are part of an overarching matrix,[21] with different sites of domination and resistance: the individual biography, the community experience and the institutional/systemic level. This explains that women from the same ethnic group, class, or family face different forms of oppression: no two individuals occupy the same social space.[22] The matrix of domination operates at different levels, expressing social divisions in institutions, organisations and the law. This approach theorises social distinctions and oppressions in a non-essentialist way. Intersectionality is about

> how exclusions and subordinations are linked to produce diverse outcomes with regard to the placement of collective subjects within the different major divisions that construct them. That is … to look at the intersections between class, ethnicity, race and gender divisions and processes within the state.[23]

Thus, understanding oppression requires asking how social divisions shape institutions and the power and personal relations of people.

An intersectional approach[24] to a social problem must identify the matrix of oppression, the interlocking systems and their particular articulations regarding

19 Patricia Hill Collins, 'Toward a New Vision. Race, Class and Gender as Categories of Analysis and Connection' in Margaret Andersen and Patricia Hill Collins (eds), *Race Class and Gender: An Anthology* (5th Edition Wadsworth 2013).

20 Collins, *Black Feminist Thought* (n 17) 226; bell hooks, *Ain't I a Woman* (n 17). This is particularly important because white feminists failed to adequately address racism and their own position of power. See also bell hooks, *Killing Rage, Ending Racism* (Penguin Books 1995) 99. "Imperial feminism" refers to the assumption of a unity of women's interest on the basis of white women's experience, Anthias and Yuval-Davis (n 3) 101. Chandra T Mohanty discusses the notion of "women's experiences": far from being a neutral unitary category, women's experiences need to be construed and interpreted, identified, and explained in their particular historical context of race/class and gender. Chandra T Mohanty, 'Feminist Encounters: Locating the Politics of Experience' in Ann Phillips (ed.), *Feminism and Politics* (Oxford Readings in Feminism, Oxford University Press 1998).

21 bell hooks, *Killing Rage* (n 20); Collins, *Black Feminist Thought* (n 17).

22 Collins, *Black Feminist Thought* (n 17). See also Aisha Gill and Avtar Brah, 'Interrogating Cultural Narratives about 'Honour'-Based Violence' (2014) 21(1) *European Journal of Women's Studies* 72.

23 Anthias and Yuval-Davis (n 3) 20; Yuval-Davis (n 18) 198.

24 Collins' provisional list of assumptions for intersectional projects comprises that: (1) race, class, gender, sexuality, and similar categories of analysis, are best understood in relational terms; and (2) these mutually constructing categories underlie and shape intersecting systems of power; (3) producing complex social inequalities that are organised via unequal material realities and distinctive social experiences; and (4) vary across time and space; (5) individuals and groups that are differently positioned within these intersecting systems of power advance different knowledge projects that reflect their social position; and (6) upholding or contesting that particular *status quo*. Intersectional knowledge projects may embrace one, some combination, or all the assumptions. Collins, 'Dilemmas' (n 13). For an alternative see Hancock (n 12).

that problem, and the unequal material realities and experiences that such articulation favours in a particular moment and place.[25] Intersectionality does not speak of identity and difference – but of power and inequality.

Sirma Bilge warns about intersectionality being subject to a "whitening" process[26] that limits its critical potential. Whitening strategies include denying the relevance of race and racism in Europe (except for the UK) and considering race an optional category; equating race to non-whiteness, "making non-whiteness as the racial modifier of gender, sexuality, class and so on". Additive models of discrimination or presenting gender (identity) as race neutral participate in this whitening strategy. Another strategy consists of taking whiteness into account as an identity dissociated from power structures.

To avoid reducing intersectionality critical potential, this chapter focuses on the role of race and racism in the conceptualisation of particular forms of VAW in the IC. Thus, the chapter avoids making non-whiteness the racial modifier of gender and class, rejects the idea that the IC provisions are race neutral, and analyses the ways in which whiteness plays a role in power structures. Today's racism is fundamentally cultural racism, that is, a practice that denies the relevance of race, but justifies discriminatory treatment on acquired characteristics. When a certain social position of a group or a certain social problem is explained in terms of culture, we should "be on the lookout for cultural racism".[27] This specially affects migrants and refugees, as well as certain practices and forms of VAW addressed as "culturally motivated".

Intersectional frameworks have been widely used to rethink social problems, including VAW.[28] Crenshaw's first analysis is particularly useful to discuss how the experiences of racialised women are the result of intersecting patterns of racism and sexism and how those experiences are excluded from the agendas of anti-racist groups and feminist groups, expressed in the legislation and policies

25 As a *work-in-progress,* an intersectional analysis limits itself to specific structures of power and specific articulations that are particular, provisional, and incomplete. See Devon Carbado, Kimberlé Crenshaw, Vickie Mays and Barbara Tomlison, 'Intersectionality. Mapping the Movements of a Theory' (2013) 10(2) *Du Bois Review* 303.

26 Bilge and Mohanty alert against the de-politising of intersectionality in the "broader context of the incorporation of various progressive struggles into market-driven and state-sanctioned diversity govermentality", Sirma Bilge, 'Whitening Intersectionality. Evanescence of Race in Intersectionality Scholarship' in Wulf Hund and Alana Lentin (eds), *Racism and Sociology* (Racism Analysis Yearbook 5, Lit Verlag-Routledge, 2014) 180. Neoliberalism turns "insurgent knowledge" into a commodity, and the epistemological and methodological claims of antiracist feminism into a privatised politics of representation. Chandra T Mohanty, 'Transnational Feminist Crossing: On Neoliberalism and Radical Critique' (2013) *Signs (Intersectionality: Theorizing Power Empowering Theory)* 38(4) 967, 971. Bilge denounces the *whitening* of intersectionality, particularly in European academic circles that present it as 'the brainchild of feminism and gender studies', omitting the constitutive character of race.

27 James Blaut, 'The Theory of Cultural Racism' (1992) 24(4) *Antipode* 289.

28 See Collins and Bilge (n 2); Collins, 'Dilemmas' (n 13).

addressing violence.[29] By "structural aspects" of VAW of colour she referred to how the varying locations of women make their experience, needs, and required remedies qualitatively different from each other. Violence as such might not be different (rape is rape) but responses that ignore the multi-layered dimensions of the subordination of racialised women fail to identify their needs, and properly allocate resources to fight "the routinized forms of domination that converge" in their lives.[30]

In this structural aspect, intersectional subordination is not necessarily intentional, but results from "the imposition of one burden that interacts with preexisting vulnerabilities to create another dimension of disempowerment".[31] Thus, structural aspects highlight the "unmet needs" and the "imposed burdens" to certain women by public responses to particular forms of VAW.

How violence is conceptualised and politicised by feminist and anti-racist groups matters, as it can be problematic to point at some forms of violence being "specific" to certain women. "Othering" the problem not only reinforces stereotypes, but can also lead to disregarding the problem as a "minority issue". Yet saying that a particular form of VAW affects "all women equally" may bring to the centre the "standard experiences of white women", further silencing minority women. Precisely because "tokenistic inclusion can be as disempowering as complete exclusion",[32] the political aspects of VAW of colour map how racism and patriarchy shape the conceptualisation of particular forms of VAW.

Finally, the representational aspects of VAW of colour draw attention to the ways in which racialised women are devaluated in cultural imaginary;[33] how stereotypes and images are construed in different narratives that "justify" the unequal treatment racialised women receive from public institutions and the law. The following sections analyse the ways in which race, migration and age intersect with gender in shaping the political, structural and representational aspects of FGM/C in the IC.

3 FGM/C in Europe

FGM/C comprises all procedures involving the partial or total removal of the external female genitalia, as well as other injuries to the female genital organs for non-medical reasons. The *Interagency Statement* acknowledges four types:

29 Crenshaw, 'Mapping' (n 4).

30 Ibid. 1245.

31 Ibid. 1249.

32 Crenshaw 'Mapping' (n 4) 1261.

33 Intersectionality differs from the critique made by black feminism for the absence of racialised women and for white feminism essentialising the category "woman". Intersectionality is grounded in the understanding that categories have a meaning and a consequence in a particular social context, and that there is power in the process of categorising. Crenshaw, 'Mapping' (n 4) 1298.

clitoridectomy, excision, infibulations and *unclassified* (Type IV).[34] FGM/C is practiced in 29 African countries, a few countries within Asia and the Middle East, as well as in some indigenous communities in Latin America. Being a practice that marks gender and ethnic identity, not all ethnic groups in the practicing countries perform FGM/C. Thus, the percentage of women aged 15 to 49 years who have undergone FGM/C can range from 8% in Iraq to 76% in Gambia or 98% in Somalia.[35] The procedures are performed by women who receive respect and recognition, have a powerful position in their communities and make a living from this and other practices. The variety and character of the procedures, and the different reasons for upholding the practice makes FGM/C a particularly complex issue.[36] The fact that some groups perform it on adult women whilst others do it on girls further complicates the discussion.

FGM/C is nowadays present in Europe mainly because of the arrival of migrants and refugees from practising African countries. Nevertheless, similar practices have been performed in Europe[37] and it remains a regular practice with intersex babies. The European Parliament considers that 500,000 women in Europe live with some form of FGM/C and that 180,000 girls are at risk every year.[38]

34 The *Interagency Statement* establishes the internationally agreed terminology and classification for FGM/C:

> Type I: Partial or total removal of the clitoris and/or the prepuce (clitoridectomy). Type II: Partial or total removal of the clitoris and the labia minora, with or without excision of the labia majora (excision). Type III: Narrowing of the vaginal orifice with creation of a covering seal by cutting and appositioning of the labia minora and/or the labia majora, with or without excision of the clitoris (infibulation). Type IV: All other harmful procedures to the female genitalia for non-medical purposes, for example: pricking, piercing, incising, scraping and cauterization.

WHO, OHCHR, UNAIDS, UNDP, UNECA, UNESCO, UNFPA, UNHCR, UNICEF, and UNIFEM, *Eliminating Female Genital Mutilation: An Interagency Statement* (World Health Organization, Department of Reproductive Health and Research 2008).

35 UNICEF, *Female Genital Mutilation/Cutting: A Statistical Overview and Exploration of the Dynamics of Change* (UNICEF 2013).

36 See Christine Walley, 'Searching for 'Voices': Feminism, Anthropology, and the Global Debate over Female Genital Operations', in Stanlie James and Claire Robertson (eds), *Genital Cutting and Transnational Sisterhood. Disputing U.S. Polemics* (University of Illinois Press 2005); IR Gunning, 'Arrogant Perception, World-Traveling and Multicultural Feminism: The Case of Female Genital Surgeries' (1992) (23) *Colum Hum Rts L Rev* 189.

37 Apparently, clitoridectomy was a "cure" for mental disorder in Europe until the nineteenth century and in the United States until at least 1937. Gunning (n 36), 195 and 207.

38 European Parliament resolution of March 24, 2009 on Combating FGM in the EU (2008/2071 (INI)).

However, the lack of systematic data collection is a main challenge in developing prevalence or incidence estimates of FGM/C in Europe.[39]

3.1 European responses before the signing of the IC

Across Europe, NGOs and community-based organisations have been working and networking on the eradication of FGM/C since the early eighties, focussing on prevention, lobbying and advocacy, and stressing the fact that a multidisciplinary approach in collaboration with potentially affected communities is crucial for behavioural change.[40] Despite this consensus, a recent exploratory survey concluded that the role of community-based organisations remains inconsistent in FGM/C interventions across Europe and is often non-existent in policy development.[41] The study identified cultural, structural, and sustainability-related barriers to the participation of potentially affected communities. The interviewed activists and professionals explained that opposing FGM/C is not easy for community members. Women may fear bringing shame on their families and communities if they speak out, and leadership can be especially difficult. Gender roles within the group may affect the options and spaces open to women for challenging strategies. However, public agencies need to find ways to support leaders and engage communities in intervention programmes.

Participants felt it is wrong to focus on FGM/C as an isolated problem because this fails to account for gendered social norms, and for other needs and

39 The European Institute for Gender Equality (EIGE) called attention to the fact that collecting prevalence data on FGM is very complicated due to limitations on the accepted method of "extrapolation-of-country of origin-prevalence-data". EIGE, *Female Genital Mutilation in the European Union Report* (EIGE 2013). Calculating "girls at risk" consists in counting the girls in a European country with parents originating from practising countries, and multiplying that number with the prevalence percentages in the concerned countries. It has been criticised as exaggerating the scope of the problem, building on essentialist views of vulnerability and disregarding the fact that migration can lead to cultural change. See Sara Johnsdotter and Birgitta Essén, 'Cultural Change after Migration: Circumcision of Girls in Western Migrant Communities' (2016) *Best Practice & Research: Clinical Obstetrics & Gynaecology* 15; Sara Johnsdotter and Ruth M Mestre i Mestre, 'Female Genital Mutilation in Europe: Public Discourse versus Empirical Evidence' (2017) (51) *International Journal of Law, Crime and Justice* 14. In 2015 a new methodology was tested in the EIGE study *Estimation of Girls at Risk of FGM in the EU* (EIGE 2015), followed by a step-by-step guide to apply the method.

40 Els Leye, Soetkin Bauwens and Owolabi Bjälkander, *Behavioral Change towards Female Genital Mutilation: Lessons Learned from Africa and Europe* (ICHR 2005) 20.

41 Elaine Connelly, Nina Murray, Hellen Baillot, et al., 'Missing from the Debate? A Qualitative Study Exploring the Role of Communities within Interventions to Address Female Genital Mutilation in Europe' (2018) 8 *BMJ Open* 1. They suggest the term "potentially affected communities" to avoid presumptions attached to "FGM practising communities" that may be inaccurate in a migration context.

violence that women suffer.[42] Finally, they complain that the participation of communities is often expected on a pro-bono basis and is inadequately funded and supported.

The lack of consistent engagement with communities has led to a failure to effectively link protection with prevention. Public efforts to reduce FGM/C have not focused on empowering women to engage in debates and create alternatives from within communities.[43] European States have developed diverse protocols and measures that are administrative or civil in nature,[44] but have focused on responses through criminal prosecutions. Despite the fact that FGM is prosecutable in all European countries (either through specific or general criminal legislation)[45] a 2015 comparative overview of FGM/C criminal court cases in eleven European countries showed few litigated cases.[46] The disparity between the number of officially estimated affected women and "girls at risk", and the scarcity of criminal court cases remains a matter of concern, and has been interpreted as a failure: a failure to detect and prosecute FGM/C and protect European girls.[47]

Unsurprisingly, supporting Member States in prosecuting FGM/C more effectively has been an explicit European policy goal since 2013.[48] Prosecution is a fair response to any act of gender-based violence because it can provide redress to the victims and supports the idea that VAW must be investigated, and the perpetrator appropriately punished regardless of the type of act and the background of the victim.[49] Prosecution can also have a deterrent effect and

42 Ibid. 7: "Participants indicated that separating FGM from issues like domestic violence was a major problem. [...] They are seen as completely separate topics or discrete topics as opposed to how these principles cut across the way we navigate our communities and navigate our spaces".

43 Moira Dustin, 'Female Genital Mutilation/Cutting in the UK: Challenging the Inconsistencies' (2010) 17(7) *European Journal of Women's Studies* 1350.

44 To my knowledge, no comparative Europe-wide study of such protective measures has been published. Studies regarding asylum procedures are general and not FGM/C specific. See n 62 below.

45 See EIGE 2013 (n 40).

46 Sara Johnsdotter and Ruth M Mestre i Mestre, *FGM in Europe: An Analysis of Court Cases and Rumours* (European Commission: Directorate-General for Justice. Publication Office of the European Union 2015). The study analysed 20 recent criminal court cases in ten EU countries and Switzerland. Around 50 FGM criminal court cases exist in Europe, and a majority of them took place in France in the eighties and nineties.

47 Johnsdotter and Mestre i Mestre, 'Public Discourse' (n 39).

48 Commission, 'Communication from the Commission to the European Parliament and the Council: Towards the Elimination of Female Genital Mutilation' (Communication) COM (2013) 833 final.

49 Or, as Susan Moller Okin put it, "When a woman from a more patriarchal culture comes to some western liberal State, she should not be less protected from violence than other women are". Susan M Okin, 'Is Multiculturalism Bad for Women? in Joshua Cohen, Matthew Howard, and Martha C Nussbaum (eds), *Is Multiculturalism Bad for Women? Susan Moller Okin with Respondents* (Princeton University Press 1999) 20.

effectively prevent future cases. However, repeated allegations of widely persisting acts of FGM/C in Europe may increase the risk of some girls undergoing the practice.[50]

Prosecution itself may entail negative effects, such as stigmatising and revictimising families and communities. Further research is needed to assess the impact that different public prosecution models have on protection against VAW in general and FGM/C in particular. Prosecution in Europe proves to be particularly difficult when the alleged act occurred in the country of origin. Since 2001, the European Parliament has required States to ensure jurisdiction for *all* offences committed *within and beyond its territory* when the offence is committed *to* or *by* one of their nationals or a person who has habitual residence in their territory, and whether the act is criminalised in the territory where it was committed or not.[51]

The reason for this lies in the fear that girls may undergo FGM/C while visiting family in the countries of origin and in the fear that families will submit the girls to the practice before migrating knowing the legal consequences in Europe. However, asserting European jurisdiction to prosecute any act of FGM/C performed by a resident, regardless of the place of commission and of the relation with Europe of the victim of such a crime is an example of symbolic criminal law focusing on migrants.

The 2015 comparative study suggested distinguishing between typical and atypical cases. Such a distinction aimed at connecting court cases to the cultural realities of the practising communities in that labelling a case as being typical or atypical requires previous knowledge about the practices and communities, and the migration status in Europe of those involved.[52]

Typical cases refer to acts of FGM by or to a European national or resident, either in or outside Europe. Evidence shows that the most typical cases under European jurisdiction are those performed in African countries to girls who have a connection with Europe.[53] Conversely, atypical cases are cases in which prosecution takes place following an *unlikely* FGM/C act, in the sense that the

50 Johnsdotter and Mestre i Mestre, 'Public Discourse' (n 39).

51 European Parliament resolution on FGM (2001/2035 (INI)).

52 For a detailed discussion see Ruth M Mestre i Mestre and Sara Johnsdotter, 'Court Cases, Cultural Expertise and "Female Genital Mutilation" in Europe' in A Sarat (ed.), *Cultural Expertise and Socio-Legal Studies: Special Issue* (2019) *Studies in Law, Politics and Society* (78) 95.

53 Nevertheless, in at least one Spanish case a resident was convicted for an FGM/C act that had occurred in an African country to a girl who was not a resident in Europe at the moment of the commission. In 2011, a woman from Senegal was accused of performing FGM on her daughter before arriving in Catalonia. The High Court (*Audiencia Nacional*) noted that because she was living in a rural area of Senegal she could not be expected to have known the laws of Spain. However, the court claimed (extraterritorial) jurisdiction because the father was living in Catalonia at the time (Spanish High Court/ Audiencia Nacional AN 13/2011). For a discussion about error in prohibition and cultural difference see Mestre i Mestre and Johnsdotter, 'Court Cases' (n 52).

alleged author or victim do not belong to a practising community; or the act does not qualify as FGM. Atypical would also be a case in which, considering the practising community the victim belongs to, it is incorrect to point to the alleged actor as responsible for the crime.

The distinction shows the relevance of cultural expertise in the legal handling of cases and in assessing the legitimacy of public intervention.[54] Atypical cases produce unfair results because stereotypes guide the interpretations of testimonies, overlooking the complex cultural, social, and gender dimensions of the issue while producing real harm.[55] The use of stereotypes disregards the fact that living in the diaspora provides women opportunities to talk with circumcised and non-circumcised women;[56] and provides all members of potentially affected communities with opportunities to redefine and reinterpret social norms.[57] This eventually produces a significant change in attitudes.

Regarding asylum, as early as 2002, the Council of Europe Committee of Ministers recommended Member States to consider the possibility of granting special protection to affected women as a threatened group for gender-based reasons.[58] In 2009, the European Parliament affirmed that FGM/C constitutes a violation of human rights, and demonstrated concern about the increasing number of asylum requests made by parents who had refused consent for their child to undergo FGM/C. Mistrust informs the 2009 Recommendation, as it encourages Member States to carefully analyse such claims, and to regularly check the daughters of those granted asylum to ensure they remain uncut.[59] Hence the apparent paradox of widely recognising FGM/C as a gendered human rights violation whilst denying asylum in national and international courts.[60]

54 Ibid.

55 See Audrey Macklin, 'The Double-edged Sword: Using the Criminal Law Against Female Criminal Mutilation in Canada' in Rogaia Mustafa Abusharaf (ed.) *Female Circumcision. Multicultural Perspectives* (University of Pennsylvania Press 2006); Mestre i Mestre and Johnsdotter, 'Court Cases' (n 53).

56 Connelly et al. (n 42) 11: "Safe, women-only spaces were considered important for women to discover for themselves the nature of their reality …" As one participant noted, "one of the mistakes we make is that we assume everyone knows that FGM is harmful whereas many women from communities or women who have experienced FGM don't see that".

57 Anna Wahlberg, Sara Johnsdotter, Katarina Ekholm Selling et al., 'Baseline Data from a Planned RCT on Attitudes to Female Genital Cutting after Migration: When Are Interventions Justified?' (2017) 7 *BMJ Open* 1.

58 The Council of Europe Committee of Ministers Recommendation Rec (2002) on the Protection of Women against Violence, para 67. See Morondo in this volume.

59 European Parliament resolution of 24 March 2009 on combating female genital mutilation in the EU (2008/2071(INI)).

60 See Council of Europe, *Gender Related Asylum Claims in Europe* (Directorate General for Internal Policies 2012). For the first FGM asylum cases see Carmen Miguel Juan, *Refugiadas* (Catarata 2016). For ECHR cases, see n 77 below.

3.2 FGM/C in the IC

The IC confirmed the homogeneous framework that the EU and Council of Europe had established. It specifically addresses FGM in Chapter V, making the 3Ps framework (prevention, protection, and prosecution) applicable.[61] This framework and the comprehensive nature of the IC can be a useful tool to address FGM/C by imposing the duties to diligently prevent, protect, and prosecute – as well as diligently support with integrated policies women and girls affected or "at risk".[62]

The different IC obligations can be adapted to the reality of FGM/C. For instance, "addressing gender stereotypes" (Article 12) relates to challenging the justifications of the practice; "protecting and supporting women through general and specific support services that are accessible and appropriate" (Articles 18, 20, and 22) may mean that States must ensure healthcare for affected women regardless of their migration status; "offering restraining protection orders for women or girls at immediate risk" (Article 53) can be done by enabling courts to withdraw travel permission when necessary and so on. Therefore, the IC provisions provide support and justification for many policies that are already being implemented.

However, FGM/C is different from other forms of VAW in ways that require closer attention. For instance, the IC does not distinguish between the needs of affected women and the needs of potentially affected girls. FGM/C is a type of violence that occurs once in a lifetime (as different from rape or stalking) and can produce life-long health and physical consequences. Families that submit their girls to the practice are not abusive families, so schemes for child protection that are not culture- and child-sensitive risk revictimising the child and the family.

The IC requires States to criminalise female genital mutilation (Article 38). More specifically, the following conducts have to be criminalised:

a. excising, infibulating or performing any other mutilation on the whole or any part of a woman's labia majora, labia minora or clitoris;
b. coercing or procuring a woman to undergo any of the acts listed in point *a*;
c. inciting, coercing or procuring a girl to undergo any of the acts listed in point *a*.

The provision addresses procedures performed on girls and women. It comprises the person performing the act itself (including medical professionals); any person

61 The drafters thought a fourth "P" for "integrated Policies" was important. Connelly et al. (n 41) propose a fifth "P" for Participation in policy making and implementation.

62 For a detailed analysis of the IC implementation regarding FGM/C see Council of Europe-Amnesty International, *The Council of Europe Convention on Preventing and Combating VAW and Domestic Violence. A Tool to End Female Genital Mutilation* (Council of Europe 2014); and the more recent Council of Europe, *Female Genital Mutilation and Forced Marriage* (Council of Europe 2018).

coercing or procuring an adult woman to undergo FGM, and "anyone, in particular parents, grandparents or other relatives" who coerce a girl to undergo the procedure.[63] Aiding or abetting and attempting the commission of the offence must also be considered an offence. The IC restates the obligation for extraterritoriality when the offense is committed *to* or *by* a national or a habitual resident of a State, without requiring double incrimination (Article 44).[64]

Article 12(5) of the IC states that culture, tradition, or custom cannot be invoked to justify any act of VAW. Further reinforcing this, Article 42 requires that criminal law and criminal procedural law prohibit the use of cultural defence in court.[65] Culture or tradition cannot be invoked in court as a justification for FGM, but the criminalisation of FGM cannot be interpreted as a restriction of cultural or religious rights and freedoms of the perpetrator,[66] thus denying the relevance of adult women's consent to undergo FGM.

4 An intersectional approach to FGM/C in the IC

Let us now very briefly explore if intersectionality could be a useful approach following Crenshaw's proposal by analysing the (1) political, (2) representational and (3) structural aspects of FGM/C in the IC. The *political aspect* requires us to explore if FGM/C has been conceptualised in disempowering ways for racialised women. The FGM/C provision not only breaks the principle of gender neutrality of the Convention (male circumcision is not criminalised), but it is the only provision referring to a racialised female subject. It specifically addresses "the traditional practice of cutting away certain parts of the female genitalia which some communities perform on their female members".[67] It is conceived as a culturally motivated crime:

> an act by a member of a minority culture, which is considered an offense by the legal system ... (but) is nevertheless, within the cultural group of the offender, condoned, accepted as normal behaviour and approved and even endorsed and promoted in the given situation.[68]

63 Explanatory Report paras 199 and 201.

64 The IC imposes the duty to allow prosecution of FGM until well after the victim has reached adulthood, although some States, such as France, have made a reservation to this provision.

65 The existing defence of *error juris* may apply. For a discussion see Mestre i Mestre and Johnsdotter, 'Court Cases' (n 52).

66 Explanatory Report para 89. See also Choudry (n 12).

67 Explanatory Report para 198. In the IC, "forced marriage" is a racialised crime that is gender neutral and "forced sterilisation" is gendered, but ethnic free. Male circumcision is not criminalised, and the rest of the provisions are gender neutral.

68 Jeroen Van Broeck, 'Cultural Defence and Culturally Motivated Crimes' (2001) *European Journal of Crime, Criminal Law and Criminal Justice* 1, 5. This terminology is used in Spain and Italy. Maria Luisa Maqueda Abreu, *Razones y sinrazones para una criminología feminista* (Dyckinson 2014); Mestre i Mestre and Johnsdotter, 'Court Cases' (n 52).

FGM/C is something "outsiders do" and different from the violence "women" suffer as a result of unequal power relations.

The exclusion of Type IV confirms the idea that the provision is racialised. Article 38 covers FGM/C Types I to III of the Interagency Statement, criminalising excision and infibulation.[69] The reference to "any other mutilation" includes clitoridectomy. However, it is doubtful that acts that do not result in a mutilation, such as pricking or piercing (Type IV) could be subsumed. Type IV puts the focus on female genital alterations that are not performed for medical reasons, nor linked to traditional practices, but are common in Western societies.

By ignoring Type IV and excluding criminal liability when valid consent has been given or a medical procedure is at stake,[70] the IC establishes a double standard regarding female genital alterations. FGM is a harmful traditional practice that cannot be excused, justified, or consented, but Western practices of genital modifications are medical procedures that can be consented. A racial differentiation of the meaning of genital alteration is created by law. The autonomy that white Western women enjoy over their bodies is denied to black migrant women.

Conceiving FGM/C as culturally motivated crimes provides a particular framework for the interpretation of acts that reinforce cultural essentialism and reifies culture. Racialised women appear as victims of their culture, rather than actors with a willingness and capacity to engage and participate in individual and collective decisions about their lives and bodies. When culture is the explanation given to violence experienced by "other women", the tension between universality of oppression and cultural diversity is resolved through the perfect *victim subject*,[71] which seems to legitimise a paternalistic and criminal response from the State.

Addressing all female genital alterations equally would have the effect of not criminalising minority groups, and would question other body modifications shaped by gender, class, and race (such as vaginoplasty). However, it risks putting white women's needs, experiences, and realities at the centre of the debate, further disempowering FGM/C-affected women. Moira Dustin proposes to apply "consistent principles of choice"; to recognise all non-therapeutic bodily modifications as cultural; and to "distinguish between adults who choose to modify their bodies and children who cannot" as a way of avoiding double standards while working towards behaviour change.[72]

69 See n 34.

70 Explanatory Report para 155.

71 Ratna Kapur, 'The Tragedy of Victimization Rhetoric: Resurrecting the "Native" Subject in International/Post-Colonial Feminist Legal Politics' (2002) (12) *Harvard Human Rights Journal* 1.

72 Dustin (n 43) 20. Male circumcision and procedures to intersex babies would also be prohibited.

Giving culture a role in cases of VAW raises specific legal questions, beyond the discussion regarding defence theories of the error of prohibition. Framing a type of violence as culturally motivated has a further disempowering effect for women, who are both victims and perpetrators. Cut mothers who fail to protect their daughters are held responsible for the mutilation caused. FGM/C affected women are not seen as women with particular needs, but as key actors for protecting potentially affected girls. FGM/C as a culturally motivated crime is disentangled from other forms of violence that potentially affected communities encounter, especially women, and it appears as if FGM/C is the only or main violence that they encounter.

Many *representational aspects* of the treatment FGM/C receives resonate with postcolonial critiques of how minority women and violence towards them is perceived in Western societies.[73] Such critiques affirm that some forms of VAW coined as cultural, such as FGM/C, receive disproportionate attention; and that creating gendered racialised categories to describe non-Western women affected by violence nourishes narratives of the powerlessness of non-Western women. "Girls at risk" is the specific FGM/C racialised female vulnerable subject. It is a category not used for girls risking any other form of violence covered by the IC, such as rape or stalking, but only for culturally motivated crimes (as FGM/C or forced marriage).[74] Perceived and construed as perfect victim subjects of their culture, women and potentially affected communities are subjected to paternalistic measures and state control without fully participating in public decisions that affect them.

Both the political and representational aspects of FGM/C result in *structural disempowerment* in a variety of ways. Structural aspects refer to unmet needs and imposed burdens that result in further disempowerment. Although FGM/C is perceived as a major problem that affected women and potentially affected girls face, there is a surprising lack of data regarding their migration status, access to healthcare, education, housing, work, or spouse in/dependence. How this subordinated location affects the way they experience VAW, including FGM/C, remains unresearched.[75] Women and potentially affected communities do not participate in the design and implementation of policies addressing VAW in general, or FGM/C in particular. Thus, public programmes risk being launched without consistently assessing their fears, needs, and priorities. Worse, the needs of affected women may be ignored with them being instrumentally included as actors protecting future generations.

73 See Lourdes Peroni, 'Violence against Migrant Women: The Istanbul Convention through a Postcolonial Feminist Lens' (2016) 24(1) *Feminist Legal Studies* 49.

74 See Council of Europe, *FGM and Forced Marriage* (n 62).

75 The Head of the Unit of Obstetrics and Gynaecology for Reconstructive Surgery at the Hospital Peset (Valencia) stated on a radio interview (21 February 2019 Á Punt Radio) that reconstructive treatments had been interrupted when women lost their regular status as migrants.

Separating FGM/C from other forms of violence connected to migration (e.g. insecure residence permits), or to intra-group power relations (e.g. social pressure on parents) puts an excessive burden on the shoulders of mothers to protect potentially affected girls from being cut. In fact, a failure in the duty to protect has been invoked in criminal cases against family members for organising the trip of a girl who returned to Europe cut.[76] The European Court of Human Rights has also confirmed the denial of asylum in several cases by arguing that the mother was able to protect her daughter if returned to her country.[77] Thus, European institutions send the message that it is women (i.e. mothers) in charge of potentially affected girls who have the responsibility to protect them, even when they ask for institutional help.

5 (Provisional) conclusions

Intersectionality means being mindful of the intersections of race, gender, migration status or culture regarding social problems concerning women's rights. This chapter has briefly analysed the ways in which migration status, race and age intersect with gender in shaping structural, political and representational aspects of FGM/C in the IC. It has explored whether the response given to FGM/C strengthens, by ignoring it, the multi-layered dimensions of the subordination of racialised women.

Regarding the political aspects, the analysis suggests that to conceive FGM/C as a culturally motivated crime is disempowering for affected women and stigmatising for potentially affected communities. This conceptualisation is grounded in a particular imaginary about racialised women, their culture and their position of subordination within such culture. These narratives of powerlessness of non-Western women are nourished with the "girls at risk" category that legitimises the paternalistic and punitive response from the State, whilst imposing a disproportionate burden on mothers to protect. Therefore, the needs of affected women dissipate into the protection of potentially affected girls, placing an excessive burden on mothers whilst displacing the responsibility of public institutions in effectively protecting minority women from violence.

The IC three "Ps" framework urgently needs to be strengthened regarding protection, policy implementation, and participation favouring the identification of needs and the allocation of resources in ways that contribute to fighting "the routinized forms of domination"[78] racialised women encounter in Europe.

76 See Johnsdotter and Mestre i Mestre, 'FGM in Europe' (n 46).

77 See *Akaziebie v Sweden* App no 23944/05 (ECHR, 8 March 2007); *Izevbekhai and Others v Ireland* App no 43408/08 (ECHR, 17 May 2011); *Omeredo v Austria* App no 8969/10 (ECHR, 20 September 2011).

78 Crenshaw, 'Mapping' (n 4).

8 Forced sterilisation in the Istanbul Convention

Remedies, intersectional discrimination and cis-exclusiveness

Daniela Alaattinoğlu[1]

1 Introduction

Surgical sterilisation is a permanent method of birth control that was introduced in many Western countries during the nineteenth and twentieth centuries. Predominantly launched with eugenic pretexts, however, the conditions under which sterilisation was allowed, even desirable, were many times determined by public authorities; not the individual – often woman – who was to be sterilised.[2] Such pretexts led to sterilisation laws and practices involving authority *force* and *coercion*.[3] Throughout the twentieth century, coercive sterilisations were allowed in many countries: starting from the United States, spreading to continental Europe (importantly Nazi Germany), to the Nordic countries, to emerging market economies (such as China, India, Puerto Rico and Singapore) and finally, to Eastern Europe.[4] Some of these eugenic and socio-political sterilisations are still on-going, such as those targeting Romani[5] women or people with disabilities.

Another form of coercive sterilisation that is often allowed, even compulsory, today is preconditioning amendment of legally registered gender with sterilisation.[6] Such sterilisations particularly target trans people, who experience a

1 I would like to thank the editors for their helpful comments on earlier versions of this chapter.

2 See, for example, Paul Weindling, 'International Eugenics: Swedish Sterilization in Context' (1999) 24(2) Scandinavian Journal of History 179.

3 In this chapter, the terms *forced*, *coerced* and *involuntary sterilisation* are used synonymously to depict sterilisations carried out contrary to the free will of the person sterilised.

4 Weindling 1999 (n 2) 186.

5 Romani is here used as an umbrella category to cover Roma, Sinti and travelling people.

6 As recognised, for example, in Council of Europe Commissioner for Human Rights, *Human Rights and Gender Identity* CoE Doc CommDH/IssuePaper(2009)2; Parliamentary Assembly of the Council of Europe, *Putting an End to Coerced Sterilisations and Castrations*. CoE Doc Res 1945 (2013).

mismatch between their birth-assigned gender and gender identity.[7] Some trans people want to undergo bodily transformations, such as genital surgery and/or sterilisation, and some do not. *Requiring* sterilisation for legal gender recognition, however, involves a Sophie's choice for many trans people. On the one hand, they can choose to preserve their fertility but not have identification documents issued in line with their gender identity, experiencing a continuous, even daily, mismatch between legal and lived gender. On the other hand, they can attain legal gender recognition by the authorities – with increased access to welfare services and the labour market – and live a life fully in line with their gender identity, but then have to undergo sterilisation, regardless of their own wishes to do so.

Emerging human rights and political prioritisation of individual over public interests are among the legal, social and cultural developments that have led to coercive sterilisation becoming increasingly questioned in many countries.[8] The Council of Europe Convention on Preventing and Combating Violence against Women and Domestic Violence (the Istanbul Convention) is the first human rights treaty to explicitly include a provision on forced sterilisation. Article 39(b), more specifically, holds that State Parties shall criminalise "performing surgery which has the purpose or effect of terminating a woman's capacity to naturally reproduce without her prior and informed consent or understanding of the procedure".[9] But how has forced sterilisation come to be included as a central violation in this significant treaty on gender-based violence?[10] What practices are conceptualised to be violations of Article 39(b) and what forms are excluded from its scope? Finally, can Article 39(b) effectively combat contemporary practices of forced sterilisation in Europe?

This chapter looks into how forced sterilisation within international law has, modelled on the Nazi atrocities, developed from a violation of international criminal law to also a (gendered) violation of international human rights law, epitomised by the Istanbul Convention. The chapter views the inclusion of forced sterilisation in the Convention as an evolution of the European Court of

7 Trans is here understood to cover a range of identities that are not cis/cisgender, i.e. people whose gender identity is not in line with their birth-assigned sex/gender. The most important group affected are probably transsexual people, that is, people who have a strong desire to assume the physical characteristics associated with the "opposite" sex. On sterilisation targeting trans people, see, for example, Daniela Alaattinoğlu, *The Path of the Law: The Establishment, Abolition and Remedy of Involuntary Sterilisation and Castration in Sweden, Norway and Finland* (European University Institute PhD thesis 2019). According to Transgender Europe (TGEU), 14 European countries still required trans people to be infertile to amend their legally registered gender in 2018. TGEU, 'Trans Rights Europe Map 2018' (21 April 2018) tgeu.org/wp-content/uploads/2018/05/MapB_TGEU 2018_Online.pdf accessed 15 October 2019.

8 Ibid.

9 The first paragraph in the article, Article 39(a), prohibits forced abortion.

10 On the definition of gender and violence in the Convention, see Niemi and Verdu Sanmartin in this volume.

Human Rights' (the ECtHR or the Strasbourg Court) emerging case law, which has focused on Romani women. Finally, it addresses the question of how comprehensively the Istanbul Convention tackles the problem of forced sterilisation in Europe today. In doing so, the chapter points out three specific problems for the Convention's effective implementation.

2 Background: the Holocaust and international criminal law

Being among the Nazi violations on trial in Nuremberg – at the heart of today's popular imagination of atrocities against the international community – forced sterilisations are considered violations of international criminal law since the end of the Second World War. To introduce the topic, a few words on the Nazi sterilisations and their context are needed. After the German National Socialist seizure of power, the Government soon introduced regulation on sterilisation through the 1933 Act for the Prevention of Hereditarily Diseased Offspring.[11] Sterilisation was seen as a way to "clean" the body of the population (*Volkskörper*) from the ones considered degenerate[12] and cost-inducing, for example, people with disabilities.[13] According to Gisela Bock, groups particularly vulnerable to the Nazi sterilisation projects were poor people, unskilled workers and their wives, house servants, farmworkers, prostitutes, unmarried mothers, women on welfare, criminals, inmates of institutions, ethnic minorities (such as Romani and Black Germans) and people who broke gender norms.[14] The Nazi sterilisation law – similarly to other Western countries' laws at the time[15] – covered both voluntary and involuntary interventions, but use of coercion and force was common to make people "consent".[16] There are no definite numbers for how many people were sterilised during the German Nazi regime, but Bock has estimated that around 400,000 people were sterilised from 1933 to 1945.[17]

At the Trials of War Criminals before the Nuremberg Military Tribunals, during which the Nazi German political, military, judicial, medical and economic leadership were tried, sterilisation experiments were among the charges. While such experiments were included in many indictments against Nazi war

11 Gesetz zur Verhütung erbkranken Nachwuchses [Act for the Prevention of Hereditarily Diseased Offspring] 1933.

12 Gisela Bock, 'Antinatalism, Maternity and Paternity in National Socialist Racism' in Gisela Bock and Pat Thane (eds), *Maternity and Gender Policies: Women and the Rise of the European Welfare States, 1880s–1950s* (Routledge 1991) 235.

13 Paul Weindling 1989 *Health, Race and German Politics between National Unification and Nazism, 1879–1945* (Cambridge University Press 1989) 441–457.

14 Gisela Bock, 'Racism and Sexism in Nazi Germany: Motherhood, Compulsory Sterilization, and the State' (1983) 8(3) *Signs* 400, 414–417.

15 For example, the laws in Sweden, Norway, Finland, Estonia and many US states.

16 Geoffrey Giles, '"The Most Unkindest Cut of All": Castration, Homosexuality and Nazi Justice' (1992) 27(1) *Journal of Contemporary History* 41; Bock 1991 (n 12) 235.

17 Bock 1991 (n 12) 235.

criminals, one of the most famous cases in which the interventions had a central role was the indictment of physicians, often referred to as "The Doctors' Trial", *United States of America v Karl Brandt et al.*[18] The medical crimes of sterilisation experiments, considered as crimes against humanity and war crimes, at Auschwitz and Ravensbruck concentration camps and elsewhere were included in the indictment and the judgment.[19] In *Poland v Höss*, the director of the Auschwitz concentration camp was found liable for genocide through sterilisation and castration.[20] Moreover, sterilisation was considered an integral part of the charges of genocide in *United States of America v Greifelt et al.*[21] Among the medical experiments and horrors carried out by Nazi officials, non-consensual sterilisation hence formed an important part of the emerging international criminal law in the immediate aftermath of the Second World War.

The Nuremberg trials became an important background model for the codification of international criminal law. The Convention on the Prevention and Punishment of the Crime of Genocide, drawn up in the post-war context, was adopted by the United Nations General Assembly in 1948. According to its Article II (d), "imposing measures intended to prevent births within the group" is listed as one form through which the crime of genocide can be perpetrated. In the *travaux préparatoires*, these measures of "biological genocide" were framed as sterilisation and/or compulsory abortion, segregation of men and women and obstacles to marriage.[22] Forced sterilisation is, hence, covered by the crime description of genocide and, as such, a violation that strikes at the heart of international criminal law.[23] Furthermore, in the 1998 Rome Statute of the International Criminal Court – the most important contemporary document of international criminal law – enforced sterilisation is included in the crime description of genocide,[24] crimes against humanity[25] and war crimes.[26]

First conceptualised as a crime against international criminal law, forced sterilisation, accompanied by forced abortion, also made its way into the 2011 Istanbul Convention. Only mentioned in passing in the protocols of the Ad Hoc Committee on Preventing and Combating Violence Against Women and

18 *United States of America v Karl Brandt et al.* [1947] US Military Tribunal Nuremberg.
19 To the extent that the defendants were found guilty of the charges.
20 *Poland v Höss* [1947] The Supreme National Tribunal in Poland. See William Schabas, *The International Criminal Court: A Commentary on the Rome Statute* (Oxford University Press 2016), 140; Dinah Shelton, *Encyclopedia of Genocide and Crimes against Humanity* (Macmillan Reference 2009) 892.
21 *United States of America v Greifelt et al.* [1948] US Military Tribunal Nuremberg.
22 UN Secretariat, *First Draft of the Genocide Convention*. UN Doc E/447 (1947); Christian Tams, Lars Berster and Björn Schiffbauer, *Convention on the Prevention and Punishment of the Crime of Genocide: A Commentary* (Hart Publishing 2014) 91.
23 See Tams et al. 2014 (n 22) 91.
24 As "[i]mposing measures intended to prevent births within the group". Rome Statute of the International Criminal Court (1998), Article 6(c).
25 Rome Statute of the International Criminal Court (1998), Article 7(1, g).
26 Ibid. Article 8 (2, b, xxii) and (2, e, vi).

Domestic Violence (CAHVIO), forced sterilisation is treated mainly as a form of violence against women during armed conflict in the *travaux préparatoires* of the Convention.[27] This depiction might, however, not correspond completely to the historical and contemporary reality. Contrastingly, forced sterilisations have globally often been carried out during times of peace, in many other contexts than Nazi Germany. The interventions have intersectionally[28] targeted diverse groups such as working-class women, racial and ethnic minorities, indigenous peoples, people with disabilities, trans people and other marginalised groups. In addition, regardless of the presence or absence of an armed conflict, practices of forced sterilisation have rarely been prosecuted as violations of international criminal law since the Nuremberg trials.[29] Rather, they are reappearing before the international community and supranational courts as human rights violations, which is also the main reason behind their inclusion in the Istanbul Convention.

3 Forced sterilisation before the European Court of Human Rights

Since the nineties, forced sterilisation has become mainstreamed as a human rights issue. The mainstreaming process started within the framework of violence against women and expanded since then.[30] Supranational human rights courts, commissions and treaty bodies have also tried individual cases of forced

27 See CAHVIO, *Report of the 1st Meeting* CoE Doc CAHVIO (2009) 5, 35; CAHVIO, *Overview of Legal Protection Against Sexual Violence Afforded to Women during Situations of Armed Conflict* CoE Doc CAHVIO (2009) 12, 2.

28 For a discussion on the meaning of the term "intersectionality", see Mestre in this volume.

29 See Alaattinoğlu 2019 (n 7) Chapter 3.

30 Forced sterilisation has been considered a violation of the prohibition of torture and cruel, inhuman or degrading treatment or punishment, and/or a violation of bodily integrity, personal autonomy, private and family life, health, and/or the prohibition of discrimination. See, for example, Human Rights Committee, *Concluding Observations on Peru* UN Doc CCPR/CO/70/PER (2000), [21]; CERD Committee, *Concluding Observations: The Czech Republic* UN Doc CERD/C/CZE/CO/7 (2007), [14]; CEDAW Committee, *Concluding Observations: Slovakia* UN Doc CEDAW/C/SVK/CO/4 (2008), [44–45]; CESCR Committee, *Concluding Observations: Brazil* UN Doc E/C.12/1/Add.87 (2003), [27]; CAT Committee, *Conclusions and Recommendations on Peru* UN Doc CAT/C/PER/CO/4 (2006), [23]; CRC Committee, *General Comment No 9: The Rights of Children with Disabilities* UN Doc CRC/C/GC/9 (2007), [60]; United Nations General Assembly, *Economic, Cultural and Social Rights. The Right of Everyone to the Enjoyment of the Highest Attainable Standard of Physical and Mental Health Report of the Special Rapporteur, Paul Hunt* UN Doc E/CN.4/2004/49 (2004), [25–27]; United Nations General Assembly, *Report of the Special Rapporteur on Torture and Other Cruel, Inhuman or Degrading Treatment or Punishment, Manfred Nowak* UN Doc A/HRC/7/3 (2008); Council of Europe Commissioner for Human Rights, *Human Rights and Gender Identity* CoE Doc CommDH/IssuePaper(2009)2; and European Torture Committee, *Report to the Czech Government* CoE Doc CPT/Inf (2007) 32, [153–154].

sterilisation during the last two decades.[31] The European Court of Human Rights has ruled on several cases of forced sterilisation.

In the early case *KH and Others v Slovakia* from 2009, the Strasbourg Court held that the applicants – sterilised Slovakian Romani women – have the right to access their medical files.[32] Such access was key to initiate further human rights litigation against Slovakia, where coercive sterilisations of Romani women have been widespread since the days of Czechoslovakian communism.[33] The Court held that the State's failure to ensure access to medical records to patients and their lawyers was an infringement of the right to respect private and family life (ECHR Article 8) unsupported by any pressing public interest, resulting in a violation of the European Convention on Human Rights.[34] Moreover, the Court considered that limiting access, including photocopying, to patients' medical records violated the applicants' access to court, a vital aspect of the right to a fair trial (ECHR Article 6).[35] The case, nevertheless, only dealt with the applicants' access to their medical files, and not with the legality of their sterilisations, which meant that it took another two years before the Court delivered a ruling on involuntary sterilisation as such.

3.1 VC v Slovakia*: a violation of the Convention, but not discrimination*

VC v Slovakia was the first ECtHR landmark case on involuntary sterilisation.[36] The applicant *VC* – Romani woman, speaking mostly the Romani language, who had finished compulsory education in the sixth grade – was 20 years old at the time of her sterilisation. She was delivering her second child through a Caesarean section at a public hospital in Slovakia in August 2000. After several hours of painful labour, she was informed by the medical staff that future pregnancies would have fatal consequences for her. She then signed a consent form to be sterilised – however, without understanding the term "sterilisation" and

31 The first supranational individual case was *María Mamérita Mestanza Chávez v Peru* [2003] IACmHR Case 12.191 (friendly settlement). Report 71/03. The CEDAW Committee has delivered recommendations in the case *AS v Hungary* [2006] Communication No 4/2004. Other supranational cases are *IV v Bolivia* [2014] IACmHR Case 12.655 (merits). Report 72/14; *IV v Bolivia* [2016] IACtHR Series C No 329; *MT v Uzbekistan* [2015] Communication No 2234/2013.

32 *KH and Others v Slovakia* App no 32881/04 (ECHR, 28 April 2009).

33 See Center for Reproductive Rights; Poradna pre obcianske a l'udské práva [Centre for Civil and Human Rights] and Ina Zoon, *Body and Soul: Forced Sterilization and Other Assaults on Roma Reproductive Freedom in Slovakia* (Center for Reproductive Rights Publications, 2003). See also Claude Cahn, *Human Rights, State Sovereignty and Medical Ethics* (Brill Nijhoff 2014).

34 *KH and Others v Slovakia* App no 32881/04 (ECHR, 28 April 2009), paras 44–58.

35 Ibid. [59–69]. Apart from costs and expenses, the eight applicants were awarded 3,500 euros each for non-pecuniary damages.

36 *VC v Slovakia* App no 18968/07 (ECHR, 8 November 2011).

after being falsely informed of the danger of future childbearing. In the hospital, moreover, the applicant was kept in a segregated room for Romani women and was prevented from using the same washroom facilities as non-Romani women. The fact that she was of Romani origin was explicitly stated several times in her hospital records. After the intervention, the applicant suffered from medical and mental harm because of her involuntary infertility: she displayed symptoms of false pregnancy, needed psychiatric treatment for psychological damage, was ostracised by the Romani community, left by her husband and finally divorced.[37]

Unable to access appropriate remedies in Slovakia, the applicant's case was brought before the ECtHR.[38] First, she stated that the intervention had amounted to inhuman and degrading treatment (ECHR Article 3), as her consent had been obtained during labour and the intervention had not been medically motivated but rather fuelled by general hostility towards Romani people.[39] Moreover, she claimed that the State's failure to conduct an effective investigation had constituted a procedural violation of the prohibition of torture and ill-treatment.[40] Second, she pointed to a violation of the right to respect for private and family life (ECHR Article 8). This claim was based on the failure of the public authorities to provide her with sufficient information on the protection of reproductive health to make an informed decision about the irreversible sterilisation.[41] Third, she claimed that there had been a violation of the right to found a family (ECHR Article 12), as the sterilisation in question had been carried out without her full and informed consent.[42] Fourth, she argued that the State had violated her right to an effective remedy (ECHR Article 13), particularly through the failure of the domestic authorities to effectively investigate the sterilisation.[43] Finally, she claimed discrimination based on sex and race (ECHR Article 14), referring to the segregation and discriminatory climate at the Slovak hospital, to the sterilisation practices targeting Romani women and to involuntary sterilisation as a form of violence against women.[44]

The Court found a substantive violation of the prohibition of torture and ill-treatment, asserting that sterilisation without informed consent is a major infringement of reproductive health, dignity, autonomy and physical integrity.[45] The Court underlined that the sterilisation had not been motivated by medical

37 Ibid. paras 9–20.

38 The applicant had initiated criminal and civil proceedings and also lodged a complaint with the Constitutional Court. Nevertheless, all her complaints had been unsuccessful (discontinued, rejected or dismissed). Ibid. paras 24–42.

39 Ibid. paras 88–91.

40 Ibid. para 121.

41 Ibid. paras 130–134.

42 Ibid. paras 156–157.

43 Ibid. paras 162–163.

44 Ibid. paras 170–171.

45 Ibid. paras 100–120.

necessity[46] and that it had provoked feelings of fear, anguish and inferiority and resulted in permanent medical, social and mental suffering.[47]

Additionally, the Court found that the applicant's involuntary sterilisation was a violation of the right to respect for private and family life, as this right also covers reproductive autonomy.[48] In particular, the Court held that the State had failed to fulfil its positive obligation to protect the applicant, taking into consideration her vulnerable position as a woman of Romani origin.[49] Importantly, the applicant's vulnerability – based on her sex/gender and race/ethnicity – was, hence, taken into consideration by the Court as a factor affecting the State's obligation to protect her from reproductive health infringements.

Regarding the prohibition of discrimination, in conjunction with the right to respect for private and family life, the Court thought that there was not enough evidence before it to establish that the Slovak doctors had acted in bad faith, that the sterilisation was part of an organised policy, or that it was racially motivated.[50] Searching for an intent to discriminate – which it was unable to find – the Court nevertheless recognised that Romani women might be particularly vulnerable to "shortcomings" in sterilisation legislation and practice.[51] This vulnerability was, nevertheless, covered within the scope of ECHR Article 8, the Court thought, concluding that it was unnecessary to also investigate whether there was a violation of the prohibition of discrimination in the case.[52] Interestingly, it did not reply to how this "vulnerability" corresponded to the concept of discrimination, creating a tension between these two concepts. The Court also dismissed the applicant's other claims.[53] The Court awarded the applicant, in light of the found violations, 31,000 euros for non-pecuniary damages.[54]

46 Ibid. para 113.

47 Ibid. para 118. The Court did not, however, find a procedural violation of the prohibition of torture and ill-treatment. Regarding the civil proceedings, the Court found that the domestic courts had dealt with the applicant's case in a reasonable time. Furthermore, regarding the necessity for domestic authorities to start a criminal investigation, the Court did not consider that the doctors had acted "in bad faith, with the intention of ill-treating the applicant", which would have warranted a criminal investigation on the State's own initiative. See paras 126–127.

48 Ibid. para 138.

49 Ibid. paras 138–155.

50 Ibid. paras 176–177.

51 Ibid. para 178.

52 Ibid. paras 178–180.

53 When it came to the right to found a family, the Court considered that the found violation of the right to respect for private and family life already covered the scope of the right in question (reproductive decisions) and did not consider it necessary to examine the relevant article separately. The Court did not find a violation of the right to an effective remedy either, as the applicant had had access to both civil and criminal remedies. See Ibid. paras 165–168.

54 Ibid. para 184.

The decision of the Court not to investigate whether the sterilisation constituted discrimination was criticised by Judge Mijovic in her partly dissenting opinion. She emphasised that discrimination was "the very essence" of the case and that the Court should have found a violation based on the principle that discrimination means treating differently without an objective and reasonable justification, laid down in previous ECtHR case law.[55] Doing so, Mijovic held that the fact that the sterilisation was motivated by the applicant being a Romani woman was "the strongest form of discrimination", which should have led to an acceptance of all the applicant's claims for just satisfaction.[56]

VC v Slovakia is a landmark judgment, which has provoked mixed views. On the one hand, it has been welcomed for condemning health care paternalism, for requiring informed consent, for recognising infertility as legal harm to be remedied and for identifying the vulnerability of the applicant.[57] One the other hand, however, the Court's reluctance to rule on the (intersectional) discrimination claim has been severely criticised. The critique has focused on the Court insufficiently conceptualising the gravity of the systematic violations targeting Romani women.[58] Critical voices have highlighted the Court's apparent disregard of evidence of sterilisations targeting Romani women presented before it.[59] Moreover, in line with Judge Mijovic's dissent, the criticism has focused on the Court wrongfully applying the burden of proof when evaluating whether the sterilisation amounted to discrimination.[60] However, regardless of the criticism of the discrimination doctrine laid down in the case – focusing on individual (criminal) intent rather than on the unjustified different treatment of Romani women – the Court has affirmed its stance in later decisions.[61]

55 *DH and Others v the Czech Republic* App no 57325/00 (ECHR, 13 November 2007); *Oršuš and Others v Croatia* App no 15766/03 (ECHR, 16 March 2010).
56 *VC v Slovakia* App no 18968/07 (ECHR, 8 November 2011), Dissenting opinion of Judge Mijovic.
57 Lourdes Peroni and Alexandra Timmer, 'Court Condemns Forced Sterilization of Roma Woman' (Strasbourg Observers, 17 November 2011) strasbourgobservers.com/2011/11/17/court-condemns-forced-sterilization-of-roma-woman/#more-1280 accessed 15 October 2019.
58 Lindsay Hoyle, 'V.C. v Slovakia: A Reproductive Rights Victory Misses the Point' (2014) 36(3) Boston College International and Comparative Law Review 17.
59 Peroni and Timmer 2011 (n 57); Hoyle 2014 (n 58); Ruth Rubio-Marín and Mathias Möschel, 'Anti-Discrimination Exceptionalism: Racist Violence before the ECtHR and the Holocaust Prism' (2015) 24(4) European Journal of International Law 881; Siobhan Curran, 'Intersectionality and Human Rights Law: An Examination of the Coercive Sterilisations of Romani Women' (2016) 16 *The Equal Rights Review*.
60 Hoyle 2014 (n 58); Rubio-Marín and Möschel 2015 (n 59).
61 *NB v Slovakia* App no 29518/10 (ECHR, 12 June 2012); *IG and Others v Slovakia* App no 15966/04 (ECHR, 13 November 2012).

3.2 ECtHR case law after VC v Slovakia*: involuntary sterilisation still not discrimination*

After *VC v Slovakia*, the ECtHR has ruled on other cases of coercive sterilisation of Romani women: *NB v Slovakia* (2012);[62] *IG and Others v Slovakia* (2012);[63] *RK v the Czech Republic* (2012);[64] *Červeňáková v the Czech Republic* (2012)[65] and *GH v Hungary* (2015).[66] In the Slovak cases, the Court found violations of the prohibition of torture and ill-treatment and the right to respect for private and family life.[67] *RK* concluded with a friendly settlement, not specifying any violations.[68] *Červeňáková* and *GH* were found inadmissible.[69] In none of the cases concerning Romani women, importantly, has the Court found a violation of the prohibition of discrimination.

There have also been cases before the ECtHR concerning involuntary sterilisation of (cis)[70] women of non-Romani origin. One example is *Joëlle Gauer v France*, a case that concerned the involuntary sterilisation of women with mental disabilities. The case was found inadmissible on procedural grounds.[71] The factual circumstances of *GB and RB v the Republic of Moldova*[72] were about a woman who had been sterilised without her informed consent during a Caesarean section. The Court considered the intervention a "serious interference" with her private and family life, constituting a violation of ECHR Article 8.[73]

Cases of compulsory sterilisation of trans people who want to access legal gender recognition have also recently appeared before the Strasbourg Court. In its important decision *AP, Garçon and Nicot v France* from 2017, the Court ruled that requiring an invasive, irreversible, physical change such as sterilisation for legal gender recognition was a violation of the right to private and family life.[74] As there is limited case law from the ECtHR to date, it is nevertheless too

62 *NB v Slovakia* App no 29518/10 (ECHR, 12 June 2012).

63 *IG and Others v Slovakia* App no 15966/04 (ECHR, 13 November 2012).

64 *RK v the Czech Republic* App no 7883/08 (ECHR, 27 November 2012).

65 *Červeňáková v the Czech Republic* App no 26853/09 (ECHR, 23 October 2012).

66 *GH v Hungary* App no 54041/14 (ECHR, 9 June 2015).

67 *VC v Slovakia* App no 18968/07 (ECHR, 8 November 2011); *NB v Slovakia* App no 29518/10 (ECHR, 12 June 2012); *IG and Others v Slovakia* App no 15966/04 (ECHR, 13 November 2012).

68 *RK v the Czech Republic.* App no 7883/08 (ECHR, 27 November 2012).

69 *Červeňáková v the Czech Republic* App no 26853/09 (ECHR, 23 October 2012); *GH v Hungary* App no 54041/14 (ECHR, 9 June 2015).

70 Cis, or cisgender, means people whose gender identity is in line with their birth-assigned sex/gender. B Aultman, 'Cisgender' (2014) 1 *Transgender Studies Quarterly* 61.

71 *Joëlle Gauer and Others v France* App no 61521/08 (ECHR, 23 October 2012).

72 *GB and RB v the Republic of Moldova* App no 16761/09 (ECHR, 18 December 2012).

73 Ibid. para 32.

74 *AP, Garçon and Nicot v France* App nos 79885/12, 52471/13 and 52596/13 (ECHR, 6 April 2017). See also the preceding *YY v Turkey* App no 14793/08 (ECHR, 10 March 2015), in which the Court condemned such sterilisation preconditions *obiter dicta*.

early to reach any conclusions on the Court's conceptualisation in cases of involuntary sterilisation targeting different groups.

Forced and coercive sterilisations, intersectionally targeting marginalised people in Europe, have not amounted to unlawful discrimination in the ECtHR's case law so far. In the Istanbul Convention, nevertheless, forced sterilisation is inherently conceptualised as discriminatory, as a practice that targets women. But who is a "woman"? Are also, for example, trans women covered by Art. 39(b)? And (how) does the Convention recognise and address the intersectional discrimination inherent in coercive sterilisations targeting, for example, ethnic minority women or women with disabilities?

4 The Istanbul Convention: forced sterilisation as gender-based violence

The Istanbul Convention was drafted as *VC v Slovakia* was pending before the Strasbourg Court. When the Convention was opened for signatures, the Court issued its landmark ruling. As a binding treaty offering wider and more general tools to address widespread human rights violations than individual ECtHR case law, the Convention conceptually responds to a European reality of coercive sterilisations, including the ones targeting Romani women in Eastern Europe. Moreover, the duty to prevent forced sterilisations is not limited to the State. Through the concept of due diligence for non-state actors, regulated in Article 5(2), the Istanbul Convention hence extends state responsibility for these acts of reproductive violence beyond state representatives to also encompass, for example, a duty to scrutinise medical professionals.

Symbolically, it is important that the Istanbul Convention lists forced sterilisation as a serious human rights violation. It can, however, be questioned how much additional supranational scrutiny the Convention in practice offers to recognise, prevent and combat such oppressive practices. In the national evaluation reports published to date by the Group of Experts on Action against Violence against Women and Domestic Violence (GREVIO), forced sterilisation has only been mentioned in passing. Moreover, rather than looking into national practices of forced sterilisation and the remedies provided to victims by State Parties, GREVIO appears to regard legislative criminalisation as sufficient remedy to combat coercive sterilisations.[75] This might be problematic, as such criminalisation might not be enforced in practice. It might also co-exist with, for example, sterilisation requirements for legal gender recognition, as these might not be seen as "forced" in the narrow sense. For the moment, GREVIO evaluation reports are, however, too few to draw further conclusions on its abilities to address forced sterilisation.

75 See, for example, GREVIO, *Baseline Evaluation Report Portugal* CoE Doc GREVIO/Inf(2018)16, para 170; GREVIO, *Baseline Evaluation Report Turkey* CoE Doc GREVIO/Inf(2018)6, para 249.

In the following, I take up three main hurdles to effective victim recognition and redress that the text of the Istanbul Convention does not resolve. The first is the limited remedial scope of the Convention. The second is the failure of the Convention to consider intersectional discrimination in the context of involuntary sterilisations. The last one is its inherent cis-exclusiveness.

4.1 Limited remedial scope

The Istanbul Convention rightly adopts a transformative approach to preventing gender-based violence, requiring States, for example, to adopt awareness-raising programmes,[76] to educate the public[77] and to train professionals[78] in order to eradicate pervasive stereotyping. This general, transformative approach is not, however, mirrored in the reparations stipulated by the Convention.[79]

The Istanbul Convention includes an obligation for States to provide remedies for victims of gender-based violence. Pursuant to Article 29(2), States are under the obligation to provide victims "with adequate civil remedies against [s]tate authorities that have failed in their duty to take the necessary preventive or protective measures within the scope of their power". Article 29 of the Convention does not further specify these civil remedies,[80] but regulates compensation as a remedial archetype in Article 30. Accordingly, compensation "shall be awarded to those who have sustained serious bodily injury or impairment of health"[81] – a formulation that includes victims of forced sterilisation. Such compensation should be provided to victims "within a reasonable time".[82]

In terms of remedies, the Convention hence focuses on financial redress, support to and protection of the person directly victimised by violence.[83] This is seen most clearly in the definition of "victim" in Article 3(e), as "any natural person who is subject to" violence against women or domestic violence. However, not only direct victims are harmed by reproductive violence such as forced sterilisation. Such violence also affects whole groups and communities targeted by state or medical authorities as inappropriate parents – for example, trans people, Romani people or people with disabilities. Moreover, it also indirectly negatively affects the reproductive choices and care obligations of the

76 Article 13.
77 Article 14.
78 Article 15.
79 On transformative remedies, see Ruth Rubio-Marín and Clara Sandoval, 'Engendering the Reparations Jurisprudence of the Inter-American Court of Human Rights: The Promise of the *Cotton Field* Judgment' (2011) 33(4) *Human Rights Quarterly* 1062.
80 The Explanatory Report states that such civil remedies depend on the national legal system and "may also include court orders that deal more specifically with acts of violence covered by the scope of this Convention, such as barring orders, restraining orders and non-molestation orders". See Explanatory Report, para 158.
81 Article 30(2).
82 Article 30(3).
83 Particularly Chapter IV.

partners and family members of the direct victim. Recognising such indirect victims and redressing communal harms are important for advancing victims' healing and for preventing further marginalisation and stigmatisation of direct victims and their communities. The ability of the remedies stipulated in the Convention to recognise and to offer redress not only to individual victims but also to other people who are indirectly victimised and negatively affected can, hence, be questioned.[84]

The Istanbul Convention, therefore, has a narrow approach to remedies. Remedies that the Convention could have included are catalogued in the 2005 United Nations resolution on *Basic Principles and Guidelines on the Right to Remedy and Reparation for Victims of Gross Violations of International Human Rights Law and Serious Violations of International Humanitarian Law* and include, for example, satisfaction[85] and guarantees of non-repetition.[86] Such remedies serve to establish more structural reforms, as they include truth commissions, investigations, public apologies, law reforms and ethics codes of conduct. They are beneficial not only to direct victims, but also to their communities and serve to fully recognise and revert the oppressive structures that caused the victimisation in the first place. Embracing such transformative measures as remedies for victims of human rights violations would also give the Istanbul Convention a meaningful link between the protection and support of individual victims and general prevention measures. This could be, for example, training health professionals to ensure free and informed consent in regions where coercive sterilisations have been found.

4.2 Failure to recognise intersectional discrimination

Forced sterilisation as gender-based violence is, according to the Istanbul Convention, based on the social and cultural gendered oppression of women. Thus, by pointing out the gender-based discrimination inherent in forced sterilisation, the Convention reaches longer than the ECtHR has done so far. Nevertheless,

84 The Explanatory Report only states that available civil remedies shall be provided for descendants "[i]n the event of the death of the direct victim". Explanatory Report, para 164. On communal harms and indirect victimisation, see Ruth Rubio-Marín, Clara Sandoval and Catalina Díaz, 'Repairing Family Members: Gross Human Rights Violations and Communities of Harm' in Ruth Rubio-Marín (ed.), *The Gender of Reparations: Unsettling Sexual Hierarchies while Redressing Human Rights Violations* (Cambridge University Press 2009).

85 United Nations General Assembly, *Basic Principles and Guidelines on the Right to a Remedy and Reparation for Victims of Gross Violations of International Human Rights Law and Serious Violations of International Humanitarian Law* UN Doc A/RES/60/147 (2006), Article 22.

86 Ibid. Article 23. CAHVIO *travaux préparatoires* bring up the *Basic Principles and Guidelines*, but only with reference to support and protection measures for direct victims. CAHVIO, *Typology of Protection for Women Victims of Violence* CoE Doc CAHVIO (2009) 11, 3.

viewing forced sterilisation as discrimination based *only* on gender prevents a full understanding of its more complex root cause.

Indeed, when carried out, involuntary sterilisations have not targeted *all* women equally. Rather, they have particularly targeted women who do not conform to the culturally hegemonic "ideal woman", the "responsible" and "desirable" mother – negatively affecting poor and marginalised women, indigenous women, ethnic minority women, trans women or women with disabilities.[87] As such, coercive sterilisations have not been solely based on the "idea of the inferiority of women or on stereotyped roles for women and men",[88] but also on the idea of the inferiority of *specific* women and the stereotyping of these women. In fact, as in the extreme case of Nazi Germany, oppressive, anti-natalist policies such as coercive sterilisation, targeting for example ethnic minority women, were carried out alongside oppressive, pro-natalist policies, such as the prohibition of abortion, targeting ethnic majority women.[89] The recognition of intersectional oppression and sub-group intersectional stereotypes – in both conceptual and remedial terms – are, hence, key to understanding and effectively combatting practices of forced sterilisation.

It should be highlighted, nevertheless, that the Istanbul Convention does not ignore the need for an intersectional approach. However, it only highlights it at an abstract level. Doing this, it points out that ratifying States "shall take into account and address the specific needs of persons made vulnerable by particular circumstances and shall place the human rights of all victims at the centre".[90] Regarding victims of forced sterilisation, the increased vulnerability of Romani women has already been recognised by the Strasbourg Court (importantly in *VC v Slovakia*). The Istanbul Convention goes further, and links forced sterilisation more clearly to gender-based discrimination. Yet, it stops at recognising "vulnerability" rather than "discrimination" on other grounds than gender. This is problematic, since recognising vulnerability without recognising (structural) discrimination obscures the role of the State in condoning the oppression of some groups of women. Moreover, not identifying and redressing the *intersectional* discrimination at play in oppressive practices such as forced sterilisation conceals the State's responsibility to revert the oppression.[91]

87 See Alaattinoğlu 2019 (n 7).
88 Article 12(1).
89 See Bock 1983 (n 14).
90 Article 12(3). It also broadly points out, in Article 4(3), that the Convention should be implemented in a non-discriminating fashion.
91 Also, CAHVIO *travaux préparatoires* point out the same problem inherent in the notion of vulnerability, namely that "[i]t is important that people are not simply labelled as 'vulnerable' and perceived only in terms of their perceived vulnerabilities and needs". Instead, "[d]elivery of economic and social rights is an obligation which must be respected by those who assume positions of authority to facilitate the exercise of agency by survivors of gender-based violence". CAHVIO 2009 (n 86), 3.

4.3 Cis-exclusiveness

The obligation imposed by the Istanbul Convention upon State Parties to criminalise forced sterilisation is seemingly limited to cis women. This is particularly problematic, as one of the main groups targeted by contemporary coercive sterilisation practices today are trans people.

The Convention does not clarify whether trans women are included in the definition of "women".[92] The Explanatory Report does not provide much guidance on the issue either, but stresses that "categories of individuals such as transgender or transsexual persons, crossdressers, transvestites and other groups of persons that do not correspond to what society has established as belonging to 'male' or 'female' categories"[93] are covered in the scope of non-discrimination in the Convention (Art. 4(3)). The Explanatory Report also states that "Parties may if they wish, extend the interpretation to individuals who are gay, lesbian, bisexual or transgender, who may also face particular forms of gender-related persecution and violence".[94]

A narrow interpretation of the Convention, hence, leaves trans women, trans men and non-binary people outside its legally binding dimensions. According to this interpretation, the protection of trans people depends on the good will of the State. However, a narrow cis-exclusive interpretation creates an uneasy tension between cis and trans women and might be difficult to justify and uphold from an inclusive human rights perspective, where the rights of every individual are equally protected. Tellingly, GREVIO goes beyond the victimisation of cis women in its reports and includes trans women to some extent in its evaluation of the Convention's implementation.[95]

The general description of forced sterilisation of women in the Istanbul Convention is tailored to the sterilisation cases of Romani women appearing before the ECtHR. As such, it depicts a situation where a woman is sterilised without *prior* and *informed* consent, for example during highly stressful situations, such as while giving birth. The text of Article 39(b) may prove limited to depict and combat the European reality where trans people are regularly subjected to preconditions of sterilisation to access legal gender recognition. For trans people, the consent to sterilisation in such situations might be both prior and informed. It is not, however, *free* consent, as sterilisation is used as a precondition to access another right. Such practices have recently been found to violate ECHR Article 8 by the ECtHR.[96] Other European institutions are also criticising sterilisation preconditions for legal gender recognition. In 2018, the European Committee of Social Rights (ECSR) found that these practices violate the right to health,

92 Article 3(f), defined as including "girls under the age of 18".
93 Explanatory Report, para 53.
94 Ibid. para 313. See also Sosa in this volume.
95 See, for example, the evaluation report on Turkey, GREVIO 2018 (n 75) para 22.
96 *AP, Garçon and Nicot v France*. App nos 79885/12, 52471/13 & 52596/13 (ECHR, 6 April 2017).

protected in Article 11 of the 1961 European Social Charter.[97] Such developments raise questions regarding how Article 39(b) of the Istanbul Convention should be interpreted.

To oblige States to criminalise situations of forced sterilisation that correspond only to those that cis women face, and not to the ones that trans women face, treats women differently based on their gender identity. Treating trans women differently by requiring them to get sterilised is predominantly based on the misconception that their parenthood would create chaos in family relations or that they would be inappropriate parents: ideas that are hardly justifiable from a human rights perspective.[98] A cis-exclusive interpretation of Article 39(b) is therefore an obstacle to addressing all practices of forced sterilisation in today's Europe in an effective and non-discriminatory manner, as many of these practices target trans people.

5 Conclusion

The inclusion of a provision on forced sterilisation in the Istanbul Convention is a welcome development since it is *inter alia* a sign of recognition of forced sterilisation as a human rights violation, as discrimination and as a phenomenon to be taken seriously by European courts and policy-makers. At the same time, however, there are some shortcomings in the Convention's ability to recognise and effectively combat contemporary practices of forced sterilisation and to provide redress to both individual victims and their communities. To effectively combat forced sterilisations, a profound understanding of the conditions and mechanisms of intersectional oppression is required. Better awareness of the intersecting inequalities that cause and enforce the practices that lead to some individuals being considered "better" or "worse" parents is needed. Equally necessary is further scrutiny of the state prerogative to decide who is apt for reproduction and who is not, or whose gender identity should be recognised and what the preconditions for this recognition should be.

97 *Transgender Europe and ILGA-Europe v The Czech Republic* Complaint No 117/2015 (ECSR, 15 May 2018).

98 See, for example, the *travaux préparatoires* of the 2018 Swedish Compensation Act to provide a financial remedy for involuntarily sterilised trans people. Swedish Government Bill 2017/18:64.

Part IV

Victim services

9 The right to adequate housing of battered women

The added value of the Istanbul Convention?

Ingrid Westendorp

1 Introduction

There is a clear connection between domestic violence and women's housing. Because of their weaker socio-economic position, many women cannot afford housing themselves and have to rely on a male partner to provide a home. This creates an unequal power relation that may be the basis for an abusive relationship. Once the battering starts, and women are both economically and psychologically dependent, it may be very difficult to leave an abusive relationship because the alternative often is an inadequate housing situation that is hard to accept, especially when children are involved.

When the main human rights instruments that contain the right for housing were drafted, there was no specific attention to the right to housing for women; housing was, and largely still is, regarded as a family right rather than as an individual right. Especially in the sixties, the idea behind the right to housing was that nuclear families consisting of a male breadwinner and a female homemaker needed a good house for themselves and their children.[1] The breadwinner was the head of the family and the main decision maker.[2] That women (and children) might need an autonomous right to housing and above all safety within their own four walls was not considered, nor did it come up when the right to housing was further clarified and interpreted.

1 The Committee on Economic, Social and Cultural Rights drew States' attention to this stereotypical thinking in its General Comment No 4, para 6 of 1991 by explaining that

> While the reference to 'himself and his family' [in article 11(1) of the ICESCR] reflects assumptions as to gender roles and economic activity patterns commonly accepted in 1966 when the Covenant was adopted, the phrase cannot be read today as implying any limitations upon the applicability of the right to individuals or to female-headed households or other such groups.

2 According to Chan Kam Wah and Patricia Kennett, "familial ideology" underpins the housing system. Housing policy and planning and the distribution of housing are based on the idea of the family as a unit. Social housing policy may give priority to families while individuals living alone may be marginalised, especially single women. Patricia Kennett and Chan Kam Wah (eds), *Women and Housing: An International Analysis* (Routledge 2011) 6.

Taking the above into consideration the research question of this chapter is: does the Istanbul Convention oblige State Parties to offer battered women better protection and support services, in particular as regards the right to housing, than other human rights instruments?

In this chapter, only the situation in the Member States of the Council of Europe is considered and the focus is on the right to housing of battered women. Although it is acknowledged that also men and children can be victims of domestic violence, this chapter concentrates on the situation of a male abuser and a female victim.

In the following pages, first the right to adequate housing is examined, as it is contained and interpreted in international and regional treaties that are important for Member States of the Council of Europe (Section 2). Next, the different solutions offered to women victims of domestic violence are debated, i.e. sending battered women to shelters and evicting the perpetrator from the family residence, as well as the housing situation of domestic violence survivors (Section 3). In Section 4, the link between domestic violence and the right to housing is under scrutiny, while Section 5 examines the potential of the Istanbul Convention, starting with the particular obligations imposed on State Parties, followed by the role of the monitoring body: the Group of Experts on Action against Violence against Women and Domestic Violence (GREVIO). Section 6 gives a short summary and the answer to the question whether the Convention has an added value as regards the housing situation of battered women.

2 The right to adequate housing in human rights law

To date, the most important interpretative work on the right to adequate housing has been done by the Committee on Economic, Social and Cultural Rights (CESCR) in General Comments Nos 4 and 7.[3] In General Comment No 4, seven conditions are mentioned that in the eyes of the Committee need to be fulfilled before housing can be called adequate. These conditions are legal security of tenure, availability of services, material facilities and infrastructure, affordability, habitability, accessibility, location and cultural adequacy.[4]

Building on General Comment No 4, the CESCR adopted General Comment No 7 with the aim of further explaining the obligations that States have in respect of forced evictions.[5]

3 The CESCR is the monitoring body of the Covenant on Economic, Social and Cultural Rights. It was established by the United Nations Economic and Social Council resolution 1985/17 of 28 May 1985.

4 CESCR General Comment No 4, The Right to Adequate Housing, 13 December 1991, para 8.

5 CESCR General Comment No 7, The Right to Adequate Housing; Forced Evictions, 20 May1997.

While these General Comments are not binding on State Parties as such, they are nevertheless considered as the most authoritative interpretation of the right to housing and their contents are acknowledged and followed by other organisations, such as the European Committee of Social Rights.[6]

Regrettably, the CESCR's comments fail to point out certain issues as regards women's housing rights that are of particular importance in the context of this chapter. Most importantly, the Committee did not link domestic violence to adequate housing and therefore did not include safety *within* the home as a condition for the adequacy of the housing situation. However, women who are battered within their own four walls are by definition inadequately housed.[7] Connected to this, is the right to privacy and respect for family life. In cases of domestic disturbance, the police may be reluctant to enter a house, and privacy protection may work in favour of the perpetrator to the detriment of the victim.[8]

The CESCR has not yet had the chance to express its views on the housing rights of battered women in a communications procedure, as no complaint concerning this situation has been received since the entry into force of the Optional Protocol to the ICESCR in 2013.

Other international human rights instruments that contain the right to housing, such as the Universal Declaration on Human Rights[9] or the Convention on the Elimination of All Forms of Discrimination Against Women (CEDAW), do not specify the content of this right. An additional problem with CEDAW is that it only mentions the right to housing in Article 14, which is a specific provision for rural women.[10]

At the European level, it is the European Social Charter (Rev.) that explicitly contains the right to housing in Article 31.[11] Unfortunately, only a limited

6 See for instance, *FEANTSA v France* Complaint No 39/2006, 4 February 2008, para 67.

7 While there are many stories describing domestic violence, for me one of the most gripping accounts is the story of Molly because it clearly depicts how unsafe home can be for a victim of domestic violence. Angela Browne, *When Battered Women Kill*, Chapter 2, Meeting Molly (Free Press 1987). Also see, Rhonda Copelon, 'Understanding Domestic Violence as Torture' in Rebecca Cook (ed.), *Human Rights of Women; National and International Perspectives* (University of Pennsylvania Press 1994) 116–152.

8 As the European Court of Human Rights stated in the *Opuz* case: "Women who go to police stations because they are subjected to domestic violence are confronted with attitudes which tend to regard the problem as a private family matter into which the police are reluctant to interfere". *Opuz v Turkey*, App no 33401/02 (ECHR 9 June 2009) para 96.

9 See Article 25 of the UDHR.

10 Paragraph (h) of Article 14 on rural women reads: To enjoy adequate living conditions, particularly in relation to *housing*, sanitation, electricity and water supply, transport and communications.

11 Article 31 reads: The right to housing. With a view to ensuring the effective exercise of the right to housing, the Parties undertake to take measures designed: 1) to promote access to housing of an adequate standard; 2) to prevent and reduce homelessness with a view to its gradual elimination; 3) to make the price of housing accessible to those without adequate resources.

number of Member States have bound themselves to this article.[12] The monitoring system of the ESC is rather weak from the perspective of individuals since it consists of a reporting system[13] and a group complaint procedure[14] entailing that national and international organisations of employers and trade unions and other NGOs can lodge complaints with the European Committee of Social Rights (ECSR).[15] So far, no complaints dealing with the violation of the right to housing of battered women have been dealt with; this will only happen if an NGO will take up battered women's plight and file a group complaint.

3 Housing solutions for battered women

If women are victims of domestic violence, the most common solution is to protect them by offering them accommodation in a shelter or safe house. In many countries, these shelters are run by NGOs or civil society organisations. Shelters offer a temporary solution and, after a certain period of time, women must choose between returning to their partners or finding their own housing.

Another solution – the prime example of which can be found in Austria – is that the perpetrator is (temporarily) evicted from the family residence in order to create a distance between him and the victim. The eviction of the batterer is usually accompanied by barring, restraining and protection orders, prohibiting the abusive partner either from entering the family abode or from being in the neighbourhood of the victim.[16]

Domestic violence survivors who have left their partners also need alternative housing, but many of them lack the economic possibilities to procure that without financial support.

12 On 1 April 2019, the following 15 States had bound themselves to Article 31: Andorra, Denmark, Finland, France, Greece, Italy, Latvia, Lithuania, the Netherlands, Norway, Portugal, Slovenia, Sweden, Turkey and Ukraine.

13 The reporting system is included in Part IV of the 1961 European Social Charter and was amended by the 1991 Turin Protocol. State Parties regularly submit reports that are examined by the ECSR. If the Committee comes to the conclusion that the national situation does not comply with the Charter, this conclusion is published, but this is not enforceable at the national level.

14 The group complaint procedure is included in the Additional Protocol to the ESC Providing for a System of Collective Complaints, Treaty No 158, 9 November 1995.

15 The complaints concerning housing that have been lodged until now can be placed into three categories: (1) States' housing policy as regards vulnerable groups, (2) Housing restitution, (3) Roma rights. Jessie Hohmann, *The Right to Housing; Law, Concepts, Possibilities* (Hart 2014) 53–66.

16 See the Austrian law to protect the family against violence: Gewaltschutsgesetz, September 2013, §38 Sicherheitspolizeigesetz, and the German private law protecting against violence and the threat thereof: Gesetz zum zivilrechtlichen Schutz vor Gewalttaten und Nachstellungen (*Gewaltschutzgesetz*), latest version 1 March 2017, Article 1.

3.1 Women's shelters

There is a marked difference between housing and shelter. Housing is meant to have a permanent character and needs to fulfil at least the seven conditions formulated by the CESCR in General Comment No 4 before it can be called adequate. Shelter, on the other hand, is meant to be temporary. The general understanding of shelter is that it is a safe haven offering protection against weather conditions as well as danger or attacks to people who have no home. Accommodation in a shelter is a far cry from adequate housing. There is no legal definition of shelter and there are no conditions that have to be fulfilled in order to qualify as "adequate" shelter. If special women's shelters are filled to capacity, battered women are often accommodated in general shelters, together with alcoholics and drug addicts. There may be a lack of space and privacy and sometimes sons of a certain age are not allowed to stay in the safe house together with their mothers.[17] However, it is clear that a shelter for battered women may provide safety and peace from the harassment of the perpetrator. Ideally, addresses are kept secret, and women are placed in a specific shelter for battered women in another town to distance them as far as possible from the batterer and to make it more difficult for the abuser to track them down.

Accommodation circumstances in shelters for battered women would improve if there would be a uniform European standard requiring that at least certain conditions need to be fulfilled in order to create "adequate" shelters.[18] Still, shelters will always remain a temporary solution and a solution that reflects traditional notions of the man being the head of the household as the main breadwinner, as well as the most important inhabitant of a house because he is supposed to bear the financial burden of the housing costs.

3.2 Eviction of domestic violence perpetrators

A solution that is more contemporary and in line with the idea of equality between men and women is that the perpetrator of an act of domestic violence has to leave the family home. Eviction is usually accompanied by barring orders and restraining or protection orders. In countries where such a solution is

17 The age at which sons are no longer allowed to stay with their mothers in a women's shelter varies per country and per shelter. In Greece the age limit that a boy is no longer welcome may be 12 http://refworld.org/cgi-bin/texis/vtx/rwmain?page=printdoc&docid=53b137394 accessed 15 October 2019, 14 in Austria <Baseline Evaluation Report Austria, GREVIO/Inf(2017)4, 27-09-2017> para 106, accessed 15 October 2019 and 15 in the Netherlands www.stichtingwende.nl/wp-content/uploads/2014/06/Stichting-Wende-Opvang-huiselijk-geweld.pdf accessed 15 October 2019.

18 Possible conditions would be safety, enough space and privacy, and the possibility for women to stay in the shelter with all their children.

possible, it is only applied in the minority of cases.[19] This may be not only because the measure is relatively new, but also because many women will be too afraid to remain in the family residence where they will feel like sitting ducks, and prefer to get away from their abuser to a place that is not known to him. Furthermore, women may have experienced a lackadaisical response of law enforcement agencies, in particular the police, downplaying the seriousness of the offence and trying to appease the situation rather than firmly handling the perpetrator.[20] Such experience may cause a loss of confidence in the authorities and induce the victim to flee. However, it should be borne in mind that with regard to many aspects, the housing situation of these women and their children will dramatically change for worse once they enter temporary housing and their leaving the family home may have repercussions for their housing situation after a divorce.[21]

3.3 Housing situation of domestic violence survivors

In case of separation or divorce, the quality of women's housing may decline in comparison to how they were housed when they were still with their partners. The result of their weaker socio-economic position will be that they will lack the money to buy or rent qualitatively good housing. Women who become dependent on social welfare may end up living with their children in neighbourhoods characterised by poverty, squalor and crime. On the contrary, many perpetrators – being the breadwinners of the family – may manage to remain in the family home or procure a home that is of the same standard as the one in which they lived with the victim.[22]

19 About half of the European States have followed Austria's example and adopted laws that make it possible to temporarily evict the perpetrator. Suzan van der Aa, Johanna Niemi et al., *Mapping the legislation and assessing the impact of Protection Orders in the European Member States* (Wolf Legal Publishers 2015) 44.

20 See e.g. Huseyin Kara et al., 'The Role of Police in Preventing and Combating Domestic Violence in Turkey' (2014) 10(20) *European Scientific Journal*, 7, and Council of Europe, *Preventing and Combating Domestic Violence against Women: A learning Resource for Training Law Enforcement and Justice Officers* (2016) para 1.5.

21 The legal position of the partner who leaves the family home may be weaker than that of the partner who remains in the home when it comes to temporary measures or even determining who will stay in the residence after separation/divorce.

22 For instance, in the Netherlands, on average, the spending power of women without children will decline by 25% after divorce and of their former male partners by 0.2%. The discrepancy in spending power between divorced women and men with children is even more pronounced. Since in the great majority of cases the children will remain with the mother, on average, the woman's spending power will decline by 26%, while the man's spending power will increase by 10%. Consequently, after divorce it is far more difficult for women to afford adequate housing. Centraal Bureau voor de Statistiek, *Trends in de financiele gevolgen van een echtscheiding voor man en vrouw*, (*Central Office for Statistics, Trends in financial consequences of divorce for man and woman*) 2017|3, 4.

4 The link between the right to housing and domestic violence

4.1 CEDAW on domestic violence and housing

Violence against women (VAW) or protection of women who are victims of violence as such is not included in CEDAW.[23] The lack of a general provision on VAW proved to be a serious problem because this kind of violence can undermine the enjoyment of virtually all other human rights a woman is entitled to, including the right to adequate housing. That is why the CEDAW Committee tried to repair this gap by adopting General Recommendations on VAW.[24] In 1992, the CEDAW Committee adopted the landmark General Recommendation No 19.[25] This Recommendation defines VAW as a form of discrimination against women, as encompassed by the definition of discrimination in Article 1 of the Convention.[26] The CEDAW Committee states that VAW violates the enjoyment of several rights, including the right to equality in the family.[27] Violence in the family is called "one of the most insidious forms of violence against women", and the Committee reminds State Parties that many women are forced to stay in abusive relationships because of their lack of economic independence.[28] That is why State Parties are recommended to provide victims with adequate protective and support services; in the context of family violence consisting among other measures of refuges and civil remedies.[29] The link between domestic violence and housing is hinted at, but not made explicit.

After 25 years, General Recommendation No 19 was updated in General Recommendation No 35.[30] In the context of this chapter, a relevant improvement is the emphasis on protective measures including "the issuance and monitoring of eviction, protection, restraining or emergency barring orders against alleged perpetrators, including adequate sanctions for non-compliance", as well as the assurance of access to *inter alia* affordable housing.[31] Still, like its predecessor, General Recommendation No 35 is far more focused on the impact of violence on victims' civil and political rights than on their economic and social rights.

23 The only form of VAW is mentioned in Article 6 concerning the prohibition of trafficking in women and exploitation of prostitution.

24 The first of these is CEDAW Committee, General Recommendation No 12, Violence Against Women, 1989. It is very short and simply draws State Parties' attention to the issue of VAW.

25 CEDAW Committee, General Recommendation No 19, Violence Against Women, 1992.

26 Ibid. para 6.

27 Ibid. para 7(f).

28 Ibid. para 23.

29 Ibid. para 24.

30 CEDAW Committee, General Recommendation No 35 on gender-based violence against women, 2017.

31 Ibid. para 31 (ii and iii).

Unfortunately, up till now, the CEDAW Committee has also failed to clearly link domestic violence to the right to housing and support for victims in its views on individual communications. Although it is true that the Committee is somewhat hindered by the fact that Article 14(h) of the Convention only mentions housing rights in connection to rural women, still, Articles 1, 2, 15 and 16 concerning non-discrimination and equality should offer an adequate legal basis to confirm the right to housing of all women in cases of domestic violence.[32]

In order to illustrate this point, it is useful to look into two of the most relevant cases.[33]

In *A.T. v Hungary*, the abusive (former) husband regularly entered the co-owned apartment and beat up the victim, who could not do anything against it because no restraining or protection orders were available and she could not go to any of the shelters because one of her children is fully disabled. While the CEDAW Committee recommended Hungary to provide A.T. with a safe home, her right to property and the violation of her right to housing were not mentioned.[34]

In the case of *Cecilia Kell v Canada*, again there was a definite link between domestic violence and the right to housing, especially because the complaint was partly based on Article 14(h) of CEDAW. Together with her husband, the victim had obtained housing on an Aboriginal community estate. This was only possible because she is an Aboriginal, but her husband is not. The victim was tricked out of her property rights over the house by her husband – who received help from the local housing authority – in a period that she was trying to escape the abusive relationship and was seeking protection in a shelter. In its assessment of the case, the CEDAW Committee acknowledged that Cecilia Kell's property rights and access to her home had been violated, but not her right to housing under Article 14(h). According to the Committee, she could not be considered as a rural woman and, being an Aboriginal, she could have obtained housing in another part of the community estate.[35] Instead of recommending restitution of the house to the victim, the Committee recommended Canada to pay her compensation and to provide her with housing commensurate in quality, location and size to the one that had been taken from her.

32 Lisa Pruitt, 'Deconstructing CEDAW's Article 14: Naming and Explaining Rural Differences' (2011) 17 *William & Mary Journal of Women and the Law*, 347, 359.

33 Until March 2019, the CEDAW Committee had published seven views concerning cases of domestic violence. These cases are: CEDAW/C/32/D/2/2003, *Ms A.T. v Hungary*, 26 January 2005; CEDAW/C/39/D/5/2005, *Şahide Goekce v Austria*, 6 August 2007; CEDAW/C/39/D/6/2005, *Fatma Yilderim v Austria*, 01-10-2007; CEDAW/C/51/D/19/2008, *Cecilia Kell v Canada*, 26 April 2012; CEDAW/C/49/D/20/2008, *Ms V.K. v Bulgaria*, 27-09-2011; CEDAW/C/61/D/24/2009, *X and Y v Georgia*, 25-08-2015; CEDAW/C/52/D/32/2011, *Isatou Jallow v Bulgaria*, 28 August 2012.

34 CEDAW/C/32/D/2/2003, *Ms A.T. v Hungary*, 26 January 2005, paras 9.2–9.4.

35 CEDAW/C/51/D/19/2008, *Cecilia Kell v Canada*, 26 April 2012, para 10.6.

4.2 The ECtHR's decisions concerning domestic violence

Although the right to housing is not included in the European Convention for the Protection of Human Rights and Fundamental Freedoms (ECHR), as this treaty focuses on civil and political rights, the European Court of Human Rights (ECtHR) has indirectly dealt with this right in the context of other provisions contained in the treaty, in particular Articles 2,[36] 3[37] and 8.[38] In several cases, the Court has decided on complaints concerning domestic violence without, however, directly linking the violence to the victims' right to housing. For victims of domestic violence, it is important that in addition to the link between the violence and their right to physical integrity, the connection between the violence and their socio-economic rights is acknowledged because only then will measures be taken to protect all their human rights, civil and political, as well as economic, social and cultural.[39]

The landmark case concerning domestic violence is *Opuz v Turkey*.[40] Nahide Opuz and her mother had been threatened and attacked by Nahide's husband H.O. in the course of eight years (between 1995 and 2002). While the women had complained about the violence to the police on several occasions, only some ineffective measures had been taken and in the few cases when H.O. was convicted of the violence, he received a very light sentence. The violence culminated in the death of Nahide's mother, who was shot by H.O. The Court explicitly stated that under the ECHR State Parties have a positive obligation to protect women against domestic violence.[41] While the Court conceded that Turkey's legislation had improved after 1998, the implementation of this legislation was thought to be faulty and ineffective. In reaction to the State's statement that the victims could have gone to a women's shelter, the Court responded by noting that, even if they would have done so, the authorities could not have guaranteed their safety in such a safe house and that would have

36 E.g. *Budayeva v Russia*, App no 15339/02 (ECHR, 20 March 2008).
37 E.g. *Marzari v Italy*, App no 36448/97 (ECHR, 4 May 1999).
38 E.g. *Fadeyeva v Russia*, App no 55723/00 (ECHR, 9 June 1995).
39 The fact that civil and political rights and economic and social rights are indivisible, interrelated and interconnected, was acknowledged by the ECHR in the *Airey v Ireland case* when the Court stated in para 26:

> Whilst the Convention sets forth what are essentially civil and political rights, many of them have implications of a social or economic nature. The Court therefore considers, like the Commission, that the mere fact that an interpretation of the Convention may extend into the sphere of social and economic rights should not be a decisive factor against such an interpretation; there is no water-tight division separating that sphere from the field covered by the Convention.

App no 6289/73 (ECHR, 9 October 1979).

40 *Opuz v Turkey* App no 33401/02 (ECHR, 9 June 2009).
41 Tarik Abdel-Monem, 'Opuz v Turkey, Europe's Landmark Judgment on Violence against Women' (2009) 17(1) Human Rights Brief 30.

been a temporary solution anyway.[42] The Court did not point out, however, that the victims had the right to stay safe in their own home, nor did it suggest the possibility of evicting the perpetrator from the family home.

In *Kalucza v Hungary*, the housing situation of the victim was the key issue, as she was out of sheer necessity sharing her flat with her violent (ex) partner while waiting for the outcome of several civil law disputes as regards the ownership of the apartment. The Hungarian authorities denied her request to remove her partner from the flat taking into account that during quarrels she had attacked him as well. According to the Court, the State had violated Article 8 of the Convention because the applicant had a right to protection against domestic violence in her own home.[43]

4.3 Concluding remarks

From the above, it has become clear that the connection between domestic violence and housing has not been easily made. While the indivisibility, interrelatedness, and interdependence of all human rights is acknowledged in legal theory, in practice the right to physical integrity and the right to housing are dealt with in different human rights instruments. Both at the international and regional levels, attempts have been made to take all rights into account when dealing with situations of domestic violence, but a clear and explicit link is still missing. The interests of victims of domestic violence will probably be best served when all their rights are included in one instrument and decisions take all rights and needs into account. That is why the next Section will examine whether the Istanbul Convention is successful in marrying all the different kinds of rights in one treaty, and thus whether it will do justice to the specifics of women's housing rights, including the housing rights of battered women.

5 Potential of the Istanbul Convention concerning the right to housing of battered women

5.1 State obligations in respect of support, housing and protection orders

The Istanbul Convention explicitly imposes an obligation upon State Parties to offer support services to victims of violence. States have to take legal or other measures to ensure that – when necessary – victims can access services that will help them to recover from the violence they have suffered; one of such services is housing.[44] Article 20 concerns general support services that are available to all victims of VAW and that are not specifically geared towards the needs of victims

42 *Opuz v Turkey*, paras 171 and 172.
43 *Kalucza v Hungary* App no 57693/10 (ECHR, 24 April 2012) para 61.
44 Istanbul Convention, Article 20(1).

of domestic violence.[45] However, this provision is potentially of great importance for long-term solutions for the survivors of domestic violence since state support may help them secure adequate housing after divorce.

Particularly for battered women and their children, States have to set up a sufficient number of specialised shelters that can provide safe accommodation around the clock.[46] From the Explanatory Report it becomes clear that such shelters are meant to provide emergency accommodation to women who had to flee an abusive relationship. In addition to serving as a temporary safe house, shelters are supposed to offer all kinds of support to help women get back on their feet so they are better equipped to lead an independent life when they leave the shelter.[47] The emphasis is on security, both of the victim and of the building. It is indeed imperative that the addresses of such shelters are kept secret and that it is well-nigh impossible for (former) partners to find out where the victim is housed in order to avoid situations where women are harassed or even attacked in front of the very safe house where they seek refuge.

As regards the implementation of the obligation to have sufficient shelters, there is still a long way to go. Ideally, there is a specialised women's shelter available for one family place per 10,000 head of population.[48] In reality, only Luxembourg, Norway and Slovenia meet this minimum standard. The Netherlands almost meets the recommended percentage, while Austria and Malta are some 10% short. Nineteen out of the 46 States examined at the request of the Council of Europe, miss 80–100% of the minimum number of shelters.[49]
While the importance of available safe houses goes without saying, it is still unfortunate that under the heading of Chapter IV, Protection and Support, only shelters are mentioned as a protection measure for women who are victims of domestic violence. Among the Convention's purposes is the elimination of discrimination against women and the promotion of substantive equality between men and women, including empowering women.[50] However, promoting shelters as the primary protection measure, rather emphasises the unequal relationship and difference in property rights between men and women, and perpetuates the traditional and stereotypical approach that it is the victim who has to leave the house.

45 Explanatory Report to the Council of Europe Convention on preventing and combating violence against women and domestic violence, Council of Europe Treaty Series, No 210, sections 125 and 126.
46 Istanbul Convention, Article 23.
47 Explanatory Report, sections 133–135.
48 This is the recommended number mentioned in the Final Activity Report of the Council of Europe Task Force to Combat Violence Against Women, including Domestic Violence, EG-TFV, 2008 p. 51. Explanatory Report section 135.
49 Council of Europe, Parliamentary Assembly, Committee on Equality and Non-Discrimination, *Promoting Best Practices in Tackling Violence against Women*, Rapporteur Ms Sahiba Gafarova, 29 September 2015, para 45.
50 Istanbul Convention, Article 1(b).

Fortunately, Chapter VI, Investigation, Prosecution, Procedural Law and Protective Measures, also mentions the possibility of restraining or protection orders, including the eviction of the perpetrator.[51] This at least offers opportunities for those women who refuse to budge and who would like to remain in the family home after the batterer has been removed from it.

What may have been expected of a modern and innovative treaty like the Istanbul Convention is, however, that much more emphasis would have been placed on such measures that put victims first and respond to perpetrators in a way that is commensurate with the idea of equality between the sexes. There do not seem to be many new ideas or approaches on how to make staying in the family home safer for women after the abuser has been removed,[52] or how to achieve long-term housing solutions for domestic violence survivors.

Furthermore, it seems that on a whole, the treaty is rather focused on criminal law and prosecution of the perpetrator, as well as on the filing of divorce and women continuing their life on their own. In practice, many female victims do not want to press charges against their partners and they do not want a divorce. They simply want the violence to stop.[53] Criminal records may reflect negatively on the whole family and incarcerating or fining the perpetrator may indirectly punish the victim and other family members because many families still depend on the man's income.[54] The consequences of criminal prosecution may present a hurdle that victims are reluctant to take until the violence has escalated and has turned into a life-threatening situation.

Instead of focusing on criminal law, Chapter VI leaves it to the discretion of State Parties to use private or administrative law measures. The prime example of a State using administrative law for this purpose is The Netherlands, where it

51 Istanbul Convention, Articles 52 and 53. Explanatory Report, pp. 45 and 46 (in particular sections 267–273). Also see Rosa Logar and Johanna Niemi, *Emergency Barring Orders in Situations of Domestic Violence: Article 52 of the Istanbul Convention. A Collection of Papers on the Council of Europe Convention on Preventing and Combating Violence against Women and Domestic Violence* (Council of Europe 2017).

52 A good example in this respect is Spain where it is possible to equip the perpetrator with an electronic device (bracelet) so the police are alerted if he comes near the family abode. Alternatively, the victim may wear an electronic bracelet that can be used for contacting the police in case of a violation of the restraining order. *Promoting Best Practices in Tackling Violence against Women*, 2015, para 60.

53 There may be many reasons why women do not want to leave their abusive partners. Some of them will be afraid of their partners, fear the disapproval of their families, or lack the financial means to live on their own. Another reason for staying may be, however, that they love their partner or that they have sympathy for him and they hope that they change him. Jason Whiting, *Eight Reasons Why Women Stay in Abusive Relationships*, Institute for Family Studies, 21 July 2016, available at https://ifstudies.org/blog/eight-reasons-women-stay-in-abusive-relationships. Also, Ingrid Westendorp, 'If Home is no Haven: Women's Right to Adequate Housing in Cases of Domestic Violence' in Ingrid Westendorp and Ria Wolleswinkel (eds), *Violence in the Domestic Sphere* (Intersentia 2005) 132.

54 Explanatory Report, section 253. Also, Westendorp (2005) 137.

is the mayor who decides on barring orders.[55] This opens up the possibility to take all kinds of measures that are commensurate with the wishes of many victims, including orders compelling the perpetrator to take anger management training or relationship therapy.[56] Maybe the law could take a step further and oblige the offender to stay in a shelter for perpetrators of domestic violence, preferably in another town. A zero tolerance, swift administrative or civil action, immediately following the first incident of violence, entailing the removal of the perpetrator and obliging him to stay in a shelter and undergo adequate therapy, would be the right signal to the offender and to society and may prevent further harm from happening. Acting in this way would also be in the offender's best interest since he will not get a criminal record, his housing situation will be taken care of, and he will be able to keep his job and hopefully benefit from therapy to such an extent that he will be able to have non-violent relationships in the future.

The Istanbul Convention is the only treaty explicitly imposing the duty of not only protecting the victims of domestic violence but also supporting them in their struggle to overcome the violence they have suffered. To what extent that will be successful will depend on how States implement these obligations and how their obligations are interpreted, assessed and monitored by GREVIO.[57]

5.2 GREVIO's role in realising the right to housing for battered women

GREVIO plays an important role because it draws up the questions for the questionnaire used for the reporting procedure and as such can steer the reporting in the direction they want it to take.[58] Evaluation procedures are based on the specific provisions selected by GREVIO.[59] If the group of experts is not satisfied with the information provided by the State Party in question, they may organise a country visit.[60] Furthermore, GREVIO has the possibility to provide more clarity on the implementation of the treaty – including clarification of terms and concepts – by authoritatively interpreting them in General Recommendations.[61] In the context of the topic of this chapter, it would be useful if

55 In practice, the Mayor will delegate this task to the police which is also the body that will execute such orders. The administrative procedure can only be used for emergency barring orders up to 28 days. If the victim wishes to prolong the eviction of the perpetrator after that, a civil law procedure has to be followed and a court fee has to be paid. Logar and Niemi (2017) 28 and 38.

56 Istanbul Convention, Article 16.

57 Ibid. Article 66.

58 Ibid. Article 68(1).

59 Ibid. Article 68(3).

60 Ibid. Article 68(9).

61 Ibid. Article 69.

GREVIO would further define and clarify adequate shelter for battered women, and the support that is needed to achieve adequate housing for female survivors of domestic violence who want to leave their partners.

The fact that national Parliaments are involved in the monitoring procedure is a big step forward in comparison to other international reporting procedures. The Concluding Observations of UN monitoring Committees hardly receive any attention of national Parliaments with the result that violations may continue and that suggestions and recommendations barely lead to improvement of legislation and policy at the national level.[62]

In May 2018, already four State reports had gone through the whole procedure as described in Article 68 of the Istanbul Convention, with the result that GREVIO has published its Baseline Evaluation Reports on these State Parties.[63] While it is still early days, these four reports may already give some insights into how the Istanbul Convention has been implemented at the domestic level. The focus of the analysis is on Articles 20 (general support services), 23 (shelters), 52 and 53 (barring orders and restraining or protection orders).

In respect of Article 20, Austria is commended for having a social housing programme that offers housing at affordable rates to people with special needs, in particular domestic violence survivors.[64] A similar programme exists in Albania for women who have left a violent partner and cannot afford adequate housing.[65] In the Danish social welfare system it is provided that a specific case worker may be assigned to victims of domestic violence whose task is to assist them with all kinds of issues, including finding housing.[66]

As regards Article 23, GREVIO utters concern about the fact that Austria has an inadequate number of shelters, especially in rural areas,[67] and that sons of fourteen years old are not welcome in some of the shelters.[68] Also in Albania, there is an inadequate number of specialised shelters and the ones available are predominantly concentrated in the capital.[69] The situation in Monaco is also not in conformity with the obligations ensuing from this article. Due to the limited size of the country, the authorities have decided not to have specific safe houses for battered women, but instead to accommodate these women in general

62 See Jasper Krommendijk, *The Domestic Impact and Effectiveness of the Process of State Reporting under UN Human Rights Treaties in the Netherlands, New Zealand and Finland. Paper Pushing or Policy Prompting?* (Intersentia 2014).

63 These State Parties are respectively, Austria, Monaco, Albania and Denmark.

64 GREVIO Baseline Evaluation Report Austria, GREVIO/Inf (2017)4, published 27 September 2017, para 95.

65 GREVIO Baseline Evaluation Report Albania, GREVIO/Inf (2017)13, published 24 November 2017, para 91.

66 GREVIO Baseline Evaluation Report Denmark, GREVIO/Inf (2017)14, published 24 November 2017, para 110.

67 In Austria 353 women had to be turned away in 2015.

68 GREVIO/Inf (2017)4 (Austria), 2017, paras 105 and 106.

69 GREVIO/Inf (2017)13 (Albania), 2017, paras 102–104.

shelters.[70] In Denmark, there are shelters exclusively reserved for women, but if they are filled to capacity, women will be offered emergency accommodation in general shelters or hotels. GREVIO recommends the State to increase the number of domestic violence shelters.[71]

With regard to barring, restraining and protection orders, the Austrian model is praised and was used as an inspiration for Articles 52 and 53.[72] In Austria, perpetrators can be banned from the home between two weeks by the police and twelve months by a civil court.[73] However, GREVIO utters criticism about the fact that protection orders are linked to places instead of to victims and therefore recommends Austria to use no-contact orders rather than no-go orders.[74]

In Monaco, barring orders are hardly ever used; they can only be applied for a very limited amount of time, and legal practitioners and victims are not really familiar with the possibility.[75] On the contrary, barring and protection orders are widely used in Albania, where the perpetrator can be removed from the family home, accompanied by an order to stay at a certain distance from the victim.[76] However, according to GREVIO, the implementation of these orders is sometimes ineffective. Due to a shortage of housing, perpetrators are occasionally ordered to live in one part of the family dwelling while the victim lives in another. Naturally, this may lead to more violence and it is therefore understandable that most victims in Albania prefer to go to a shelter instead of staying in their own homes.[77]

Barring orders and other protection orders are included in the Danish legislation, but are hardly used because victims prefer to go to a shelter.[78] Denmark is criticised for the fact that exceptions to protection orders are possible so the perpetrator can have contact with his children. GREVIO points out that this creates a risk for violence against the partner.

From the assessment of the first four countries, it becomes clear that these countries are doing their best to live up to the obligations contained in the Istanbul Convention. There is attention to securing independent housing for domestic violence survivors, but there is no indication concerning the quality of such housing. While there are differences among the States, on a whole, GREVIO is not satisfied with the number of specialised domestic violence shelters, and all four countries are recommended to increase their efforts. As regards barring and other protecting orders, only Austria is doing well. In practice, these orders are hardly ever used in the other three countries because they are

70 GREVIO/Inf(2017)3 (Monaco), published 27 September 2017, para 71.
71 GREVIO/Inf(2017)14 (Denmark), 2017, paras 115–116.
72 GREVIO/Inf(2017)4 (Austria), 2017, para 171.
73 GREVIO/Inf(2017)4 (Austria), 2017, para 172.
74 GREVIO/Inf(2017)4 (Austria), 2017, paras 172–173.
75 GREVIO/Inf(2017)3 (Monaco), 2017, paras 151–152.
76 GREVIO/Inf(2017)13 (Albania), 2017, para 183.
77 GREVIO/Inf(2017)13 (Albania), 2017, paras 184–186.
78 GREVIO/Inf(2017)14 (Denmark), 2017, paras 204–207.

still too new, unknown to the public at large, or can only be imposed for a very short period. The implications may be that women prefer going to a shelter instead of remaining in their own homes.

6 Conclusion

The Istanbul Convention is unique in that it explicitly poses obligations upon State Parties to protect all kinds of rights of victims of domestic violence including support services for domestic violence survivors. It is also the first instrument that directly links domestic violence to the right to housing. This is a great improvement in comparison to other international and European instruments that deal with only one of these issues and fail to make the link. However, basic concepts and terms, such as adequate shelter or adequate housing for domestic violence survivors, still need to be clarified and defined. Moreover, the empowerment and substantive equality between men and women should be emphasised by explaining that women have an autonomous right to housing and are entitled to accommodation that is at least equally adequate if compared to the housing of their (former) abusers. This is a task that GREVIO could discharge by adopting a general recommendation under Article 69 of the Convention.

While preference for shelters as the first and foremost solution to protect battered women is understandable in countries where barring, restraining and protection orders are new and women may feel too unsafe to make use of them, it is important that shelters are seen as the last resort. Creating distance between the batterer and the victim ideally entails that the perpetrator is removed from the family residence whereas his wife/partner and children are not uprooted, but continue living in their own home. It is evident that such orders need to be paired to better protection in practice so that victims feel confident that there is no need to flee. Innovative techniques, such as GPS systems checking the whereabouts of the perpetrator or alarm systems that can be used by victims, need to be improved and deployed so that women feel safe to stay in the family home.[79] If women and men are convinced that the police will immediately act in cases of threats of violence, or when protection orders are encroached upon, the need for women's safe houses will decrease. Furthermore, creating shelters where perpetrators will be forced to stay makes more sense and will be cost-effective since only one person of a family needs to be accommodated instead of the victim and her children. In addition, this also solves the predicament that boys of a certain age are not allowed to stay with their mothers in a safe house.

79 This is already possible in Spain based on the Organic Act 1/2004 of 28 December 2004 on Integrated Protection Measures against Gender Violence. Since the introduction of the Electronic Monitoring of Restraining Measures System in 2009, more than 1,800 devices have been activated. Parliamentary Assembly, Committee on Equality and Non-Discrimination, *Promoting best practices in tackling violence against women*, Rapporteur Ms Sahiba Gafarova, 29 September 2015, para 60.

In conclusion, it can be said that the question whether the Istanbul Convention has an added value if compared to other international and European human rights instruments can be answered in the affirmative. The Convention certainly has the potential to improve the protection of and support for battered women, particularly as regards their right to housing. However, as always, much will depend on the interpretation of the obligations by the monitoring body, and the implementation by State Parties.

10 Support to battered women in Sweden

Non-profits and public authorities collaborating, counteracting and competing

Ulrika Andersson and Sara Bengtson[1]

1 Introduction: from private to public to multiple conflicts

The promotion of women's rights has in many ways been essential to the Swedish welfare state project.[2] Policies such as free education, free school meals, parental leave and individualised social security rights have all contributed to making Sweden and its Nordic neighbours world champions of gender equality.[3] Against this backdrop of state feminism,[4] one might assume that the implementation of the Council of Europe Convention on preventing and combating violence against women and domestic violence (the Istanbul Convention) would face few obstacles in Sweden. However, if the concept of welfare is expanded to also encompass bodily integrity, the image of a woman-friendly Sweden changes.[5] The issue of violence against women was long considered to be a private matter.[6] The dominant view was that gender equality was achieved in particular through reforms of the labour market.[7]

1 We would like to thank the editors for valuable comments.
2 Compare Johanna Niemi, 'Law and Gender' in Kimmo Nuotio, Sakari Melander, Merita Huomo-Kettunen, *Introduction to Finnish Law and Legal Culture* (Forum Iuris 2012), 274f.
3 Compare ibid., 274f.
4 Compare Johanna Kantola, Judith Squires, 'From State Feminism to Market Feminism?' (2012) 33 *International Political Science Review* 382–400.
5 Compare Gun Hedlund, 'Att samverka i ideologiskt laddade frågor – exemplet kvinnofrid' in Gun Hedlund and Stig Montin (eds), *Governance på svenska* (Santérus Academic Press Sweden 2009), 88.
6 See Maria Wendt Höjer, *Rädslans politik – Våld och sexualitet i den svenska demokratin* (Liber AB 2002).
7 Wendt Höjer, 155. See also Sara Helmersson, 'Mellan systerskap och behandling. Omförhandlingar inom ett förändrat stödfält för våldsutsatta kvinnor' (DPhil thesis, Lund University 2017), 77; Maud Eduards, 'The Women's Shelter Movement' in Gunnel Gustafsson, Maud Eduards and Malin Rönnblom (eds), in *Towards a New Democratic Order?: Women's Organizing in Sweden in the 1990s* (Norstedts Juridik AB 1997), 163; and Viveka Enander, Carin Holmberg and Anne-Li Lindgren, *Att följa med i samtiden – kvinnojoursrörelse i förändring* (Atlas 2013), 19f.

Until the eighties, violence against women was thus not seen as a societal problem: a view that was reflected in its absence from public policy and legislation.[8] Once the non-interventionist attitude towards violence against women was abandoned in the early eighties, other tensions followed. This chapter explores some of these tensions as they have played out in the context of support to battered women, with a view to discussing them in relation to the Istanbul Convention, whose Article 23 obliges its State Parties to provide for "the setting-up of appropriate, easily accessible shelters in sufficient numbers to provide safe accommodation for and to reach out pro-actively to victims, especially women and their children".

The main tension surrounding the issue of violence against women in Sweden has concerned the conceptualisation of violence. The women's shelter movement, which for a long time was the primary actor providing support and shelter to battered women, has promoted a structurally oriented feminist view, which describes violence against women as an expression of an unequal gender order. According to this view, men's violence restricts all women, and all men benefit from men's superior position in society – a position which simultaneously produces and is a result of men's violence.[9] This understanding of violence has been controversial, even within the movement itself. Nevertheless, it eventually came to influence public policy, where, however, it has competed with individualist and relational perspectives that focus on the individual perpetrators and the relation between the man and the woman, respectively.

The different conceptualisations of violence against women imply different ways of organising society's response to such violence, the debate over which is also full of tensions. Should support to battered women be informed by separatism, where only women help other women? Or should it be informed by cooperation – between women and men and between shelters and social services? Should it be guided by sisterhood or professionalism? Should it aim at empowerment or treatment? In Sweden, these conflicts have been intensified as the responsibility of municipalities has increased thanks to several legislative amendments since the late nineties. Expanded state responsibility has meant increased funding for support work – but also more bureaucratisation and professionalisation, which breaks with the traditional working methods of the women's shelter movement.

In this chapter we explore the tensions described above, on the one hand by revisiting the development of the Swedish women's shelter movement, and on the other by examining Swedish legislative material, in particular major reforms

8 In 1982, domestic violence became subject to public prosecution. This enabled the police to investigate and detain batterers, which previously they could not do unless the victim herself reported the violence. Other examples during this period include Restraining Orders Act in 1988, which prohibited a perpetrator from visiting or contacting someone he had previously battered.

9 Compare Eduards, 156.

to victim support. How do the shelter movement and the legislator conceptualise violence? How do they imagine the response to violence? How has the relationship between the shelter movement and the State changed as municipalities have been given increasing responsibility for battered women?[10] The Istanbul Convention places violence against women in the context of gender inequality. It requires that a contracting State take interest in and actively work against violence against women; it requires that the State acknowledge the violence as a public problem, which public authorities are accordingly responsible to combat. The Swedish case illustrates that increased public responsibility may sometimes entail dilemmas for feminist goals and perspectives.

2 Conceptualisations of violence

2.1 The Istanbul Convention

The preamble of the Istanbul Convention describes the understanding of violence against women that informs the instrument. Violence against women is "a manifestation of historically unequal power relations between women and men, which have led to domination over, and discrimination against, women by men and to the prevention of the full advancement of women". The preamble further recognises "the structural nature of violence against women".

The Convention thus acknowledges violence against women as an expression of an unequal gender order, in which men as a collective have more power than women as a collective. To overcome the inequality that simultaneously *produces* (equality is "a key element in the prevention of violence against women") and *is a result of* ("violence against women is one of the crucial social mechanisms by which women are forced into a subordinate position compared with men") violence against women, the State Parties are obliged to "take the necessary legislative and other measures to protect the right of everyone, particularly of women, to live free from violence in both the public and the private spheres". States are accordingly under an obligation to institutionalise the issue and responses to it, through legislative or other measures.[11]

2.2 Within the Swedish women's shelter movement

The first non-profit women's shelter in Sweden opened in Gothenburg in 1978 and was soon followed by more. From the start, the women's shelter movement's conceptualisation of violence against women was heterogenous. Many of

10 Some important aspects of this development, such as the recent years' focus on honour-related violence and intersectional perspectives, are omitted due to the space they would require to do them justice.

11 See further on how the Convention conceptualises violence against women in Niemi and Verdu Sanmartin in this volume.

the non-profit women's shelters subscribed to a structurally oriented feminism. This type of feminism was also what eventually came to inform the national umbrella body, Roks (National Organization for Women's and Young Women's Shelters in Sweden), established in 1984. Alongside sexual violence, prostitution and pornography, violence against women was seen as an expression of a societal structure in which men have more power than women. Solutions to the issue of violence thus had to be sought at an overarching, societal level.[12] Next to providing support and shelter to battered women, engaging in political advocacy was therefore an utterly important task for the shelter movement.

However, factions within the movement disagreed with the structurally oriented feminist understanding of violence and accompanying ideas about how to counter it. They objected with dread to what they perceived as radical feminists' hatred towards men. Their approach to shelter work was more informed by philanthropism, or they saw themselves as a complement to social services.[13]

When the structurally oriented feminist shelters embraced the work of the sociologist Eva Lundgren towards the end of the eighties, tensions within the movement increased. Lundgren adopted a structural perspective on violence against women. Central to her theory was the idea of the "normalisation process". She described domestic violence as a process in which a battered woman eventually accepted, expected and even defended the violence committed against her. According to Lundgren, the roots of the violence lay in the fact that the violent man saw women as inferior to men. He resorted to violence to manifest his superior position as a man and make the woman correspond to his imagination of womanhood.[14]

Lundgren's normalisation theory corresponded to many shelter workers' experience of the workings of violence. Her work gave their knowledge scientific legitimacy, and this, according to Gabriella Nilsson, was a crucial factor in making fighting male dominance the primary goal of Roks in 1994.[15] Those who disagreed with the structurally oriented feminist view have described how other perspectives were marginalised.[16] They found support in the dissertation of Margareta Hydén, who argued that power relations were created in the specific relationships, rather than the result of an unequal gender order.[17]

12 Helmersson, 79; and Enander, Holmberg and Lindgren, 11.

13 See Gabriella Nilsson, 'Könsmakt eller häxjakt? Antagonistiska föreställningar om mäns våld mot kvinnor' (DPhil thesis, Lund University 2009), 178; Enander, Holmberg and Lindgren, 46, and Amy Elman, 'Refuge in Reconfigured States: Shelter Movements in the United States, Britain, and Sweden' in Lee Ann Banaszak, Karen Beckwith and Dieter Rucht (eds), *Women's Movements Facing the Reconfigured State* (Cambridge University Press 2003), 99.

14 See for Lundgren's thinking Eva Lundgren, 'Våldets normalisering och andra våldsförståelser' (Roks 2012).

15 Nilsson, 184.

16 Enander, Holmberg and Lindgren, 46.

17 As recaptured in Nilsson, 186.

By 1996, the conflict within Roks had reached the point where some local shelters split from the organisation and established a second umbrella organisation for women's shelters, Skr (the Swedish Association of Women's Shelters and Young Women's Empowerment Centres), today called Unizon. The women's shelter movement was thereby formally split into two factions, where one understood violence against women as a structural problem (men use violence because of their socially constructed superiority), and the other understood it as a social, relational and psychological issue (*some* men use violence because of factors attributable to the individual and to the individual relationship).[18]

The tensions between different perspectives on violence against women within the women's shelter-movement would eventually permeate also public policy on the issue.

2.3 In Swedish legislative material

When violence against women first gained attention in the eighties, it was not singled out or understood differently from violence against other groups.[19] Its roots, like those of violence in general, were associated with individual factors such as alcohol use, socio-economic circumstances and psychology.[20] By the late eighties, Roks had gained considerable influence in the public debate and became an important consulting body in law-drafting processes.[21] The perspective of women working in the shelters was considered important for formulating adequate responses to violence against women. Preparatory works referred to the "normalisation process", as described by "research [on women's issues]".[22] On the cusp of the nineties, legislators seemed ready for the entry of a feminist, structurally oriented, analysis into public policy.

In 1990, a legislative bill for the first time acknowledged violence against women as a matter of gender equality,[23] and "power" was used to describe the relations between men and women in society.[24] In 1993, the minister of social affairs, Bengt Westberg, established the Commission on Violence against Women. The instructions to the Commission described the roots of violence as outdated images of women and the unequal distribution of power between the sexes in society.[25] In its report, "Women's Integrity", the Commission

18 Helmersson, 80.
19 Hedlund (n 5), 91. Wendt Höjer, 95.
20 Wendt Höjer, 105ff.
21 Nilsson, 177.
22 See e.g. Kommittédirektiv 1993:88, 'Kommission om våld mot kvinnor' (Commission on Violence Against Women) and SOU 1995:60, 'Kvinnofrid' (Women's Integrity), 52.
23 Prop. 1990/91:113, 'Om en ny jämställdhetslag, m.m.' (On a New Law on Gender Equality), 48.
24 Ibid. 48.
25 Commission on Violence Against Women.

categorically referred to the problem as *men's* violence against *women*,[26] and distinguished it from other types of violence.[27]

The structural perspective, however, was not hegemonic. In contrast to the Commission itself, the 1993 instructions to the Commission never spoke of *men's* violence.[28] The roots of violence were outdated images of *women*; the generality of the abusing man was not as accepted.[29] Maria Wendt Höjer notes that the government bill based on the "Women's Integrity" report acknowledged the link between male culture and violence against women, but simultaneously stressed that not all men resort to violence, that the problem in Sweden was minor compared to other countries, and that women also harass men.[30] The debate about the bill in the Riksdag followed the same pattern. It was controversial to qualify violence as male.[31]

Nevertheless, although toned down at times, the structural perspective continued to figure in legislative materials until the early 2000's. In the Power bill from 2005, it was dominant.[32] This bill described violence against women as the most extreme consequence of men's superior and women's inferior position in society. The connections between domestic violence and other forms of violence, such as rape and sexual harassment, were pointed out. It was important, the government further held, to speak in gendered terms about violence: to speak of *men's* violence against *women*, instead of gendered violence or sexualised violence.[33]

Things would change quickly, however. In 2005, Swedish public television broadcast a documentary entitled *Könskriget* (The Gender War).[34] The show portrayed the women's shelter movement as a man-hating sect that had infiltrated the Swedish government. Many scholars have observed that this documentary brought about a backlash against Swedish feminism.[35] The backlash was arguably reflected in the Action Plan adopted by the Liberal-Conservative government in 2006.[36] The plan completely lacked a structural perspective.

26 SOU 1995:60A, 'Women's Integrity'. See also Wendt Höjer, 159.
27 Compare Wendt Höjer, 160, 167 and 174.
28 Compare Enander, Holmberg and Lindgren, 74.
29 See also Eduards, 156.
30 Prop. 1997/98:55,'Kvinnofrid' (Women's Integrity), 22f.
31 Wendt Höjer, 161.
32 Prop. 2005/06:155, 'Makt att forma samhället och sitt eget liv – nya mål i jämställdhetspolitiken' (The Power to Shape Society and Your Own Life: Towards New Gender Equality Policy Objectives, hereinafter the Power bill).
33 Ibid. 51f.
34 Evin Rubar, 'Könskriget' (2005).
35 See, among many, Enander, Holmberg and Lindgren, Helmersson, Nilsson, and, Jenny Westerstrand, 'Konstig, isolerad och extrem' (2012) 3–4 Bang.
36 Skr. 2007/08:39, 'Handlingsplan för att bekämpa mäns våld mot kvinnor, hedersrelaterat våld och förtryck samt våld i samkönade relationer' (Action Plan to Counter Men's Violence Against Women, Honor Crimes and Oppression and Violence in Same-Sex Relations).

There was no reference to a gender order.[37] It called for explanations of why "some men" resort to violence.[38] According to the Liberal minister Nyamko Sabuni, a power-based analysis of violence against women would risk obscuring other types of violence.[39]

In one of the bills that followed in the wake of the Action Plan, the government did speak of *men's* violence, and, in a short passage, noted that this violence was a gender equality issue.[40] This was, however, the only remaining vestige of a structural perspective. The contrast with the Power bill is striking. In the Action Plan, the analysis of violence was limited to the observation that violence was not of a private nature. Violence was, however, not spoken of in terms of power.[41] It was classified as a social problem, as a problem that is costly for society, and as a public health problem.[42] In 2014, the latter became the explicit title of a report by the newly appointed National Coordinator on Domestic Violence,[43] which explained that domestic violence stemmed from the unequal balance of power between the sexes.[44] Simultaneously, the need of treatment for perpetrators was underlined.[45]

After the general election in 2014, the language of structural feminism was again in full bloom in the new government's policy. Violence against women was again viewed as the most extreme consequence of men's superior and women's inferior position in society.[46] It was also declared that conceptions of gender, power and sexuality are fundamental to all sorts of men's violence against women.[47]

During the nineties the views advocated by Roks thus achieved a breakthrough in public policy. The perspective of Roks was acknowledged by parties from the entire political spectrum. Gender neutrality and psychology moved over and made space for structural explanations of violence. These explanations were continuously challenged. But with the election in 2014 of a new "feminist" government, composed of the Social Democrats and the Green Party, the structural language was back. The following sections examine the implications

37 Enander, Holmberg and Lindgren, 85. Gun Hedlund, *Samverkan under frihet eller tvång* Roks rapport 1/2009, 22.
38 The Action Plan, 9.
39 As quoted in an interview with Enander, Holmberg and Lindgren, 105.
40 Prop 2006/07:38, 'Socialtjänstens stöd till våldsutsatta kvinnor' (Support from the Social Services for Women Subjected to Violence).
41 Ibid. 8.
42 Ibid. 8f.
43 SOU 2014:49, 'Våld i nära relationer – en folkhälsofråga' (Domestic Violence – A Public Health Issue).
44 Ibid. 19.
45 Ibid. 14 and 260ff.
46 Skr. 2016/17:10 'Makt, mål och myndighet – feministisk politik för en jämställd framtid' (Power, Policy Objectives and a New Government Agency – Feminist Politics for an Equal Future).
47 Ibid. 33.

of these different views on violence for formulating responses to violence. Is the acknowledgment of structural feminism reflected in how support to battered women is arranged?

3 Support for battered women: female separatism or cooperation?

3.1 The approach of the Istanbul Convention

The Istanbul Convention promotes a comprehensive and integrated policy including various measures to counteract violence against women. This implies, among other things, a tension embedded in the Convention between the above-mentioned structural approach to violence against women and the more individually oriented one.[48] Further, the Convention's emphasis on services, the multiagency cooperation and the acknowledgement of civil society organisations means that Swedish shelters, with a similar organisational structure are highly relevant to discuss in relation to the Istanbul Convention.

3.2 Organisational differences within the Swedish shelter movement

Whereas the feminism of Roks helped to institutionalise the issue of violence against women and introduce power analysis into policy-making, we can see how the agenda of the pragmatic, cooperation-minded Unizon corresponded to and was reflected in policy-makers' responses to the problem in the late nineties and onwards. But what would cooperation eventually mean?

Roks' structural feminism entailed female separatism. Accordingly, there were and are no men at their shelters.[49] Shelters are meant to be "free zones" for women, where they do not have to meet men, who symbolise patriarchal oppression.[50] Female separatism is based on the idea of the shared experience of female vulnerability and lives restricted by men's violence and male threat. Solidarity and exchange between women generate the knowledge and strength to make violence visible and to create change.[51] Female separatism is thus essential to the *method* of the women's shelters within Roks, both as a form of empowerment and as a producer of knowledge.[52]

In a broad sense, the separatism of Roks was a reason for the internal division that led to the establishment of a second national organisation for women

48 Article 1(1)(e), Istanbul Convention.

49 www.Roks.se/om-Roks. Accessed 15 October 2019.

50 Helmersson, 186.

51 Ibid. 186. See also Chrystal Kunosson, 'Ideella organisationer' in Gun Heimer, Annika Björck, Chrystal Kunosson (eds), *Våldsutsatta kvinnor – samhällets ansvar* (Studentlitteratur AB 3rd edition 2014), 271.

52 Although Sara Helmersson's work shows that separatism is questioned within Roks. Helmersson, 206.

shelters. The founders of Unizon wanted to be more open. They wanted to expand the focus to *subgroups* of women, and, importantly, to children, including boys. They wanted to expand the number of actors with whom women's shelters could cooperate. Men, and men's organisations against male violence, were potential partners.[53] It was thought that these multiple perspectives would eventually work to the benefit of the women and children Unizon served.[54] At Unizon, men thus were and are welcome. Men as a group were conceptually fragmented; all men were not responsible for the violence of some.[55] Unizon's perspective corresponded to the traditional Swedish consensus-oriented view on how to achieve gender equality, according to which men and women work together.[56]

Unizon's openness further meant that they were open to cooperation with the State and municipalities. Through its insight into the state apparatus, via its connections within the Social Democratic party, Unizon was able to adapt to and influence emerging trends in public policy.[57] Its interaction with state actors was reflected in the "Women's Integrity" report of 1995 and the subsequent government bill, several parts of which were in line with Unizon's ambitions. Important among these elements were the focus on children and subgroups of women, and the emphasis on cooperation among different actors.[58]

3.3 Increased responsibility for municipalities

During the "Women's Integrity" process in the 1990s, the responsibility for victims of domestic violence came to rest with municipalities. Until that point, women's shelters had been the main providers of support to battered women. Municipalities supported the shelters financially, but the extent of this support varied across the country. Now the State increased its own financial support as well as its pressure on the municipalities to support shelters and to engage in support to victims.[59]

The Women's Integrity bill highlighted the value of women's shelters as an *alternative* to support provided by the State. It emphasised the value of volunteers and volunteer engagement; the ability of shelters to provide anonymity; the opportunity for victims of violence to meet others in the same situation. According to the bill, it was important that women's shelters keep their autonomy. Although shelters were dependent on public funding, public authorities should not try to govern them.

53 Enander, Holmberg and Lindgren, 69.
54 Ibid. 44.
55 Enander, Holmberg and Lindgren, however, point out that Unizon was loyal to the original movement in the sense that the group continued to talk about "men's violence". Ibid. 93.
56 Ibid. 92.
57 Ibid. 92.
58 Ibid. 80.
59 Prop.1997/98:55, Women's Integrity, 61.

At the same time, the bill emphasised the responsibility of the State. In particular, it stressed that women often brought children to shelters. Therefore, cooperation between shelters and local social services was important.[60] Consequently, local social services set up specialised units for victims of violence, which offered therapy and, sometimes, sheltered housing.[61] The main responsibility for battered women remained, however, with the women's shelters.[62]

By the turn of the millennium, the field of violence against women had thus undergone important developments. The issue had become institutionalised, and incorporated elements (if somewhat toned down) of Roks' structurally oriented feminism. The ideological and organisational approach of Unizon simultaneously grew strong. So did the focus on children. The actors who provided support to victims had changed. In a field formerly dominated by non-state actors – the shelters – the State now took on an important role. What would this multiplication of actors mean for the work of supporting battered women?

3.4 The women's shelters: moving from an "alternative" to a "complement" to "social services"

At the beginning of the 2000s, the government continued to encourage cooperation between state and non-state actors. Municipalities were encouraged to learn from the shelters' long experience.[63] The shelters' autonomy towards the municipalities was still emphasised. Municipalities were not allowed insight into the personal data of women staying at the shelters.[64] In the Power bill from 2005, the government increased funding to combat men's violence against women. Municipalities and women's shelters were encouraged, although not obliged, to apply for funding jointly.[65]

In the Liberal-Conservative government's Action Plan from 2007, the manner of describing women's shelters changed. The order of presenting the actors was altered. The women's shelters were no longer "an alternative" to the support provided by the State – they were "a complement".[66] This indicates the shift in understanding of the relation between the State and the shelters that was underway: the former was now the main provider of support to victims of violence.

When the State assumed more responsibility, a new emphasis on *quality* was introduced.[67] Quality meant that *review* of the work with battered women was

60 Ibid. 61f.
61 Helmersson, 17.
62 See SOU 2004:121, 'Slag i luften. En utredning om myndigheter, mansvåld och makt' (Inquiry on Government Agencies, Men's Violence, and Power), 115.
63 Ibid. 17.
64 The Power bill, 76.
65 Prop. 2005/06:155, 75.
66 The Action Plan, 5.
67 See in particular Support from the Social Services for Women Subjected to Violence.

necessary, including the work done by women's shelters.[68] In an article from 2008 authored by the presidents of the two umbrella organisations and gender equality minister Nyamko Sabuni, reviewing the work of the shelters was portrayed as a way of spreading awareness for their activities.[69] In an interview with Sabuni, another picture emerged, as Sabuni underlined the importance of quality and evidence-based methods. If the State was to pay for the "service" the women's shelters provide, she said, there must be guarantees that their work was of sufficient quality.[70] The knowledge possessed by the women's shelters was thus no longer authoritative.

Another consequence of political developments from the year 2006 onwards was that the work of women's shelters increasingly became governed by administrative law. This too resulted in new demands for reviews of the shelters. According to an agreement from 2008, a municipality and a women's shelter could enter into an agreement according to which the municipality could refer women to the shelter and pay for their stay there.[71] In such cases, the shelter was formally performing social services. Consequently, shelters were obliged to follow the rules guiding the work of social services, and the ultimate responsibility for the quality of the work lay with the municipal social services.[72] The autonomy of the shelters, which in the Women's Integrity bill prevented municipalities from dictating how shelters should arrange their work, had been reduced to the power to decide whether to "provide services according to the Social Services Act" or not.[73]

As a result of the laws on social services, shelters are now obliged to ***document*** their work, including the keeping of journals.[74] Sara Helmersson describes how this has changed the daily work at shelters, as administration has become an integral part of the work.[75] The increased administrative burden puts pressure on the women working in shelters, Helmersson writes, since they lack sufficient

68 The Action Plan, 19. In 2008, the government tasked the National Board of Health and Welfare with conducting the review, the results of which are presented in Socialstyrelsen, 'Utvärdering av socialtjänstens och ideella kvinnojourers insatser för våldsutsatta kvinnor' (Review of the Social Services' and the Women's Shelters' Support to Women Subjected to Violence) (2011).

69 Nyamko Sabuni, Carina Ohlsson, Gunilla Westny, 'Regeringen öppnar för starkare kvinnojourer' *Göteborgsposten* (Gothenburg, 26 June 2008).

70 Enander, Holmberg and Lindgren, 119.

71 'Överenskommelse mellan regeringen, ideburna organisationer inom det sociala området och Sveriges Kommuner och Landsting' (Agreement Between the Swedish Government, National Idea-Based Organisations In the Social Sphere and the Swedish Association of Local Authorities and Regions, hereinafter the Agreement).

72 See ibid. 36, and the Social Services Act, chapter 3, section 3.

73 Meddelandeblad nr 2/2012, 'Socialnämnders respektive ideella föreningars ansvar för god kvalitet m.m. vid utförandet av insatser enligt socialtjänstlagen'(The Social Services' and Non-Government Organizations' Responsibility for Qualitative Support According to the Social Services Act), 8.

74 See ibid. 9.

75 Helmersson, 91ff.

competence to navigate the complicated bureaucratic system of which they now form a part.[76] Paradoxically, increased funding has rendered the work more insecure, as it is accompanied by complicated application processes demanding both time and know-how.[77]

The new administrative framework means, moreover, that when a woman is referred to the shelters by social services, the shelters are obliged to report to social services if they suspect that an accompanying child has been harmed.[78] Both Enander, Holmberg and Lindgren and Helmersson write that, overall, neither Roks nor Unizon shelters consider reporting problematic.[79] However, a dilemma arises when a battered woman wants to avoid contact with social services, since reporting harm to a child would mean revealing the identity of the mother.[80] Helmersson discerns an ambivalent attitude among the shelters to this problem. Some take a clear stand against the mother.[81] Others underline the importance of the mother's consent. They may encourage a mother to establish contact with social services, but ultimately, she must make the decision.[82]

These documenting and reporting requirements challenge the traditional shelter value of *anonymity*.[83] They further break with the understanding expressed in the Women's Integrity bill of the shelters as an *alternative* to state support: a place where women can go if they do not want to have contact with public authorities. And they move even further from the idea of a women's shelter movement *in opposition* to the State. A risk of depoliticisation is also inherent in the lack of time and opportunity to engage in advocacy due to new administrative duties, as described by Helmersson.[84] The reporting obligation can also break with the shelter-value of *sisterhood*. An unproblematised approach to reporting may be read as acceptance of the interpretation that the best interest of the child always includes contact with social services, in contrast to an approach that trusts the woman's perception.[85]

76 Ibid. 101.
77 Helmersson, 93.
78 Social Services Act, chapter 14, sections 1 and 1c.
79 Enander, Holmberg and Lindgren, 137, and Helmersson, 113. Within Roks, children have received increased attention in their own right since around 2010. Helmersson interprets this as a reaction to the prosecution in the early 2000's of shelter workers who for years had helped a woman hide her children from a father with custody. She writes that the shelter workers, by being positive toward reporting and thus avoiding even the suspicion of a similar scandal, appeared to protect the legitimacy of the shelter movement.
80 Enander, Holmberg and Lindgren, 133.
81 Helmersson, 116.
82 Ibid. 117.
83 Compare Eduards, 152.
84 Helmersson, 91ff.
85 Compare for a similar reflection Helmersson, 120.

4 Support for battered women: sisterhood or professionalism?

The new "qualitative" support to battered women has additional consequences. Support work should be *professional*: that is, carried out by trained staff and documented.[86] This challenges both the methods and the epistemological foundations of the shelters, which are informed by *sisterhood*.

Sisterhood as a method means that the shelters offer a space where women are believed. Women working in shelters listen to, confirm and avoid questioning a battered woman. They help the victim to understand that she is not to blame for the violence she has suffered. By unconditionally supporting the battered woman, they seek to *empower* her, so that she finds strength to leave the abusive relationship.[87] This empowerment is also one of the goals expressed in Chapter IV of the Istanbul Convention, Art 18.1–3.

Helmersson's study provides an example of what professionalism means at the municipalities' specialised units. Certainly, they too underline the importance of listening to women, but they do so to understand the women's "perspective". And they also listen to and try to understand other family members. According to Helmersson, this way of describing listening indicates that the same story can have many narratives. She analyses this approach as informed by an ideal of *neutrality*.[88] Similarly, Enander, Holmberg and Lindgren write that professionalisation makes the women working in the shelters more like social services employees and less like women who support other women.[89] Professional caretakers, rather than sisters.

Neutrality, Helmersson further claims, implies a relational understanding of violence. According to this understanding, violence is not a product of an unequal gender structure, but rather released in an individual conflict.[90] Such an ideology points to a different method than the one used by structurally oriented feminism, of standing loyally by women's side to empower them. It entails a *therapeutic* way of working, in which the woman has to engage in self-examination and take responsibility for not putting herself and her children in unsafe situations. She is also responsible for the future, for not ending up in yet another violent relationship.[91]

Sisterhood and professionalism contain opposing understandings of what constitutes relevant *knowledge*. Sisterhood implies that knowledge is gendered. Women are particularly equipped to listen to other women and to be experts on men's violence against women, as all women share the experience of being restricted by the threat of men's actual violence. Professionalism, in contrast, is

86 The Action Plan, 6.
87 See Helmersson, 127; Eduards, 151.
88 See Helmersson, 128ff.
89 Enander, Holmberg and Lindgren, 170.
90 See Helmersson, 129.
91 Ibid. 137ff.

not explicitly gendered. The Social Services Act, which, following the 2008 Agreement mentioned above, sometimes applies also to women's shelters, stipulates that social work be performed by professionals with adequate education and experience.[92] Professionals treating victims of violence "should" have a degree in social work.[93] An academic degree is thus more important than being a woman. Following Eduards, such an approach "removes [violence against women] from the context of women's politics [and turns] it into an issue of professional care".[94]

In the Explanatory Report for the Istanbul Convention, the drafters' understanding of Article 23 also reflects tension between sisterhood and professionalism. On the one hand, women's shelters are supposed to provide support and to help women regain their self-esteem, both of which could be associated with sisterhood.[95] On the other hand, they stressed that all shelters should apply a set of standards, thus implying a more professionally oriented approach.[96]

5 Conclusion: dilemmas of institutionalisation

Curiously, in Sweden, the institutionalisation of work to combat violence against women has undermined a structural perspective of the kind the Convention advocates. Institutionalisation has resulted in increased acknowledgment of the issue, broad engagement among all political parties, more funding to women's shelters and the opening of municipal shelters. But institutionalisation has also resulted in the public review of, and application of administrative law to, non-governmental organisations. The reforms challenge core shelter values such as anonymity and sisterhood, both of which are derived from a structurally oriented feminist analysis of an unequal gender order. It has also entailed a way of conducting support work that promotes the ideals of the Swedish democratic order – neutrality and openness; that is, that men and women can work together towards gender equality. These ideals, too, run counter to the ideals flowing from the shelter movement's structural feminist analysis – to stand by the side of battered women unconditionally, and to honour the knowledge that women have by virtue of being women.[97] As we see it, structural feminism was successful in making violence against women into a high-priority political issue in Sweden. Its language has survived to some extent and parties across the political spectrum have used it to varying degrees. But its emphasis on men and women as two separate groups with separate interests has been too provocative to be allowed to inform public policy responses to violence against women.

92 Social Services Act, chapter 3, section 3.
93 SOSFS 2014:4, 6.
94 Eduards, 153.
95 The Explanatory Report, 25.
96 Ibid. 25.
97 Compare for this last point Eduards, 152.

Lastly, the social movements face a dilemma and a difficulty in maintaining their radical character, when the State finally has acknowledged, and eventually embedded, their claims.[98] The perils of institutionalisation include an impact both on how radical work can be conducted and formulated, and on the ability to criticise the State. In the present case, feminism may get excellent help from the Istanbul Convention in making violence against women a universal concern. Nevertheless, the institutional structures of every State have an impact on the implementation of the Convention: an impact in no way unpolitical. When the agenda of social movements increasingly is embedded in the State, who will point out its politics – and who will contest them?

98 See, for example, Hedlund (n 5), 44.

Part V

Migration and asylum

11 Protection beyond victimisation

The significance of the Istanbul Convention for migrant women

Fulvia Staiano

1 Introduction

Migrant and refugee women in Europe are particularly at risk of experiencing, and, in fact, experience with particular frequency, various forms of violence. This issue has been widely recognised in the European context. Already in 2009, the Parliamentary Assembly of the Council of Europe stressed the importance of taking into account the specific needs of this group in Member States' responses to violence against women.[1] In relation to migrant women in particular, the International Organisation for Migration has stressed the link between migration status and violence – both in Europe and worldwide.[2] Language barriers, legal status, limited knowledge of their rights, inadequate access to appropriate jobs and social isolation have been identified as decisive factors in increasing the likelihood of experiencing violence for migrant women.

In relation to migrant women in Europe, however, the problem is not simply and not mainly the absence of protective norms. Rather, law in this field plays a complex role because of a narrow focus on criminal law and *ex post* responses to violence against women. In other words, substantive law is much more preoccupied with offering protection to women victims of violence than with eliminating the sources of vulnerability within the legal frameworks applicable to migrant women. This focus has overshadowed the need for a more comprehensive approach that also takes into account immigration law and the ways in which it contributes to create imbalances of power within key family and employment relationships that are conducive to violence.

On the grounds of this premise, this chapter analyses how family reunification and labour migration law generate vulnerability to violence for migrant women in particular. To do so, it draws meaningful examples from Italy, where the ratification of the Istanbul Convention was carried out in a political and

1 Parliamentary Assembly of the Council of Europe, Resolution 1697(2009), *Migrant Women: at Particular Risk from Domestic Violence*, 20 November 2009.

2 International Organisation for Migration (IOM), *Taking Action against Violence and Discrimination Affecting Migrant Women and Girls*, 2013 https://publications.iom.int/books/taking-action-against-violence-and-discrimination-affecting-migrant-women-and-girls.

legal climate of great concern over the phenomenon of violence against women. The ultimate aim of this chapter is then to enquire into the potential of the Council of Europe Convention on Preventing and Combating Violence against Women and Domestic Violence (Istanbul Convention)[3] to effectively expose and remedy the negative effects of immigration law norms on migrant women's right to live free of violence.

Some features of the Istanbul Convention would encourage an optimistic view of this matter. First, the Convention devotes its entire Chapter III to prevention. Second, its Article 59 is specifically devoted to migration and establishes State Parties' obligation to ensure access to an autonomous residence permit for victims of violence. However, this chapter will emphasise the need for specific attention to the question of prevention within substantive law, which the Istanbul Convention does not directly address. Indeed, state obligations of prevention established in Chapter III are mostly focused on awareness-raising activities and education programmes directed at stakeholders and civil society at large, or on treatment programmes for perpetrators. Chapter V on substantive law, on the other hand, overlooks the question of prevention entirely – let alone the question of possible normative sources of vulnerability for women in general and migrant women specifically. This chapter of the Istanbul Convention instead deals with violence against women after its occurrence, establishing state obligations with respect to the adoption of civil remedies, the criminalisation of certain conducts and matters of jurisdiction.

The question of whether the more general provisions of the Istanbul Convention concerning state obligations of prevention of violence against women (particularly those under Article 12) can support or even demand changes in State Parties' domestic immigration law remains open. This chapter will explore the potential of the Istanbul Convention to produce significant impact on the protection of migrant women from violence by broadening the scope of substantive law beyond the narrow focus of criminal law to cover other crucial areas of prevention such as family migration law and labour migration law.

Section 2 of this chapter, in particular, will offer a critical analysis of the obligations of prevention enshrined in the Istanbul Convention as well as of the specific protective measures prescribed by this treaty with respect to migrant women in particular. Section 3 will then move on to argue, through an analysis of the Italian implementation of the Istanbul Convention, that a comprehensive and effective legal framework aimed at the prevention and repression of violence against migrant women cannot merely focus on *ex post* remedies. Lastly, Section 4 will draw some conclusions on the potential of the Istanbul Convention to foster holistic legal responses by its State Parties with respect to prevention of violence against migrant women.

3 Council of Europe Convention on Preventing and Combating Violence against Women and Domestic Violence [2011] CETS 210.

2 The obligations to prevent violence against women

It has been rightly noted that obligations of prevention of violence against women permeate the entire Istanbul Convention.[4] Article 5(2) of the Convention, for instance, enshrines an obligation of due diligence to prevent acts of violence perpetrated by private actors. Furthermore, the general obligations established by Article 12 also include the requirement for the State Parties to take all necessary measures (legislative or other) to prevent violence against women, as well as the obligation to address "the specific needs of persons made vulnerable by particular circumstances".

The Explanatory Report to the Convention clarifies the meaning of this expression, stating that such persons include, among an heterogeneous array of categories, undocumented migrants and refugees (without specifying their gender).[5] It is observed, in particular, that positive action is required by State Parties to address the needs of these and other categories because perpetrators may choose to target them knowing that "they are less likely to be able to defend themselves, or seek prosecution (…) and other forms of reparation, because of their situation".[6] The qualification of migrants and refugees as inherently vulnerable to violence due to "their situation" has rightly attracted criticism. In particular, it has been noted that the Explanatory Report overlooks the important fact that the cause of such a vulnerability does not simply lie in the inherent characteristics of certain groups but rather within structural and institutional barriers that hinder access to justice and existing forms of protection.[7]

Furthermore, neither the Istanbul Convention nor the Explanatory Report mention the fact that the "particular circumstances" making certain individuals vulnerable may be created by the law itself, and that such circumstances may coincide with a precarious residence or employment status. Yet migrant women's vulnerability to violence and their capability to respond to it can be severely affected by their legal status not only when they are refugees or undocumented, but also when they hold residence permits that impose a certain degree of dependence on their spouses or employers.

This crucial aspect appears to be overlooked even by Article 59, which is devoted to the residence status of victims of violence. Two main areas of concern emerge from an analysis of this Article. They will be further discussed in the following sections of this chapter using the Italian case as an illustration.

4 Lisa Grans, 'The Istanbul Convention and the Positive Obligation to Prevent Violence' (2018) 18 *HRLR* 133, 144.

5 Explanatory Report to the Council of Europe Convention on Preventing and Combating Violence against Women and Domestic Violence, Council of Europe Treaty Series No 210, 11 November 2011.

6 Ibid. 87.

7 Lourdes Peroni, 'Violence against Migrant Women: The Istanbul Convention Through a Postcolonial Feminist Lens' (2016) 24 *Feminist Legal Studies* 49, 61–64.

First, Article 59(1) establishes an obligation of result for State Parties to ensure the granting of an autonomous residence permit to women whose residence status depends on that of their spouses or partners according to domestic law, in case of dissolution of the marriage or the relationship and in the event of particularly difficult circumstances. This provision, which recognises that residence status might constitute an additional hurdle for migrant women victims of violence and might even prevent them from reporting their situation, is an important step forward in the current European human rights law framework.

However, the entire focus of Article 59(1) concerns the response of domestic immigration law to violence that has already taken place, entirely overlooking the matter of prevention through family reunification schemes that do not tie sponsors and spouses indefinitely. Setting aside the equally important issue of the limited scope of application of this provision,[8] another important shortcoming relates to the absence of obligations or even recommendations to State Parties to eliminate unnecessarily long periods of legal dependence of migrant women on their sponsors as a preventive measure.

Second, Article 59(3) provides that State Parties must issue a renewable residence permit to victims of violence when national authorities assess that their stay is necessary owing to their personal situation or for the purpose of their cooperation in investigations or criminal proceedings. This norm, which is applicable to situations of violence beyond the family realm, is a further illustration of an *ex post* approach that fails to consider that some of the causes of such a violence might reside in the very same domestic law to which their protection is entrusted.

As clarified by the Explanatory Report, Article 59(3) was inspired by Article 14(1) of the Council of Europe Convention on Action against Trafficking in Human Beings.[9] This fact, together with the reference to cooperation during investigations or criminal proceedings, suggests a criminal law approach that – while commendable in its effort to provide redress to victims – is inevitably incomplete due to its failure to address how labour migration schemes or visa regimes might generate vulnerability for migrant women in the first place. This might occur, for instance, when residence status is made dependent on continuous employment from the same employer, or in all those cases where the employer is granted with great control over the validity of the residence and work permit of a migrant worker.

Such difficulties have been partially acknowledged by the Explanatory Report. Precisely in relation to Article 59 of the Istanbul Convention, the Report observes that "fear of deportation or loss of residence status is a very powerful

8 This matter has been dealt with extensively in Vladislava Stoyanova, 'A Stark Choice: Domestic Violence or Deportation? The Immigration Status of Victims of Domestic Violence under the Istanbul Convention' (2018) 20 *EJML* 53.

9 Explanatory Report (n 6), para 307.

tool used by perpetrators to prevent victims of violence against women and domestic violence from seeking help from authorities or from separating from the perpetrators".[10] Nonetheless, it further confirms the strictly *ex post* approach of Article 59. In relation to domestic violence, for instance, the Report expresses the view that residence permits granted under Article 59(1) "will allow victims to obtain the necessary protection from authorities without fearing that the perpetrator will retaliate by withdrawing or threatening to withdraw residence benefits under the perpetrator's control".[11]

In sum, despite the inclusion of a significant preventive dimension in the Istanbul Convention, its provisions specifically directed at migrant women victims of violence appear to adopt a quite narrow approach. Article 59, in particular, merely includes a list of preconditions for granting autonomous residence permits, without addressing the ways in which migrant women may be disempowered and made vulnerable by domestic immigration law. To illustrate these points, the next paragraph will comment on the impact of the Istanbul Convention on the Italian system, paying special attention to its effects beyond national criminal law and jurisprudence. The Italian case will be analysed as an important example of the unforeseen but damaging effects of national immigration law and policy on the effective protection of migrant women victims of violence.

3 Immigration law as a source of vulnerability to violence

The ratification of the Istanbul Convention by Italy occurred at a time when political and media attention to violence against women had gained particular momentum.[12] Italy was the fifth State to ratify the Convention, with Law No 77 of 27 June 2013.[13] The ratification contributed to strengthening the public focus on this phenomenon, and domestic law soon followed to ensure compliance with the provisions of the Convention, in the form of Law Decree No

10 Ibid. 301.

11 Ibid. 304.

12 Flavia Laviosa, 'Killing in the Name of Love. Violence against Women in Italy' (2015) 8 *JOMEC Journal* 6; Alessandra Gribaldo, 'The Paradoxical Victim: Intimate Violence Narratives on Trial in Italy' (2014) 41 *American Ethnologist* 743, 745.

13 Legge 27 giugno 2013, n. 77, Ratifica ed esecuzione della Convenzione del Consiglio d'Europa sulla prevenzione e la lotta contro la violenza nei confronti delle donne e la violenza domestica, fatta a Istanbul l'11 maggio 2011. (Law of 27 June 2013, No 77, Ratification and Implementation of the Council of Europe Convention on Preventing and Combating Violence against Women and Domestic Violence, signed in Istanbul, on 11 May 2011.)

93 of 14 August 2013.[14] The approach of the Italian legislator in this field suggests the characterisation of violence against women as a national emergency. The title itself of Law Decree 93/2013 referred to "urgent measures on the matter of security and for contrast of gender-based violence".

Another important feature of the Italian implementation of the Istanbul Convention was its marked focus on criminal law and on the adoption of repressive measures against perpetrators of violence against women. This focus on criminal law responses in the implementation of the Istanbul Convention is by no means a peculiarity of the Italian case. Country reports presented to the Group of Experts on Action against Violence against Women and Domestic Violence (GREVIO) show that a similar focus on *ex-post* criminal repression is also present in legislative reforms adopted by other State Parties with the aim to ensure compliance with the Convention.[15] In this light, the approach of the Italian legislator in the implementation of the provisions of the Istanbul Convention devoted to substantive law emerges as an illustration of a general tendency shown by State Parties rather than an odd exception.

Beyond criminal law, the only two other areas touched upon by the general reform introduced by Law Decree 93/2013 consisted in the regulation of anti-violence centres and, within immigration law, the introduction of special residence permits for victims of violence as required by Article 59 of the Convention. Italy's ratification of the Istanbul Convention prompted an important legislative reform of the main immigration law in this country (the so-called *Testo Unico Immigrazione*). A special residence permit for victims of violence, which had been lacking until that point, was introduced as a result.

Article 18-*bis* of the *Testo Unico* now establishes that when situations of violence or abuse against a foreigner are ascertained in the context of police operations, investigations or proceedings for criminal offences related to domestic

14 Decreto-Legge 14 agosto 2013, n. 93, Disposizioni urgenti in materia di sicurezza e per il contrasto della violenza di genere, nonché in tema di protezione civile e di commissariamento delle province. (Law-decree of 14 August 2013, No 93, Urgent Provisions on Safety and for the Fight against Gender-based Violence, as well as on Civil Protection and Compulsory Administration of Provinces.) The Law Decree was then converted into law by legge 15 ottobre 2013, n. 119, Conversione in legge, con modificazioni, del decreto-legge 14 agosto 2013, n. 93, recante disposizioni urgenti in materia di sicurezza e per il contrasto della violenza di genere, nonché' in tema di protezione civile e di commissariamento delle province. (Law of 15 October 2013, No 119, Conversion into Law, with Modifications, of Law-decree of 14 August 2013, No 93, Urgent Provisions on Safety and for the Fight against Gender-based Violence, as well as on Civil Protection and Compulsory Administration of Provinces.)

15 See in particular Report submitted by Portugal pursuant to Article 68, paragraph 1 of the Council of Europe Convention on Preventing and Combating Violence against Women and Domestic Violence (Baseline Report), received by GREVIO on 8 September 2017; Report submitted by France pursuant to Article 68, paragraph 1 of the Council of Europe Convention on Preventing and Combating Violence against Women and Domestic Violence (Baseline Report), Received by GREVIO on 5 April 2018, 44ff.

violence and there is an actual risk for the physical integrity of victims "as a consequence of the choice to escape such violence or of their statements during preliminary investigations or proceedings", victims will be granted a one-year residence permit "for special cases". The same permit is released when situations of violence or abuse are detected in the context of assistance provided by anti-violence centres or social services. The permit will be revoked whenever the victim adopts a conduct which is "incompatible with the aims of the permit" or when the conditions that justified its release no longer exist.

The addition of Article 18-*bis* was a welcome development brought by the ratification of the Istanbul Convention. Before then, the only explicitly available protection for migrant women victims of violence within the *Testo Unico* was the special residence permit regulated by Article 18, which however covers only individuals whose physical integrity is put at risk "due to efforts to subtract oneself from the influence of a criminal organisation (…) or of declarations made in the context of preliminary investigations or of proceedings". Thus, the Italian system of protection of migrant women against violence significantly improved thanks to the ratification of the Istanbul Convention.

Nonetheless, one important limitation of the Italian response after the ratification of the Istanbul Convention was the exclusive provision of *ex-post* remedies to situations of violence against migrant women (consisting in the establishment of a special residence permit) rather than the adoption of comprehensive prevention strategies that include targeted reforms of family and labour migration laws. This paragraph will illustrate the limitations of this approach, analysing how immigration law can generate vulnerability to violence for migrant women by creating an unnecessarily prolonged and strict relationship of dependence on other individuals, namely spouses and employers.

Instances of dependence generated by disproportionate legal requirements for the validity of residence permits suggest that an effective implementation of the Istanbul Convention should encompass targeted reforms of domestic immigration law and policy. State Parties should translate the holistic approach of the Convention to this specific area, rather than exclusively focusing on the establishment of residence permits for victims of violence as required by Article 59. There is indeed little doubt that while this provision is specifically devoted to migrant women, all the general obligations established by the Convention – including those concerning the prevention of violence against women – also include this category within their scope. Through a critical review of the Italian example, this paragraph aims to convey the idea that an effective prevention of violence against migrant women can only be realised through the orderly coordination of the different legal frameworks applicable to them.

3.1 Cohabitation requirements in family reunification law

Family reunification schemes in Europe generally entail some form of dependence of the family members' permit on that of the sponsor. While such schemes also generally envisage the possibility of obtaining an independent permit for victims of violence, problems persist. First and foremost, domestic legislation usually requires an active participation of victims of violence in judicial proceedings against perpetrators. As clarified earlier, this is also one of the two cases where Article 59(3) of the Istanbul Convention establishes an obligation for State Parties to grant an autonomous residence permit.

However, reporting to the authorities might be neither a feasible option nor an immediate reaction for victims of violence in general and for migrant women in particular. Lack of trust in the authorities or unwillingness to remove oneself from imminent danger might be just two of the reasons why victims' first reaction might not be reporting the violence, but rather interrupting cohabitation. For this reason, in addition to a residence permit, it is crucial that victims are also granted the possibility to end or suspend cohabitation without repercussions on their residence status. Nevertheless, the latter is rarely recognised by domestic immigration systems that instead may require cohabitation as a precondition for the continuous validity of residence permits issued for the purpose of family reunification.[16] Undoubtedly, this requirement responds to the aim of deterring sham marriages contracted with the sole aim of obtaining residence permits.

It is, however, questionable whether imposing a prolonged cohabitation between spouses is an effective or proportionate means to fulfil this aim. Finding alternative ways to ensure the genuine character of spousal relationships that do not impair women's possibility to leave the conjugal home can be crucial to ensure an effective protection of migrant women victims of violence, but it is also an important matter of prevention. Unfortunately, the focus adopted by Article 59 of the Istanbul Convention on *ex post* responses to violence against migrant women rather than including preventive measures within its scope has not encouraged State Parties to eliminate such cohabitation requirements.

The Italian case is a telling example of the limited impact of the Istanbul Convention on this matter. On the one hand, the Istanbul Convention produced a notable effect in the Italian order by prompting the introduction of the abovementioned Article 18-*bis* of the *Testo Unico*, which allows migrant women victims of violence to obtain residence permits regardless of their willingness to initiate judicial proceedings against perpetrators. It should be noted that offences related to domestic violence, such as that of abuse within the family

16 EMN Synthesis Report for the EMN Focussed Study 2016, *Family Reunification of Third-Country Nationals in the EU plus Norway: National Report*, 40, https://ec.europa.eu/home-affairs/sites/homeaffairs/files/00_family_reunification_synthesis_report_final_en_print_ready_0.pdf. The Report highlights that, as a general rule, family members' residence rights are no longer recognised in case of separation between the spouses. Moreover, in several Member States an autonomous right of residence may be granted only after a certain number of years of residence. Not all of these States provide exceptions in cases of domestic violence. Lastly, in Germany, Norway and Spain a minimum period of cohabitation with the spouse or partner – ranging from two to three years – is established as a prerequisite to acquire an independent right of residence.

envisaged by Article 572 of the Criminal Code, can be prosecuted *ex officio* and do not require filing of a report by victims or their cooperation in the ensuing investigation and proceedings.

On the other hand, the ratification of the Istanbul Convention in Italy has produced substantive law reforms focused on redress rather than prevention. At present time, Article 30 of the *Testo Unico* still requires cohabitation as an essential precondition for maintaining residence permits issued on the grounds of marriage with Italian or EU citizens. Article 30(1)(b), in particular, establishes such requirements for foreigners who have regularly resided in Italy for at least a year and who have married Italian or EU citizens or regular resident third-country nationals on Italian territory.

In addition to failing to mention domestic violence as a specific ground of legal protection for holders of residence permits for family reasons, Article 30 establishes a problematic link between cohabitation and the maintenance of residence permits. More specifically, pursuant to Article 30(1-*bis*), residence permits for family reasons granted to foreign spouses of Italian, Union, or third-country citizens "will be immediately revoked if it is ascertained that an actual cohabitation did not follow the marriage, except when children were born from the marriage". As clarified above, this measure pursues the legitimate aim of ensuring that the residence permit for family reasons is not exploited through sham marriages.

However, requiring cohabitation for an indefinite period of time is neither the only nor the best means to fulfil this aim. A more proportionate measure is envisaged by the very same Article 30(1-*bis*) with respect to holders of family reunification visas. For this specific category, residence permits for family reasons will be refused or not renewed "if it is ascertained that the marriage (…) [has] taken place only in order to allow the interested person to reside on the national territory". Here, therefore, cohabitation is not considered a necessary requisite for the purpose of proving that one's marriage is genuine. Instead, a specific assessment of individual situations is required to reach this conclusion.

Another example of an alternative and less disempowering solution for migrant women holding residence permits on the grounds of marriage is provided by Article 12 of Legislative Decree No 30/2007.[17] This norm, which is applicable to spouses of EU or Italian citizens, establishes that the mere lack of cohabitation is not sufficient in itself to justify the revoking of residence permits for family reasons. Instead, a concrete assessment of the actual fraudulent aim of the marriage is necessary.

Neither Article 59 nor other articles of the Istanbul Convention require the elimination of cohabitation requirements from the national family migration regimes. Nonetheless, the inevitable relationship of dependence generated by

17 Legislative Decree No 30 of 6 February 2007, Attuazione della direttiva 2004/38/CE relativa al diritto dei cittadini dell'Unione e dei loro familiari di circolare e di soggiornare liberamente nel territorio degli Stati membri, *GU* No 72 of 27 March 2007.

the legal requirement of continuous cohabitation can foster situations of vulnerability to domestic violence, which sits uneasily with the protective aims of Article 59 of the Convention as well as of Article 18-*bis* of the *Testo Unico*. A combined reading of the latter provision with Article 30 of the *Testo Unico* suggests that migrant women who leave violence or the household without turning to social services, to anti-violence centres or to police authorities will jeopardise their residence status unless their situation is autonomously detected and proceedings are initiated *ex officio*. More broadly, by requiring cohabitation for an indefinite period of time not only is Italian immigration law failing to strike a fair balance between the interest to fight sham marriages and migrant women's human rights, but Italy may also be in breach of its positive and negative obligations under the Istanbul Convention, especially those concerning the effective prevention of violence against migrant women.

Unfortunately, Italian jurisprudence so far has not provided any indications on the relationship between Article 18-*bis* and Article 30(1-*bis*) of the *Testo Unico*. Given this uncertainty, it is only possible to hope that the two norms will be interpreted in a coherent manner in the light of Italy's obligations of prevention of domestic violence under the Istanbul Convention. More generally, the Italian jurisprudence on Article 18-*bis* is quite sparse.[18] As a result, there have been very few clarifications on the scope of the requirement of cohabitation for spouses of third-country nationals who regularly reside in Italy.

A partial corrective to this situation has been provided by the extensive interpretation by Italian courts of Article 30(5) of the *Testo Unico*, which allows for the possibility to convert residence permits for family reasons into permits on the grounds of employment, autonomous work or study in case of widowhood, separation and divorce. By doing so, de facto separation has been included within the scope of this provision.[19] However, in case of lack of employment, autonomous work or study reasons, administrative tribunals have continued to enforce the rule under Article 30(1-*bis*) whereby residence permits are immediately and automatically revoked in case of lack of cohabitation.[20]

The imposition of strict cohabitation requirements as a precondition for the regularity of residence is only one example of the often implicit ways in which immigration rules can foster migrant women's vulnerability to violence. Labour

18 An isolated but notable exception in this respect is provided by Court of Cassation, Sixth Criminal Section, *Criminal Proceedings Against K.K. and K.F.*, judgment No 16498 of 1 March 2017. This judgment rejected as manifestly illogical the argument of a lower court which had dismissed criminal prosecution for domestic violence on the grounds that the victim's statements were ultimately aimed at obtaining a residence permit pursuant to Article 18-bis.

19 Consiglio di Stato, Third Section, *X v Ministry of the Interior*, Judgment No 390 of 28 January 2015; see also Consiglio di Stato, Third Section, *Ministry of the Interior v M.C.*, Judgment No 4433 of 22 September 2015.

20 TAR Milano, Judgment No 1938 of 8 September 2015; TAR Genova, Judgment No 1521 of 11 December 2013; TAR Firenze, Judgment No 1471 of 28 October 2015.

migration law is another area where regulation of entry and residence of migrant workers can generate relationships of dependence on employers. Such dependence can create a favourable environment for psychological, economic and even physical violence especially in the context of professions that take place in private realms. The next section will delve into this matter with specific reference to two sectors of the European labour market that are characterised by a high degree of dependence on employers, i.e. the entertainment sector and domestic work.

3.2 Ties with employers in labour migration law

Migrant domestic workers and entertainers have been identified by human rights jurisprudence and scholarship as particularly vulnerable to violence and abuse by employers.[21] By taking place in private realms, such professions isolate workers from the host society and aggravate eventually pre-existing cultural and language barriers. Already in 2000, the UN Special Rapporteur on contemporary forms of slavery observed that the concentration of women in unskilled sectors of the labour market (including domestic work and entertainment) characterised by low salaries, few labour rights and low job security formed "the basis for forced, servile and exploitative working conditions".[22]

It is therefore not surprising that the recognition of breaches of the prohibition of slavery, servitude and forced labour under Article 4 ECHR against migrant women in the case law of the European Court of Human Rights (ECtHR) has concerned precisely these two sectors. This jurisprudence conveys a worrying picture of the different forms of violence experienced by migrant women in entertainment and domestic work. These forms range from trafficking for the purpose of sexual exploitation uncovered in the judgment of *Rantsev v Cyprus and Russia*[23] to economic and psychological violence implicit in the form of domestic servitude in *Siliadin v France*,[24] *C.N. and V. v France*[25] and *C.N. v the United Kingdom*.[26] It is worth stressing that all such forms of violence come within the scope of Article 3(a) of the Istanbul Convention. Because the described forms of violence occur in sectors where workers are predominantly

21 Siobhán Mullally, 'Migration, Gender and the Limit of Rights' in Ruth Rubio Marín (ed.), *Human Rights and Immigration* (OUP 2014).

22 Report of the United Nations Special Rapporteur on violence against women, its causes and consequences on trafficking in women, women's migration and violence against women of 29 February 2000, 40. On migrant domestic workers specifically, see also Report of the United Nations Special Rapporteur on contemporary forms of slavery, including its causes and consequences of 27 July 2018, available at https://undocs.org/A/HRC/39/52.

23 *Rantsev v Cyprus and Russia* ECHR 2010-I.

24 *Siliadin v France* ECHR 2005-VII.

25 *C.N. and V. v France* App no 67724/09 (ECHR, 11 October 2012).

26 *C.N. v the United Kingdom* App no 4239/08 (ECHR, 13 November 2012).

female and thus affect women disproportionately, they may also be qualified as gender-based violence for the purpose of Article 3(g).

In the *Rantsev* judgment, the ECtHR recognised Cyprus' responsibility for a breach of Article 4 ECHR (among other things) also because of its failure to put in place an appropriate legislative and administrative framework to protect holders of "artiste" visas against trafficking and sexual exploitation. In particular, the ECtHR recalled the fact that cabaret managers and not the artistes themselves were required to apply for an entry permit, and that the former were required to lodge a bank guarantee to cover potential repatriation expenses. In *Siliadin v France*, *C.N. and V. v France* and *C.N. v the United Kingdom*, the ECtHR identified the existence of forced labour (defined as work exacted under the menace of any penalty) precisely because of employers' abuse of the vulnerable positions of applicants stemming from their irregular status.[27] The discussed judgments revealed factual triggers of vulnerability to employers' abuse against migrant workers, including residence status and nationality. However, the specific role of domestic immigration law in creating such a vulnerability was acknowledged by the ECtHR only in the case of *Rantsev*.[28]

The general principle established by the ECtHR whereby "a State's immigration rules must address relevant concerns relating to encouragement, facilitation or tolerance of trafficking"[29] has not yet found any equivalent application in other instances of violence against migrant women beyond trafficking. However, the *Rantsev* judgment raised the crucial issue of prevention of all forms of violence against migrant women through the elimination of immigration law measures that unnecessarily link employees to employers. This judgment unveiled how immigration law and visa policies might themselves generate vulnerability to violence for women.

Despite the lack of follow-up judgments by the ECtHR on state responsibility in relation to prevention of violence against migrant women through immigration law and policy, the matter is still very much relevant in contemporary Europe. The Italian regulation of all types of labour migration, for instance, still manifests features that recall those on which the ECtHR relied to identify a breach of Cyprus' obligation to prevent trafficking against migrant women in the *Rantsev* judgment. Article 22 of the *Testo Unico* envisages a procedure for hiring third-country nationals that is entirely under the control of the employer. The latter is required to initiate an online procedure for the issue of a visa for the purpose of

27 Beyond domestic work, the importance of assessing the existence of instances of forced labour in the light of the link between irregular residence status and increased vulnerability to labour exploitation has been highlighted in *Chowdury and Others v Greece* App no 21884/15 (ECHR, 30 March 2017). On this judgment, see Vladislava Stoyanova, 'Sweet Taste with Bitter Roots: Forced Labour and *Chowdury and Others v Greece*' (2018) 1 *EHRLR* 67.

28 Lourdes Peroni, 'The Borders that Disadvantage Migrant Women in Enjoying Human Rights' (2018) 36 *NQHR* 93, 106–108.

29 Ibid. 284.

employment, specifying the terms of the employment relationship in a proposal of contract that will be signed by the prospective employee. Moreover, employers are required to commit to covering eventual repatriation costs.

In addition to presenting problematic features in its general regulation of labour migration, Italian law establishes an even stronger dependence on employers for certain categories, such as entertainers. Dancers, artists and musicians to be employed in entertainment clubs are among the professions for which Article 27 of the *Testo Unico* allows entry beyond the yearly quota system established for migrant workers in general. In addition to requiring employers to apply for their entry, Italian law prevents entertainers to move on to other sectors of the labour market or to change qualification. Changing employer is equally prohibited by the law, since an eventual renewal of the work and residence permit for entertainers is only allowed for continuing the employment relationship with the same employer.

Several aspects of the described provisions increase the risk of abuse from employers for third-country nationals holding entertainers' permits. The tight links with employers and with the specific profession established by this framework appear particularly noteworthy, especially if considered in connection with the strong control granted by Italian law in general to employers over application procedures and their obligation to cover workers' repatriation expenses. A 2011 CEDAW Shadow Report on Italy voiced concerns over the risk of trafficking implied by the described rules. In particular, the Report stressed that

> entry in Italy with a residence permit for entertainers (the limited duration of which is linked to the willingness of the employer to maintain the contract) creates a situation of dependence on club managers which is often conducive to exploitation.[30]

Similar observations can be made in relation to special labour migration schemes established for migrant domestic workers, which often imply a high degree of dependence on employers. I have commented elsewhere that this feature was present in the Italian regularisation programmes for domestic workers and more recently in the United Kingdom's Overseas Domestic Workers Visa.[31] In both cases, the strong control granted by domestic legislation

30 Italian Platform 'CEDAW: Work in Progress', CEDAW Shadow Report www.aidos.it/wp-content/uploads/2017/06/ItalyCEDAWShadowReport.pdf, 43. On the relation between the limited validity of work and residence permits in this sector and vulnerability to trafficking, see Federico Lenzerini, 'International Legal Instruments on Human Trafficking and a Victim-Oriented Approach: Which Gaps Are to Be Filled?' (2009) 4 *Intercultural Human Rights Law Review* 205, 233ff.

31 Fulvia Staiano, *The Human Rights of Migrant Women in International and European Law* (Giappichelli – Eleven 2016) 79ff. On this matter, see also Siobhán Mullally and Clíodhna Murphy, 'Migrant Domestic Workers in the UK: Enacting Exclusions, Exemptions and Rights' in Siobhán Mullally (ed.) *Care, Migration and Human Rights: Law and Practice* (Routledge 2015).

to employers over their employees' residence status could generate severely imbalanced employment relationships and make migrant workers vulnerable to psychological or even physical abuse. Indeed, not only women migrant workers who work and reside irregularly in their host countries, but also workers whose residence status is entirely dependent on continuous work with the same employer might be severely discouraged from reacting to situations of abuse. In Italy, for instance, the Court of Cassation has dealt with at least two cases of sexual violence by employers against domestic workers characterised by forms of exploitation of their irregular residence status.[32]

The establishment of a special residence permit for victims of violence is an important but insufficient remedy to such vulnerability. It is certainly crucial to ensure that migrant women are given the possibility to report abusive employers to the authorities of their host country without fear of jeopardising their residence status or of exposing their irregular status. The recognition and the actual enforcement of basic labour and socio-economic rights to all migrant workers appear an equally important measure of prevention of violence against migrant women in the context of employment relationships. Such rights should include, at the very least, all labour protections granted to citizen workers – including in particular the right to decent working conditions – as well as the right to change employer. Ensuring that migrant women actually enjoy these rights is a form of prevention of violence that complements the *ex post* protection granted by residence permits for victims of violence under Article 59 of the Istanbul Convention.

Against this background, it is important to consider the potential of the Istanbul Convention to highlight the links between the regulations of work and residence permits (as well as work visas) and the increased risk of suffering violence at the hands of employers, particularly for certain categories of workers hidden from the public eye such as entertainers and domestic workers. State Parties of the Istanbul Convention should be pushed to address these issues from a perspective of prevention of violence in the employment realm (such as sexual exploitation and domestic servitude through threats and psychological submission).

The Convention's general provisions contain an obligation for State Parties to adopt and implement policies encompassing all relevant measures for prevention of violence against women (Article 5(2)). Such policies can be understood to include also immigration policies. This interpretation should not be taken for granted, since States may choose to exercise their discretionary power to choose the means to fulfil their due diligence obligations through other avenues. This point has been very effectively made in the context of the implementation of

32 Court of Cassation, Third Criminal Section, *Criminal Proceedings Against L.G.*, judgment No 9131 of 27 May 2015; Court of Cassation, Third Criminal Section, *Criminal Proceedings Against G.C.*, judgment No 14817 of 13 February 2018.

Article 4 ECHR precisely in relation to the possibility for migrant women's right to change employer.[33]

It is crucial that legislators and policy-makers are made aware of the unforeseen and perverse effects of some rules governing visa schemes and residence permits so that the main sources of legislative precariousness and vulnerability for migrant women are eliminated. In this context, the monitoring work of GREVIO can play an important role, offering clarifications to State Parties on how to strike a fair balance between their interest to control and regulate labour migration, on the one hand, and their obligations under the Convention, on the other. By doing so, the measures necessary for the effective application of the Istanbul Convention to migrant women would be significantly expanded beyond the narrow scope of the right to residence permits recognised by Article 59(3).

4 Concluding observations

Far from representing an exception, the Italian case exemplifies how immigration law can significantly contribute to migrant women's vulnerability to violence and affect their capability to react to it without fearing to jeopardise their residence status. The domestic legislation of State Parties discussed in this chapter suggests that despite the momentum gained by the legal response to violence against women around the time of the ratification of the Istanbul Convention, prevention remains an overlooked aspect of the implementation efforts. This might also be due to the narrow focus of Article 59 of the Convention on States' obligation to grant residence permits. Neither Article 59 nor the broader Article 5 specifies which preventive measures should be adopted for this category of women.

It will be up to the GREVIO – hopefully – to offer important clarifications to State Parties on how to ensure that the holistic approach required by the Convention does not exclusively benefit citizen women. Furthermore, this approach would also foster a welcome departure from a quite common narrative in legal discourses depicting migrant women as helpless victims of violence rather than as individuals in need of socio-economic and legal empowerment. By doing so, migrant women would also be fully included within the scope of the obligation of result as formulated by Article 18(3) of the Convention, which envisions that State Parties should "aim at the empowerment and economic independence of women victims of violence".

GREVIO might have the chance to make such clarifications quite soon in its country-monitoring activities. The first round of baseline reports submitted by State Parties reveal an unsatisfactory situation from the point of view of compliance with positive and negative state obligations under the Istanbul

33 Vladislava Stoyanova, *Human Trafficking and Slavery Reconsidered: Conceptual Limits and States' Positive Obligations in European Law* (CUP 2017) 387–394.

Convention. In particular, it is possible to observe a general overlooking by State Parties of the particular circumstances that make migrant women vulnerable to violence, let alone of the fact that such circumstances may be created by their own immigration laws.

At the time of writing, GREVIO has issued evaluation Reports concerning only eight State Parties. None of them offers clarifications on specific preventive measures to be taken with respect to migrant women within family or labour migration law and policy. However, the evaluation activities of GREVIO are at a too early stage to allow for any conclusions on whether and to what extent this monitoring body will encourage the adoption of a comprehensive approach to the issue of violence against migrant women, and will push State Parties to consider specific questions of prevention in relation to this category of women. For now, one may only note that important encouragements in this direction have recently come from soft law sources.[34] Among them, it is particularly interesting to recall General Recommendation No 35 of the Committee for the Elimination of Discrimination against Women, which recommends that State Parties to CEDAW repeal all "restrictive immigration laws that discourage women, including migrant domestic workers, from reporting [gender-based] violence".[35]

It remains to be seen whether and to what extent these perspectives will be assimilated in the supranational and domestic interpretation and enforcement of the Istanbul Convention. There is no doubt that the incorporation of a construction of migrant women's vulnerability to violence as contingent and dependent also on the regulation of their entry and residence in host countries is a crucial aspect of the effectiveness of any measure of prevention.

34 Siobhán Mullally, 'Migrant Domestic Workers and Continuums of Exploitation: Beyond the Limits of Antitrafficking Laws' (2018) *AJIL Unbound – Symposium on Framing Global Migration Law*, 501–502.

35 Committee on the Elimination of Discrimination against Women, General Recommendation No 35 on gender-based violence against women, updating General Recommendation No 19, 14 July 2017, CEDAW/C/GC/35, 31, let c).

12 Gender-based violence against women and international protection needs

The contribution of the Istanbul Convention

Dolores Morondo Taramundi

1 Introduction

It is widely acknowledged that, notwithstanding the gender-neutral definition of refugee in international law,[1] asylum has largely been seen through a male lens, and asylum systems have been developed as a response to men's experiences of persecution.[2]

Since the eighties, it has been increasingly understood that international conventions and national asylum policies have tended to overlook the specific position of female asylum seekers and the gendered nature of refugee situations, preventing women from being adequately protected by the Refugee

1 Both Article 1A(2) of the Convention Relating to the Status of Refugees (1951) and its 1967 Protocol define a refugee as

> a person who, owing to a well-founded fear of persecution for reasons of race, religion, nationality, membership of a particular social group or political opinions, is outside the country of his nationality and is unable or, owing to such fear, is unwilling to avail himself of the protection of that country.

2 European Parliament, Committee on Women's Rights and Gender Equality, *Draft Report on the situation of women refugees and asylum seekers in the EU* (2015/0000(INI), 16 November 2015, Rapporteur Mary Honeyball; UNHCR, Guidelines on International Protection No 1: Gender-related Persecution within the context of Article 1A(2) of the 1951 Convention and/or its 1967 Protocol relating to the Status of Refugees, HCR/GIP/02/01, 7 May 2002 (Guidelines on Gender-related Persecution).

Convention.[3] The recognition that sexual and gender-based violence can fall under the definition of persecution in refugee law has emerged slowly, in line with a broader development resulting from the struggle of feminist and women's groups to have women's rights recognised under international law and, in particular, to see violence against women acknowledged as a form of human rights violation.[4]

The Office of the United Nations High Commissioner for Refugees (UNHCR)[5] and the Committee on the Elimination of Discrimination against Women (CEDAW Committee)[6] have given detailed recommendations about different aspects of the refugee process where gender makes a difference, and where gender-sensitiveness could improve asylum procedures and ensure that they are more responsive to women's needs and claims regarding asylum. These

3 Karen Musalo and Stephen Knight, 'Asylum for Victims of Gender Violence: An Overview of the Law, and an Analysis of 45 Unpublished Decisions' (2003) *Immigration Briefings* 1. Besides reports by international organisations, there is a growing field of scholarly research on gender and asylum. See, for example, Lisa Frydman and Kim Thuy Seelinger, '*Kasinga*'s Protection Undermined? Recent developments in Female Genital Cutting Jurisprudence' (2008) 18 *Bender's Immigration Bulletin* 1073; Alice Edwards, 'Transitioning Gender: Feminist engagement with international refugee law and policy 1950–2010' (2010) 29(2) *Refugee Survey Quarterly* 21; Siobhán Mullally, 'Migration, Gender, and the Limits of Rights' in Ruth Rubio-Marín (ed.), *Migration and Human Rights*, Collected Courses of the Academy of European Law (OUP 2013); Helen Bailot, Sharon Cowan and Vanessa Munro, '"Hearing the Right Gaps": Enabling and Responding to Disclosures of Sexual Violence within the UK Asylum Process' (2013) Edinburgh School of Law Research Paper 2013/36 www.research.ed.ac.uk/portal/files/14559850/Hearing_the_Right_Gaps.pdf; Efrat Abel, Catherine Dauvergne and Jenni Millbank (eds), *Gender in Refugee Law: From the Margins to the Centre* (Routledge 2014); Karen Musalo, 'Personal Violence, Public Matter: Evolving Standards in Gender-Based Asylum Law' (2014) *Harvard International Review* 45; Melanie Randall, 'Particularized Social Groups and Categorical Imperatives in Refugee Law: State Failures to Recognize Gender and the Legal Reception of Gender Persecution Claims in Canada, the United Kingdom, and the United States' (2015) 23 *American University Journal of Gender, Social Policy & the Law* 529.

4 Mullally (n 3); Edwards (n 3).

5 Besides the Guidelines on Gender-related Persecution: UNHCR, *Handbook on Procedures and Criteria for Determining Refugee Status under the 1951 Convention and the 1967 Protocol relating to the Status of Refugees*, HCR/IP/4/Eng/REV.1 [1979, reed. January 1992]; UNHCR, *Handbook for the Protection of Women and Girls* [2008]; UNHCR, *Improving Asylum Procedures: Comparative Analysis and Recommendations for Law and Practice: Key Gender Related Findings and Recommendations* (2010).

6 Committee on the Elimination of Discrimination against Women, 'A Call for Gender Equality for Refugees and Stateless Persons', Statement on the Anniversaries of the 1951 Convention Relating to the Status of Refugees and the 1961 Convention on the Reduction of Statelessness, 19 October 2011; Committee on the Elimination of Discrimination against Women, General recommendation No 32 on the gender-related dimensions of refugee status, asylum, nationality and statelessness of women, CEDAW/C/GC/32, 14 November 2014 (General Recommendation No 32).

guidelines and recommendations, as well as numerous studies and reports,[7] cover a variety of issues which can be grouped under three main headings: (a) questions regarding gender bias in the assessment of women's claims to asylum;[8] (b) women's needs and conditions in transit situations and reception places;[9] and (c) issues relating to gender-related persecution and the determination of refugee status.

This chapter will focus on the last point, namely gender-based persecution and gender-based violence against women as grounds for claiming asylum. This focus includes exploring the challenges that female asylum seekers might experience in the procedures for determining their refugee status on those grounds, and the measures provided by the Istanbul Convention for their international protection. First, the next section will address the challenges faced by gender-related persecution in asylum claims. Second, the role played by Articles 60 and 61 of the Istanbul Convention will be examined in relation to the identified challenges or gaps, and taking into account the wider international protection framework.

7 For example, Hana Cheikh Ali, Christel Querton and Elodie Soulard, *Gender Related Asylum Claims in Europe: A Comparative Analysis of Law, Policies and Practice Focusing on Women in Nine EU Member States* (European Parliament 2012); Gabor Gyulai, *Información sobre el país de origen en el procedimiento de asilo: La calidad como requisito legal en la UE* (Comité Helsinki de Hungría 2011); Amnesty International End FGM Campaign, ILGA-Europe and the European Women's Lobby, *En-Gendering the European Asylum Support Office* February 2011; ILGA-Europe *Policy paper on the recast of the EU Asylum Procedure and Reception Directives* July 2011; Asylum Aid, *Unsustainable: The quality of initial decision-making in women's asylum claims* 2011; CEAR, CIR and FTDA, *Exchange for Change: Guide for an effective protection of refugee victims of gender-related persecution in Europe* 2010; Human Rights Watch, *Fast-tracked Unfairness: Detention and Denial of Women Asylum Seekers in the UK* 2010; Yakin Ertürk, *15 years of the United Nations Special Rapporteur on Violence against Women, Its Causes and Consequences* (United Nations 2009); Heaven Crawley and Trine Lester, *Comparative Analysis of Gender-related Persecution in National Asylum Legislation and Practice in Europe* (UNHCR 2004); Radhika Coomaraswamy, *Integration of the Human Rights of Women and the Gender Perspective, Violence against Women* (UN doc. E/CN.4/2000/68, 29 February 2000).

8 For example, a tendency to regard women's and girls' claims as being included in the claims made by their husbands, fathers or any other male family members, even when they have suffered the same persecution as the male applicant has. In women's claims for asylum, oral testimony tends to play a bigger role, given the lack of documentary evidence of the persecution, which makes credibility assessments crucial to their applications. Women also tend to have less access to information, poorer language skills and less confidence in dealing with bureaucratic procedures and public officials.

9 Recommendations include gender-sensitive reception procedures and support services, such as appropriate accommodation for pregnant and lactating women and families with children, sex-segregated accommodation and toilet facilities, lockable rooms and adequate lighting, guard protection (including female guards), information to women and girls on gender-based violence and assistance services, and crisis counselling and medical care for survivors of sexual violence.

2 Specific challenges regarding gender-based persecution

The UNHCR Guidelines on Gender-related Persecution begin by acknowledging that the term "gender-related persecution" does not have a legal meaning per se. It is used to "encompass the range of different claims in which gender is a relevant consideration in the determination of refugee status".[10] In these Guidelines, gender-related claims typically comprise acts of sexual violence, family/domestic violence, coerced family planning, female genital mutilation, punishment for transgression of social mores, and human trafficking. The Guidelines state, nevertheless, that "mere discrimination" might not be sufficient to amount to persecution. A pattern of discrimination which, on cumulative grounds, leads to consequences of a substantially prejudicial nature, or to a pattern of discrimination in state protection of certain individuals from certain types of harm, might give the right to international protection.[11]

A variety of expressions to refer to the phenomenon of gender-related persecution, as well as various classifications can be found both in policy documents and in relevant scholarship. Women and girls may experience persecution because of gender[12] and persecution which takes a gendered form. The former comprises forms of harm inflicted on women and girls because of repressive social and legal norms, discriminatory legislation or cultural practices. Among the latter, the use of rape and other forms of sexual violence are paramount as means to inflict harm on women and girls.[13]

Since gender-related persecution claims differ from traditional asylum claims, they have historically faced significant challenges. In what follows, five challenges will be assessed. The first three were discussed by Musalo and Knight in the early 2000s,[14] whereas the last two have been developed by scholars and practitioners more recently.

10 Guidelines on Gender-related Persecution, para 1.

11 Guidelines on Gender-related Persecution, paras 14 and 15.

12 The notion of persecution because of gender includes not only forms of harm inflicted on women, but also those inflicted on other gendered groups, such as homosexuals and transgender persons, on the basis of their sexual and gender identities. In a comprehensive understanding of gender, men who (unlike women and homosexuals) are not normally gendered, *in specific circumstances* can be demeaned and humiliated through certain gender constructions. For example, this was the case for some soldiers or prisoners detained in the Abu Ghraib prison that were raped or subjected to sexual forms of humiliation during the Second Iraq War. See Sandesh Sivakumaran, 'Sexual Violence against Men in Armed Conflict' (2007) 18 *European Journal of International Law* 253. Increased attention is being paid to other gendered practices regarding men, such as, for example, punishments for failing to adhere to the normative standards of masculinity. See Melanie Griffiths, '"Here, Man Is Nothing!" Gender and Policy in an Asylum Context' (2015) 18 *Men and Masculinities* 468.

13 Similarly, Heaven Crawley's distinction between gender-related and gender-specific persecution. Heaven Crawley, *Refugees and Gender: Law and Process* (Jordans 2001), 7–8.

14 Musalo and Knight (n 3).

2.1 Gender as a ground of persecution in the Refugee Convention

According to Musalo and Knight, the absence of an explicit reference to gender in the refugee definition provided in the 1951 Refugee Convention is the first factor that has hindered the recognition of gender-related claims.[15] Even when gender-based violence is severe enough to amount to persecution, the determination of refugee status requires that actual or feared persecution be "for reasons of race, religion, nationality, membership of a particular social group or political opinion". These are the grounds to be established in order to qualify for refugee status. Gender is not included among the listed grounds. Therefore, even when adjudicators find that persecutory acts have taken place, they may deny refugee protection for the lack of nexus to one of the grounds.

Consequently, some authors have favoured the inclusion of gender as an additional ground of persecution in Article 1A(2).[16] This emphasises that gender-related persecution and violence are as serious as other forms of persecution, and promotes the visibility of the phenomenon, which is currently under-reported.[17] General Recommendation No 32 of the CEDAW Committee, while commending a gender perspective in the application of all five grounds of persecution in the Refugee Convention, encourages States to "further introduce other grounds of persecution, namely sex and/or gender, into national legislation and policies relating to refugees and asylum seekers".[18]

The UNHCR, however, has maintained that the definition in the 1951 Refugee Convention covers gender-related persecution if "properly interpreted" (that is, construed in a gender-sensitive manner), and that therefore there is no need to add a new ground.[19] However, research indicates that this standpoint is problematic when taking into account the rejection rate of applications for asylum made by women victims of gender-related persecution.[20] While both the European Parliament and the UNHCR have supported an interpretation of Article 1(A)2 of the Refugee Convention that includes both women who are victims of persecution because of their gender and women who face persecution for violating social norms, this is not a generally accepted position among national legislators and judges.[21]

15 Musalo and Knight (n 3).

16 Doreen Indra, 'Gender: A Key Dimension of the Refugee Experience' (1987) 6(3) *Refuge* 3; Natalie Oswin, 'Rights Spaces: An Exploration of Feminist Approaches to Refugee Law' (2001) 3 *International Feminist Journal of Politics* 347; Crawley (n 13); Jane Freedman, *Gendering the International Asylum and Refugee Debate* (Palgrave Macmillan 2007).

17 The lack of statistics is considered an important barrier for assessing the phenomenon and designing mechanisms to tackle it. UNHCR, Position Paper on Violence against women and girls in the European Union and persons of concern to UNHCR, PC.DEL/824/14, 9 July 2014, 5. See also Cheikh Ali, Querton and Soulard (n 7).

18 General Recommendation No 32, paras 30 and 38.

19 Guidelines on Gender-related Persecution, para 6.

20 Freedman (n 16).

21 Freedman (n 16); Cheikh Ali, Querton and Soulard (n 7).

2.2 Specificity of the harm inflicted upon women

A second challenge in the recognition of gender-related protection claims concerns the types of harm inflicted on women. Some of these, such as female genital mutilation and oppressive social norms, are often regarded as cultural norms and duties incumbent upon women, rather than as forms of persecution. The traditional understanding of the public/private divide plays a fundamental role in rendering the power that men exercise over women a private, family, or personal matter, rather than a political one. The idea that gender-related types of harm are private or cultural issues, rather than forms of persecution, is further reinforced by the gendered role distributions that place men in the public/political sphere and women in the private/domestic sphere. Recently, US Attorney General Jeff Sessions used this argument in a decision that reversed an immigration appeal court ruling that had granted asylum to a Salvadoran woman sexually abused by her husband: "an alien may suffer threats and violence (…) for any number of reasons relating to her social, economic, family or other personal circumstances. Yet the asylum statute does not provide redress for all misfortune".[22]

As argued by Crawley, this elaboration of persecution fails to understand the way in which the concepts of politics and belonging, political space and participation are already gendered. Individual actions by women do not seem to fit in the construction of individual rights in the public space, because they are understood as belonging to a different sphere (i.e. the private and personal). The UNHCR Guidelines on gender-related persecution make reference to how dominant gender roles might determine women's involvement in political activities and how this is perceived. For example, women may be involved in low-profile activities (more difficult to prove in asylum claims) and may be persecuted because they are associated with the political activities of male relatives.[23] Furthermore, harm suffered by women in the private sphere, as well as action taken by women to alter their condition in their private family or close community relations, has a political or public dimension. Both the UNHCR and the CEDAW Committee have highlighted that opinions on gender roles and activism in favour of women's rights need to be understood within the ground of political opinion in asylum claims.[24]

2.3 Non-state actors as persecutors

The third challenge to the recognition of gender-related protection claims examined by Musalo and Knight refers to the persecuting agents involved. In many cases of gender-related harm, the persecutor is not an agent of the State, but a non-state actor. Harm perpetrated by non-state actors amounts to

22 Matter of A-B-, 27 I&N Dec. 316 (A.G. 2018), 318.
23 Guidelines on Gender-related Persecution, para 33.
24 Guidelines on Gender-related Persecution, para 32; General Recommendation No 32, para 15.

persecution when the State is unable or unwilling to prevent such harm or to protect the claimant because of discriminatory governmental policies or practices.[25] Although many countries now recognise those who flee persecution by non-state actors where the government cannot or will not control these actors as refugees, this recognition has been slow to come.[26]

Recognition of non-state actors as persecutors is further hindered when these actors are not armed guerrilla groups, rebel military forces or territory-controlling criminal organisations such as mafias or *maras*, but the applicant's own closest relations. In some forms of gender-related persecution such as marital violence, forced marriage, female genital mutilation or enforcement of oppressive social mores, the persecutor is the applicant's husband, father or other members of her family or community.[27] This has led adjudicators to characterise these forms of persecution as "personal" in nature, rather than public and political. In the already cited decision of Attorney General Sessions in July 2018, it was required that "[w]here the persecutor is not part of the government, the immigration judge must consider both the reason for the harm inflicted on the asylum applicant and the *government's role in sponsoring or enabling such actions*".[28] By requiring a more robust appreciation of the role of the government (sponsoring or enabling), this instruction strengthens the public/private divide. Most of the victims of gender-related persecution have, at best, country of origin reports or reports by international organisations which show the lack of effectiveness of the government's measures against gender-based violence. These reports may be enough to argue that the State is in fact unable to prevent harm or protect the victims. Yet they may not be able to sustain that the State "sponsors" or "enables" gender-based violence. This more exacting requirement means, in fact, that in cases where the persecutor is a non-state actor, violence must be characterised by some public dimension: by the State taking active part in it as a "sponsor" or "enabler", and not just by not being capable of or effective in controlling gender-based violence.

2.4 *The role of pervasive and structural gender inequalities*

The previous three challenges identified by Musalo and Knight could be seen as resulting from a traditional elaboration of the definition of persecution in terms of violations of individual rights or, even more restrictedly, of negative

25 Guidelines on Gender-related Persecution, para 19.

26 Cheikh Ali, Querton and Soulard (n 7). In the abovementioned decision by US Attorney General, it was stated that "[t]he mere fact that a country may have problems effectively policing certain crimes – such as domestic violence or gang violence – or that certain populations are more likely to be victims of crime, cannot itself establish an asylum claim." Matter of A-B- (n 22), 319.

27 Freedman (n 16), 83.

28 Matter of A-B- (n 22), 318 (emphasis added).

freedoms.[29] This limitation causes asylum systems to "offer only limited redress in cases where there is pervasive and structural denial of rights, such as those cases were rights are denied because of pervasive and structural gender inequalities".[30] The more pervasive and structural violence is (as in the case of gender-based violence), the lower the ability of the asylum system to perceive the particular instances of violence as persecution cases.

This tension between the individualistic understanding of persecution in the Refugee Convention and the structural character of gender inequality appears as a "discomfort with gender",[31] noticeable, for example, in the text of the Guidelines on gender-related persecution. On the one hand, this discomfort taints the language of gender sensitiveness. Gender sensitiveness – understood as awareness of or perspective on the ways that gender discrimination works – is certainly necessary in asylum adjudication. Nevertheless, the language of the Guidelines seems to point to the idea that the lack of recognition of gender-related persecution by receiving countries' adjudicators is not related to gender inequality or sexist assumptions in those countries, but rather to a lack of sensitivity, empathy or compassion. When asylum systems are unable to grasp the structural character of gender inequality, a gender-sensitive interpretation runs the risk of detecting gender inequality in third countries in stereotyped (and racialised) ways.[32] At the same time, it runs the risk of being unobservant of gender biases and gender inequality in the action of asylum systems themselves.

On the other hand, this tension is also noticeable in disclaimers such as the one in paragraph 4 of the Guidelines: "Adopting a gender-sensitive interpretation of the 1951 Convention does not mean that all women are automatically entitled to refugee status". This disclaimer has attracted criticism for pampering to the "spectre of hordes of women" ready to claim asylum, a form of moral panic statements very common in some political discourses on asylum.[33] But more importantly, it seems to understand "gender" as being a euphemism to refer to women and not to the sexual division of power. In this sense, the Guidelines reproduce, in the particular area of asylum law, a wider difficulty of anti-discrimination law exposed by Iris Marion Young:[34] structural understandings of

29 David Bartram, 'Forced Migration and "Rejected Alternatives": A Conceptual Refinement' (2015) 13 *Journal of Immigrant & Refugee Studies* 439.

30 Freedman (n 16).

31 Sharon Pickering, 'Gender Persecution: A Response to the UNHCR Guidelines' in *Stemming the Tide or Keeping the Balance: The Role of the Judiciary* (International Association of Refugee Law Judges 2002), 348.

32 Lourdes Peroni, 'The Protection of Women Asylum Seekers under the European Convention on Human Rights: Unearthing the Gendered Roots of Harm' (2018) 18 *Human Rights Law Review* 347.

33 Yet, as Sharon Pickering has noted, the UNHCR has not endorsed this kind of discourse for other grounds of persecution and has not felt the need to placate governments or the public with similar disclaimers on race, nationality or religion. Pickering (n 31) 348–349.

34 Iris M. Young, *Justice and the Politics of Difference* (Princeton UP 1990).

inequality as oppression are incommensurable with the language of liberal individualism; in the present case, with the notion of individualised persecution based on delimited grounds or causes.[35]

2.5 *The application of the notions of "safe countries" and "internal flight alternative"*

A final challenge in relation to gender-related persecution refers to the application of the notions of "safe country" and "internal flight or relocation alternative". These notions limit the determination of refugee status by taking into account whether claimants have the possibility of moving to another area of their home country where there is no well-founded fear of persecution, and where they "could reasonably be expected to establish him/herself and live a normal life".[36] The UNHCR adopted guidelines on the internal flight alternative in 2003 to promote a more consistent approach and to stop the increasingly divergent practices observed within and among jurisdictions.

In the cases of asylum claims filed by women victims of gender-related persecution, the understanding of the possibility of internal flight or relocation alternatives tends to be tainted by the public/private divide as well. Women need to show that they would not be safe in any part of their own country of nationality or residence. Yet the idea that their persecutors are private individuals, and that their persecution is not fully political or public in nature leads adjudicators to consider that women victims of gender-related persecution can protect themselves by simply moving away from their persecutors. Whereas the public sphere is a social realm, the private sphere is seen as an individual realm and, therefore, it can be abandoned, construed and re-construed by individuals, provided that there is no interference from the State. Without proper recognition of the structural character of gender-based violence, women's claims, especially in cases of persecution by non-state actors, are easily dismissed as unfortunate situations which can, however, be remedied privately.[37]

35 Specifically, Young's analysis draws attention away from the element of "intention" in the definition of oppression. Young (n 34), 41. In the area of asylum, Alexander Betts has suggested that the causes of the displacement should not be the focus; instead, a threshold of human rights should be identified which, if unavailable in the country of origin, should grant a right that the individual could not to be returned ("survival migration"). Alexander Betts, 'State fragility, refugee status and "survival migration"' (2013) 43 *Forced Migration Review* 4.

36 UNHCR, Guidelines on International Protection No 4: 'Internal Flight or Relocation Alternative' within the Context of Article 1A(2) of the 1951 Convention and/or 1967 Protocol relating to the Status of Refugees, HCR/GIP/03/04, 23 July 2003.

37 Lourdes Peroni has shown these difficulties in the inadmissibility decisions of the ECtHR, where internal relocation is considered an available option for rejected asylum claimants by downplaying the structural character of gender inequality and overemphasising the private resources of the applicants (their own or their families') to protect themselves. Peroni (n 32).

3 Violence against women as grounds for asylum in the Istanbul Convention

By the time the Istanbul Convention was drafted, most of these challenges were known and discussed by academics, activists and decision-makers. Since the early nineties, the Steering Committee for Equality between Women and Men within the Council of Europe (CoE) has undertaken a series of initiatives to promote the protection of women against violence. Most notably, in 1998, the CoE called upon all Member States to eliminate gender discrimination among refugees and to adapt the treatment of women refugees to their specific situation and requirements.[38]

The Istanbul Convention contributes to this tracked effort with two provisions specifically dedicated to asylum. Article 60 deals with "gender-related asylum claims". It calls on Parties to have gender-based violence recognised as a form of persecution within the meaning of Art. 1A(2) of the Refugee Convention; to ensure that a gender-sensitive interpretation is given to the Convention grounds; and to develop gender-sensitive reception procedures and services, including the procedures for refugee status determination and application for international protection. Article 61 is focused on the principle of *non-refoulement* (which is reaffirmed), and on the prohibition of returning victims of violence against women in need of protection to countries where they might fear for their lives or be at risk of torture or inhuman or degrading treatment or punishment.

3.1 Addressed challenges: gender-based violence and harm as grounds for asylum

Of the challenges faced by the gender-related asylum claims previously enumerated, Article 60(1) addresses the first one, as it calls upon Parties to "take the necessary legislative or other measures to ensure that gender-based violence against women may be recognised as a form of persecution within the meaning of Article 1A(2), of the 1951 Convention relating to the Status of Refugees and as a form of serious harm giving rise to complementary/subsidiary protection". Article 60(1) does not require State Parties to introduce gender as a ground of persecution, in line with the recommendation of the CEDAW Committee.[39] Rather, it remains closer to the UNHCR's interpretation that gender-related persecution is covered by the definition of refugee if properly interpreted.

In fact, the Explanatory Report to the Istanbul Convention, while criticising the "gender blindness" of asylum law, which has prevented asylum systems from

38 Council of Europe Parliamentary Assembly, Recommendation 1374 on the Situation of Refugee Women in Europe, 20 May 1998, para 5.

39 General Recommendation No 32, paras 13 and 38.

grasping "why and how" women experience persecution,[40] considers that Article 60(1) consecrates what is already a practice. The added value or the contribution of the Istanbul Convention would be, then, that it includes an obligation of the Parties to recognise that gender-specific violence may amount to persecution, and that gender-based violence may constitute serious harm. This recognition should cause the granting of the right to international protection. It is worth noticing that in Article 60(1) "international protection" is not limited to the recognition of the refugee status under the Refugee Convention, but may also be provided under other "well established international and regional standards" such as the ECHR and EU instruments.[41]

Furthermore, the second challenge discussed by Musalo and Knight (the traditional consideration of gender-based violence as a private or personal matter, or as a social or cultural norm, instead of as a form of persecution) is addressed also in Article 60(2). This provision requires State Parties to ensure a gender-sensitive interpretation of each of the Refugee Convention grounds. The Explanatory Report further clarifies the notion of gender-sensitive interpretation, which "implies recognising and understanding how gender can have an impact on the reasons behind the type of persecution or harm suffered".[42] It also provides enough examples of gender-related violence which can be used as forms of persecution and have been traditionally considered private matters or cultural and religious norms. Examples include female genital violence, dowry-related violence, forced marriage, serious domestic violence, and so-called "honour" crimes for not conforming to religious norms or customs.

The notion of gender-sensitive interpretation in the Istanbul Convention falls in line with the development at the UN. On the one hand, a "gender-sensitive interpretation" is mandated by the general application of the principle of non-discrimination.[43] CEDAW General Recommendation No 32 speaks of a "comprehensive international human rights legal framework"[44] whereby the CEDAW provisions "reinforce and complement" the international protection offered by the Refugee Convention, "especially because explicit gender equality provisions are absent from (…) the 1951 Convention".[45] In the Istanbul Convention, Article 6 contains a general obligation for Parties to ensure that a gender perspective is adopted in the design and evaluation of all the measures taken to implement the Convention. The gender perspective in compliance with the

40 Council of Europe, Explanatory Report to the Council of Europe Convention on preventing and combating violence against women and domestic violence (2011) (Explanatory Report).

41 Explanatory Report, para 311.

42 Explanatory Report, para 312. See also Crawley (n 13).

43 E.g., Article 14(1) of the Universal Declaration of Human Rights, which states that "everyone has the right to seek and to enjoy in other countries asylum from persecution", must be read together with the general anti-discrimination clause in Article 2, which includes sex as a prohibited ground of discrimination.

44 General Recommendation No 32, para 9.

45 General Recommendation No 32, para 10.

Convention itself places "an obligation on Parties that goes beyond the specific measures to be taken"[46] and is linked to the Convention's purposes, i.e., promoting substantive equality and empowering women.

In relation to asylum law and procedures, the notion of gender-sensitive interpretation has also been substantively developed beyond the general application of the principle of non-discrimination.[47] One of the earliest documents, in 1985, introduced the possibility that States

> in the exercise of their sovereignty, [...] adopt the interpretation that women asylum-seekers who face harsh or inhuman treatment due to their having transgressed the social mores of the society in which they live may be considered as a "particular social group" within the meaning of Article 1A(2) of the 1951 United Nations Refugee Convention.[48]

The Executive Committee of the UNHCR later called upon the High Commissioner to support States in developing and implementing criteria and guidelines on responses to persecution specifically aimed at women[49] and persecution on conventional grounds "including persecution through sexual violence or other gender-related persecution".[50]

The CoE has also been concerned about having a gender-sensitive interpretation of asylum law applied in its Member States. A Parliamentary Assembly Resolution of 2010 called on Member States to "ensure that gender-based violence is taken into account under the five different grounds of persecution (...) and that 'gender' is specifically included in the notion of a 'particular social group' (...) preferably by law, or at least in practice".[51] The Explanatory Report

46 Explanatory Report, para 62.

47 As early as in the eighties, the UNHCR Executive Committee (ExCom) began to produce a series of specific documents on gender-based claims in order to promote a "gender-sensitive" interpretation of the Refugee Convention. Besides the ExCom conclusions and recommendations, the UNHCR produced a number of policy documents and guidelines, as well as a handbook on refugee women. See also the UNHCR, Guidelines on International Protection No 2: Membership of a particular social group within the context of Article 1A(2) of the 1951 Convention and/or its 1967 Protocol relating to the Status of Refugees, HCR/GIP/02/02, 7 May 2002; the UNHCR, Guidelines on International Protection No 6: Religion-based refugee claims under Article 1A(2) of the 1951 Convention and/or the 1967 Protocol relating to the Status of Refugees, HCR/GIP/04/06, 28 April 2004, particularly paras 24, 28 and 30; and the UNHCR, Guidelines on International Protection No 7: The application of Article 1A(2) of the 1951 Convention and/or 1967 Protocol relating to the Status of Refugees to victims of trafficking and persons at risk of being trafficked, HCR/GIP/06/07, 7 April 2006.

48 UNHCR, Executive Committee Conclusions No 39 (XXXVI), Refugee Women and International Protection [1985].

49 UNHCR, Executive Committee Conclusions No 77 (XLVI) (1995]).

50 UNHCR, Executive Committee Conclusions No 77 (XLVI) (1995); UNHCR, Executive Committee Conclusions No 79 (XLVII) [1996].

51 CoE, Parliamentary Assembly Resolution 1765 (2010), Gender-related claims for asylum, 8 October 2010, para 8.1.

to the Istanbul Convention, however, seems to show more concern about the fact that gender-based violence is often seen to fall within the ground of "membership of a particular social group", and that other grounds are therefore overlooked.[52] It thus encourages Parties to adopt a gender perspective on the grounds of race, nationality and religion, and to include opinions regarding gender roles and non-conforming behaviour as political grounds for persecution.[53]

3.2 Missed opportunities and lingering challenges

The Istanbul Convention either remains silent or does not provide sufficient input on the other challenges discussed in Section 2. Persecution by non-state actors is only fleetingly referred to in the Explanatory Report: "[t]here is no doubt that rape and other forms of gender-related violence (...) are acts which have been used as forms of persecution, *whether perpetrated by state or non-state actors*".[54] Adjudicators differ in the appreciation of the role of the State in cases of non-state actors of persecution. In cases of gender-related persecution by non-state actors, specifically serious domestic violence or trafficking for sexual exploitation, on some occasions adjudicators have decided that there was no persecution because those are criminal actions persecuted by the State.[55] However, according to the UNHCR guidelines, the mere enactment of laws prohibiting persecutory practices is not in itself sufficient to render an asylum claim without merit. State responsibility may be established if it condones or tolerates discriminatory practices or is unable to provide effective protection from them.[56]

Second, the Istanbul Convention shows the same "discomfort with gender" that can be identified in the UNHCR Guidelines on gender-related persecution, as discussed above. The tension between the understanding of persecution in terms of violation of individual rights and the structural character of gender inequality emerges clearly in the uneasiness shown in the Explanatory Report about the implications of adopting a gender perspective. On the one hand, there is no mention of gender inequality in relation to Articles 60 and 61. The historical lack of recognition of women's asylum claims, which the Explanatory Report denounces, is attributed not to gender inequality but rather to gender

52 Explanatory Report, para 313. This concern had been expressed in 2002 in the Guidelines on Gender-Related Persecution, para 7.

53 Explanatory Report, para 313.

54 Explanatory Report, para 310 (emphasis added).

55 In Spain, for example, victims of trafficking for sexual exploitation have not entered the procedures for international protection for this reason, and have tended to be re-directed to the protection measures accorded to those who cooperate with the judicial system in dismantling criminal organisations.

56 Guidelines on Gender-related Persecution, para 11.

blindness.[57] On the other hand, disclaimers play a noticeable part in the text of the Explanatory Report, in an attempt to limit the consequences of including a gender perspective in the treatment of asylum cases at this point. These disclaimers include that the recognition of gender-based violence as a form of serious harm does not imply that all gender-based violence is automatically considered serious harm (para 311); that the adoption of a gender-sensitive interpretation does not mean that all women will automatically be entitled to refugee status (para 312); and two repetitions that Article 60(1) is not intended to overrule the provisions of the Refugee Convention on the conditions for granting asylum (paras 300 and 311).

Another reason for concern is the lack of references in the Istanbul Convention to the last challenge mentioned in the previous section, namely the internal flight alternative. This absence of references is especially concerning because this is one of the main arguments in inadmissibility decisions by the European Court of Human Rights (ECtHR) in gender-related persecution cases.[58] Furthermore, at the time the Istanbul Convention was adopted, this particular challenge had already been addressed both by the Parliamentary Assembly of the CoE and by the EU asylum system. In Resolution 1765, the Parliamentary Assembly called on Member States to "restrict the use of internal flight alternatives for asylum seekers who invoke gender-related claims" and to take into account a series of elements in the consideration of internal flight alternatives, namely the availability of State protection in the area of relocation, the safety of the route, the prevailing social and cultural conditions in the country and the possibilities to earn a living.[59] None of this made its way to the Istanbul Convention.[60]

Finally, an additional point of concern is paragraph 300 of the Explanatory Report. It guides the interpretation of Articles 60 and 61 to ensure that they are

57 In fact, gender inequality as a structural cause is never mentioned, either in the two provisions or in the corresponding paragraphs of the Explanatory Report.

58 For example, the Court has declared some cases regarding female genital mutilation inadmissible. Some cases are *Collins and Akaziebie v Sweden* App no 23944/05 (ECHR, 8 March 2007); *Izevbekhai et al. v Ireland* App no 43408/08 (ECtHR, 17 May 2011); *Omeredo v Austria* App no 8969/10 (ECHR, 20 September 2011) and a number of cases regarding trafficking or the risk of re-trafficking, such as *V.F. v France*, App no 7196/10 (ECHR, 29 November 2011); *Idemugia v France* App no 4125/11 (ECHR, 27 March 2012) and *F.A. v the United Kingdom* App no 20658/11 (ECHR, 10 September 2013). For a detailed assessment of the Court's argumentation in such cases, see Peroni (n 37).

59 CoE, Parliamentary Assembly Resolution 1765 (2010), Gender-related claims for asylum, 8 October 2010, para 10.5.

60 This kind of requirements to the possibility of invoking internal protection were introduced, for example, by the EU's recast Qualification Directive. This instrument, which was adopted also in 2011, also addresses the question of protection by non-state actors. Directive 2011/95/EU of the European Parliament and of the Council of 13 December 2011 on standards for the qualification of third-country nationals or stateless persons as beneficiaries of international protection, for a uniform status for refugees or for persons eligible for subsidiary protection, and for the content of the protection granted (recast) [2011] OJ L337/9.

compatible with the 1951 Refugee Convention and with Article 3 of the ECHR (prohibition of torture and inhuman or degrading treatment or punishment), as interpreted by the ECtHR. This requirement of compatibility between the interpretation and the application of different but related human rights instruments is reasonable and very common in international instruments and judgments. Yet paragraph 300 contains a more problematic insertion. According to this paragraph, the provisions of the Istanbul Convention referring to asylum and other forms of complementary or subsidiary international protection do not go beyond the scope of application of the Refugee Convention and the ECHR, but only grant them a practical dimension.

Yet if the intention was only to provide them with a practical dimension, an opportunity may have been missed to offer concrete guidelines on the challenges that keep women from being granted adequate international protection in cases of gender-based violence. The practical dimension of guaranteeing effective international protection to gender-persecution claimants lies on issues on which Articles 60 and 61 of the Istanbul Convention remain silent: structural gender inequality; stereotyping; clear and effective limits to the application of the internal flight or relocation alternative; requirements for considering private actors as capable of protecting victims in the internal flight alternative; criteria for determining when a State fails to fulfil its obligation to protect; and guidelines for adjudicators containing standards for assessing different aspects of the claims. When the Istanbul Convention was adopted, some of these "practical dimension" standards had been established by the Qualification Directive, and three years later by CEDAW General Recommendation No 32. The Istanbul Convention may have foregone a chance to make a contribution and confront practical obstacles for gender-related persecution claims that exist in the practice of asylum claims adjudicators.

4 Conclusions

This chapter has reviewed the contribution made by the Istanbul Convention to some lingering challenges and open questions regarding gender-based violence against women as grounds for claiming asylum. Gender bias and the lack of recognition of women's claims in international asylum law have been a growing concern for the past decades. As the Istanbul Convention became part of this debate, some practices and interpretations which give recognition and visibility to gender-based violence against women as serious forms of human rights violations have been strengthened. Although the Convention does not require Parties to introduce gender as a ground of persecution in itself, and stipulates that its provisions do not expand the scope of application of the 1951 Refugee Convention, Articles 60 and 61 do reinforce the position of victims of gender-related persecution. First, because they require States to acknowledge, either by law or at least in adjudication, that different forms of gender-based violence are not private matters, but rather serious violations of human rights which might amount to persecution by state or non-state actors. Second, because they require Parties to interpret conventional grounds of persecution in a manner that includes how women might be persecuted and the ways in which gender affects the grounds of persecution. In this respect, examples of harm, forms of persecution, and ways of understanding the conventional grounds contained in the Explanatory Report might be very useful. They are not a novelty, but they explain the binding obligations of signatory Parties.

The Istanbul Convention, nonetheless, has missed an opportunity to guide other open questions in gender-related persecution claims and to reinforce victim protection. The most serious gap in protection may be the re-introduction of the public/private divide. While it has been rejected in the interpretation of violence suffered by women, it has been allowed to return when protection is discussed. In fact, the Istanbul Convention has not introduced guarantees to regulate the possibility that States may invoke the internal flight alternative or other forms of private protection (i.e. protection by non-state actors). Furthermore, the structural dimension of gender inequality does not appear in the asylum provisions of the Convention. Individualised and exception-like approaches to gender-related persecution claims are favoured instead. Finally, the Istanbul Convention seems to be aimed at reinforcing the idea of a gender-sensitive interpretation, rather than at offering concrete guidelines to overcome the practical barriers encountered when seeking to have gender-related persecution claims acknowledged.

Part VI

National responses to the Convention

13 The Istanbul Convention in Poland

Between the "war on gender" and legal reform

Katarzyna Sękowska-Kozłowska

1 Introduction

The Council of Europe Convention on Preventing and Combating Violence against Women and Domestic Violence (the Istanbul Convention) is a well-known human rights treaty – and certainly the most recognised women's human rights treaty – in Poland. Although Poland has been a State Party to the Convention on the Elimination of All Forms of Discrimination against Women (CEDAW) since 1980, CEDAW has been virtually invisible in the public sphere and hardly recognised by law makers and practitioners.

In part, this is due to the fact that the socio-political circumstances in Poland have changed dramatically since the eighties, when Poland ratified CEDAW. When Poland accessed CEDAW, it was a satellite of the Soviet Union and followed a policy of gender equality as one of the slogans of socialist ideology.[1] In contrast, when it accessed the Istanbul Convention, it had become a democratic country bound by human rights values due to its membership in the Council of Europe and the European Union. In light of its human rights commitments, it can be expected that Poland's engagement with gender equality has become much stronger than ever. However, the Istanbul Convention has given rise to controversies and has been an object of hostility, particularly by the Catholic Church and by conservative politicians who claim that it promotes "gender ideology".[2]

1 Agnieszka Zembrzuska, 'The Socialist Model of Woman in Poland and its Soviet Prototype' in Dorothy Rogers, Joshua Wheeler, Marína Zavacká and Shawna Casebier (eds), *Topics in Feminism, History and Philosophy, IWM Junior Visiting Fellows Conferences*, Vol. 6 (IWM 2000).

2 "The concept of gender ideology is a right-wing invention that intentionally misrepresents feminist, queer, and gender theory in order to justify discrimination against women and LGBTQ people. It was concocted by the Vatican in the mid-nineties, and has since spread globally. The Right claims gender ideology is being peddled by Western elites who want to destabilise the traditional family and the natural order of society", Gillian Kane, 'Right-Wing Europe's War on "Gender Ideology"', *The Public Eye*, Spring 2018.

This unprecedented campaign against the ratification of the Istanbul Convention has given a basis to the so-called "war on gender" in Poland,[3] a phenomenon related to the concept of "anti-genderism". This concept can be traced back to the early nineties, particularly in the Vatican's activity.[4] According to Korolczuk and Graff, "antigenderism" is a coherent ideological construction consciously and effectively used by right-wing and religious fundamentalists worldwide.[5] Against this background, the attacks on the Istanbul Convention in Poland are just the tip of the iceberg. A backlash against gender equality has appeared in other EU countries as well as worldwide.[6] The list of countries that still have not ratified the Istanbul Convention due to the "war on gender" is long. It includes Bulgaria, Croatia, the Czech Republic, Hungary, Latvia, Lithuania, the Slovak Republic and Ukraine.[7] Thus, the

3 See e.g. Agnieszka Graff, 'Report from the Gender Trenches: War against "Genderism" in Poland' (2014) 21(4) *European Journal of Women's Studies* 431. It must be noted that Graff uses the expressions "war on gender", "war on 'gender ideology'", or "war against genderism" interchangeably. The terms "war on gender" (Polish: *wojna o gender*) or "war against gender" (Polish: *wojna z gender*) are widely used in Polish journalistic and academic writings. For more, see, e.g. Maciej Duda, *Dogmat płci. Polska wojna z gender* (Katedra 2016).

4 Mary Anne Case, 'Trans Formations in the Vatican's War on "Gender Ideology"' (2019) 44 *Signs: Journal of Women in Culture and Society*.

5 Elżbieta Korolczuk and Agnieszka Graff, 'Gender as "Ebola from Brussels": The Anticolonial Frame and the Rise of Illiberal Populism' (2018) 43(4) *Signs: Journal of Women in Culture and Society* 798.

6 See e.g. Borbála Juhàsz, Enikő Pap, *Backlash in Gender Equality and Women's and Girls' Rights*, Study requested by the FEMM committee, June 2018.

7 See e.g. Ruzsha Smilova, *'Promoting "Gender Ideology": Constitutional Court of Bulgaria Declares Istanbul Convention Unconstitutional'* (2018) http://ohrh.law.ox.ac.uk/promoting-gender-ideology-constitutional-court-of-bulgaria-declares-istanbul-convention-unconstitutional/ accessed 15 October 2019; Laura Nacyte, *Debating the Istanbul Convention in Lithuania: The Term 'Gender' is not Alien* (2018) https://ilg2.org/2018/07/13/debating-the-istanbul-convention-in-lithuania-the-term-gender-is-not-a-lien/ accessed 15 October 2019; Michael Mustillo, *Latvia Bristles against the Istanbul Convention Combating Violence against Women* (2018) www.baltictimes.com/latvia_bristles_against_the_istanbul_convention_combating_violence_against_women/ accessed 15 October 2019; Elise Ketelaars, *When "European values" Do not Count: Anti-gender Ideology and the Failure to Comprehensively Address GBV in Ukraine* (2018) http://blogs.lse.ac.uk/gender/2018/09/26/when-european-values-do-not-count-anti-gender-ideology-and-the-failure-to-comprehensively-address-gbv-in-ukraine/ accessed 15 October 2019; Hana Stelzerová, *The Istanbul Convention – Experience from the Czech Republic* (2018) https://czlobby.cz/en/news/istanbul-convention-experience-czech-republic accessed 15 October 2019; Georgi Gotev, *After Bulgaria, Slovakia too Fails to Ratify the Istanbul Convention* (2018) www.euractiv.com/section/future-eu/news/after-bulgaria-slovakia-too-fails-to-ratify-the-istanbul-convention/ accessed 15 October 2019; Miguel Alcalde and Josipa Šarić, *The Istanbul Convention in Croatia: Attending to the Anxiety in the Intersection of Belief and Policy-making* (2018) http://blogs.lse.ac.uk/religionglobalsociety/2018/04/the-istanbul-convention-in-croatia-attending-to-the-anxiety-in-the-intersection-of-belief-and-policy-making/ accessed 15 October 2019; Balázs Pivarnyik, *Family and Gender in Orbán's Hungary* (2017) www.boell.de/en/2018/07/04/family-and-gender-viktor-orbans-hungary accessed 15 October 2019.

experience of Poland, where the Istanbul Convention has been ratified but its implementation is still affected by the "war on gender", may be of broader relevance.

This chapter presents two contexts in which the Istanbul Convention operates in Poland. The first one is the socio-political context of the "war on gender", in which the Istanbul Convention is perceived as a threat to the family and traditional Christian values. This discourse on the Convention – which is very much present in the media and in public debate in Poland[8] – has overshadowed the second context I will examine, namely the legal context. This chapter attempts to demonstrate, by focusing on sexual and domestic violence, that the Istanbul Convention has far-reaching implications for Polish law and practice. Although some positive developments within the legal context have been achieved, a number of challenges still remain.

2 Historical and social background: gender (in)equality in Poland

When discussing gender issues in Poland it is necessary to look back and sketch out some factors that impede the implementation of women's human rights in the country today. Over the years, Poland has developed its own model of womanhood. During its long, 123-year struggle to regain independence,[9] the ethos of the "Polish Mother" evolved. This is the figure of a heroic woman who is capable of great sacrifices for the good of the homeland and the family. This ethos still strongly influences the position of women in the family and society today, as well as women's own perception of their roles and duties, particularly regarding motherhood.[10]

In communist times, the figure of the "Polish Mother" was confronted with the Soviet prototype of the emancipated woman building a new regime hand-in-hand with men, while home duties such as childcare were institutionalised and transferred to the public realm.[11] As a result of the Polish tradition and

8 See e.g. Dariusz Baran, 'Echoes of the CE Convention in Most Noteworthy Polish Press and the Internet Media' in Anna Frątczak (ed.) *Gender Mainstreaming in Polish Media Discourse as Exemplified in the Debate Concerning the Convention on Preventing and Combating Violence against Women and Domestic Violence* (Andrzej Frycz Modrzewski Krakow University 2014).

9 This was the so-called "period of partitions"; whereby parts of the former Poland were incrementally annexed by surrounding powers, and Poland as a nation-state ceased to exist from 1795 to 1918.

10 Agnieszka Imbierowicz, "The Polish Mother on the Defensive? The Transformation of the Myth and its Impact on the Motherhood of Polish Women' (2012) 1 *Journal of Education Culture and Society* 140–153.

11 Agnieszka Zembrzuska, 'The Socialist Model of Woman in Poland and its Soviet Prototype' in Dorothy Rogers, Joshua Wheeler, Marína Zavacká and Shawna Casebier (eds), *Topics in Feminism, History and Philosophy, IWM Junior Visiting Fellows Conferences*, Vol. 6 (IWM 2000).

antipathy towards Soviet domination and its imposed rules, Polish women, although outwardly empowered in the labour market and in public life, remained attached to traditional and patriarchal roles such as home-making and childcare. According to Drweski, during the communist era there was a strong perception of a dichotomy between the private sphere of the home and the public sphere of the State. The domestic sphere was perceived as a haven of refuge from the all-encompassing socialist environment, where women were idealised as homemakers and care providers. In a continuance of the traditional image of the "Polish mother", women were pushed to put the needs of others and the fulfilment of this idealised role above their own needs. Approximating this ideal of self-sacrifice was a main way in which Polish women gained social power.[12]

Women's subordination in Poland has been entrenched by the strong influence of the Roman Catholic Church. As a major force for preserving Polish nationhood during the times of partition[13] and as a pillar of support for the anti-communist resistance movement, the Catholic Church has become an important player in Polish political and social life. After 1989, the relationship between the Polish State and the Roman Catholic Church has become institutionalised, including its official presence in schools, where religious education is conducted. In 1993, Polish law on abortion was severely restricted.[14]

The discourse on abortion presaged the "war on gender" in Poland. John Paul II, the first Polish pope, introduced the concept of "culture of life" in opposition to "culture of death", which was allegedly supported by countries where abortion was permitted. The concept of "culture of life" was an element of the Pope's broader plan to re-create moral rules for post-communist societies and to promote Christian revival.[15] Poland was charged with the mission of implementing these moral values and of promoting them throughout the world, especially in the European Union.[16] In recent decades, the Roman Catholic Church has been an active voice in the public debate in Poland, expressing its

12 Abby Drwecki, 'A Woman's Nature: Addressing Violence Against Women through Femininity in Poland' (2010) 11(4) *Journal of International Women's Studies* 97–114.

13 See footnote 9.

14 See e.g. Jacqueline Heinen and Stéphane Portet, *Religion, Politics and Gender Equality in Poland, Final Research Report prepared for the project Religion, Politics and Gender Equality*, United Nations Research Institute for Social Development (UNRISD) and Heinrich-Böll-Stiftung 2009.

15 Andrzej Kulczycki, 'Abortion Policy in Postcommunist Europe: the Conflict in Poland' (1995) 21(3) *Population and Development Review* 471.

16 Wanda Nowicka, 'The Struggle for Abortion Rights in Poland' in Richard Parker, Rosalind Petchesky and Robert Sember (eds), *SexPolitics. Reports from the Front Lines* (Sexuality Policy Watch 2007).

criticism not only of abortion, but also of contraception, sex education, in-vitro fertilisation, cohabitation and homosexuality.[17]

At the same time, there have certainly been positive developments over the years in securing gender equality in Poland. For example, due to Poland's aspiration to join the European Union, labour law included protections against sex discrimination and sexual harassment in the workplace. The electoral law introduced gender quotas.[18] However, there is no national mechanism or institution that could secure the implementation of women's rights and coordinate gender equality policies at all levels. Substantive gender equality is yet to be achieved in many fields, as has been regularly pointed out by international human rights bodies, including the Committee on the Elimination of Discrimination against Women (CEDAW Committee).[19] One of the main problems is the prevalence of violence against women. According to an EU Fundamental Rights Agency (FRA) Survey published in 2014, 19% of women in Poland have experienced physical and/or sexual violence and only 28% of them reported the most serious incidents to the police.[20] Other research demonstrates that 87% of Polish female respondents have experienced some form of sexual violence, whereas 22% were raped, mostly by their ex- or present partners.[21]

To summarise this overview, the current social and legal status of women in Poland has been shaped by various factors, including the turbulent past and the fight for nationhood; the communist legacy; Roman Catholicism; the attachment to family values; and Polish membership in the European community, with its democratic and human rights values. The process of acceding to the Istanbul Convention has clearly demonstrated that even in the case of violence

17 See e.g. Dorota Gozdecka, 'The Polish Catholic Church and the Regulation of IVF in Poland: Polarised Political Discourses and the Battle over "Proper2 Reproduction' (2012) 2(1) *feminists@law* Retrieved from https://journals.kent.ac.uk/index.php/feministsatlaw/article/view/26; Dorota Hall, 'Religion and Homosexuality in the Public Domain: Polish Debates about Reparative Therapy' (2017) 19(5) *European Societies* 600–622; Monika Mynarska, Laura Bernardi, 'Meanings and Attitudes Attached to Cohabitation in Poland: Qualitative Analyses of the Slow Diffusion of Cohabitation among the Young Generation' (2007) 16 *Demographic Research* 519–553; Joanna Sieracka, 'The Church and Polish Feminism: Forever Enemies? A Secular Feminist Perspective' (2017) 21(1) *Prace Kulturoznawcze* 123–144.

18 See e.g. Marta Warat, 'Development of Gender Equality Policies in Poland. A Review of Success and Limitations' (2014) Gender equality and quality of life – how gender equality can contribute to development in Europe. A study of Poland and Norway. Working paper No 2.2. Gender Equality Policy in Poland www.geq.socjologia.uj.edu.pl/documents/32447484/80907944/WP2.2Warat_gender_equality_in_Poland.pdf accessed 15 October 2019.

19 See e.g. Committee on the Elimination of Discrimination against Women, Concluding Observations (2014), CEDAW/C/POL/CO/7-8.

20 Violence against Women: an EU-wide Survey. Results at glance, EU Fundamental Rights Agency 2014.

21 Magdalena Grabowska, Agnieszka Grzybek (eds), *Przełamać tabu. Raport o przemocy seksualnej* (Fundacja STER 2016).

against women – which should be recognised as a human rights violation regardless of any ideological disputes – the underlying tensions between these various factors are difficult to overcome.

3 Polish accession to the Istanbul Convention and the launch of the "war on gender"

Poland participated in drafting the Istanbul Convention from the very beginning and was present in all meetings of CAHVIO.[22] As it appears from reports of the CAHVIO meetings during the preparation of the Convention in 2008–2010,[23] and confirmed by interviews with experts who participated in these meetings,[24] the concept of gender equality was at that time taken for granted by all governments and there were almost no controversies surrounding this issue.[25]

Public discussion over Poland's accession to the Istanbul Convention erupted in the spring of 2012 with a statement by Jarosław Gowin, then Minister of Justice and representative of the ultraconservative wing of Platforma Obywatelska (Civic Platform or PO), which was then the governing party. The government was run by PO, a liberal-conservative and Christian democratic party whose representatives took part in the process of drafting the Istanbul Convention and officially supported Poland's accession to this treaty. PO was, however, confronted by some of its ultraconservative member politicians, including Gowin. He declared that Poland should not sign the Convention because of its definition of gender. According to him, the Istanbul Convention was "an expression of feminist ideology", which undermined the traditional role of the family, jeopardised the institution of heterosexual marriage and promoted same-sex partnerships. Article 12 of the Convention, aimed at combatting stereotypical gender roles, appeared to be the most contested provision. In Gowin's opinion, this provision would lead to discouraging women from fulfilling their roles as mothers and wives, which contradicted the Polish Constitution.[26]

Gowin's statement marked the beginning of the "war on gender" in Poland. Some right-wing politicians, activists, media outlets, and dignitaries of the Roman Catholic Church strongly supported the discourse against "gender ideology". This rhetoric was contested in a heated public debate, particularly

22 CAHVIO reports of 1st to 9th meetings available at www.coe.int/en/web/istanbul-convention/cahvio accessed 15 October 2019.

23 Ibid.

24 Informal consultations were carried out by the author with experts who participated in the CAHVIO meetings.

25 Besides the reservations expressed by the delegations of the Russian Federation and Lithuania regarding references to sexual orientation and gender identity in Article 4 of the Convention, Report of 8th CAHVIO meeting, CAHVIO (2010) 27 rev, para 8.

26 Magdalena Grzyb, 'Why Violence against Women is such Politically Controversial Issue? The Polish Struggle to Ratify the Istanbul Convention' (2012/2013) 20 *Biuletyn PTK* 75.

by liberal politicians, the media, and activists dealing with human rights and women's issues. For example, Gowin faced opposition within the PO government, particularly from Agnieszka Kozłowska-Rajewicz, who as then Government Plenipotentiary for Equal Treatment, was actively lobbying for the Convention to be signed and ratified.[27] The Convention was finally signed by Poland in December 2012.

When Poland signed the Convention, it lodged several declarations.[28] One of them states that: "The Republic of Poland declares that it will apply the Convention in accordance with the principles and the provisions of the Constitution of the Republic of Poland".[29] This declaration was attached as a compromise to assuage the dissenting voices within the government and to enable Poland's accession to the Convention. Austria, Finland, the Netherlands, Norway, Sweden and Switzerland objected to this declaration and indicated that it amounted to a reservation that sought to limit Poland's responsibilities under the Convention and raised doubts as to its commitment to the object and purpose of the Convention.[30] Poland also attached some reservations to the Convention, the compatibility of which with the Convention may be questionable.[31]

It took more than two years for Poland to ratify the Convention: the ratification took place in April 2015, shortly before the electoral defeat of the above-mentioned ruling Civic Platform party. In October 2015, the government in Poland was taken over by Prawo i Sprawiedliwość (The Law and Justice party or PiS), a right-wing populist national-conservative party that had also won the presidential elections earlier in the year. This electoral result sparked a series of deep political and legal changes aimed at dismantling institutional checks on the government, thus eroding a number of civil and political rights.[32] The rhetoric used by PiS to maintain popularity has been based on, *inter alia*, creating a fear of "Others", such as refugees, migrants and homosexuals. This rhetoric also stresses the necessity to defend Polish society against the harmful "gender ideology" imposed by the EU. Alongside this rhetoric, PiS introduced a strategy of strong family-support measures, including financial benefits for families with children.

The introduction of the "gender ideology" issue changed the debate on Poland's accession to the Convention. Before 2012, only a narrow group of

27 Magdalena Grzyb, 75.
28 Which were confirmed in 2015 when Poland ratified the Convention.
29 www.coe.int/en/web/conventions/full-list/-/conventions/treaty/210/signatures?p_auth=UB27ggxf accessed 15 October 2019.
30 www.coe.int/en/web/conventions/full-list/-/conventions/treaty/210/signatures?p_auth=UB27ggxf accessed 15 October 2019.
31 For more: see Burek in this volume.
32 More: Wojciech Sadurski, 'How Democracy Dies (in Poland): A Case Study of Anti-Constitutional Populist Backsliding' (2018) Sydney Law School Legal Studies Research Paper No 18/01.

officials and experts discussed the conformity of Polish law with the Convention. Afterwards, violence against women became an element of visible political game. Similar to access to abortion, violence against women has been perceived mostly as a political and ideological issue, whereas women's rights and dignity have been overlooked. It has to be noted, however, that the controversies surrounding the Convention have given it an unprecedented amount of attention in Polish media and society. This rising public awareness can be viewed as a positive side effect of the "war on gender",[33] although at the same time meaningful discussions on important legal issues and measures to secure women's human rights have been overshadowed by the ideological discourse.

Since the takeover of power by PiS, negative attitudes towards "gender ideology" have been openly present in politics, including in sectors like education and academia. In December 2016, the press revealed that the Ministry of Justice had prepared a draft motion for Poland's withdrawal from the Convention.[34] As a result of an official inquiry of the Ombudsman, the government confirmed that consultations regarding this matter had been initiated, but denied that it had intended to withdraw from the Convention.[35]

Since December 2016, the current government has repeated that it does not intend to withdraw from the Convention.[36] However, public statements by state officials reveal their reluctance to comply with its provisions. For instance, President Andrzej Duda stated in a television interview that it was not necessary to apply the Convention in practice because Polish law on counteracting violence was very good.[37] Prime Minister Mateusz Morawiecki said that he did not agree with the Convention's stance that gender inequality or traditional gender roles have been a source of violence against women. In his opinion

> there is no violence where family bonds are cared for, where there is a normal home and love. Violence occurs more often in de facto relationships, relationships other than those recognised by law. This is why I do not want this harmful gender ideology to cover up the real problem of domestic violence against women and children.[38]

33 Magdalena Grzyb, 76.

34 Robert Kowalski, 'Rząd PiS przygotowuje wypowiedzenie konwencji antyprzemocowej' (*OKO.press* 2 December 2016), https://oko.press/rzad-pis-przygotowuje-wypowiedzenie-konwencji-antyprzemocowej/ accessed 15 October 2019.

35 DSO.SORT.18.4.1.216.MD.

36 https://wpolityce.pl/polityka/381632-rafalska-resort-rodziny-nie-pracuje-nad-wypowiedzeniem-konwencji-antyprzemocowej accessed 15 October 2019.

37 https://vod.tvp.pl/video/warto-rozmawiac,02022017,28601628 accessed 15 October 2019.

38 www.gosc.pl/doc/4408019.Wychowalem-sie-w-trojkacie-bermudzkim accessed 15 October 2019.

It has become evident that the "war on gender" is part of a large right-wing mobilisation at both the local and transnational levels.[39] Korolczuk and Graff argue that today's global Right, while selectively borrowing from the liberal Left and feminist discourses, is in fact constructing a new universalism – an illiberal one that replaces individual rights with the rights of the family as a basic societal unit and depicts religious conservatives as an embattled minority.[40] Thus, the "war on gender" has to be perceived in the wider context of the illiberal transformation in Poland and other States. As Grzebalska and Pető observe, family mainstreaming and anti-gender policies have been one of the main pillars on which the illiberal State has been erected, and through which security, equality and human rights have been redefined.[41] Examples from other Member States of the Council of Europe where the Convention was either rejected or seriously contested demonstrate that the experience of Poland is not an isolated local aberration, but a forerunner of serious problems undermining gender equality and human rights more widely in Europe.

While the controversies surrounding the Istanbul Convention have impeded its implementation by Poland, this does not mean that the Convention was ratified in vain. As discussed below, the Istanbul Convention has had an impact on Polish law and some positive changes have been achieved, although much remains to be done. Since it is not possible to address all the issues in this chapter, the next part will focus on sexual violence and domestic violence. The most important developments have taken place in these areas, while the most burning challenges remain.

4 Implications of the Istanbul Convention for domestic law: sexual violence

This section examines the most important legal implications of the Istanbul Convention for Polish substantive and procedural law on sexual violence, including the challenges to substantive law (namely ensuring conformity of the definitions of rape and sexual harassment with the Convention) and the amendments to procedural law as a result of Poland's accession to the Convention.

39 Agnieszka Graff and Elżbieta Korolczuk, '"Worse than Communism and Nazism Put Together": War on Gender in Poland' in Roman Kuhar and David Paternotte (eds), *Anti-gender Campaigns in Europe: Mobilizing against Equality* (Rowman & Littlefield International, 2017) 175.

40 Elżbieta Korolczuk and Agnieszka Graff, 'Gender as "Ebola from Brussels": The Anticolonial Frame and the Rise of Illiberal Populism' (2018) 43(4) *Signs: Journal of Women in Culture and Society* 798.

41 Weronika Grzebalska and Andrea Pető, 'The Gendered Modus Operandi of the Illiberal Transformation in Hungary and Poland' (2018) 58 *Women's Studies International Forum* 164–172.

4.1 Definition of rape

In its definition of sexual violence, the Istanbul Convention refers to acts to which the victim has not consented. As explained in Article 36(2) of the Convention, "consent must be given voluntarily as the result of the person's free will assessed in the context of the surrounding circumstances". The lack of consent is thus a key element under the Convention in the definition of sexual violence, including rape.

Pursuant to Article 197(1) of the Polish Penal Code, "whoever, by force, illegal threat or deceit, subjects another person to sexual intercourse shall be subject to the penalty of the deprivation of liberty for a term of between 2 and 12 years". The national definition of rape also embraces acts of making another person submit to a sexual act or perform such an act by force, illegal threat or deceit (Article 197(2)).

The absence of consent is widely discussed in Polish legal literature and case law and is sometimes called "a hidden element in the definition of rape".[42] According to some experts, there is no need for an explicit reference to consent; the issue is sufficiently resolved by well-established jurisprudence so there is no need to amend the law.[43] At the same time, it has been argued that due to the various interpretations by courts regarding the elements of rape it is necessary to amend the law so that it would be evident that *any* sexual conduct without the victim's consent falls under the definition of rape.[44] It has been pointed out that both the law and its application in Poland focus on the conduct of the perpetrator – whether there was "use of force, illegal threat, or deceit" – and not on establishing whether there was voluntary consent by the victim.[45] However, no concrete proposals for amendments to the definition of rape have so far been initiated. The government is of the opinion that the definition of rape established in the Polish Penal Code "is open to interpretation in accordance with the Istanbul Convention" and thus no amendment is needed.[46]

42 Appeal Court of Gdańsk, 9 February 2017, II AKa 294/16.

43 Wojciech Zalewski, 'Article 36. Przemoc seksualna, w tym gwałt' in Ewa Bieńkowska and Lidia Mazowiecka (eds), *Konwencja o zapobieganiu i zwalczaniu przemocy wobec kobiet i przemocy domowej. Komentarz* (Wolters Kluwer 2016), 442.

44 Eleonora Zielińska, *Konwencja o zapobieganiu i zwalczaniu przemocy wobec kobiet i przemocy domowej, jej ogólna ocena oraz celowość przystąpienia do niej przez RP* (Instytut Wymiaru Sprawiedliwości 2012), 67.

45 Monika Płatek, 'Przestępstwo zgwałcenia w świetle prawa i z perspektywy osób poszkodowanych' in Joanna Piotrowska and Alina Synakiewicz (eds), *Dość milczenia. Przemoc seksualna wobec kobiet i problem gwałtu w Polsce* (Feminoteka 2011) 30.

46 www.sejm.gov.pl/Sejm8.nsf/interpelacjaTresc.xsp?documentId=06753E25D9317746C125827300497EA9&view=S accessed 15 October 2019.

4.2 Sexual harassment

Article 40 of the Istanbul Convention obliges State Parties to "take the necessary legislative or other measures to ensure that any form of unwanted verbal, non-verbal or physical conduct of a sexual nature with the purpose or effect of violating the dignity of a person, in particular when creating an intimidating, hostile, degrading, humiliating or offensive environment, is subject to criminal or other legal sanctions". As explained by the drafters, criminal or "other" legal sanctions means that State Parties may choose to deal with sexual harassment via criminal or administrative law, or sanctions under civil or labour law.[47]

In Polish law, sexual harassment is a form of discrimination based on sex covered by the Labour Code[48] and by the law on equal treatment, which implements EU anti-discrimination directives.[49] It would thus appear that the requirements established by the Convention are satisfied. However, the scope of protection against sexual harassment in the above-mentioned laws is limited to the area of employment and vocational training. Thus, Polish law does not offer specific protection against sexual harassment in other areas, such as public spaces, schools and universities. The civil or penal remedies are not adequate, particularly in cases of verbal and non-verbal behaviours such as sexist speech, jokes, gestures or images. Specific legal amendments that fully implement the Convention would therefore be welcomed.[50]

4.3 Introduction of ex officio *proceedings*

The introduction of *ex officio* proceedings regarding rape has been the most visible amendment in Polish legislation to ensure compliance with the Istanbul Convention. Prior to 2014, a victim had to file a complaint to trigger the investigation of the sexual crimes specified in Articles 197–199 of the Penal Code.[51] These crimes included rape committed by abusing the vulnerability of another person, including her/his mental disability, as well as sexual abuses committed in a relationship of dependence or by taking advantage of another person's critical situation. The rationale behind the requirement of an official complaint by the victim, which originated in 1932, was to respect the autonomy and intimacy of the victim and to allow her to avoid the shame of rape, which is still classified in the Polish Penal Code as an "offence against sexual liberty and decency".

47 Explanatory Report to the Council of Europe Convention on Preventing and Combating Violence against Women and Domestic Violence, para 207, https://rm.coe.int/16800d383a accessed 15 October 2019.

48 Ustawa z dnia 26 czerwca 1974 r. – Kodeks pracy, Dz.U. 2018, poz. 917, Art. 18^{3a} § 6.

49 Ustawa z dnia 3 grudnia 2010 r. o wdrożeniu niektórych przepisów Unii Europejskiej w zakresie równego traktowania, Dz.U. 2016 poz. 1219, Art. 3.

50 Eleonora Zielińska, 71.

51 Ustawa z dnia 6 czerwca 1997 r. – Kodeks karny, Dz.U. 1997, Nr 88, poz. 553 ze zm.

While the discussion over the introduction of *ex officio* proceedings in rape cases was initiated by Polish experts long before the Convention was adopted, Poland's accession to the Convention speeded up the process of introducing this change in Polish law.[52] This amendment was discussed in the Sejm (the lower house of the Polish Parliament) in the period of 2012–2013, i.e. at the time when "gender ideology" was already present in the political debate. During this time period, however, there was no polarisation – 444 members of Parliament voted for this change, with no votes against and only one abstention.[53]

It seems that for ultraconservatives the provisions regarding sexual violence have been easier to accept than other regulations of the Convention. As Gowin admitted, the requirement of *ex officio* proceedings in rape cases was "something valuable in the Convention".[54] Also the present PiS government has demonstrated its eagerness to counteract rapes. The Ministry of Justice aims to radically expand penalties for rapes.[55] However, no serious prevention measures have been undertaken, such as mandatory and modern sexual education at schools. It seems that the populist agenda involves mainly a superficial fight against sexual violence designed to gain votes.

Data provided by the police indicates that the introduction of *ex officio* proceedings has significantly increased the number of investigations of rape. Between 2009–2013, approximately 1,750 and between 2014 and 2017 approximately 2,400 investigations were initiated annually.[56] This increase, however, does not correspond with the number of rape convictions, which has slightly decreased – from 1,400 annually between 2009–2013 to 1,200 per year in the period of 2014–2017.[57]

4.4 Protection of victims during investigation and judicial proceedings

Other amendments introduced into Polish law have contributed to the implementation of Article 56 of the Istanbul Convention, which secures the protection of victims during investigations and judicial proceedings. Article 56 "[enables] victims to testify, according to the rules provided by their internal law, in the courtroom without being present or at least without the presence of the alleged perpetrator, notably through the use of appropriate communication technologies, where available". Following revision of the criminal procedure in

52 Agnieszka Renkowicz, Magda Duniewska, 'Zasadność ścigania z urzędu przestępstwa gwałtu' (2015) 11 *PWSZ IPiA Studia Lubuskie* 8.

53 www.sejm.gov.pl/Sejm7.nsf/PrzebiegProc.xsp?nr=532 accessed 15 October 2019.

54 www.wprost.pl/kraj/316552/Gwalt-bedzie-scigany-z-urzedu-Gowin-pracujemy-nad-tym.html accessed 15 October 2019.

55 www.sejm.gov.pl/Sejm8.nsf/druk.xsp?nr=2154 accessed 15 October 2019.

56 http://statystyka.policja.pl/st/przestepstwa-ogolem/przestepstwa-kryminalne/zgwalcenie/122293, Zgwalcenie.html accessed 15 October 2019.

57 Ibid.

2013, a victim of rape should be interrogated only once during the entire pre-trial and trial proceedings.[58] Interrogation has to be conducted in the presence of a psychologist and has to be recorded.[59] To protect the victim from being interrogated again in court, the recorded testimony can be played at the trial.

Some issues still need to be tackled, however. For instance, the professionals present during the interrogation need not be of the same sex as the victim, apart from a psychologist which may be of the same sex if a victim so requests. Article 50 of the Convention requires State Parties to ensure that the responsible law enforcement agencies respond promptly and appropriately to all the forms of violence included in the Convention by offering adequate and immediate protection to victims. This obligation includes hearing the victims without delay by specially trained, and where appropriate, female staff in premises designed to establish a relationship of trust between the victim and law enforcement personnel.[60]

Another problem is the length of time before the proceedings take place. As required by Article 49 of the Istanbul Convention, investigations and judicial proceedings should be conducted "without undue delay". According to the Polish Ombudsman, in some cases victims have to wait up to three months for their interrogation after the rape was reported, which obviously affects their psychological well-being and ability to recall details; this period of waiting may also lead to re-victimisation.[61] In 2017, the Ministry of Justice declared that the procedure will be changed to secure that victims of rape are interrogated no later than fourteen days after the court receives the motion to conduct an interrogation.[62] This amendment has been passed in 2019.

5 Implications of the Istanbul Convention for Polish law: domestic violence

This section examines some shortcomings vis-à-vis the requirements imposed by the Istanbul Convention regarding domestic violence. It focuses on the definition of domestic violence in Polish law as a gender-neutral phenomenon, on the definition of a perpetrator, and on the necessity to introduce immediate protection orders and other measures to secure victims' rights and safety.

58 There is, however, a significant exception to this rule – an accused person may request interrogation of the victim again during the trial if the accused was not represented by a lawyer when a victim was interrogated for the first time. Since victims are usually interrogated at an early stage of the proceedings, when often no suspects are established yet, this exception may be widely used in practice.

59 Ustawa z dnia 6 czerwca 1997 r. – Kodeks postępowania karnego, Dz.U. 1997, Nr 89, poz. 555.

60 Explanatory Report, para 258.

61 RPO 2016, BPK. 518.5.2015.

62 http://prawo.gazetaprawna.pl/artykuly/1064736,sadownictwo-przesluchanie-ofiar-gwaltu.html accessed 15 October 2019.

5.1 Definition of domestic violence and absence of gender-sensitivity

Prevention of domestic violence in Poland is regulated by the 2005 Act on counteracting domestic violence.[63] The then-Government Plenipotentiary for Equal Status of Women and Men had initiated the Act in response to the efforts of many women rights' activists since the early nineties.[64] The draft for the law intended to emphasise that domestic violence is not gender-neutral, since it affects mostly women, and to introduce measures based on Austrian regulations, including strong measures such as restraining orders and immediate eviction orders.[65] The proposal for the Act was supported by women's and human rights activists, but contested by conservative politicians who opposed excessive interference in "family matters".[66] The final version of the Act was a compromise, without an explicit gender content and without a strong perpetrator-restraining pillar.

As a result, domestic violence is perceived in Polish law as a purely gender-neutral problem. This has prompted the CEDAW Committee to forward a recommendation to Poland to "include a definition of violence against women in the Act on countering domestic violence so as to ensure that relevant laws and policies are implemented in a gender-sensitive manner".[67]

Additional important elements are missing in the national definition of domestic violence as compared to the definition formulated in Article 3 of the Istanbul Convention. Specifically, Polish law does not mention economic violence, nor does it refer to economic harm when it defines domestic violence. Although there are some provisions of civil and penal law that may be used by victims claiming economic harm, there is no specific tool dedicated to protect them against economic abuse, such as controlling expenditures or preventing a partner from acquiring resources. Thus, in practice economic violence is weakly recognised as a form of domestic violence.[68]

5.2 Definition of perpetrator

The Polish legislation deviates from the Istanbul Convention with respect to the definition of a perpetrator. According to Polish law, domestic violence is committed by a next-of-kin who is defined as "a spouse, ancestor, descendant,

63 *Ustawa z dnia 29 lipca 2005 r. o przeciwdziałaniu przemocy w rodzinie, Dz.U. 2005, Nr 180, poz. 1493 ze zm.*

64 *Andrea Kirzsán, Conny Roggeband,* The Gender Politics of Domestic Violence. Feminists Engaging the State in Central and Eastern Europe (Routledge 2018) 1.

65 See Section 5.3 of this chapter.

66 Sylwia Spurek, *Przeciwdziałanie przemocy w rodzinie. Komentarz,* (Wolters Kluwer 2012) 56 et. seq.

67 Committee on the Elimination of Discrimination against Women concluding observations (2014), CEDAW/C/POL/CO/7-8, para 24.

68 Jagoda Tkacz-Dral, *Przemoc ekonomiczna. Opracowania tematyczne OT-639* (Kancelaria Senatu 2015), 8.

sibling, relative in the same line or degree, person related by adoption or the spouse or partner thereof"[69] or by another person who shares residence or runs the household with a victim.[70] This definition embraces a wide category of persons in line with Article 3 of the Istanbul Convention, where domestic violence is "violence that occurs within the family or domestic unit" irrespective of biological or legal family ties.[71]

At the same time however, Polish law does not fully cover intimate partner violence in line with the Istanbul Convention, as it does not embrace a former spouse or partner. He (or she) may be convicted for domestic violence only if he (or she) still shares the same residence with the victim.

5.3 Immediate protection of victims

Polish law is sorely lacking when it comes to the immediate protection of victims. According to the Istanbul Convention, State Parties are required to establish emergency restraining orders, including barring a perpetrator from accessing the residence. The aim of such emergency restraining order is to grant the competent national authorities

> the power to order, in situations of immediate danger, a perpetrator of domestic violence to vacate the residence of the victim or person at risk for a sufficient period of time and to prohibit the perpetrator from entering the residence of or contacting the victim or person at risk.[72]

The Istanbul Convention does not define the authorities with the power to issue emergency restraining orders, but requires that these authorities are able to respond immediately to a domestic violence call.

In practice, several models of providing immediate protection to victims exist in different Member States, such as Austria, Bulgaria, Spain and the Netherlands.[73] Pursuant to the Austrian model – probably the most widely acclaimed – the police issue an emergency restraining order. In other countries, other authorities are in charge, such as courts or prosecutors; in all cases, however, the authorities have to react immediately or within a very short span of time, such as 24 or 72 hours.[74]

69 Ustawa z dnia 6 czerwca 1997 r. – Kodeks karny, Dz.U. 1997, Nr 88, poz. 553 ze zm., Art. 115§11.
70 Ustawa z dnia 29 lipca 2005 r. o przeciwdziałaniu przemocy w rodzinie, Dz.U. 2005, Nr 180, poz. 1493 ze zm., Art. 2.
71 Explanatory Report, para 41.
72 Article 52, Istanbul Convention.
73 Rosa Logar and Johanna Niemi, *Emergency Barring Orders in Situations of Domestic Violence: Article 52 of the Istanbul Convention. A Collection of Papers on the Council of Europe Convention on Preventing and Combating Violence Against Women and Domestic Violence* (Council of Europe 2017).
74 Ibid. 28–44.

In Poland the police are not equipped with the power to issue emergency restraining orders during an immediate intervention following a domestic violence call. Such a measure may be imposed only when criminal proceedings have been initiated or after trial, as a penal or probation measure. In addition, while a civil procedure allows the court to issue an eviction order against a perpetrator of domestic violence, this is not an emergency order since the court has one month to issue a decision. Moreover, in practice the duration of the proceedings is usually much longer.[75] Thus, Polish law and practice sorely need to be amended in order to implement Article 52 of the Istanbul Convention.[76]

5.4 Other measures protecting victims

The Ombudsman and other specialists on domestic violence have indicated other systemic problems concerning national legal standards on shelters, specialist support services for victims, and treatment programmes for perpetrators. In particular, the number of shelters is not sufficient and most of them are not fully accessible to persons with disabilities.[77] Victims living in shelters are not provided with adequate legal and psychological support,[78] and treatment programmes for perpetrators are very limited.[79]

Poland has not introduced a mechanism for risk assessment and/or risk management, as required by Article 51 of the Istanbul Convention to ensure the effective protection of victims of domestic violence.[80] Another concern is the use of mediation proceedings in domestic violence cases. Although Polish law – in accordance with Article 48(1) of the Istanbul Convention – prohibits mandatory alternative dispute resolution in domestic violence cases, research indicates that in practice a large number of cases are treated as a "family conflict" and automatically directed by the courts to mediation proceedings, regardless of the situation of victims and the scale of harm.[81]

Enhanced protection of migrant women victims of domestic violence is also recommended. This includes the establishment of a legal mechanism in line with Article 59 of the Istanbul Convention,[82] and the recognition in asylum procedures that gender-based violence against women is a form of persecution. Although Polish law appears on its face to be in line with Article 60 of the

75 RPO 2017, IV.7214.62.2014.DZ.
76 RPO 2015, XI.518.47.2015.AM.
77 RPO 2016, III.518.16.2016.JA.
78 Ibid.
79 RPO 2017, IX.517.3085.2016.MK.
80 Urszula Nowakowska, 'Ocena ryzyka w sprawach o przemoc w rodzinie' in Lidia Mazowiecka (ed.), *Jak skutecznie chronić ofiary przemocy w rodzinie* (Wolters Kluwer 2013).
81 Małgorzata Czarkowska, *Przeciwdziałanie przemocy wobec kobiet w rodzinie w praktyce organów ścigania, wymiaru sprawiedliwości i innych instytucji* (Lexis Nexis 2014), 290–296.
82 Witold Klaus, *Przemoc ze strony najbliższych w doświadczeniach życiowych uchodźczyń. Analiza kryminologiczna* (Scholar 2016), 279–280.

Istanbul Convention, in practice there have been no cases where refugee status has been granted solely on the basis that a woman was a victim of gender-based violence.[83]

So far, the Istanbul Convention has had a rather minor impact in counteracting domestic violence in Poland. However, the Convention is visible in public and political debates concerning the issue, and the Ombudsman[84] as well as members of opposition parties[85] refer to it when addressing the government. In addition, the Convention has contributed to the creation of some concrete tools, such as a state-wide 24/7 emergency phone line free of charge, which has been operating since 2017 and was set up to comply with Article 24 of the Istanbul Convention.[86] On the other hand, some steps undertaken by the government are alarming. In December 2018, a draft amendment to the domestic violence law was revealed which aimed to change the definition of domestic violence so that only recurring acts, but not a single action, could be recognised as domestic violence.[87] The draft was rapidly withdrawn following the loud and immediate reaction of the press and civil society. It can, however, be perceived as a clear signal that the current Polish government aims to preserve family unity at the expense of the safety and rights of victims.

6 Conclusions

The Istanbul Convention plays a major role in Poland in two interrelated contexts. In the socio-political context, it has a symbolic value for both sides of the polarised society. For the ultraconservatives and populists, it has become a symbol of "Ebola from Brussels",[88] an emanation of liberalism, multiculturalism, and other trends "from the West".[89] On the other hand, the necessity to defend the Convention has to some extent motivated the liberal, pro-democratic and human rights movements. If it were not for the controversies surrounding its ratification and implementation, probably only a narrow group of women's

83 Ibid. 220–224.

84 See footnotes 34, 57, 58, 59.

85 See e.g. www.sejm.gov.pl/Sejm8.nsf/interpelacja.xsp?documentId=EF9996DCEF60F6AC C125823A004E4D59 accessed 15 October 2019.

86 www.rpo.gov.pl/pl/content/rpo-sprawdza-jak-dziala-telefon-dla-ofiar-przemocy-w-rodzinie accessed 15 October 2019.

87 Karolina Nowkowska, Raz to nie przemoc? PiS zmienia ustawę o przeciwdziałaniu przemocy w rodzinie (*Gazetetaprawna.pl* 2 January 2019), https://prawo.gazetaprawna.pl/artykuly/1389977,zmiany-w-utawie-o-przeciwdzialaniu-przemocy-w-rodzinie.html accessed 15 October 2019.

88 Elżbieta Korolczuk and Agnieszka Graff, 'Gender as "Ebola from Brussels": The Anti-colonial Frame and the Rise of Illiberal Populism' (2018) 43(4) *Signs: Journal of Women in Culture and Society* 798.

89 Even though the cold war ended almost 30 years ago, countries of the so-called "old EU" are still frequently associated, particularly by older generations, with "the West", and thus as a strange and "other" culture.

rights activists and specialists would have knowledge of or interest in this treaty. Thus, in Poland the Convention has become a symbol of modern, European values worth fighting for.

At the same time, in the legal context the Convention has had some important implications for Polish law, which however have not resulted in a sufficient number of important legal developments. The most important achievement has been the introduction of *ex officio* proceedings in rape cases. This legal amendment constituted a breakthrough development because it challenged the perception of sexual violence as a form of shame and stigma for victims. Moreover, some significant measures aimed at protecting rape victims during proceedings were introduced. Other aspects of counteracting sexual violence, however, still require action, including the re-definition of rape and sexual harassment.

It may fairly be said that no major reform in the field of counteracting domestic violence has taken place. Paradoxically, this area seems to be more ideologically sensitive than sexual violence. This could be attributable to the fact that sexual violence is stereotypically perceived as committed by "strangers", not relatives.[90] Since for ultraconservatives the protection of family unity and identity is a primary concern, the current Polish government is not likely to undertake any measures that could interfere in family matters.

The first evaluation report of GREVIO on Poland is to be published in January 2021.[91] Its outcome will strongly depend on the political situation in Poland then. So long as the Istanbul Convention is blatantly disrespected by the Polish authorities, any major amendments of Polish law in order to implement the Convention seem rather unlikely.

This work was supported by National Science Centre (Poland), Grant Number 2019/33/B/HS5/01634.

90 See e.g. Timothy Fortney, Jill Levenson, Yolanda Brannon and Juanita N. Baker, 'Myths and Facts about Sexual Offenders: Implications for Treatment and Public Policy' (2007) 2 *Sexual Offender Treatment* 1.

91 www.coe.int/en/web/istanbul-convention/timetable accessed 15 October 2019.

14 Reservations and declarations under the Istanbul Convention

Wojciech Burek

1 Introduction

The International Court of Justice (ICJ) Judge José M. Ruda observed back in 1975 that "the question of reservations to multilateral treaties has been one of the most controversial subjects in contemporary international law".[1] In subsequent years, this statement has become even more legitimate. Most of the problems and controversies manifest themselves in the context of human rights treaties, in particular of those treaties that remain silent on reservations or regulate them in very general terms. The volume, characteristics, and far-reaching effect of the reservations made by many States to human rights treaties (especially those adopted within the UN human rights system) have provoked reactions from human rights monitoring bodies,[2] and triggered an ongoing academic debate over the subject.[3] Some of these problems are also related to the so-called "interpretative declarations" formulated with respect to treaties.

In 1993, the UN International Law Commission (ILC) included in its agenda the law and practice relating to reservations to treaties. The work commenced the following year with the appointment of Alain Pellet as a Special Rapporteur. The ILC needed 18 years to conclude its work and the final product is massive in size and scope. The ILC Guide to Practice on Reservations to the Treaties[4] is, together with its commentaries, more than six hundred pages long. It has a mixed legal character, or as Alain Pellet observed

1 José M Ruda 'Reservations to treaties' (1975-III) 146 RCADI, 101.

2 The Human Rights Committee's General Comment No 24, UN Doc. CCPR/C/21/Rev.l/Add. 6 (1994).

3 See, *inter alia* Liesbeth Lijnzaad, *Reservation to UN Human Rights Treaties: Ratify and Ruin?* (Nijhoff 1995); JP Gardner (ed.), *Human Rights as General Norms and a State's Right to Opt Out: Reservations and Objections to Human Rights Conventions* (British Institute of International & Comparative Law 1997); Yogesh Tyagi, 'The Conflict of Law and Policy on Reservations to Human Rights Treaties' (2000) 71 *Brit. Y.B. Int'l* 181; Ryan Goodman, 'Human Rights Treaties, Invalid Reservations, and State Consent' (2002) 95 *Am. J. Int'l* 531; Ineta Ziemele (ed.) *Reservations to Human Rights Treaties and the Vienna Convention Regime: Conflict, Harmony or Reconciliation* (Brill/Nijhoff 2004).

4 Guide to Practice on Reservations to Treaties. *Yrbk ILC* (2011), II, Part 2.

> the guidelines have very different legal values, from pure recommendations to fully binding rules – not because they appear in the Guide, but because they have acquired (independently of the Conventions and, *a fortiori*, of the Guide) the status of customary rules.[5]

Despite its non-binding nature, the ILC Guide to Practice has acted from its adoption as a point of reference in most of the discussions on reservations or interpretive declarations to treaties. The ILC document contains a comprehensive and universally-accepted definition of a reservation and interpretative declarations.[6]

The drafters of the 2011 Istanbul Convention[7] were able to draw from the wide-ranging experiences with reservations regimes under other international treaties and available solutions concerning how (or whether) to regulate reservations and interpretative declarations, including the ongoing work of the ILC on this topic. The available solutions range from remaining silent on reservations (and declarations), as for example in the 1948 Genocide Convention,[8] to the explicit prohibition of reservations, as for example in Article 3 of the 2002 Protocol No 13 to the European Convention on Human Rights and Fundamental Freedoms,[9] with a whole range of options in between. In the end, however, the reservation regime enshrined in Articles 78 and 79 of the Istanbul Convention seems to be, at least partially, unique.

Article 78(1) of the Convention states that no reservations may be made to the treaty with some exceptions as regulated under Article 78(2). The latter provision lists the Convention Articles that may be object of reservations. In this regard, the system under the Istanbul Convention can be compared to the one

5 Alain Pellet, 'The ILC Guide to Practice on Reservations to Treaties: A General Presentation by the Special Rapporteur' (2013) 24 *Eur. J. Int'l* 1061,1073.

6 Reservation:

> a unilateral statement, however phrased or named, made by a State or an international organization when signing, ratifying, formally confirming, accepting, approving or acceding to a treaty, or by a State when making a notification of succession to a treaty, whereby the State or organization purports to exclude or to modify the legal effect of certain provisions of the treaty in their application to that State or to that international organization.
>
> (Guideline 1.1)

Interpretative declaration: "a unilateral statement, however phrased or named, made by a State or an international organization, whereby that State or that organization purports to specify or clarify the meaning or scope of a treaty or of certain of its provisions" (Guideline 1.2).

7 The Council of Europe Convention on Preventing and Combating Violence Against Women and Domestic Violence, ETS No 210.

8 The Convention on the Prevention and Punishment of the Crime of Genocide, 78 UNTS 278.

9 The Protocol No 13 to the European Convention on Human Rights and Fundamental Freedoms, Concerning the Abolition of the Death Penalty in All Circumstances, ETS No 187.

established under the 1967 Protocol Relating to the Status of Refugees.[10] In particular, Article VII of the latter lists also the provisions which can be subject to reservations or interpretative declarations. The novelty of the Istanbul Convention reservations regime is rather its Article 79, which emphasises the temporary nature of reservations formulated in accordance with Article 78, via the required renewal of reservations every five years. The Group of Experts on Action Against Violence against Women and Domestic Violence (GREVIO) plays a role in this procedure as clarified by Article 79. In contrast to explicit regulation of reservations, the Convention is however silent on interpretative declarations.

Section 2 of this chapter will present the list of provisions that may be object of reservations under Article 78, as well as a discussion of the legal effect of impermissible reservations. Section 3 will engage with the procedure for lodging both reservations and interpretive declarations. Section 4 will deal with state practice concerning reservations to the Istanbul Convention. This will be followed by an assessment of the reservations formulated so far, with the main finding being that only Poland's reservation to Article 30(2) gives rise to serious doubts as to its compatibility with international law. Section 5 accordingly will review the existing state practice concerning both unilateral statements and interpretative declarations to the Istanbul Convention, which will be again followed by an assessment of the formulated statements and declarations. Here, special attention will be given to the practice of some States (Croatia, Latvia, Lithuania and Poland) to formulate vaguely worded interpretative declarations with reference to domestic law. Information on the reactions from other States will be also presented in this section.

2 Permissible and invalid reservations under the Istanbul Convention

Before turning to an analysis of the practice of States under the Istanbul Convention, the Istanbul Convention provisions that may be object of reservations will be presented, followed by a discussion of the legal effect of invalid reservations. This discussion offers a response to the following question: What happens if a State has submitted a reservation that, under the terms of Article 78(1), can be qualified as impermissible?

2.1 Expressly authorised reservations

Under Article 78(2) parties to the Convention may "reserve the right not to apply or to apply only in specific cases or conditions" several explicitly indicated provisions.

10 The Protocol Relating to the Status of Refugees, 606 UNTS 267.

The first one is Article 30(2), which addresses the issue of state compensation supplementing compensation from the perpetrator or insurance for "those who have sustained serious bodily injury or impairment of health". Parties to the Convention may also introduce reservations in relation to several paragraphs of Article 44, which deals with jurisdiction (i.e. 1(e), 2 and 4). Another provision that may be object of reservations is Article 55(1) in connection with Article 35, regarding minor offences only. As a result of this reservation, minor physical violence may be exempted from investigation if the victim does not report it or withdraws her report.

Article 58 of the Convention, read in conjunction with Articles 37, 38 and 39, can be also object of reservations. By formulating this reservation States may be under no obligation to extend the time for initiating legal proceedings in cases of forced marriage, female genital mutilation, or forced abortion and forced sterilisation after the victim has reached the age of majority. Finally, Article 78(2), read in conjunction with Article 59, allows for reservations in relation to States' obligations to grant residence status to victims who are migrants. Article 78(3) that allows for the possibility to "reserve the right to provide for non-criminal sanctions, instead of criminal sanctions" for psychological violence (Article 33) and stalking (Article 34) needs to be also added to the list of provisions that can be object of reservations.

The reason for choosing the specific provisions from the Istanbul Convention listed in Article 78(2) is revealed in its Explanatory Report. The latter explains that they are all:

> provisions for which unanimous agreement was not reached among the drafters despite the efforts to achieved in favour of compromise. These reservations aim at enabling the largest possible ratification of the Convention, whilst permitting Parties to preserve some of their fundamental legal concepts.[11]

The Explanatory Report provides a similar rationale for allowing reservations under Article 78(3) – preservation of the criminalisation of psychological violence and stalking, "while allowing flexibility where the legal system of a Party provides only for non-criminal sanctions in relation to these behaviours".[12] This kind of rationale, i.e. allowing reservations in relation to selected provisions, follows the dominant general justification for reservations to treaties. In particular, many scholars link the growing acceptance of reservations with the change of the procedure for adopting texts of multilateral treaties – from the rule of unanimity to majority voting. In the latter case, there is always a

11 Council of Europe, *Explanatory Report to the Council of Europe Convention on preventing and combating violence against women and domestic violence* (2011) (Istanbul 11 May 2011), 381.

12 Explanatory Report, paras 181 and 186.

possibility of an overruled minority. In such a case "[i]n order to secure the final adoption of and wide participation in the convention, States dissenting on one or another provision must be given the possibility of ratifying or adhering with reservations".[13]

In light of the above-described system that allows reservations, the following questions arise: How should reservations which are outside the scope of Article 78 of the Convention be dealt with? What are the legal effects of impermissible reservations?

2.2 The legal effect of invalid reservations

The wording of Article 78 is clear: reservations may only be lodged in relation to the provisions from the Convention explicitly listed by this provision. As a consequence, any reservation that does not concern one of the provisions expressly stated in Article 78 should be treated as invalid. But what are the consequences of non-compliance with Article 78? What happens if a State has submitted a reservation that under the terms of Article 78 can be qualified as impermissible?

These two questions refer to the legal effects of invalid reservations. This is an issue that has been at the centre of the debates on reservations to treaties, especially human rights treaties. Two main opposing positions can be identified within these debates: the "permissibility school" and the "opposability school".[14] The former school argues that an invalid reservation (i.e. a reservation that is incompatible with the object or purpose of the treaty or a reservation that is not specifically authorised by the treaty) is without legal effect. As a result, the formulating State cannot benefit from it, even in cases when other contracting States do not react (i.e. object) to it. The permissibility doctrine has been endorsed by, *inter alia*, the UN Human Rights Committee,[15] the European Court of Human Rights,[16] and several States, especially pioneering Nordic States.[17]

13 Karl Zemanek, 'Some Unresolved Questions in the Vienna Convention on the Law of Treaties' in Jerzy Makarczyk (ed.), *Essays in International Law in Honour of Judge Manfred Lachs* (Brill 1984), 327.

14 See, *inter alia*, Konstantin Korkelia, 'New Challenges to the Regime of Reservations under the International Covenant on Civil and Political Rights' (2002) 13 *Eur. J. Int'l* 437, 452–453.

15 UN Human Rights Committee (HRC), *CCPR General Comment No 24: Issues Relating to Reservations Made upon Ratification or Accession to the Covenant or the Optional Protocols thereto, or in Relation to Declarations under Article 41 of the Covenant*, 4 November 1994, UN Doc. CCPR/C/21/Rev.1/Add.6.

16 See, *inter alia*, the *Belilos v Switzerland* case – App. No 10328/83, Belilos v Switzerland, 29 April 1988, Series A No 132.

17 Jan Klabbers, 'Accepting the Unacceptable? A New Nordic Approach to Reservations to Multilateral Treaties' (2000) 69 *Nord. J. Int'l* 179.

In contrast, the "opposability school" argues that all reservations are valid unless they are objected to by other contracting parties. An objection may preclude the entry into force of the treaty between the objecting party and the party that has formulated the reservation. However, an objection has no bearing on treaty relations between the reserving State and other non-objecting States. It follows that the only situation whereby reservations will not have any legal effect is when all other contracting parties submit objections aimed at precluding the entry into force of the convention between them and the reserving States. The opposability doctrine has been supported by some States.[18]

The ILC Guidelines on the consequences of invalid reservations follow the permissibility doctrine. Under Guideline 4.5.1: "[a] reservation that does not meet the conditions of formal validity and permissibility (...) is null and void, and therefore devoid of any legal effect". Additionally, "[t]he nullity of an invalid reservation does not depend on the objection or the acceptance by a contracting State or a contracting organization".

As it will be shown below, so far all the formulated reservations were lodged to the provisions directly listed in Article 78(2) of the Istanbul Convention. However, at least some of the formulated "interpretative declarations" give rise to serious doubts and may in fact be treated as invalid reservations. In this regard, as will be further elaborated below, the doctrine of permissibility may play an important role also in the context of the Istanbul Convention.

3 The Istanbul Convention procedure for reservations and declarations

3.1 Reservations

The procedure for lodging reservations is regulated by Articles 78 and 79 of the Istanbul Convention. More specifically, reservations shall be addressed and transmitted to the Secretary General of the Council of Europe (CoE), who acts as the depository of the Istanbul Convention. They can be formulated in writing at the time of signature or when a State deposits its instrument of ratification, acceptance, approval or accession. This implies that reservations need to be formulated before a State or the European Union becomes a contracting party to the Convention. Under Article 78(4), the Secretary General of the CoE shall be also informed in cases of whole or partial withdrawal of reservations.

Every reservation formulated in accordance with Article 78(2) and (3) is valid for five years, with a possibility for further renewals for the same period. The procedure governing renewal in Article 79(2) can be described as favourable for the reserving party. Not only is there an obligation upon the Secretary General

18 See, *inter alia*, the observations by the United Kingdom, the United States, and France on the UN Human Rights Committee's General Comment No 24 – published in: Gardner (n 4) 193–207.

to inform the reserving party about the upcoming expiry, but even if there is no reaction by the State the reservation is automatically extended for another six months. Only a failure on the part of a reserving State to notify (during this extended period) the Secretary General of its intention to uphold or modify the reservation, causes invalidation of the reservation.

Pursuant to Article 79(3), GREVIO plays an important role in the procedure since the State Parties are under the obligation to present an explanation to GREVIO before renewal of a reservation or upon request from GREVIO. The Explanatory Report offers the following clarification as to the reasons underlying the system for renewal of reservations: "[T]the drafters considered it appropriate to provide for a periodic review of the reservations in order to encourage Parties to lift them or to indicate the reasons for maintaining them".[19] The role of GREVIO is limited to receiving explanations only when a reserving party decides to renew its reservation. GREVIO does not play a role when a party initially decides to formulate a reservation. It is regrettable that GREVIO is consulted only *ex post* at the point when a reservation might be renewed, and not at the moment when the prospective State Party to the Convention makes its decision on formulating reservations.

3.2 Declarations

As the Convention remains silent on interpretative declarations, there is nothing on the procedural aspects of lodging these kinds of declarations. Hence to address this, a reference should be made to general international law doctrine on interpretative declarations. For this purpose, it is important to refer to the ILC's Guide to Practice that deals with interpretative declarations in a comprehensive manner. Guideline 3.5 states that "[a] State or an international organization may formulate an interpretative declaration unless the interpretative declaration is prohibited by the treaty". This can be regarded as a generally accepted rule. Donald M. McRae confirmed its general acceptance in his influential 1978 article by presenting a sufficient number of examples from state practice.[20] It follows that the permissibility of interpretive declarations to the Istanbul Convention is not controversial.

3.3 State practice concerning reservations

So far 21 States out of the 46 States that have signed the Convention[21] have made use of Articles 78(2) and or 78(3). Nine of them have formulated reservations to only one article, and the rest to two or more. All of them are presented in the table below.

19 Explanatory Report, para 384.

20 Donald M. McRae, 'The Legal Effect of Interpretative Declarations' (1978) 49 *Brit. Y.B. Int'l* 155.

21 The Convention has been signed by 46 States and by the European Union. Currently 33 States are parties to the Convention (i.e. after ratification or accession).

Table 14.1 Reservations formulated under Article 78

	Reservations without clarification[a]	*Reservations with added clarifications*
Article 30(2) – state compensation supplementing compensation from the perpetrator or insurance for "those who have sustained serious bodily injury or impairment of health".	**Andorra, Armenia, Croatia, Cyprus, Georgia, Malta, Monaco, Romania, Serbia, Slovenia**	**Poland** – "shall be applied solely in regard of victims who are citizens of the Republic of Poland or the European Union and in accordance with a procedure provided for by national law", **The former Yugoslav Republic of Macedonia (FYROM)** – only in specific cases (Law on the Children's Justice).
Article 44(1)(e) – criminal jurisdiction when the offence is committed outside the territory of a State Party but "by a person who has her or his habitual residence in their territory".	**Cyprus, the Czech Republic, Greece, Poland, Romania, Serbia, Slovenia, and Switzerland**	**France** "only in specific cases and conditions", **Malta** not to apply Article 44(1)(e) when the offence is committed by a person holding permanent residence, **Germany** only pursuant to the conditions stipulated in Section 7(2) No 2 of the German Criminal Code.
Article 44(3) – in case of particular offences, i.e. sexual violence, including rape, forced marriage, female genital mutilation, forced abortion and forced sterilisation, jurisdiction should not be "subordinated to the condition that the acts are criminalised in the territory where they were committed".	**Cyprus, Greece, Romania, Serbia, Slovenia, Sweden**	**France** "only in specific cases and conditions", **Denmark** will not apply with respect to Articles 36, 37 and 39 of the Convention, **Switzerland** will not apply "with regard to sexual violence against adults (Article 36 of the Convention) and to forced abortion and forced sterilisation (Article 39 of the Convention)", **FYROM** will apply the jurisdiction rules and requirements in its legislation (Chapter 12 of the Criminal Code of the Republic of Macedonia).

Article 44(4) – criminal jurisdiction when the offence is committed outside the State Party by one of its nationals or "by person who has her or his habitual residence in" its territory, is not subordinated to the reporting by the victim or "by the State of the place where the offence was committed".	**Cyprus, Greece, Romania, Serbia, Slovenia**	**France** "only in specific cases and conditions".
Article 55(1) – *ex officio* proceedings with respect to Article 35 (physical violence) regarding minor offences	**Latvia, Poland, Romania, Slovenia**	**Finland** – will not to apply "to petty assault when the offence is committed against a person other than a person referred to in the Finish Criminal Code", **Switzerland** – "only in specific cases or conditions", **FYROM** "until the alignment of the provisions of the relevant legislation of the Republic of Macedonia with the provisions of the present Convention".
Article 58 – commensurate statutes of limitations with respect to Articles 37 (forced marriage), 38 (female genital mutilation) and 39 (forced abortion and forced sterilisation).	**Poland, Slovenia, Sweden**	**France**, in all cases where these offences are qualified as crimes by French Law and in specific cases or conditions where these offences are qualified as torts (délits) by French law.
Article 59 – obligation to facilitate the process of granting residence status for victims who are migrants	**Cyprus, Romania and Slovenia**	**Germany** narrowed its reservation only to Article 59(2) and (3), **Monaco** will not apply this provision "in whole or in part", **Switzerland** only in specific cases or conditions, **FYROM** will not apply "until the alignment of the provisions of the relevant legislation of the Republic of Macedonia with the provisions of the present Convention".

continued

Table 14.1 Continued

	Reservations without clarification[a]	*Reservations with added clarifications*
Non-criminal sanctions, instead of criminal sanctions, for the behaviours referred to in Articles 33 (psychological violence)	**Romania**	
Non-criminal sanctions, instead of criminal sanctions, for the behaviours referred to in Articles 34 (stalking)	**Romania, Denmark**	

Note
a These States have decided not to apply this provision without adding any clarifications to justify their choice.

The above-mentioned reservations fulfil all the formal criteria for the validity of reservations under international law. Under the terms of Article 78(2) and (3) certain reservations are expressly authorised by the Convention and, as the above Table 14.1 shows, States have taken advantage of this possibility. Thus, these States are not per se in violation of international law.[22] However, it cannot be excluded that upon closer examination some of the submitted reservations may give rise to doubts. This might be the case for those reservations which include references to national law (e.g. Germany's reservation to Article 44(1)(e) or Finland's reservation to Article 55(1)). Only after an examination of the national legislation mentioned therein can the exact scope of the reservation(s) be revealed and assessed. In order to assess these possible doubts, the role of GREVIO, as the body to which, under Article 79(3), State Parties present explanations when deciding to renew a reservation, might be of considerable importance. As was mentioned above, unfortunately GREVIO is consulted only *ex post*, i.e. at the point when a reservation might be renewed.

It remains to be seen how GREVIO, which held its first meeting only a few years ago, will use its competences with respect to the renewal of reservations, or more generally with respect to reservations as such. In the case of the former, so far only Malta has informed the Secretary General of its intention to wholly uphold its reservation for a period of another five years. However, neither Malta's explanation nor GREVIO's assessment has been released. In the case of the latter, GREVIO's main procedure, namely country monitoring and evaluation based on country reports, has been completed only with respect to six State Parties. Only two of them had formulated reservations (Denmark and Monaco). However, in both cases the scope of the formulated reservations is clear, and as such they do not give rise to any doubts from the perspective of international law.[23]

The only formulated reservation which raises doubts from the point of view of international law, without further examination of the national legislation, is the reservation formulated by Poland with respect to Article 30(2). Poland stated that Article 30(2) of the Convention "shall be applied solely in regard to

22 This is indirectly confirmed by the fact that the so far formulated reservations have not been met with responses (i.e. objections) from the other contracting parties.

23 GREVIO in its Baseline Evaluation Reports on Denmark and Monaco noted all the reservations and reminded these countries of their obligation to provide an explanation prior to the prospective renewals of their reservations. Only as regards Monaco's reservation with respect to Article 59(2) did GREVIO offer a more detailed assessment. In particular, GREVIO stated that it

> invites the authorities to ensure that the conditions governing the right of residence in Monaco and renewal of residence permits are enforced so as to take into account the difficulties, particularly financial, that foreign women who are victims of violence may experience when they no longer have the resources of their spouse or partner

– *see* GREVIO Baseline Evaluation Report. Denmark, GREVIO/Inf(2017)14, paras 10 and 173; GREVIO Baseline Evaluation Report. Monaco, GREVIO/Inf(2017)3, para 165.

victims who are citizens of the Republic of Poland or the European Union and in accordance with a procedure provided for by national law". This means that in all cases (even when the perpetrator has Polish nationality), victims of domestic violence who are third-country nationals are excluded from supplementary compensation. This exclusion raises various concerns.

First of all, provisions authorising reservations shall not be interpreted in isolation from the other provisions of the Convention. Poland's reservation might be incompatible with Article 4(3) of the Istanbul Convention, which enshrines the prohibition on discrimination. Article 4(3) includes a non-exhaustive list of grounds, including migration status, based on which discrimination is not allowed. Article 4(3) is part of Chapter 1 of the Convention, which contains, *inter alia*, the purposes of the Convention, its scope, and the general obligations of State Parties, and as such should be treated as a core provision of the Istanbul Convention. This assessment of Article 4(3) can be also justified by the fact that combating discrimination against women and achieving gender equality is one of the main goals of the Convention. Having this in mind, it is difficult to accept the idea that State Parties to the Convention, being under the obligation to fight one type of discrimination, may discriminate on other grounds. This is linked to the notion of the compatibility of reservations with the object and purpose of the treaty.

Since the adoption of the 1951 ICJ advisory opinion on *Reservations to the Convention on the Prevention and Punishment of the Crime of Genocide*,[24] most of the debates on the permissibility of reservations have focused on the notion of their compatibility with the object and purpose of the treaty.[25] In other words, in cases of reservations not expressly authorised by the treaty, or which fall outside the scope of what is permissible, they can only be treated as valid subject to the condition that they are formulated with respect to rather minor provisions of the treaty, i.e. outside its core provisions. The clarification added by Poland in relation to its reservation suggests that the factual scope of its reservation undermines one of the core provisions of the Convention – Article 4(3). The ILC Guide to Practice also confirms that the notion of compatibility with the object and purpose of the treaty is applicable in cases similar to the Istanbul Convention reservations regime, i.e. to permissible reservations expressly authorised in the treaty.[26]

24 *Reservations to the Convention on the Prevention and Punishment of the Crime of Genocide*, Advisory Opinion [1951] ICJ Rep. 24.

25 This notion is also at the centre of the 1969 Vienna Convention on the Law of Treaties (1115 UNTS 331.) and has been set out in several human rights treaties. (see, e.g. Article 28(2) of the 1979 Convention on the Elimination of Discrimination Against Women (CEDAW) – 1249 UNTS 13, and Article 46(1) of the Convention on the Rights of Persons with Disability – 2515 UNTS 18).

26 *See* Guideline 3.1.4: "Where the treaty envisages the formulation of specified reservations without defining their content, a reservation may be formulated by a State or an international organization only if it is not incompatible with the object and purpose of the treaty".

Furthermore, the Explanatory Report suggests an additional constraint: "[t]his possibility of reservations [with respect to Article 30(2) – author] is without prejudice to the obligations of the Parties pursuant to other international instruments in this field (…)".[27] There are many human rights treaties to which Poland is a party and which prohibit discrimination and require equal treatment. The situation arising from Poland's reservation with respect to Article 30(2) seems especially to contradict Article 26 of the International Covenant on Civil and Political Rights ("all persons (…) are entitled without any discrimination to the equal protection of the law"), which provides an autonomous right to non-discrimination and includes a non-exhaustive list of statuses.[28] The refusal to grant supplementary compensation to a victim who is a third-country national – while at the same time under the relevant legislation victims with Polish (or other EU Member State) nationality are entitled to this type of benefit – is a clear breach of the obligation to guarantee equal protection under the law. The latter implies that persons similarly situated must be similarly treated.

Nowak, in his commentary to the ICCPR, rightly observes that its Article 26 encompasses all four pillars of the principle of equality: equality before the law; equal protection of the law; prohibition of discrimination; and protection against discrimination, which together form the unified and related obligation to "to ensure substantive equality by way of legislation".[29] The same author further notes that equal protection of the law contains both a negative and a positive aspect. The negative aspect obliges State Parties to "refrain from any discrimination when enacting laws".[30] In this regard, the exclusion of third-country nationals from compensation, depending on the particular circumstances of a given case, might be treated as a form of prohibited discrimination on several grounds (e.g. national origin or migrant status).

At the same time, however, the reader needs to be reminded that the ICCPR monitoring body, the UN Human Rights Committee, in its General Comment No 18 confirmed the well-established rule in human rights law that "not every differentiation of treatment will constitute discrimination, if the criteria for such differentiation are reasonable and objective and if the aim is to achieve a purpose which is legitimate under the Covenant".[31] In light of this rule, the question remains whether the provision of compensation by the State falls within the scope of Article 26 of the ICCPR. The Human Rights Committee's jurisprudence seems to confirm that it does. For instance, in its decision *Joseph Frank Adam v Czech Republic*,[32] the Committee confirmed that the application of a provision of law concerning cases of property confiscation by

27 Explanatory Report, para 171.

28 The 1966 International Covenant on Civil and Political Rights (ICCPR) – 999 UNTS 171.

29 Manfred Nowak, *U.N. Covenant on Civil and Political Rights: CCPR Commentary* (N.P. Engel 1993), 469–461, 469.

30 Ibid. 468.

31 UN Doc. HRI/GEN/1/Rev.1 at 26 (1994), para 13.

32 UN Doc. CCPR/C/57/D/586/1994.

the State – whereby property might be subject to restitution or compensation only when claimants are Czech citizens – constituted a violation of Article 26 of the ICCPR. In my opinion the differentiation of the legal position of victims of domestic violence based on their nationality cannot be considered as reasonable and aimed to achieve a purpose that is legitimate under the ICCPR.

This opinion seems to be confirmed in relation to the concerns put forward by Stoyanova in a slightly different context (i.e. compensation for the victims of human trafficking and slavery). The author indicates that in many cases national legislation provides for a distinction based on, *inter alia*, nationality, concerning access to certain rights, also noting that national legislators argue that in some cases the notion that a certain degree of discretion must be afforded to States in relation to aliens might prevail over the notion of equal treatment.[33] However, in refutation of this argument Stoyanova relies on the relevant provision of the Council of Europe Convention on Action against Trafficking in Human Beings (Article 15(4),[34] which "refers to victims without any further qualifications" and provides that "victims of trafficking have to have access to compensation (…), and victims' residence and migration status should not bar this access".[35] The wording of Article 30(2) of the Istanbul Convention ("compensation shall be awarded to those who have sustained serious bodily injury") justifies the same conclusion, and reference to Article 26 of the ICCPR only reinforces this reasoning.

In sum, the Polish reservation to Article 30(2) gives rise to serious doubts as to its compatibility with international law.

4 State practice concerning (interpretative) declarations

Formulated declarations to the Istanbul Convention can be divided into two groups: on the one hand, unilateral statements, and, on the other hand, those which are considered by the declaring States as interpretative declarations.

4.1 Unilateral statements

Some States have formulated statements concerning several issues either specifically mentioned in the Convention or of a rather general character. Belgium, Estonia and France clarified which official national body would be a co-ordinating body within the meaning of Article 10. Two countries, the Netherlands and Denmark made declarations delimiting the application of the Convention in such parts of the country that have some degree of self-governance. Spain formulated

33 Vladislava Stoyanova, *Human Trafficking and Slavery Reconsidered. Conceptual Limits and States' Positive Obligations in European Law* (Cambridge University Press 2017), 173.

34 The Council of Europe Convention on Action against Trafficking in Human Beings, ETS No 197.

35 Stoyanova (n 35), 179.

two unilateral statements: one on the specific status of Gibraltar, and a second one declaring that it "will make the necessary changes to its domestic legislation in order for the Convention to be applied in its entirety".[36]

Guideline 1.5 from the ILC Guide to Practice stipulates that "[u]nilateral statements formulated in relation to a treaty which are not reservations nor interpretative declarations (…) are outside the scope of the present Guide to Practice". However, such declarations, or similar ones, are quite common in international practice and should be treated as uncontroversial and admissible.[37]

4.2 Interpretative declarations

Five declarations, by four States, are considered as interpretative declarations. Three States (Poland, Lithuania and Latvia) lodged almost identically worded declarations that the Convention will be applied in conformity with "the principles and provisions" of their constitutions. Lithuania and Latvia formulated this declaration when they signed the Convention, but they have not yet ratified it; accordingly, their declarations have been neither accepted, confirmed, nor objected to by the other parties. In contrast, Poland confirmed its declaration when depositing the instrument of ratification, and several parties to the Convention reacted by submitting objections (which are discussed below).

A second declaration by Poland was also included in the instrument of ratification. This declaration aims to clarify the way in which Poland intends to interpret Article 18(5) of the Convention. The latter provision obliges State Parties to "take the appropriate measures to provide consular and other protection and support to their nationals and other victims entitled to such protection in accordance with their obligations under international law". The Polish declaration declares that under the Polish international obligations, the consul of the Republic of Poland in principle can take actions of consular protection only towards Polish nationals or, in special circumstances, nationals of other EU Member States. The lack of any reaction by the other parties to the Convention indicates that this declaration can be considered as permissible and valid.

However, the same cannot be said about the Polish declaration which states that the Convention will be applied "in accordance with the principles and provisions of the Constitution". Similarly worded declarations were lodged by Lithuania and Latvia. Six States lodged objections to this declaration: Austria, Finland, the Netherlands, Norway, Sweden and Switzerland. All of the objecting States justified their objections using very similar arguments, which correctly reflect the three concerns this declaration has raised. First, the formulated

36 The text of all declarations, as well as reservations and objections is available on the website of the Council of Europe's Treaty Office www.coe.int/en/web/conventions/home accessed 15 October 2019.

37 Guide to Practice (n 5) 89.

declaration constitutes, in fact, a reservation.[38] Second, as a reservation, the "declaration" is prohibited by the Convention since it is not authorised by Article 78.[39] Third, the "declaration" is of a general and indeterminate scope, and as such should be treated as incompatible with the object and purpose of the Convention.[40] All the objecting States declared in the texts of their objections that the objectionability of the Polish "declaration" shall not preclude the entry into force of the Convention between them and Poland. Four States (i.e. Finland, Norway, Sweden and Switzerland) followed the so-called "severability" doctrine and suggested that the Polish "declaration" shall be treated as null and void.[41]

In the light of above considerations, the Polish "declaration" should be treated as an invalid reservation.[42] Apart from its formal invalidity, there are also doubts concerning the rationale underpinning "the declaration" as presented by Poland. More specifically, it is difficult to imagine a viable conflict between a human rights treaty, like the Istanbul Convention, and a modern constitution that recognises basic human rights, like the Polish Constitution of 1997.[43] These kinds of declarations should be perceived more as a political gesture in the imaginary fight against the so-called "gender ideology",[44] aimed more at protecting the traditional family model rather than a manifestation of an actual legal issue.

38 This position has been taken by, *inter alia*, Finland, which stated that "the [Polish] declaration seems to constitute a reservation as it limits the scope of the application of the Convention".

39 In this sense the Netherlands, for instance, correctly observed that according to Article 78(1) of the Convention, "reservations are only permitted with regard to a limited and specified number of Articles".

40 Norway, for example, stated that

> [b]y invoking a general reference to the national Constitution without further description of its content, the Republic of Poland exempts the other States Parties to the Convention from the possibility of assessing the full effects of the declaration (…) the reservation in its present form (…) may cast doubts as to the commitment of the reserving State to the object and purpose of the Convention.

41 For example, Finland stated that "[t]he Convention will thus become operative between the two States without the Republic of Poland benefitting from this reservation".

42 The ILC, in its Guide to Practice, recognised a specific form for formulating a reaction to interpretative declarations – i.e. "recharacterisation" defined as

> a unilateral statement made by a State or an international organization in reaction to an interpretative declaration in respect of a treaty formulated by another State or another international organization, whereby the former State or organization purports to treat the declaration as a reservation.
>
> (Guideline 2.9.3)

43 The Constitution of Republic of Poland of 2 April, 1997 (*Journal of Laws of the Republic of Poland* 1997, No 78, item 483 as amended).

44 See Sekowska-Kozolowska's chapter in this volume.

Having detailed the objections to the Polish "declaration", the following question still remains open: Who is entitled to make a final and binding assessment of a declaration/reservation? The ILC Guide to Practice leaves room for manoeuvre in this respect. Guideline 3.2 states, *inter alia*, that contracting States and treaty monitoring bodies "may assess, within their respective competence, the permissibility of reservations". Guideline 3.2.1 further clarifies that a "treaty monitoring body may, for the purpose of discharging the functions entrusted to it, assess the permissibility of reservations formulated by a State (...)" and "[t]he assessment made by such a body in the exercise of this competence has no greater legal effect than that of the act which contains it". Since the Istanbul Convention's monitoring body, GREVIO, does not have the power to render decisions or resolutions binding upon the contracting States, its assessment on formulated reservations/declarations must also be considered as also non-binding.

In my opinion, the doubtful Polish "declaration" should be treated as an invalid reservation, which is null and void by operation of law, regardless of other State Parties' reactions. However, given that GREVIO's opinion is without binding legal effect, the only possibility to finally clarify the ambiguities connected to the Polish "declaration" is to persuade Poland to withdraw it.

Similar concerns might be put forward with respect to Croatia's declaration formulated in June 2018. The first part of Croatia's declaration is directed against the so-called "gender ideology" and aimed at protecting the "traditional form of marriage": "[t]he Republic of Croatia considers that the provisions of the Convention do not include an obligation to introduce gender ideology into the Croatian legal and educational system, nor the obligation to modify the constitutional definition of marriage".

The second part of the declaration can be described as a moderated version of the declarations entered by Poland, Latvia and Lithuania. It reads that

> [t]he Republic of Croatia considers that the Convention is in accordance with the provisions of the Constitution of the Republic of Croatia, in particular with the provisions on the protection of human rights and fundamental freedoms, and shall apply the Convention taking into account the aforementioned provisions, principles and values of the constitutional order of the Republic of Croatia.

This second part alone justifies a reaction similar to those of Austria, the Netherlands, Finland, Norway, Sweden and Switzerland to the above discussed Polish "declaration".

The specific reference to "gender ideology" in the first part of the Croatian "declaration" could also raise concerns and, as a consequence, it could possibly be treated as a form of an invalid reservation which aims to restrict at least two core provisions of the Istanbul Convention. These are more specifically Article 6 (gender-sensitive politics) and Article 12(1) of the Convention. The latter stipulates that the State Parties shall:

> take the necessary measures to promote changes in the social and cultural patterns of behaviour of women and men with a view to eradicating prejudices, customs, traditions and all other practices which are based on the idea of the inferiority of women or on stereotyped roles for women and men.

The fight against the so-called "gender ideology", which is on-going in some States (mostly in Central and Eastern Europe) and includes criticism of the Istanbul Convention, is founded on manipulative arguments. In particular, these arguments are based on a mixture of prejudices against homosexuality, same-sex marriages and a "third-sex".[45] However, apart from the possible interpretation of one of the general preventive measures stipulated in the above-mentioned Article 12(1), none of these issues are directly included in the Convention. It seems that the mere reference to "gender" included in the Convention has triggered attacks against the Istanbul Convention in general in some States, sadly undermining the whole idea of the fight against violence against women and domestic violence, and that by using a twisted logic the mere reference to violence against women and domestic violence is perceived by some as an attack on "traditional family and values".

In sum, out of the five interpretative declarations communicated so far, four give rise to serious issues and may in fact be invalid reservations. In this context, the absence of a clause prohibiting interpretive declarations in the text of the Istanbul Convention is regrettable.

5 Conclusions

It should be applauded that the drafters of the Istanbul Convention adopted a rather strict approach to reservations. The reservation clause with its exhaustive list of provisions to which reservations may be formulated, is next to a complete prohibition on reservations. The clause thus represents the most desirable response to the controversial practice of reservations to human rights treaties. As the Explanatory report to the Convention notes, the provisions in the list are those in relation to which "unanimous agreement was not reached among the drafters despite the efforts achieved in favour of compromise".

Perhaps only the reservation by Poland with respect to Article 30(2) raises some doubts from the perspective of other provisions of the Convention and other human rights treaties. The other reservations formulated so far by other

45 For a short commentary on these fears in Bulgaria, see Ruzha Smilova, 'Promoting "Gender Ideology": Constitutional Court of Bulgaria Declares Istanbul Convention Unconstitutional' (*Oxford Human Rights Hub*, 22 August 2018) http://ohrh.law.ox.ac.uk/promoting-gender-ideology-constitutional-court-of-bulgaria-declares-istanbul-convention-unconstitutional/ accessed 15 October 2019; and in Croatia, see Johanna Niemi, 'Gender Violence – A Hot Topic?' (*ASLA – Actors, Structures, Law*, 7 August 2018) https://blogit.utu.fi/asla/2018/08/07/gender-violence-a-hot-topic/ accessed 15 October 2019.

States seem to be within the scope of the Article 78, and as such should be treated as permissible.

This positive assessment of the reservations regime of the Istanbul Convention is also justified when compared to the regime under other treaties on women's rights, in particular the 1979 Convention on the Elimination of All Forms of Discrimination Against Women (CEDAW).[46] Far-reaching reservations undermine the way CEDAW is implemented in many States. In this context, one must agree with McQuigg that, in contrast to CEDAW, the drafters of the Istanbul Convention adopted a stricter approach to the issue of reservations and that "[t]he adoption of such a narrow approach to the issue of reservations may well serve to increase the effectiveness of the convention, although it could of course also deter some States from signing up to this instrument."[47]

However, the current practice regarding interpretative declarations shows that the Convention's silence on this issue is most unfortunate. The vague wording and the references to domestic law in four out of the five lodged interpretative declarations rightly gave rise to opinions that this type of declarations amount to invalid reservations. So far only six States have formulated such an opinion in response to the Polish 'declaration', while it is highly expected that some States will react in the same manner to the declarations formulated by Croatia, Lithuania and Latvia. Given that GREVIO cannot render binding decisions, even strong and well-reasoned objections by some States do not resolve all the controversies surrounding these declarations. The exertion of political and diplomatic pressure on Poland, Croatia, Lithuania and Latvia to withdraw their declarations seems to be the most desirable path forward.

46 For an overview of the reservations formulated to this Convention see, *inter alia*, Belinda Clark, 'The Vienna Convention Reservations Regime and the Convention on Discrimination against Women' (1991) 81 *Am. J. Int'l* 281; Lijnzaad (n 4) 298–370.

47 Ronagh J.A. McQuigg, 'What Potential Does the Council of Europe Convention on Violence against Women Hold as Regards Domestic Violence?' (2012) 16 *Int. J. H.R.* 947, 959.

Index

For Product Safety Concerns and Information please contact our EU representative GPSR@taylorandfrancis.com
Taylor & Francis Verlag GmbH, Kaufingerstraße 24, 80331 München, Germany

www.ingramcontent.com/pod-product-compliance
Ingram Content Group UK Ltd.
Pitfield, Milton Keynes, MK11 3LW, UK
UKHW020018200926
475702UK00014B/1956
* 9 7 8 1 0 3 2 1 7 3 5 3 5 *